Migration in a mature

Cambridge Studies in Population, Economy and
Society in Past Time 3

Series Editors:
PETER LASLETT, ROGER SCHOFIELD and
E. A. WRIGLEY
ESRC Cambridge Group for the History of Population and
Social Structure

and DANIEL SCOTT SMITH
University of Illinois at Chicago

Recent work in social, economic and demographic history has revealed much that was previously obscure about societal stability and change in the past. It has also suggested that crossing the conventional boundaries between these branches of history can be very rewarding.

This series will exemplify the value of interdisciplinary work of this kind, and will include books on topics such as family, kinship and neighbourhood; welfare provision and social control; work and leisure; migration; urban growth; and legal structures and procedures, as well as more familiar matters. It will demonstrate that, for example, anthropology and economics have become as close intellectual neighbours to history as have political philosophy or biography.

Migration in a mature economy

Emigration and internal migration in England and Wales, 1861–1900

DUDLEY BAINES
Department of Economic History,
London School of Economics and Political Science

The right of the
University of Cambridge
to print and sell
all manner of books
was granted by
Henry VIII in 1534.
The University has printed
and published continuously
since 1584.

CAMBRIDGE UNIVERSITY PRESS

Cambridge
London   New York   New Rochelle
Melbourne   Sydney

PUBLISHED BY THE PRESS SYNDICATE OF THE UNIVERSITY OF CAMBRIDGE
The Pitt Building, Trumpington Street, Cambridge, United Kingdom

CAMBRIDGE UNIVERSITY PRESS
The Edinburgh Building, Cambridge CB2 2RU, UK
40 West 20th Street, New York NY 10011–4211, USA
477 Williamstown Road, Port Melbourne, VIC 3207, Australia
Ruiz de Alarcón 13, 28014 Madrid, Spain
Dock House, The Waterfront, Cape Town 8001, South Africa

http://www.cambridge.org

First published 1985
First paperback edition 2002

A catalogue record for this book is available from the British Library

Library of Congress Cataloguing in Publication data
Baines, Dudley, 1939–
Migration in a mature economy.
(Cambridge studies in population, economy, and society in past time; 3)
Bibliography.
Includes index.
1. England – Emigration and immigration – History – 19th century.   2. Wales –
Emigration and immigration – History – 19th century.   3. Migration, Internal –
Great Britain – History – 19th century.   I. Title.   II. Series.   JV7614.B35
1985   325.42   85-7777

ISBN 0 521 30153 X hardback
ISBN 0 521 89154 X paperback

For Mary

Contents

Tables

Figures

Acknowledgements

In the twenty years in which I have been (discontinuously) working on this project I have incurred many intellectual and personal debts. I had decided, as a matter of principle, to do all the work myself and to ask neither for research funding nor for the aid of a research assistant. I was very reliant on criticism and encouragement from friends and colleagues – particularly since the technical and methodological problems were far more serious than I expected. I cannot remember all the people who have helped me over the years – or much of their advice – but I would particularly like to mention Charlotte Erickson, Tony Wrigley and the late David Glass. Mary Morgan did most of the work on the model and Carol Hewlett wrote the main programme. The manuscript (sic) was typed by many people but I would like to thank Joan Lynas, Moira O'Shaughnessy, Penny Ewles, Gail Martin and Tess Truman. Finally, my wife, Mary Russell, has given me constant support and encouragement and has shown the forbearance that authors always mention but I suspect do not always receive.

I was able to present papers on various aspects of the work at Conferences in Salford in 1967, Harvard in 1973 and Cambridge in 1977 and at seminars at the Universities of Manchester, Leeds, Leicester, New South Wales, New England, Melbourne, Oxford, Warwick and Cambridge, at the Institute of Historical Research (three times), Birkbeck College (twice), L.S.E. and at Monash, La Trobe and Flinders Universities. To my critics on these occasions I offer thanks.

1

Introduction: the scope of the study

The emigration of between 44 and 52 million people[1] from Europe overseas between the end of the Napoleonic Wars and the outbreak of the First World War was a phenomenon of outstanding importance which has attracted a large literature.[2] In the last two decades, however, the direction of research into the history of European emigration has shifted. With some important exceptions, the majority of the books and papers published before 1960 were written from the viewpoint of the receiving countries. They were frequently concerned with the settlement and assimilation of nineteenth and early twentieth-century immigrants in overseas countries and also with the rigours of the passage from Europe. Less attention was paid to the social and economic conditions in those parts of Europe from which the emigrants came. The effect of this bias in the literature was that emigration from, say, Italy, Sweden, Ireland and Britain was often regarded as if it were part of a single phenomenon which was caused by population pressure, changes in (rural) society and the development of inland and overseas transport.[3] In the last two decades, research on European

[1] Forty-four million emigrants were reported to have left European countries for overseas destinations between 1816 and 1915 and 52 million were reported to have arrived. See I. Ferenczi and W. F. Willcox, *International migrations* (National Bureau of Economic and Social Research, New York, 1929–31), Table 6, pp. 235–88.

[2] The most recent general paper is J. D. Gould, 'European inter-continental emigration, 1815–1914: patterns and causes', *Journal of European Economic History*. 8 (3), 1979, pp. 593–679. The most important general works are mentioned in chapter 2.

[3] This tendency was pointed out by Frank Thistlethwaite in a paper at the Historical Congress in Stockholm in 1960. This paper was very influential and many Scandinavian historians, for example, have said that it was a turning point in migration studies. F. Thistlethwaite, 'Migration from Europe overseas in the nineteenth and twentieth centuries', pp. 32–60. *XIe Congrès International des Sciences Historique, Stockholm, 1960, V: Historie Contemporaine* (Almqvist and Wiksell, Stockholm, 1960). Hansen's *Atlantic migration* was an important exception to the generalisation that the older books tended

1

emigration has tended to proceed along two main lines. The relationship between the annual rate of emigration and the social and economic characteristics of the sending and receiving countries has been
subjected to formal econometric analysis.[4] But more important, interest has centred on the detailed scrutiny of the local background and
the social and econòmic structure of particular groups of emigrants.[5]
This has directed attention towards the study of the emigration flow
itself. Important issues in the literature have been: the sources of information available to potential emigrants, the extent to which emigrants
moved along chains that had been established by the previous movement of others and the relation between internal migration (in particular, towards the cities) and emigration. These issues are discussed
in chapter 2 which summarises the most important issues in the current literature on the history of emigration from Europe before the
First World War.

It would be fair to say that the quantitative importance of emigration
from Britain has not been reflected in the literature. About one-fifth
of all European emigrants in the hundred years after the Napoleonic
Wars were British[6] but relatively less is known about them than, say,
about Swedish emigrants.[7] The main reason for our relative ignorance
about British emigrants is that the government largely lost interest

---

to neglect the European background of emigration. M. L. Hansen, *The Atlantic migration, 1607–1860* (Harvard University Press, Cambridge, Mass., 1940).

[4] A recent survey of the econometric work is contained in L. Neal, 'Cross spectral
analysis of long swings in Atlantic migration', pp. 260–97, in P. Uselding (ed.),
in Economic History, vol. 1 (Greenwich, Connecticut, 1976).

[5] There are good short bibliographies in P. A. M. Taylor, *The distant magnet* (Eyre and
and Spottiswoode, 1971), and C. Erickson (ed.), *Emigration from Europe, 1815–1914.
Select documents* (Adam and Charles Black, 1976).

[6] For example, the bibliography contains only sixteen books about Britain which include
'emigration', 'emigrants' and 'overseas migration' in their titles. Of these, six are
predominantly about the experience of emigrants in their country of destination;
two are about the Atlantic Economy and two about government policy. On the other
hand the bibliography contains eight large-scale works on emigration from Scandinavian countries which, in general, contain far more information about the characteristics
of the emigrants than the books on English, Welsh and Scottish emigration. (Needless
to say the bibliography contains a larger proportion of the work on British than Scandinavian emigration.) Total emigration from the five Scandinavian countries in the
100 years after 1815 was about 3 million compared with 10 million from Britain in
the same period.

[7] There have been more detailed studies of the origins of Swedish emigrants than
of emigrants from any other country. This is partly because the data are fuller but
also because the finance and skilled manpower for detailed analysis have been
available. See I. Semmingsen, 'Emigration from Scandinavia', *Scandinavian Economic
History Review*, 20 (1), 1972 pp. 45–60 and H. Rundblom and H. Norman (eds.), *From
Sweden to America. A history of the migration* (University of Minnesota Press,
Minneapolis, 1976 and Acta Universitatis Upsaliensis, 1976).

in emigration in the 1850s, that is, before the large-scale emigration of the latter part of the century. This meant that when emigration from Britain was at its peak in the 1880s and early twentieth century, relatively little data were being collected about it. In addition, some of the data published by the British government on the occupations of emigrants are seriously deficient.[8] The bulk of the original lists which counted the number of passengers outward bound from British ports has not survived, and there are no data that show the birthplaces of individual British emigrants. Not unnaturally, research on British emigration has tended to concentrate on the earlier part of the nine-teenth century about which more material is available. Hence, research has tended to be biased towards assisted emigration and colonisation schemes which were relatively more important in the earlier years. Much less is known about the majority of British emigrants who left later in the century and who were unassisted by government.[9]

The most important work on British emigration in the second half of the nineteenth century has been carried out by Charlotte Erickson and by Brinley Thomas. Professor Erickson has published a series of papers[10] based mainly on the enumeration of incoming passengers in the American ships' lists. Among other things, Professor Erickson was able to show the importance of the urban areas of Britain as a source of emigrants in the decade of the 1880s when emigration was very heavy. The approach associated with Professor Brinley Thomas depends on the inferences he has drawn from aggregate demographic and economic data.[11] Professor Thomas's views have been very influential, in particular the relationship he has shown between the building cycle in Britain and the United States, the internal and international flow of investment and the rate of emigrations and internal migration. Both the work of Charlotte Erickson and that

[8] In particular, the failure to record the occupations of females, and the failure to distinguish agricultural labourers from general labourers who did not work in agriculture and probably lived in towns.

[9] Good data on the number of assisted passages are not available, but it is doubtful if more than 10% of all emigrants between 1815 and 1914 were assisted by a government, or a trade union or a charity. Most of the assisted passages occurred before 1850 and after 1910.

[10] Charlotte Erickson, 'Who were the English and Scottish emigrants in the 1880s?' pp. 347–81, in D. V. Glass and R. Revelle (eds.), *Population and Social Change* (Arnold, 1972); Charlotte Erickson, 'Who were the English emigrants of the 1820s and 1830s? A preliminary analysis' (Unpublished research paper, California Institute of Technology, 1977). Charlotte Erickson, 'Emigration from the British Isles to the USA in 1831', *Population Studies*, 35, 1981, pp. 175–97.

[11] B. Thomas, *Migration and economic growth. A study of Great Britain and the Atlantic Economy* (NIESR, Cambridge University Press, 1954, second edition, 1973). B. Thomas, *Migration and urban development* (Methuen, 1972).

of Brinley Thomas has had the effect of putting urban growth in Britain into the forefront of British emigration research. This is hardly surprising, since Britain was the most urbanised country. The literature on the characteristics of British emigrants is discussed in chapter 3.

The main gap in the literature on British emigration is probably the shortage of cross section studies. There have been a number of studies which relate the annual rate of emigration from Britain to a set of social, economic and demographic variables in both Britain and the countries to which British emigrants normally went.[12] But, so far there have been few studies which show the areas of Britain from which the emigrants came, and for example, show their occupations and ages. The short fall of cross section studies is particularly important because they are likely to throw doubt on the results of studies which treat all British emigration as part of a single stream. It has long been known, for example, that emigration rates were much higher from some parts of European countries than from other parts.[13] There are two likely explanations for the differences in regional emigration rates. They could simply reflect the fact that the inhabitants of one region had more cause to emigrate than others. Alternatively, the rate of emigration may have been related to the amount of information available to potential emigrants – information about job opportunities, for example – and their response to it. Since letters home from previous migrants and the experience of migrants who had returned, were probably the most important source of information available to potential migrants it is likely that the emigration from a particular region would be partly a consequence of previous emigration. It will be shown in chapter 6 that the social and economic characteristics of the individual English and Welsh counties seem not to explain the wide differences in emigration rates from those counties. This gives considerable support to the view that the flow of information was important.

The studies of Charlotte Erickson, which have been referred to,

[12] I am referring to studies based on data that cover a large number of emigrants. There have been several important micro studies based on letters and trade union records, for example, but it is difficult to draw any conclusions about the mass of British emigrants from them. Examples of econometric studies are L. E. Gallaway and R. K. Vedder, 'Emigration from the United Kingdom to the United States 1860–1913', *Journal of Economic History*, 31, 1971, pp. 885–97; H. W. Richardson, 'British emigration and overseas investment, 1870–1914', *Economic History Review*, 25, 1972, pp. 99–113.

[13] The Italians, for example had long been aware of the importance of the Arbruzzi, Calabria and Sicily in Italian emigration because of the issue of emigration passports. See R. F. Foerster, *The Italian emigration of our times* (Harvard University Press, Cambridge, Mass., 1919) p. 38.

and which will be discussed in detail in chapter 3 are, so far, the only substantial work which shows the parts of Britain from which the emigrants were drawn. Unfortunately, this work is very laborious and Professor Erickson's team have only been able to cover a relatively small number of British emigrants.[14] An additional problem is that the ships' lists show only the last residence of emigrants. It is impossible to tell from the lists if the emigrants had been born in the towns and villages from which they departed. This is an important issue in the Scandinavian literature. Urban emigration from Scandinavia was frequently relatively higher than rural. But how far had the urban emigrants been born in the towns and cities, or were they 'stage-emigrants' who had previously moved to the cities from the rural areas or from another urban area?[15]

There is only one other method of analysing the characteristics of British emigrants which yields general results. This is to estimate the place of birth of all English and Welsh emigrants from the enumeration of the county of birth in the published census volumes. Usable data exist for the period 1861–1900. In essence, the method used here to estimate the county of birth is very simple. It consists of estimating the number of deaths of natives of each of the fifty-two counties of England and Wales distinguishing those that occurred in the county in which the individuals had been born and those that occurred in the other counties of England and Wales.[16] Since the number of births, the number of natives still living in their place of birth and the number living in the other counties is known, we can calculate migration of natives out of each county and the migration into the other fifty-one counties in each decade. The difference between the two flows must be the number of natives of each county who went overseas. This calculation can be stated another way. If we know the number of Cornishmen who died in England and Wales in each decade we must also know the number who died overseas. The latter is virtually identical with the emigration of Cornishmen net of returns.[17] Unfortunately,

[14] Her work, which only covers emigrants who went to the United States, has so far been based on samples drawn from the 1880s and the 1830s. Work on the 1850s is in progress. Her total observations number about 20,000 out of a total emigration of some 10 million before 1914, of which about 6 million went to the United States. (Her samples are largely of adult males, however.) Erickson, 'Who were?' (1972), 'Who were?' (1977).

[15] This point is discussed in Semmingsen, 'Emigration from Scandinavia'. Nilsson has made an important contribution to the debate. F. Nilsson, *Emigrationen från Stockholm till Nordamerika, 1880–93* (Studia Historica Upsaliensis, Stockholm, 1973).

[16] For data reasons, London and Middlesex had to be combined to make one county and migration to Scotland and Ireland could only be distinguished from migration overseas by indirect methods.

[17] 'Overseas' deaths would include deaths at sea, for example.

this method, although simple in concept, is rather difficult in practice. In the first place, the data contained in the census and in the Registrar General's returns are not usable in their raw state. And second, the estimation of migrant deaths involves several important issues of technical and historical judgement. Chapter 4 shows the methods used by the author to estimate the number of emigrants by county of birth for each of the fifty-two English and Welsh counties in the period 1861–1900. Chapter 4 discusses the quality of the data in detail, the problems of analysis and the significance of possible estimation and data errors.

Our new data made it possible to answer several important questions about English emigration and about the characteristics of English and Welsh emigrants in the later nineteenth century. Some of these questions, like the importance of stage emigration, for example, are subjects of lively debate in the European literature to which historians of English emigration have been able to make relatively little contribution. Chapter 5 discusses return migration to Britain. It is possible to estimate the rate of return of English and Welsh emigrants in the 1860s and 1870s which is not available in the official returns of emigration. It was discovered that the rate of return increased markedly in the 1870s which was the decade when virtually all emigrants were carried by steamship across the North Atlantic.

Chapter 6 shows the variation in the rate of emigration from the fifty-two English and Welsh counties for the period 1861–1900 as a whole. A large number of social, economic and demographic variables are used to explain the differential emigration rates. Typical variables are the proportion of the county's population that worked in agriculture, the wages of unskilled labour and the proportion of young adults in the population. No significant correlation could be found between county emigration rates and economic and social conditions in the individual counties insofar as they are captured by these and other variables. This result could be held to support the view that is often stated in the European literature, that the decision to emigrate was determined more by the information available to the potential emigrants and less by the particular conditions in the areas from which the emigrants came.

The contribution of different counties to the exceptionally high emigration in the 1880s and the exceptionally low emigration in the 1890s is analysed in chapter 7. It was found, for example, that the majority of the additional emigrants in the 1880s came from the more urban counties. It was also found that many of these emigrants came from counties with no recent tradition of high emigration. This result has important implications for the view that the spread of information was a major cause of emigration.

Chapter 8 considers the view that many potential emigrants from Britain considered the alternative of moving to another part of the country. That is, that internal migration (particularly to the urban areas) and emigration were substitutes. This view is part of an important concept associated with Professor Brinley Thomas and others. As we mentioned above, this view relates fluctuations in urban growth, the building cycle and home and overseas investment with fluctuations in the rate of internal and overseas investment and what is usually called 'the Atlantic economy'. We found evidence that emigration in some decades from English and Welsh counties was *unrelated* to migration to other counties. Only partial support could be found for the proposition that internal migration in England and Wales was related to the Atlantic economy.[18]

Chapter 9 considers an important refinement to the view that emigration and internal migration were substitutes. This is the view that many emigrants from the urban areas originally came from the (nearby) rural areas. The chapter shows the author's method of estimating the maximum number of emigrants from the urban areas of England and Wales, in the period 1861–1900, who could have been born in rural areas. It was found that rural-urban stage emigration cannot have been very important. Hence, emigration from England and Wales seems to have been very different from emigration from Scandinavia, for example.[19]

Chapter 10 examines the thesis (also associated with Brinley Thomas) that the Welsh followed a radically different migration pattern to the English largely because the Welsh economy was distinct from the English economy.[20] The author's new estimates of emigration and internal migration from Welsh counties provide no evidence whatever for this view. Wales was not a distinct migration region and its migration pattern offers no evidence for the existence of a distinct Welsh economy.

---

[18] See Thomas, *Migration and economic growth* and *Migration and urban development*.

[19] See, for example, Semmingsen, 'Emigration from Scandinavia'.

[20] B. Thomas has stated his views most recently in *Migration and urban development*, chapter 6. See also B. Thomas 'Wales and the Atlantic economy', *Scottish Journal of Political Economy*, 1959, pp. 169–92, and B. Thomas (ed.), *The Welsh economy. Studies in expansion* (University of Wales Press, Cardiff, 1962), chapter 1.

2

Issues in the history of European emigration, 1840–1914

I

We pointed out in the introductory chapter that there has been not only a great increase in research on European emigration in the last two decades, but that the research has tended to move in relatively new directions. There has been an increase in the use of quantitative data, much of which had been little exploited before, and a shift in emphasis towards research on the causes of emigration – in other words towards the social and economic changes in the countries and regions of emigration. A paper read by Frank Thistlethwaite in Stockholm in 1960, was almost certainly an important turning point.[1] Thistlethwaite's paper encouraged historians to turn away from the conditions of settlement and assimilation in overseas countries, with which many had been concerned, and to look at the factors in the sending countries which affected the decision to emigrate. The key issue, of course, was why only some individuals decided to emigrate, and not others. This may have been because conditions in one area were more conducive to emigration than in another area, or it could be that some people were more likely to consider emigration than others, even if, for the sake of argument, the benefits of emigration would be the same for all.[2] Historians had been interested in these issues before, of course. For example, Marcus Hansen published, in 1940, the first volume of a study which laid great emphasis on the European background of emigrants.[3] But it was only when historians

---

[1] F. Thistlethwaite, 'Migration from Europe'.

[2] That is, the *perceived* difference between their social and economic condition in Europe and their expected social and economic condition in an overseas country was identical.

[3] M. L. Hansen, *Atlantic migration*. (Hansen died before he could write a second volume.)

acquired the taste and the facilities to handle quantitative data, that they began to tease out the partial life histories of individual migrants and the social and economic structure of the areas from which the migrants came. In turn, these studies – the bulk of which have come from Scandinavia – have led to important changes in the way historians look at emigration.

II

The broad dimensions of European emigration in the nineteenth and early twentieth centuries are well known. The most comprehensive collection of the emigration statistics of European countries was published between 1929 and 1931, in a monumental work by Ferenczi and Willcox.[4] About 44 million emigrants were recorded as having left European countries for overseas destinations between 1821 and 1915. This was about a quarter of the natural population increase. In the same period, the receiving countries recorded about 52 million immigrants. The shortfall between recorded emigration and recorded immigration is because a smaller proportion of all outward-bound passengers were classified as 'emigrants' in Europe than were classified as 'immigrants' on arrival. In addition, there was some unrecorded emigration from Europe in the early years, part of which was clandestine.[5]

The data collected by Ferenczi and Willcox show that about 10 million of the 44 million recorded emigrants came from Britain, 8 million from Italy, 6 million from Ireland, nearly 5 million from Germany or its constituent states and just over 4.5 million from Spain and Portugal. Assuming that the rate of under-recording was roughly the same in each country, these data imply that about 23% of the emigrants came from Britain, 18% from Italy, 14% from Ireland, 11% from Germany and about 10% from Iberia. Less than a quarter of the emigrants in the century before the First World War came from the rest of Europe, that is, from Russia, Eastern Europe, France, the Low Countries and Scandinavia.[6] Emigration rates are more difficult to place in rank order

---

[4] Ferenczi and Willcox, *International migrations*, Table 6, pp. 236–88. This book is an essential starting point for emigration history. Much of the material is repeated in M. R. Davie, *World migration* (Macmillan, New York, 1949). The first comprehensive statistical survey of European emigration was by Gustav Sundbärg, *Emigrationsutredningen*. Bilaga IV, Utvandringsstatistik (Stockholm, 1910).

[5] Not unnaturally, the collection of statistics did not occur in some countries until emigration became an important issue. Clandestine emigration was often to evade military service. The under-recording of emigration from Britain before 1850 is discussed in chapter 3.

[6] Ferenczi and Willcox, *International migrations*, pp. 236–88.

Table 2.1. *Overseas emigration (outward sailings) by citizens of European countries, 1851–1913 (average annual rate per 1000 population)*

	1851–60	1861–70	1871–80	1881–90	1891–1900	1901–10	1913
Ireland	14.0	14.6	6.6	14.2	8.9	7.0	6.8
Norway	2.4	5.8	4.7	9.5	4.5	8.3	4.2
Scotland	5.0	4.6	4.7	7.1	4.4	9.9	14.4
Italy			1.1	3.4	5.0	10.8	16.3
England and Wales	2.6	2.8	4.0	5.6	3.6	5.5	7.6
Sweden	0.5	3.1	2.4	7.0	4.1	4.2	3.1
Portugal		1.9	2.9	3.8	5.1	5.7	13.0
Spain				3.6	4.4	5.7	10.5
Denmark			2.1	3.9	2.2	2.8	3.2
Finland				1.3	2.3	5.5	6.4
Austria–Hungary			0.3	1.1	1.6	4.8	6.1
Switzerland			1.3	3.2	1.4	1.4	1.7
Germany			1.5	2.9	1.0	0.5	0.4
Netherlands	0.5	0.6	0.5	1.2	0.5	0.5	0.4
Belgium				0.9	0.4	0.6	1.0
France	0.1	0.2	0.2	0.3	0.1	0.1	0.2

Source: Adapted from Ferenczi and Willcox, *International migrations*, vol. II, pp. 200–1. 75% of emigrants from English ports 1851–2 were assumed to be Irish. See p. 49. The rank order is the mean emigration rate of the four heaviest decades.

because some countries, like Italy, only emerged as important sources of emigrants at the very end of the period. If we define a high emigration rate as 4% of the population in a decade, then Ireland lost at least 4% in all six decades between the 1850s and the First World War, Norway lost at least 4% in five, Britain in three and Italy, Sweden, Spain and Portugal in two (Table 2.1). The basis of Table 2.1 is a rather arbitrary way of measuring emigration, not least because there was great variance in the total population of the states subsumed within the larger countries (like 'Germany') where the rate of emigration was substantially greater than from the country as a whole. But the table does give a reasonable picture of the relative levels of gross emigration from the European countries, although it does not of course show the national composition of the emigrants from the multi-national empires, like Austria–Hungary.

The heavy emigration from Europe in the nineteenth and early twentieth centuries has often been seen as a phenomenon caused by a set of circumstances that were unique to the period – the growth of population in Europe, the development of the New World and Australasia and major improvements in transport and communications.[7] It is obvious that these factors must have affected virtually all emigrants from Europe in some way. But economic and social conditions in the countries of greatest emigration varied considerably throughout the period, and more important, were very varied when the different European countries entered the stage of mass emigration. Consequently, the view that European emigration can be seen as a single phenomenon can only superficially be true.

Secondly, emigration was not a phenomenon that was unique to the nineteenth and early twentieth centuries. Emigration was established from Britain, Ireland and some German states in the eighteenth century. This emigration was quantitatively much less important than later, of course, but the fact remains that emigration cannot have been caused by factors unique to the nineteenth century. More important, emigration continued well into the twentieth century and did not decrease because individuals chose not to move, but because decisions which were essentially *political*, made it more difficult for them to do so.

The significance of population growth as a cause of emigration rests largely on the observation that unprecedented population growth, which was caused by falling mortality while fertility remained at earlier levels, spread eastward through Europe in a similar way to the onset of large-scale emigration.[8] When emigration affected a large proportion of the population, as it did in Württemberg in the 1840s, Sweden and Norway in the late 1860s, and Italy in the 1890s, that country was experiencing an acceleration in population growth or had recently done so. Moreover, France which did not experience rapid population growth in the nineteenth century because fertility was falling, was not a country of large-scale emigration. The writers who stress the

---

[7] Most general books on European emigration have focused on emigration to the U.S.A. Taylor, *Distant magnet*, Hansen, *Atlantic migration*. Erickson, *Emigration from Europe* is an important collection of documents many of which appear in English for the first time. See also, United Nations, *The determinants and consequences of population trends* (New York, 1953). An important general paper is Gould, 'European inter-continental emigration'.

[8] Birth rates exceeded death rates by at least 10 per 1000 p.a. in Scandinavia, Germany and Britain by the 1840s. D. V. Glass and E. Grebenik, 'World population 1800–1950', in H. J. Habakkuk and M. Postan (eds.), *The Cambridge Economic History of Europe*, vol. VI (Cambridge University Press, 1966), Table 9, pp. 68–9. Evidence on the course of birth and death rates in eastern Europe is sparse, but the population of the Balkans and Austria–Hungary was probably increasing at 10 per 1000 p.a. from the 1880s. Glass and Grebenik, 'World population', Table 8, p. 62. See also, W. R. Lee, (ed.), *European demography and economic growth* (Croom Helm, 1979).

importance of population growth as a cause of emigration argue that the main mechanism was that it became increasingly difficult for many European peasants and labourers to obtain land, either by inheritance or purchase. The effect was either that an increasing proportion of the rural population had no land[9] or that the land was subdivided into smaller holdings which, even with the introduction of new crops like potatoes, could become insufficient to maintain a family.[10]

Few writers have been prepared to argue that Malthusian pressure on rural resources was a sufficient cause of European emigration in the period. An important additional factor was the effect of transport development, particularly the spread of railways. In some parts of Europe the initial effect of cheaper transport worked to the disadvantage of the peasants and rural labourers, because the railways increased the opportunity to sell agricultural produce in the towns. This tended to intensify the competition for land. This happened in Germany east of the Elbe, for example.[11] But in the long run, commercial agriculture in many parts of Europe was itself threatened by the development of an international market in the most important agricultural commodities. According to one view, the consequence of cheap grain was a rapid increase in emigration from the higher cost agricultural countries of Europe. The emigration continued until one of two things happened. The agricultural crises were averted by tariffs as in the case of Germany, or a shift within agriculture took place so that cheap grain became an input of an expanding livestock industry as in Denmark and Britain.[12] But it is frequently argued that the more important effect of transport development on rural society was not the effect on agriculture but on rural industry. Examples are the effect of the growth of Berlin on rural industry in East Pomerania, of the growth of Lodz on Southern Poland and the effect of Manchester on Ulster. Industrial production became more concentrated in the

---

[9] Semmingsen, 'Emigration from Scandinavia'. S. M. Eddie, 'The changing pattern of landownership in Hungary', *Economic History Review*, 20 (2), 1967, pp. 293–310.

[10] Polish Galicia, southern Germany and parts of Italy were affected by subdivision of holdings. J. Zubrzycki, 'Emigration from Poland in the nineteenth and twentieth centuries', *Population Studies*, 6, 1953, pp. 248–72. M. Walker, *Germany and the Emigration, 1816–1885* (Harvard University Press, Cambridge, Mass., 1964). J. S. MacDonald, 'Some socio-economic emigration differentials in rural Italy 1902–13', *Economic Development and Cultural Change*, 8 (1), 1958, pp. 59–60.

[11] In parts of eastern Germany the nobility were able to dispossess the peasants. The nobles then farmed the land themselves with a landless labour force and migrant labour from the Polish provinces. Walker, *Germany and the Emigration*, pp. 164–5.

[12] For example, the price of rye in Sweden halved between 1881–7, because of Russian imports. Tariffs were imposed in 1888.

urban areas. This reduced earnings from small-scale industry in rural areas, which was an important additional source of family income.

The development of international transport and communications not only changed the rural economy of parts of Europe to the disadvantage of many of their inhabitants. It also provided the means for them to escape. The growth of the overseas countries that have collectively been called the 'regions of recent settlement' (e.g. the U.S.A, Argentina, Canada, Australia and Brazil) was not only a consequence of their ability to export land-intensive products to Europe but also because it was possible to transfer European capital and labour to them.[13] With the exception of the Irish, the majority of the earliest immigrants entered agricultural occupations. On the other hand, when the great emigrations from eastern and southern Europe began in the 1880s, agricultural employment in the regions of recent settlement was expanding much more slowly than employment in industry and services.[14] Even if the eastern European emigrants had wanted to remain in agriculture, relatively few could have done so.[15] The dominant emigration streams became rural–urban, just like the dominant streams of internal migration.

III

It is obvious from our discussion so far that the extensive emigration from Europe in the hundred years before the First World War was related to the growth of population, structural changes in agriculture, urban and industrial growth and the development of transport and communications. The difficulty is that these factors affected almost the whole of Europe; yet emigration rates varied very considerably between European countries. Nor can the variance in emigration rates be explained by the relative importance of these factors in different

[13] 93% of all emigration was to these five countries in the period 1821–1915; approximately 31.9 million migrants entered the U.S.A., 4.7 million entered Argentina, 3.4 million entered Brazil, 4.2 million entered Canada, and 3.7 million entered Australia. Ferenczi and Willcox, *International migrations*, Table 6, pp. 236–88.

[14] See, for example, Walker, *Germany and the Emigration*, p. 65. C. Erickson, 'Agrarian myths of English immigrants', pp. 59–80, in O. F. Ander, (ed.), *In the track of the immigrants* (Augustana College, Rock Island, Illinois, 1964).

[15] For example, the number of foreign born working in American agriculture fell by 2.5% between 1850–1900 but the number of foreign born rose by 28.8% in trade and transport and 18.5% in manufacturing. By 1900, there were twice as many foreign born in the two latter groups as there were in agriculture. Some groups, notably Scandinavians, still had more migrants working in agriculture than in trade, transport and manufacturing. E. P. Hutchinson, *Immigrants and their children, 1850–1950* (S.S.R.C., Chapman and Hall, New York, 1956), Table 31, p. 159.

countries – even assuming that the factors could be properly weighted. For example, population density was high in the southern Netherlands, yet emigration from the Netherlands was always low.[16] This is puzzling, since the port of Rotterdam was of great importance in the Atlantic trade, and Dutch interests in the U.S.A. were very strong. In addition, Rotterdam was the main port of embarkation for the large emigration from southern Germany and Switzerland.[17] In fact, the correlation between long-standing overseas trading links and the onset of large-scale emigration may be low.[18]

The reason that population growth has been in the forefront of the general explanations of European emigration in the nineteenth century is, as we have said, because of the effect of increasing numbers on the supply of land in the rural areas. But, in fact, it is difficult to find countries where the problem of obtaining land (leading perhaps to excessive sub-division of holdings) was a *sufficient* cause of rural emigration. Consider emigration from Scandinavia. Between 1860 and 1870, which was the first decade of substantial emigration from Scandinavia, the gross emigration rate from Norway and Sweden averaged about 5.8 per 1000 p.a. and 3.1 per 1000 p.a. respectively, while emigration from Finland and Denmark was negligible (Table 2.1). In the same decade the population of Norway increased by about 11%, Sweden by about 8%, Denmark by about 11% and Finland by about 1%.[19] The population growth includes the effect of emigration, of course. Hence, the rate of natural population increase in Scandinavian countries must have predicted the rank order of emigration rates in the decade when emigration became quantitatively important. It would be difficult therefore to argue that population pressure was not an important cause of emigration. But we cannot be sure that it was a sufficient cause, without examining the changes in (rural) society in the individual countries, in particular what was happening

---

[16] For Dutch emigration see Robert P. Swierenga and H. S. Stout 'Social and economic patterns of migration from the Netherlands in the nineteenth century', pp. 298–333 in Uselding, *Research in Economic History*, vol. 1 and Henry S. Lucas, *Netherlanders in America* (University of Michigan Press, 1955).

[17] For example, recorded emigration from the Rhenish Palatinate between 1848 and 1856 was 10% of the population and emigration from Württemburg between 1852 and 1854 was 3% of the population. Walker, *Germany and the Emigration*, p. 157. Walker thought that clandestine emigration could have been as much again.

[18] For example, early Swedish emigration was from the eastern provinces, not from the western provinces which had the greater contacts with Göteborg and the U.S.A. H. Norman, 'Causes of emigration. An attempt at a multivariate analysis', pp. 149–63, in Rundblom and Norman, *From Sweden to America*.

[19] B. R. Mitchell, *European historical statistics, 1750–1975* (Macmillan, 1981), Table B1, pp. 29–33.

to rural incomes. But, there is little evidence, for example, that rural incomes were declining in Norway and Sweden which had the highest emigration in the 1860s and subsequent decades.[20] In addition, recent research on emigration from individual Swedish parishes has shown that the ownership of land may not have been an important variable.[21] Of course, the belief that population pressure was a sufficient cause of emigration from the European countries as a whole rests on an implicit assumption that the main features of European society (in particular peasant proprietorship) were similar throughout Europe, an assumption which is clearly false. For example, the bulk of the inhabitants of the Hungarian plain in the 1880s, when emigration from Hungary became important, were not peasants but agricultural labourers, and they had been agricultural labourers for years. Many of the Hungarian emigrants in the 1880s were labourers from the plains.[22] If population pressure had been a sufficient cause of emigration from that part of Hungary, it must have affected rural society in a quite different way than, for example, in those parts of Sweden that were dominated by peasant agriculture. In general it seems that population pressure was only an important cause of emigration from European countries when it occurred in conjunction with several other factors.

The general view that emigration was related to a lack of industrial development in a particular country is also not necessarily true. This view implies that after some point the industrial development of a country would begin to provide sufficient opportunities at home which would make it unnecessary for people to seek them abroad. This seems to have happened in Germany. The rate of emigration fell from the 1880s as more migrants from the rural east were absorbed in the rapidly growing industrial areas of western Germany.[23] But the opposite was true of England where the rate of emigration rose as the country became more urban and industrial.[24] And in the Scandinavian countries, emigration rates from many urban areas exceeded those from the rural areas.[25]

[20] Semmingsen, 'Emigration from Scandinavia', pp. 46–7.
[21] Norman, 'Causes of emigration', pp. 149–63.
[22] Most Hungarian peasants had never had sufficient land to keep a family, nor had they any anticipation of obtaining it. The land was not redistributed to the cottiers on the abolition of serfdom in 1848 and they become a rural proletariat. See John Kosa, 'A century of Hungarian emigration 1850–1950', *American Slavic and East European Review*, 16, 1957, pp. 501–14, Doreen Warriner (ed.), *Contrasts in Emerging Societies* (Athlone Press, 1965), p. 11.
[23] See Hilde Wander 'Migration and the German economy', pp. 197–214 in Brinley Thomas (ed.), *The economics of international migration* (Macmillan, 1958).
[24] The relationship between urban growth and emigration is discussed in chapter 8.
[25] Semmingsen, 'Emigration from Scandinavia', p. 52.

IV

The relative contribution of factors like population growth, changes in rural society, industrial development in Europe and transport development, to the rate of emigration from European countries, is an issue which, in theory, is eminently suitable for econometric analysis and there have been quite a large number of studies.[26] The commonest method has been to take the annual outward movement of emigrants as the dependent variable and a measure of the level or the changes in a set of economic and social variables as the independent variables. It would be fair to say, however, that the results so far have been disappointing. There seem to be several important problems. The first is that the dependent variable, which in most studies is the gross outward movement of persons, may not measure emigration correctly. There are also some important technical difficulties, not least because the trend of many of the variables is similar. But most important, very few of the models have been able to capture the effect of previous migration upon the decision of those who remained behind.

Quantitative work on emigration has naturally been concerned with the marked fluctuations in the outward flow of emigrants from Europe which were superimposed on the strong upward trend (taking one peak with another, most countries had an increasing rate of emigration). The peaks of emigration from Europe before the First World War occurred in 1849–54, 1869–73, 1882–3 and 1903–7. The fluctuations in the flow of emigrants were common to nearly all countries. That is, when new countries began to lose appreciable numbers of emigrants, it was at a time when emigration was at a high level from those countries where it was already established.

There has been a long discussion concerning how far the fluctuations in the rate of emigration were determined by the 'pull' of conditions in the U.S.A. and the other countries of immigration, and how far by the 'push' of conditions in Europe. In practice, it is very difficult to say that emigrants were 'pushed' or 'pulled'. Obviously, if the emigrants were unaware of conditions in the countries to which they were going, then their decision to emigrate can only have been affected by the 'push' of European conditions. But it is likely that the first flow of emigrants was followed by a flow of information about the opportunities in the new country. It is unrealistic to assume that potential emigrants paid no regard to this information, except possibly in the case when the cost of remaining at home was starvation. For most potential emigrants, the decision to leave must have involved

[26] The best, and most recent, survey of the quantitative studies is in Gould, 'European inter-continental emigration'.

a balance between the expectation of the benefits to be derived from moving and the expectation of the disadvantages of remaining behind. Over a period, of course, the relative weight that individual emigrants were placing on the 'push' factors and on the 'pull' factors would change – not least because the journey became easier and cheaper. However, this leaves us with the observation that the fluctuations in the rate of European emigration were, in general, common to all the European countries. It is unlikely, for example, that conditions in most European countries deteriorated simultaneously. Hence, it appears that short-run changes in the economies of the overseas countries had a considerable effect in many parts of Europe on the decision to emigrate. It would be very difficult to argue otherwise. It is generally believed that at least a quarter of the emigrants before the First World War were financed from overseas, frequently by a member of the family sent abroad for that purpose.[27] When employment was high and/or incomes were rising, emigrants could afford to send larger remittances home and were more likely to encourage other members of the family to join them. Livi Bacci showed, for example, that in the peak years of Italian emigration to the United States, the proportion of women and children was lower than average.[28] This can be interpreted to mean that when conditions in the United States improved, some Italian families immediately sent a young man. If he made some money, he either returned with it to Italy or sent for other members of his family. But even if the response of European emigrants to the 'pull' of overseas conditions was widespread and immediate, it does not follow that the overseas conditions were *autonomous* determinants of the rate of emigration. The general propensity to emigrate (that is, the willingness of people to consider emigration) could largely have been produced by the conditions they were facing within Europe, while the fluctuation of opportunities abroad could largely have determined the precise years in which that emigration occurred.

The first important contribution to the long quantitative discussion of the relative importance of the 'push' from Europe and the 'pull' from overseas was made by H. Jerome in 1926.[29] Jerome showed that the level of immigration into the U.S.A. was positively correlated with

[27] R. A. Easterlin, 'Influences in overseas emigration before World War I', *Economic Development and Cultural Change*, 9 (3), 1961. pp. 341–4.

[28] M. Livi Bacci, *L'Immigrazione e l'assimilazione degli Italiani negli Stati Uniti secondo le statistiche demagrofiche Americana (Guiffre, Milan, 1961) pp. 18–9.* Quoted in Gould, 'European inter-continental emigration', p. 642.

[29] H. Jerome, *Migration and business cycles* (National Bureau of Economic Research, New York, 1926), p. 208.

the American business cycle (the correlation was particularly close after 1870). This conclusion was modified by Dorothy Swaine Thomas in a book published in 1941. She found that emigration from Sweden to the U.S.A. peaked when an industrial depression in Sweden coincided with an upturn in the U.S.A. Her conclusion was that there was a latent 'push' out of Swedish agriculture, but that the rate of emigration was determined by the *relative* attractiveness of industry in Sweden and the U.S.A.[30] This raised a large number of new questions.

The understanding of the relationship between conditions in some of the countries of emigration and conditions in some of the countries of immigration was improved by the apparent discovery of 'long swings' of about twenty years' duration in many economic and demographic variables.[31] The most important of these variables were the rate of population growth and the level of home and overseas investment.[32] The most important contribution to the study of European emigration, using the explanatory device of the long swing, has been made by Professor Brinley Thomas.[33] He showed that the turning points in the long swings of 'population sensitive investment' in the U.S.A., by which he meant construction and railroad building, nearly coincided with the turning points in the four great waves.[34] He thought that the timing of these four great waves of migration was determined by birth cycles in European countries through the effects of fluctuations in the number of births on the age structure of the population. In turn, this affected the relative profitability of 'population sensitive' investment in Europe and in the United States.[35]

[30] Dorothy Swaine Thomas, *Social and economic aspects of Swedish population movements 1750–1933* (Macmillan, New York, 1941), pp. 166–9.
[31] See S. Kuznets, 'Long swings in the growth of population and related variables', *Proceedings of the American Philosophical Society*, 102 (1), pp. 31–6, for a summary of his views.
[32] It should be mentioned that not all economic historians accept the existence of long swings. The identification of long swings in, for example, population growth and investment depends on the prior identification of a trend and the measurement of deviations from that trend. The difficulty is that the trends that have been fitted to the main economic and demographic series are parabolic in form. There is some suspicion that the deviations from trend depend on the slope of the particular trend identified.
[33] Thomas, *Migration and economic growth* (1st edn 1954, 2nd edn 1973, and *Migration and urban development*.
[34] After 1871, the turning points in construction and railroad building lagged behind those in immigration, whereas before 1871 they had preceded them, but this is not a serious problem.
[35] Thomas, *Migration and economic growth*, pp. 158–74. The important relationships between home and overseas investment and internal and overseas migration are discussed in chapter 8.

More recent quantitative research has not, in the main, been concerned with the so-called long swing. There have been a few cross-section studies, notably by Easterlin[36] and J. A. Tomaske[37] but the most common approach has been to use time series analysis. The dependent variable is usually the gross (occasionally net) annual rate of outflow from one European country. This is explained in terms of a set of independent variables which attempt to capture the relevant economic and demographic conditions in both the sending and the receiving country. There are well known studies by Kelley,[38] Richardson,[39] Gallaway and Vedder,[40] Wilkinson,[41] Quigley,[42] and Moe.[43] In addition there are some important critiques of the methodology and the data used in these studies by Gould,[44] Pope,[45] Poulson and Holyfield,[46] Neal[47] and Williamson.[48] Moe's work on Norwegian emigration to the U.S.A is probably the most sophisticated. The hypothesis tested was that in the long run migration depended on the previously observed income differential between Norway and the U.S.A., the pool of persons in the mobile age groups and the pool of previous emigrants in the U.S.A. In the short run, emigration depended on transport costs and on differential employment opportunities in Norway and the U.S.A., as measured by an estimate of unemployment.

[36] Easterlin, *Influences in overseas emigration.*
[37] J. A. Tomaske, 'The determinants of inter-country differences in European emigration 1881–1900', *Journal of Economic History*, 31 (4), 1971, pp. 840–53.
[38] A. G. Kelley, 'International migration and economic growth, Australia, 1865–1935', *Journal of Economic History*, 25, 1965, pp. 333–54.
[39] Richardson, 'British emigration'.
[40] Gallaway and Vedder, 'Emigration from the United Kingdom to the United States'.
[41] M. Wilkinson, 'Evidences of long swings in the growth of Swedish population and related economic variables'. *Journal of Economic History*, 27 (1), 1967, pp. 17–38. See also his 'European migration to the United States, an econometric analysis of aggregate labour supply and demand', *Review of Economics and Statistics*, 52, 1970, pp. 272–9.
[42] J. M. Quigley, 'An econometric model of Swedish emigration', *Quarterly Journal of Economics*, 86 (1), 1972, pp. 111–26.
[43] T. Moe, 'Some economic aspects of Norwegian population movements: an econometric study', *Journal of Economic History*, 30 (1), 1970, pp. 267–70. This is a summary of his thesis, *Demographic developments and economic growth in Norway, 1740–1940. An econometric study* (Ann Arbor, University Microfilms, 1970).
[44] Gould, 'European inter-continental emigration'.
[45] D. Pope, 'The push-pull model of Australian migration', *Australian Economic History Review*, 16 (2), 1976, pp. 144–52.
[46] B. W. Poulson and J. Holyfield, 'A note on European migration to the United States: a cross spectral analysis', *Explorations in Economic History*, 2 (3), 1974, pp. 299–310.
[47] L. Neal, 'Cross spectral analysis', pp. 260–97.
[48] J. G. Williamson, 'Migration to the New World: Long term influences and impact', *Explorations in Economic History*, 2 (4), 1974, pp. 357–89. This is reprinted in a somewhat different form in his book, *Late nineteenth-century American development: A general equilibrium history* (Cambridge University Press, 1974).

These variables explained about 87% of the observed variation in emigration. But it should be pointed out that Moe used the emigration of young adults as the dependent variable. He excluded dependents. This makes it difficult to relate his work to the other studies. However, if Moe's work is probably the most sophisticated and interesting, it stands among a series of studies which have been (to say the least) extremely disappointing. There has been no agreement, so far, on any of the important issues; for example, on the relative importance of the 'push' from Europe and the 'pull' from overseas in the decision to emigrate. But, as we know, this was a distinction which the bulk of potential emigrants would have had considerable difficulty in appreciating. On the other hand, the lack of consensus between the studies is not of any great importance, because many of the studies are seriously flawed both in their use of data and in their methodology.

The first problem is that there is no agreement about the relevant variables. For example, some studies use differential wage rates, some do not use a wage differential at all and some use differential employment opportunities. These imply very different things about potential emigrants. If emigrants considered the wage differences between their own country and, say, the U.S.A. (discounting the search costs) it implies that the two countries were part of the same labour market. Since the employment variables perform better than the income variables we could reject the first proposition as unrealistic and assume that it was the chance of finding employment that was uppermost.[49] But the problem is that there are no good measures of the availability of jobs in the nineteenth century in either European countries or overseas. Even the unemployment data are very deficient. Hence, we could regard the superior performance of the variables that are intended to capture this effect as spurious.

The estimation problems would seem to be of two kinds. In cross section studies the slope of the regression line could be determined by very few observations in the case where emigrants were moving from a number of European countries to one destination – e.g. the U.S.A. This is because there is more likely to be variation in the data about several countries than in data about one country.[50] The problem

[49] It would have to be assumed that potential emigrants were receiving information about employment opportunities from letters and personal contacts. In this case their knowledge would be very localised. But then the other variables in the model would be inappropriate since they are based on national aggregates.

[50] Neal claimed that if a model considers many sending countries and one receiving country, the use of non-parametric techniques will show pull influences to be dominant (e.g. Easterlin) and parametric techniques will show push influences to be dominant (e.g. Wilkinson). The opposite is true if the study is of one sending country and many receiving. Neal, 'Cross spectral analysis', p. 262.

with the time series studies is similar. If there is no trend in the level of emigration then a variable with considerable fluctuations – such as a proxy for unemployment – could 'explain' a large part of the variation. Finally, there is the obvious point that if there is a time trend in the dependent variable as there was, for example, in the rate of emigration from some southern and eastern European countries in the twenty years before the First World War then it is bound to be highly correlated with a similar trend in an independent variable.[51]

A more important problem is that the dependent variable, which is usually the rate or number of emigrants from a European country (overseas), is critically dependent on the definition of 'emigrant' adopted at the time. In some countries the emigration data were generated by the issue of emigration passports or the control of shipping contracts.[52] But elsewhere (notably in Britain) the data do not distinguish emigrant passengers from non-emigrants. Many of the outward-bound passengers were clearly not emigrants and others were going to places that would not have been considered emigrant destinations. It is unlikely that the fluctuations in the outward movement of non-emigrants were the same as those of emigrants. Hence, it cannot be assumed that all passenger movement is a proxy for 'emigration'. A more serious, but related, problem is the failure of many studies to distinguish between gross and net emigration. Since most models use variables that are designed to capture the differential between, say, income in a European and an overseas country it is illegitimate to use gross emigration as the dependent variable.[53] Unfortunately, in many cases the annual rate of return is unknown. There are no data on annual returns to Britain before 1876, for example. But even in the few cases when annual net emigration is known it is not clear that it would be the appropriate variable. To use net emigration would in effect imply that only those emigrants who failed to return were true emigrants. It is usually assumed that at least a quarter of all people who would have been classed as emigrants when they left Europe, subsequently returned. The problem is that net emigration cannot be considered as a proxy for all emigration because the annual rate of return was not a constant proportion of outward movement. For example, net overseas emigration from England and Wales was about 490,000 in the 1860s and about the same in the 1870s. Gross outward movement was 605,000 in the 1860s and 972,000 in the 1870s.

---

[51] Gould, 'European inter-continental emigration', p. 670.
[52] Passports were characteristic of Italy and Hungary. Swedish and Danish data come from the compulsory contract made between the emigrants and the ship's master.
[53] For example, Richardson, 'British emigration'.

The number of return emigrants must have increased by about 370,000 – i.e. by about the same as the increase in 'emigrants' as defined by outward sailings.[54] Hence, the extent of net emigration can be seriously affected by the decision to return. But all the studies mentioned here assume either that there were no returns or that the decision to return was governed by the same factors that determined the original decision to emigrate.

The geographical coverage of the current quantitative literature is very narrow. It is largely concerned with emigration from the 'old' countries (Britain, Sweden, Norway) to the U.S.A. (and occasionally Australia). Emigration from the 'new' countries of southern and eastern Europe was rather different. For example, emigrants from Italy and the Balkans had always had a high probability of returning.[55] This was not true of emigrants from northern Europe. Does this mean that there was a general case of European emigration and deviations from the 'norm' are a consequence of quantifiable factors such as the development of ocean transport? Or are the factors affecting emigration unique to particular countries or groups of countries? A related problem is that the emigrants did not all go to the same destination. Presumably, nearly two-thirds of European emigrants in the period went to the United States because it was the cheapest to reach and because it was always much more developed than any of the alternative countries. But this merely raises the question of why more than a third of the emigrants did *not* go to the United States. Does this mean they were not maximising the benefits of emigration? (If this were true it would have serious implications for the majority of the quantitative work.) A related and more important problem is that many of the studies ignore internal migration – except insofar as it is captured by the income or employment level in the sending countries. In the years before the First World War virtually all countries had at least one region (often the capital city) where there was net in-migration. In theory, a potential migrant was faced with a choice of going overseas, of going to another part of his own country or even, like the Irish and the Italians, another European

---

[54] The author's estimates of return migration to England and Wales are discussed in chapter 5.

[55] See, for example, M. Palairet, 'The "New" migration and the newest; Slavic migration from the Balkans to America and industrial Europe since the late nineteenth century', pp. 43–65 in T. C. Smout (ed.), *The search for wealth and stability. Essays in Economic and Social History presented to M. W. Flinn* (Macmillan, 1979), pp. 45–7. Palairet shows that the behaviour of many Yugoslav emigrants to the U.S.A. meant that they had always intended to return.

country. A model that ignores internal migration assumes that emigration and internal migration were not alternatives.

The final and most important issue concerns the population from which the potential emigrants were drawn. The most consistently successful variable in the models is the level of previous emigration.[56] This may be because the most important factor in the decision to emigrate was the flow of information.[57] Potential emigrants received information about overseas countries in several ways, for example, from emigrants who had returned and from letters to relatives and friends.[58] We will examine below, how much of the emigration did not take place from country to country but probably depended on relationships that had been built up between individual communities, in Europe and overseas. For example, the decision of many people to emigrate was not likely to have been based on their perception of average employment conditions in the U.S.A., but on the employment conditions in those (relatively few) parts of the U.S.A. to which emigrants from that particular area customarily went.[59]

This means that the data that are commonly used to capture economic and social conditions in both the sending and the receiving countries are likely to be too aggregated. It also means that the greatest chance of increasing our understanding of European emigration is probably through the detailed (quantitative) analysis of the local migration flows.[60]

V

The existence of considerable variation in the emigration rates from different regions of European countries has been known for many

[56] See Williamson, 'Migration to the New World', Quigley, 'Swedish emigration' and Kelley, 'International migration and economic growth'.

[57] Gould, 'European inter-continental emigration', p. 660.

[58] See, M. Curti and K. Birr, 'The immigrant and the American image in Europe, 1860–1914', *Mississippi Valley Historical Review*, 37, 1950, pp. 203–30. The sources of information to potential emigrants are discussed below.

[59] For example, about 70% of Norwegian born in the U.S.A. in 1850 were living in Wisconsin. A further 19% were in Illinois. As late as 1890 about 70% of Norwegian immigrants were in Wisconsin, Illinois, Iowa and Minnesota. R. K. Vedder and L. E. Gallaway, 'The settlement preferences of Scandinavian emigrants to the United States, 1850–1960', *Scandinavian Economic History Review*, 18 (2), 1970, pp. 213–26. L. E. Gallaway, R. K. Vedder and V. Shulka, 'The distribution of the immigrant population in the United States: an economic analysis', *Explorations in Economic History*, 2, Spring 1974. I. Semmingsen, 'Norwegian emigration in the nineteenth century', *Scandinavian Economic History Review*, 7, 1960, p. 157.

[60] This was one of the conclusions of Thistlethwaite's well known paper. Thistlethwaite, 'Migration from Europe'.

Table 2.2. *Overseas emigration from some important regions (gross outward movement and annual average rate per 1000 mean population)*

	period		per 1000 p.a.	% of all emigration	% of population
Arbruzzi	1901–13	689,000	34	7.9	4.3
Basilicata	1901–13	202,000	34	2.3	1.4
Calabria	1901–13	614,000	37	7.0	4.1
Sicily	1901–13	1,125,000	26	12.9	10.7
All Italy	1901–13	8,742,000	20		
Galicia	1881–1910	859,000	10	47.7	28.2
All Austria	1881–1910	1,799,000	2		
S. Ostrobothnia	ª1860–1930	120,000	7	33.0	9.6
All Finland	ª1860–1930	360,000	2		
West Prussia	1871–95	321,000	7	13.5	3.0
Pomerania	1871–95	222,000	6	9.4	3.3
All Germany	1871–95	2,371,000	2		

Note: a = mainly after 1900.
Sources: Knodel, *Decline of fertility*, p. 195; Toivonen, *Emigration from S. Ostrobothnia*, pp. 292–3; Chmeler, *Austrian emigration*, p. 319; Mitchell, *European historical statistics*, pp. 57–63; Foerster, *Italian emigration of our times*, p. 38; MacDonald, *Agricultural organisation in rural Italy*, p. 581.

years. Emigration from some of the well-known regions for which data are known is summarised in Table 2.2. It shows the gross outflow of emigrants from the region and the proportion of the emigration that came from a particular region within those countries.

The table shows that one-third of Finnish emigrants came from one province (the area around Vaasa) that contained less than 10% of the population[61] and that nearly half of Austrian emigrants in 1881–1910 came from one province (Galicia combined with the Bukovina) with just over a quarter of the total population.[62] German emigration was also concentrated. Nearly a quarter of German emigrants

[61] Anna-Zeena Toivonen, *Etëla-Pohjanmaan Valtamoren – takeineen Sürtolaisuus 1857–1930* (*Emigration overseas from South Ostrobothnia*) (Suomen Historiallisia Tutkimuksia, Helsinki, 1963) fig. 1, p. 29. See also Reino Kero, *Migration from Finland to North America in the years between the United States Civil War and the First World War* (Yliopisto Turun, Turku, 1974), p. 91.
[62] J. Chmelar, 'The Austrian emigration, 1900–1914', *Perspectives in American History*, 7, 1973, p. 318.

in the peak years 1871–95 came from West Prussia and Pomerania,[63] states that at that time held less than 7% of the population. Curiously, the famous emigration region of Sicily was not losing emigrants very much faster than the average for all of Italy in the early twentieth century, but the three southern provinces of the Basilicata, the Arbruzzi and Calabria had emigration rates nearly double the national average.[64] In addition, it is known that a large proportion of Norwegian and Swedish emigrants came from an almost contiguous strip that ran from south-central Norway to eastern Sweden.[65] In the second half of the nineteenth century 48% of Irish intercontinental emigrants came from six of the thirty-two counties, all of which were in the west and south-west.[66] We will show that there were also distinct emigration regions within England and Wales, for example, the West of England.[67] This is not to say that national boundaries were irrelevant in emigration history, of course. The fact that a particular region was located in one country and not in another could be important, if only because nations had very different policies towards emigration. For example, the bulk of the emigrants from Russia, Romania and Bulgaria were from national or racial minorities.[68] But, because emigration was essentially regional the rate of emigration could be very varied between different parts of the same country, particularly if that country was large. For example, Germany produced nearly 5 million or about 10% of Europe's emigrants and contained several regions of exceptional emigration yet it ranks only eleventh when the emigration is deflated by total population.[69]

[63] G. Sundbärg, *Emigrationsutredningen*, Bilaga IV, p. 99. This table is reprinted in Erickson, *Emigration from Europe*, p. 29.

[64] Foerster, *Italian emigration of our times*. J. S. Macdonald, 'Agricultural organisation, migration and labour militancy in rural Italy', *Economic History Review*, 16 (1), 1963, p. 58.

[65] Sten Carlsson, 'Chronology and composition of Swedish emigration to America' in Norman and Rundblom, *From Sweden to America*, pp. 133–4 and the maps on Scandinavian emigration, pp. 128–9. Semmingsen, 'Norwegian emigration', pp. 150–60.

[66] Arnold Schrier, *Ireland and the American emigration, 1850–1900* (University of Minnesota Press, Minneapolis, 1959), p. 4.

[67] See below, pp. 157–62.

[68] Ferenczi and Willcox, *International migrations*, Table 148, p. 416. The Poles were probably the most numerous of the emigrants from Austria–Hungary. Between 1900 and 1914, 18.7% of Austria–Hungarian emigrants were Poles, 15.4% Slovaks and 14.2% Croats and Slovenes. It is also thought that about 20% or 1 million of the German emigrants between 1881 and 1910 were from the Polish parts of Prussia. C. Bobinska and A. Pilch, (eds.), *Employment seeking emigrations of the Poles world wide XIXth and XXth centuries* (Polonia educational research centre, 1976).

[69] Sundbärg, *Emigrationsutredningen*, p. 99, John E. Knodel, *The decline of fertility in Germany, 1871–1939* (Princeton University Press, 1974), p. 55.

The difference in regional emigration rates within a country possibly could be explained by the variance in economic and social characteristics of the regions. But studies of this type have so far achieved relatively limited success, even where sufficiently disaggregated data are available. This is probably because emigration was a self-reinforcing process. The majority of emigrants may have moved from one community to another and depended on the extension of contacts between the communities. The higher the emigration, the greater the flow of information, money and returned migrants. If emigration did flow from one community to another it would mean that an important cause of an individual's first move was the previous move of someone else. This phenomenon is usually called 'chain' migration. This is linked to another hypothesis, usually called 'stage' migration. This states that once an individual had made an initial move – if only to another part of his own country – his decision to move again was related to his previous move.[70] There is a very great deal of evidence from both nineteenth-century and more recent sources that chain migration was (and is) extremely important. We pointed out in Section IV that the most consistently successful variable in the econometric work has been the previous rate of emigration. The chain migration hypothesis implies, of course, that a so-called emigration region is largely a collection of communities with links overseas. This means, presumably, that in some cases all the communities in the region were affected by emigration but that in other cases there was considerable variance in emigration rates between individual towns and villages.

VI

The view that the bulk of migrants moved along paths that had already been taken by friends and relations is similar to that shown by more recent studies of many parts of the world.[71] A quite well known exam-

[70] A great deal of the Scandinavian literature has been concerned with this problem, notably the relation between rural–urban migration and emigration. See, *inter-alia*, Rundblom and Norman, *From Sweden to America*, Semmingsen, 'Emigration from Scandinavia', Nilsson, *Emigrationen från Stockholm* and K. Hvidt, *Flight to America. The social background of 300,000 Danish emigrants* (Academic Press, New York, 1975).

[71] See, for example, Ezra F. Vogel, 'Kinship structure, migration to the city and modernisation' in R. P. Dore (ed.), *Aspects of social change in modern Japan* (Princeton University Press, 1967). E. A. Wilkening, Jao Bosco and Jose Pastor, 'Role of the extended family in migration and adaptation in Brazil' *Journal of Marriage and the Family*, 30, 1968, pp. 689–95. W. A. Hance, *Population, migration and urbanisation in Africa* (New York, 1970), James S. Brown, Harry K. Schwartzweller and J. F. J. Mangalam, 'Kentucky mountain migration and the stem family', *Rural Sociology* 28, 1963, pp. 48–69. I am grateful to Charlotte Erickson for these references.

ple is provided by the village of San Giovanni Incario which lies in the mountains roughly halfway between Rome and Naples. In the 1950s, the village, which had a population of about 4,000, still had virtually no contact with the surrounding area. No outsiders had married or settled in the village. Yet there were about 3,000 people who had been born in San Giovanni Incario in two American suburbs (one of Boston and the other of Providence, Rhode Island).[72]

The census returns of countries of large-scale immigration showed that the distribution of most foreign-born populations was highly clustered.[73] In extreme cases, a migration flow from (say) a European village has been related to a particular street in an American city.[74] There is also some evidence that when European emigrants had to state their destination, the destinations were highly specific. For example, 60% of Danish emigrants to the U.S.A. between 1868 and 1914 stated on departure that their destination was a particular rural settlement.[75] We also know that the number of letters from emigrants rose with the growth of emigration.[76] The letter was almost certainly the most important source of information about emigration prospects that was available in Europe.[77] Letters from overseas often contained, besides personal matters, detailed information about the employment

[72] C. C. Zimmerman, 'American roots in an Italian village', *Genus* XI (1955) quoted in H. Mandras 'The rural exodus and industrialisation' *Diogenes*, 30, 1960, pp. 104–19. An important question is whether the extremely high emigration rate from San Giovanni Incario was because the village had no contact with the rest of Italy or whether it was despite it. Tederbrand's study of Vasternoerland, a province of northern Sweden with about 225,000 population in 1900 is probably the best historical study of a migration region. L. G. Tederbrand, *Vasternoerland och Nordamerika, 1875–1913* (Studia Historica Upsalensia, XLII, Almqvist and Wiksell, Uppsala, 1972).

[73] See, for example, the evidence of the dispersion of Norwegian immigrants in the U.S.A. quoted in footnote 59. About 80% of them were usually found in only six states before 1900.

[74] This does not mean that the culture of a particular village was transferred unchanged. For example, the unity of the Italian–Americans and the relative homogeneity of the Italian enclaves in American cities was probably created in the U.S.A. Italian society was based on the family and was more fragmented. H. S. Nelli, 'Italians in America', *International Migration Review*, New Series (1), 1967, pp. 38–55. (Special issue on Italian Emigration.) For some good descriptions of individual immigrant life styles in the U.S.A., see L. Adamic, *From Many Lands* (Harper and Row, New York, 1940).

[75] Hvidt, *Flight to America*, pp. 161–2.

[76] For example, letters from the U.S.A. to Denmark rose from 3.6 p.a. for each Danish-born person in the U.S.A. in 1875–85, to 7.1 p.a. in 1905–14. Hvidt, *Flight to America*, p. 187.

[77] See Curti and Birr, 'The immigrant and the American image'. In Britain, letters were complemented by local newspapers from America and elsewhere, which were often placed in the public libraries of towns with overseas connections.

opportunities, wages and prices in a particular overseas town.[78] If
the home population was illiterate, the letters might become public
property. This seems to have been common in the west of Ireland,
for example.[79] The letters were supplemented by remittances – some
of which were used to help the emigrants' families but some were
used to purchase tickets for further emigration. The flow of money
to Europe must have been very large. Remittances are known to have
been more than enough to finance the total movement overseas from
some countries (although it is not known what proportion was actually
used for that purpose).[80] We do not know the total number of emigrants who travelled on pre-paid tickets. But it seems to have been
at least a quarter of Scandinavian emigrants, for example.[81]

The influence of returned emigrants was almost certainly profound.
Between a quarter and a third of all emigrants from Europe before
the First World War seem to have returned, and return migration
was by 1900 probably common among all groups except the Irish and
the Jews.[82] In most areas emigration from a particular place seems
to have been relatively quickly followed by a counter flow of returned
migrants and visitors. The effect was twofold. In the early years, the
material condition of the returned emigrants was so superior, that
it induced an immediate rush to emulate their success, as in the so-
called 'American fever' which swept Norway and Sweden in the 1850s
and 1860s.[83] In the long run, however, the returned emigrants' more

---

[78] Two important collections of emigrant letters are W. I. Thomas and F. Znaniecki,
The Polish peasant in Europe and America (Knopf, New York, 1918), and Charlotte
Erickson, *Invisible Immigrants* (Weidenfeld and Nicholson, 1972). The latter book contains a valuable discussion of the kind of people who were most likely to write
letters home, and hence the strength and weakness of the emigrant letter as evidence.

[79] Schrier, *Ireland and the American emigration*, p. 41.

[80] At least $260 million were sent from the U.S.A. to the U.K. by postal and money
orders between 1885 and 1937. F. D. Scott, 'The study of the effects of emigration',
Scandinavian Economic History Review, 8, 1960, p. 164. Remittances to Italy were enough
to finance half of the country's trade deficit. But known remittances only relate to
money and postal orders. The amount sent in cash, either through the post or in
the care of friends is unknown.

[81] It is known that 30.1% of Finnish emigrants travelled on pre-paid tickets between
1891 and 1914; more than 50% of Swedish emigrants in the mid 1880s; about 40%
of Norwegians between 1872 and 1874 and between 13% and 32% of Danish emigrants in each year between 1877 and 1895. Relatively more women travelled on
pre-paid tickets. Kero, *Migration from Finland*, pp. 177–8. The Dillingham Commission
estimated that 32.1% of all immigrants into the U.S.A. between 1908–14 were financed
by previous immigrants. See Jerome, *Migration and business cycles*, p. 77.

[82] This is no more than an educated guess but it is accepted by most authorities. See
Gould, 'European inter-continental emigration', p. 609.

[83] Semmingsen, 'Emigration and the image of America in Europe', pp. 26–54 in
H. S. Commanger (ed.), *Immigration and American history. Essays in honour of Theodore
C. Blegen* (University of Minnesota Press, Minneapolis, 1961).

important function was to convey information about both the costs and benefits of emigration. Obviously, if the bulk of the returned emigrants had been failures they would have been less likely to induce the emigration of others. There is little direct evidence about returned migrants but the few scraps that exist suggest that the returned migrants were by no means less prosperous than those who had remained.[84] The indirect evidence is considerable, however. For example, in the years 1900–14 (taken as a whole), the rate of outward movement from most European countries was at its peak. Yet return migration was probably at least a third of outward in most countries by 1900 *and was increasing*.[85] This suggests that the returned migrants were not failures or if they were their experiences must have been heavily discounted by potential emigrants. It is much more likely, of course, that many emigrants left Europe with the specific intention of returning.[86] Moreover, re-emigration from some countries was common. For example, 10% of Italian immigrants into the United States in 1904 were entering for the second time.

It is obvious that the flow of information from previous emigrants could not have been the initial cause of a particular emigration flow which must, in one sense, have been caused by factors external to the flow itself. Not much is known about the very earliest emigration, but there is evidence that material conditions (like the level of agricultural income) were not a sufficient cause. For example, many of the migrations from the German states in the 1830s and from Scandinavia in the 1850s were connected with Pietist religious movements that felt they were under attack at home.[87] These migrations established

---

[84] See T. Saloutos, *They remember America, The story of the repatriated Greek–Americans* (University of California, Berkeley, 1956), pp. 33–4, 117–31. Semmingsen, 'Norwegian emigration', p. 160. Foerster, *Italian emigration of our times*, pp. 454–5. See also footnotes 106 and 107.

[85] See Gould, 'European inter-continental emigration', pp. 606–9 for the most recent assessment.

[86] Some writers have argued that the increase in the propensity to return was a consequence of the shift in emigration towards the countries of south and south-east Europe, where attitudes to emigration and settlement were quite different from those in the 'old' countries of north and west Europe. This view was commonly held at the time, particularly in the United States. But it may have been more a consequence of change in the quality of transport. It will be argued that the propensity of English emigrants to return was little less after 1870 than it was to Italy after 1900. See Palairet, 'The "New" immigration and the newest'. J. D. Gould, 'European inter-continental emigration. The road home. Return migration from the U.S.A.', *Journal of European Economic History*, 9 (1), 1980, pp. 41—112: and chapter 5 below.

[87] Walker, *Germany and the Emigration*, pp. 12–14, 78–80. T. C. Blegen (ed.), *Land of their choice. The immigrants write home* (University of Minnesota Press, Minneapolis, 1955), p. 3, and P. E. Hammond, 'The migrating sect: an illustration from early Norwegian immigration', *Social forces*, 41 (3), 1963, pp. 275–83. Rundblom and Norman, *From Sweden to America*, pp. 116–18.

flows which remained important even when the religious fervour had cooled.

It is not implied that a particular emigration flow always went to the same destination. If the information flow was an important determinant of the direction and the rate of emigration, it seems likely that after a time potential emigrants would begin to receive signals that told them of a more attractive destination, and in the long run the direction of part or all of the flow would change. This raises the issue of the relation between movement between European countries or within European countries and overseas migration. It is thought, for example, that international harvest migration from parts of eastern Germany, Finland, Italy, Spain and Ireland was sometimes a transitional stage in the development of emigration flows.[88] The most famous of these was the annual migration of the 'golondrinas' who followed the harvest from Italy to the River Plate.[89]

The development of close links between individual communities did not mean that the migration flow was continuous. On the contrary, it led to a quicker response to changing opportunities at home and abroad. A general mechanism of emigration could be stated as follows. At a given point in time there was always a family – or a group of individuals – who had already decided to emigrate, and were merely awaiting favourable conditions (in the medium term).[90] When this marginal family thought that relative opportunities had improved sufficiently, the group emigrated – or one member emigrated to prepare the way for the others to follow. Another group might not have considered emigration, but could be converted to it by the success or the example of the first group. On the other hand, the first group justified its decision to emigrate by persuading another to do the same. In each phase of emigration the average rate tended to rise because emigration spread to new areas. But, eventually, the medium term prospects in the U.S.A., or some other country, tended to deteriorate and/or the medium term prospects at home tended to improve.[91]

---

[88] See, for example, J. H. Johnson, 'Harvest migration from nineteenth-century Ireland', *Transactions of the Institute of British Geographers*, 41, 1967, pp. 97–112. Walker, *Germany and the Emigration*, pp. 53–8. Toivonen, *Emigration from South Ostrobothnia*, p. 287. Foerster, *Italian emigration of our times*, pp. 131–4, 173.

[89] 'Golondrina' is Spanish for swallow. C. Diaz Alezandro, *Essays on the economic history of the Argentine Republic* (Yale University Press, New Haven, 1970), p. 22. The number of 'golondrinas' who went to Argentina was of the order of 30,000 p.a. between 1900 and 1914. See Gould, 'Return emigration from the U.S.A.', pp. 93–5.

[90] Medium run conditions are defined as those which determine the *year* in which emigration takes place. Within any one year emigration from rural areas tended to occur after the harvest had been sold.

[91] Needless to say, an individual family could respond to a very different set of stimuli

Then the flow of remittances would slow down, families would be less likely to join sons or fathers,[92] and returned migrants would become more numerous. More important, some of the returned emigrants would have been unsuccessful overseas. The demonstration effect would then become negative.

VII

The generalised picture of a migration flow which we are presenting is subject to three important qualifications. Firstly, the generalisation does not apply to crisis emigration, for example, during a famine or pogrom. Secondly, in the long run, the proportion of the emigrants travelling as members of a family group tended to fall, and the proportion of young single adults tended to rise. Thirdly, the development of steam shipping enormously reduced the financial and emotional costs that the emigrants had to face.

In a crisis, like the Irish Famine of 1845–8, the decision to emigrate had to be made very quickly. People fled a famine in families, or if they did send a member in advance, the rest of the family followed very quickly indeed. The costs of remaining at home were so high relative to the benefits of emigration that there was no point in waiting for the best medium run conditions abroad. It should be remembered, however, that many of the famous crisis emigrations were not aimless, but confirmed links that had *already* been made with some place or places overseas. This seems to have been partly true of the Irish Famine, for example.[93]

In the early years of European emigration, the flows were often dominated by the emigration of whole families, parents with their children. But in the later years, when the rate of emigration was much higher, the age structure of the emigrants became very skewed. More-

at home or abroad. But these were usually related to the medium term state of the economy, and hence, the stimuli affecting each family tended to act in the same direction.

[92] There is evidence that pre-paid passages to the U.S.A. peaked just after the peaks of emigration. See Hvidt, *Flight to America*, pp. 191–4.

[93] Much of Irish emigration during the Famine did not come from the most seriously affected areas – the west and the south-west. The explanation of this phenomenon is complex, and is partly related to the incentives for landowners to evict tenants, and partly to the condition of local industry. But an important factor is that the western Irish had little previous experience of emigration. See S. M. Cousens, 'The regional pattern of emigration during the great Irish Famine', *Transactions of the Institute of British Geographers*, 28, 1960, pp. 119–34. In Sweden emigration in years of famine was relatively far greater from län with an established tradition of emigration. Rundblom and Norman, *From Sweden to America*, p. 123.

over, with the important exceptions of Swedish emigration, which
had a relatively large number of men, and Irish, which usually had
a relatively large number of women, male emigrants outnumbered
females by about two to one.[94] The typical ages of first time emigrants
were between seventeen and twenty-five.[95] This is not surprising.
Emigration involved an investment decision. Current income (in the
widest sense) was foregone in the expectation of a higher income
in the future.[96] The total return was therefore greater for young persons than for older. Another reason why emigrants were so young
is because migration was (and still is) often related to particular stages
in the life cycle – in particular when a young man or woman left
the parental home to set up on their own. This is why many writers
have argued that the ability to obtain land was often an important
factor in European emigration. The ability to obtain land was obviously
important but, as far as we have seen, the available quantitative data
suggest that it is unlikely that it was a sufficient cause of emigration.

'Individual' emigrants were usually not common in the early stages
of each migration flow, but became important once the flow had been
established. For example, only about a third of all Norwegian emigrants in the great wave of 1866–70 were men aged fifteen to thirty,
but by 1911–15 this group constituted more than three-quarters of
all Norwegian emigrants.[97]

The main reason that most emigrants travelled in families in the
early years is that they were pioneers who had little expectation of

---

[94] In post-famine Ireland, on the other hand, many of the sons of the larger farmers
were encouraged to emigrate to maintain the size of the family farm and hence
the income considered by a farmer to be necessary. Farmers' daughters were also
encouraged to emigrate since only a small number could marry a farmer's son. The
most recent book on this recurrent theme in Irish history is R. E. Kennedy, *Ireland:
fertility, emigration and marriage since the Famine* (University of California Press, Los
Angeles, 1974). See also K. H. Connell, 'Peasant marriage in Ireland: its structure
and development since the Famine', *Economic History Review*, 14, 1962, pp. 502–23.

[95] In the years 1840–1930 between 65% and 75% of the immigrants who arrived in
the U.S.A. each year were aged 15–40. Ferenczi and Willcox, *International migrations*,
vol. II, p. 114.

[96] 'Income' is taken to include a range of social and economic benefits. It does not
imply that income differentials (strictly defined) were the key differentials in a migration flow.

[97] Semmingsen, 'Norwegian emigration', pp. 53–4. About 50% of Danish emigrants
travelled in family groups 1868–81, but from 1882 the percentage fell continuously
until it was less than 25% in 1900. Hvidt, *Flight to America*, p. 98. Naturally, both
family and individual emigration was occurring in the later years. For example, many
families left Vasternoerland in Sweden in the early twentieth century because of
the decline of certain industries. They rarely returned, but at the same time there
was heavy emigration of individuals from the same province who were very likely
to return. Tederbrand, *Vasternoerland och Nordamerika*, pp. 311–12.

returning. And, as we have noticed, many of the very early emigrants were members of religious sects who emigrated to avoid persecution or to find a new life remote from disturbing influences in their own country. The Mormons are an obvious example.[98] Although common, the religious component was not necessary. It was simply that the earliest emigrations from Europe were largely composed of people who were transferring their existing society to a new country.

The transition from 'family' or 'folk' emigration to 'individual' emigration occurred for two reasons.[99] Firstly, the development of the migration stream and the growth of contacts between the communities at either end, made it possible for potential emigrants to contemplate returning within a relatively short period. Secondly, the economies of the receiving countries changed.

There is, however, an important distinction between western Europe and the rest of Europe. Emigration from westen Europe predated emigration from other parts of Europe, which means that we would expect the emigration streams from southern and eastern Europe to have been still in the 'folk' stage when western European emigration had reached the 'individual' stage. But in eastern European countries, where there was a transition, the stage of family emigration was very brief. In the case of Italy, the majority of emigrants were nearly always single men with a very high rate of return. This was partly because when emigration from southern and eastern Europe was high, in the late nineteenth century, there was little hope of setting up pioneer agricultural settlements in the overseas countries. But it was also because of the development of railways and steam shipping. We do not know if a transition from family to individual emigration would have occurred in eastern and southern Europe as it occurred in Scandinavia, Germany, Ireland and Britain, because the steamships (even more than the railway) changed the nature of the decision to emigrate. The main influence of the steamship, of course, was that it allowed the emigrant to return. A four or five week crossing of the Atlantic by sail was so awful that few chose to repeat it.[100] But

---

[98] For Mormon emigration from England, see P. A. M. Taylor, *Expectations Westward* (Oliver and Boyd, Edinburgh, 1965), and Hvidt, *Flight to America*, pp. 148–55, for Mormon emigration from Jutland.

[99] This terminology is used by most Scandinavian historians.

[100] For the rigours of the passage by sail see T. Coleman, *Passage to America* (Hutchinson, 1972), E. Guillet, *The great migration* (Toronto University Press, Toronto, 1937) chapter 8. Conditions on sailing ships were such that the British government could use its power to impose safety regulations to control the rate of emigration. See M. Jones, 'The role of the United Kingdom in the trans-Atlantic emigrant trade', D.Phil. thesis, Oxford University, 1955. The improvement in the Atlantic passage occasioned by the introduction of steamships is very well documented in Taylor, *Distant magnet*.

once a regular steam route was established (and, for example, through-tickets could be purchased from eastern Europe via Bremen or Trieste), it became much easier for an emigrant to think about returning.[101] Hence, the decision to embark on the outward journey was less final. Nor was the crossing by steam significantly dearer than by sail, if the earnings that the emigrant forwent during the voyage are included.

A very important issue in migration history is the extent to which the rate of emigration and its characteristics were determined by the transport improvements, by changes within the countries of emigration (for example, urbanisation), and by forces indigenous to the development of the emigration flows.[102] For example, it is probable that the development of the European railway system and of the trans-atlantic emigrant trade was an exogenous factor in the growth of emigration from eastern and southern Europe in the period 1880–1914. That is, part of the emigration was caused by the improvement in travel and communication. If this view is correct, it implies that the large emigrations from western Europe in the period 1847–55 would have been much greater, and their characteristics would have been different, but for the difficulty of emigration by sailing ship. This would be less true of the emigrations in the 1840s and 1850s that were 'crisis' emigrations, because presumably the problems and dangers of the voyage were relatively less inhibiting to emigrants who were starving. But, as we have mentioned, the concept of a pure 'crisis' emigration is hard to substantiate. In the mid nineteenth century, England, Scotland, Ireland and Germany had links with the U.S.A. that had been developing since the eighteenth century. It seems likely that if safe, reliable passages had been available, the rate of emigration from western Europe in the 1850s would have been greater, and a large proportion of the emigrants would have been young single adults, with a high probability of returning home. We will show that in the years between 1860 and the First World War (when most emigrants went by steamship), large numbers of emigrants from England and Wales were footloose individual migrants with a high propensity to return.[103] In this respect the British emigrants of the period 1860–1914 do not seem to have been dissimilar from the so-called 'new' emigrants

---

[101] T. W. Page, 'The transportation of immigrants and reception arrangements in the nineteenth century', *Journal of Political Economy*, 19, 1911, pp. 732–49.

[102] In practice it is, of course, difficult to distinguish between exogenous changes in transport and those changes that came about through the development of the migration flow itself.

[103] See Charlotte Erickson, 'Emigration from the British Isles' and 'Who were?' (1972).

who entered the U.S.A. from eastern and southern Europe from the 1890s.[104] In other words, the British seem to have entered the stage of mass emigration in the 1850s, but since the journey was so hard, the outflow was relatively modest compared with, say, the great waves from eastern Germany in the 1880s or Austria–Hungary in the 1900s.

VIII

It is quite common for historians to regard emigrants as 'deviant'. This is because they were, by definition, more dissatisfied with the place that they left than those who chose not to emigrate. But it is less easy to regard emigrants as deviant when they came from a community that had a long tradition of emigration.[105] Presumably, at some stage in their life cycle all the (young) members of the community were faced with the decision to emigrate or to remain at home. In this case the total population of the community could be considered to be potential emigrants and the emigrants at any point of time would be only those who chose to go that year, not a group who were distinct from the rest of the population. For those people migration would be more like a demographic phenomenon, akin to birth or death. It was often experienced, but not everyone experienced it at the same time.

The importance of returned migrants has already been mentioned in connection with emigration models. It was pointed out that it is incorrect to regard the bulk of returned migrants as failures. The characteristics of an increasing proportion of European emigrants in the 1880s and afterwards, which were discussed above, make it clear that large numbers of emigrants left with the specific intention of returning. And the behaviour of many returned emigrants suggests that they had been successful. For example, there is evidence that many Italians and Greeks returned to live on their capital.[106] It is

---

[104] An objection to this argument is that the characteristics of earlier Western European emigration were determined by conditions in the receiving countries. In other words, initially they could only absorb 'folk' migrants because there were few urban jobs. But the Irish never went into American agriculture and large numbers of 'individual' migrants went to the Argentine in the 1880s and early 1890s when that country was little more developed than the U.S.A. had been in the 1850s.

[105] In fact, many early 'folk' migrations were likely to be 'deviant'. They often occurred in order to preserve a way of life which was subject to pressure at home. Erickson, 'Agrarian myths', pp. 70–80, and M. Walker, *Germany and the Emigration*, pp. 8–15, 78–9.

[106] In one of the few substantial works on returned emigrants, Saloutos showed that the bulk of Greek repatriates had not failed in the U.S.A. But the Greek government was becoming very anxious about the effects of emigration, and gave maximum

known that Norwegians and Finns often returned home to farm, and
it seems that their farms were often more efficient than those of non-
emigrants.[107] Even in the countries where return migration was rare
– as in Ireland – the returned migrants were rarely failures.[108]

On the other hand, the contemporary literature and, until relatively
recently, much of the historical writing, did assume that the emigrants
were deviant. This was one of several important errors made by the
United States Immigration Commission of 1907–10, for example.[109]
The Commission drew a distinction between the young, single (male)
adults who were coming to the U.S.A. from eastern Europe in the
early twentieth century and who had a high rate of return, and the
families who had come in earlier years from north west Europe. They
saw that emigration had become 'one of the biggest business ventures
of all time',[110] and one of the main conclusions was that emigration
into the United States at that time was artificial because it had been
stimulated by shipping companies looking for business and by labour
contractors. The Commission's view was that the 'old' emigration
from north west Europe had been comprised largely of families who
had settled permanently. This conclusion was related to the view,
since denied, that the 'new' immigrants were a net economic and
social cost.[111] In fact, very little evidence has been found to substantiate
the view that shipping companies promoted emigration.[112] Few papers

publicity to those emigrants who had failed – for example, those who returned
penniless from the United States in 1907–8. Saloutos, *They remember America*, pp.
33–4 and 117–31. On the returned Italians, see Foerster, *Italian emigration of our
times*, pp. 454–5.

[107] Semmingsen, 'Norwegian emigration', p. 160. Scott, 'Effects of emigration', p. 165.
[108] Schrier, *Ireland and the American emigration*, pp. 129–41.
[109] United States Immigration Commission (Dillingham Commission), U.S. Senate
Documents, 1907–10.
[110] H. A. Citröen, *European emigration overseas, past and future* (Research group in European Migration problems, The Hague, 1951), p. 10.
[111] Despite that, on the Commission's own evidence, dependency was lower among
the 'new' immigrants. As is well known, the main criticism of the 'new' immigrants
rested on a simple correlation between the absolute growth of urban problems (like
overcrowding), and the spacial distribution of the most recent immigration communities. See Taylor, *Distant magnet*, pp. 239–50.
[112] Hvidt showed that emigration from Denmark in the early twentieth century was
(negatively) correlated with the level of fares on the Copenhagen–New York route.
He concluded that emigration had been stimulated by aggressive marketing. But
similar fluctuations on the Goteberg–New York route in the same period were not
correlated with fluctuations in Swedish emigration. K. Hvidt, 'Danish emigration
prior to 1914. Trends and problems', *Scandinavian Economic History Review*, 14, 1966,
pp. 175–8. Birgitta Oden, 'Scandinavian emigration prior to 1914', *Scandinavian Economic History Review*, 20, 1972, pp. 89–94. It is also doubtful if shipping companies
were able to promote emigration from Italy in the early twentieth century. Curti
and Birr, 'The immigrant and the American image', p. 211.

of shipping agents have survived, but Brattne was able to show that the firm of Larrson Bros. in Stockholm, which handled about 10% of Swedish emigration, confined their propaganda to conditions at sea and did not mention conditions in the U.S.A.[113] Similarly, the extent of labour recruitment by American firms or government agencies in Europe seems to have been low. Emigration to the U.S.A. under a direct labour contract was relatively rare, even before it became illegal.[114] Direct methods to recruit immigrants were probably ineffective because it was difficult to succeed in an overseas country without some personal contacts.[115] Of course, the activities of shipping companies and emigration agencies may have had an indirect effect. Individuals may have come to consider emigration when in the absence of advertising they would not. But in such cases the role of 'artificial' stimulants to emigration would have been little different from the informal effect of letters, newspapers and the like.

IX

A great deal of the recent work on emigration has been concerned with the relation between urban growth within Europe and the rate of emigration. The majority of the early emigration must have been rural–rural, either of families hoping to set up a family farm, which was the case of emigrants from the German states, Britain and Scandinavia or of individuals going overseas to work in agriculture. (Some of the latter were temporary migrants like the 'golondrinas'.) But as the nineteenth century progressed the proportion of emigrants going to the urban areas of the United States, Canada, Argentina, Australia and the other countries of immigration rose and the proportion going to the rural areas fell. By the late nineteenth century opportunities in agriculture were relatively scarce. It was becoming difficult to set up a family farm in the United States where the available land was

---

[113] Larssons were the Swedish representatives of the British Guion line. Berit Brattne was also able to show that Larssons' replies to those who had requested information were very stereotyped. Larssons were not recruiting *via* their correspondence. She estimated that about 100,000 Swedes had corresponded with emigration agents and *not* emigrated. Berit Brattne, *Bröderna Larsson. En studie i svensk emigrantagentverksamhet under 1880–talet. (The Larsson Brothers. A study of the activities of Swedish emigrant agencies during the 1880s.)* Studia Historica Upsaliensis, Almqvist and Wiksell, Uppsala, 1973), pp. 276, 285, 287, 289.

[114] Charlotte Erickson, *American industry and the European immigrant 1860–1885* (Harvard University Press, Cambridge, Mass., 1957), pp. 88–105.

[115] This is the conclusion, for example, of Lars Ljingmark, *For sale, Minnesota. Organised promotion of Scandinavian immigration, 1866–1873* (Scandinavian University Books, 1971).

expensive and remote. There had never been a great deal of small-scale
agriculture in Australia and Argentina.[116] Of the main emigrant destinations, only Canada could be said to have an accessible frontier by
the turn of the century, and even there it was difficult for emigrants
to set up farms without access to considerable capital.[117]

The decline of opportunities for immigrants in the rural sector was
paralleled by the rise of employment opportunities in the urban sector.[118] The continued expansion of industry and commerce in the New
World and Australasia created jobs in those parts of industry and
services which were relatively difficult to mechanise, and hence were
rather badly paid by local standards. The natives, or the established
immigrants, were able to take the more productive jobs, thus leaving
an entrée for the new arrivals who could push their way into the
labour market at low wages. By 1900 about 40% of the population
of the U.S.A. was living in urban areas – and about 50% of the
Australian population.[119] Substantial numbers of emigrants were still
leaving the rural areas of Europe. Hence, there was a considerable
increase in the numbers of rural–urban emigrants.

The shift towards rural–urban emigration raises an important issue,
because urban growth was occurring in Europe. A potential migrant
could choose between moving to a city in his own country (or in
another European country) or going overseas.[120]

Traditionally, the European cities have been seen as a kind of reservoir. Migrants came from the countryside. If the towns were not able
to absorb them the migrants went abroad. For example, relatively
slow urban growth is often cited as a major reason for the high rates
of emigration from Italy and from Ireland.[121] Similarly, Walker and

---

[116] In the main, frontier agriculture in the Argentine, Uruguay and Australia was too
capital intensive and carried out on too large a scale to offer openings for the majority
of immigrants. See W. A. Sinclair, *The process of economic development in Australia*
(Cheshire, Melbourne, 1976), pp. 4–6; R. C. Jackson, *Australian economic development
in the nineteenth century* (A.N.U. Press, Canberra, 1977), pp. 107–8; A. Ferrer, *The
Argentine Economy* (Cambridge University Press, 1967), pp. 97–9.

[117] N. Macdonald, *Canada, Immigration and Colonisation, 1841–1903* (Aberdeen University
Press, 1966), pp. 25–9, 269–71.

[118] There was considerable fluctuation in the growth of urban employment. For example,
Argentina and Australia suffered serious depressions in the 1890s and immigration
was severely restricted.

[119] Only 7% of the United States population lived in cities of more than 2,500 in 1820.
Bureau of the Census, *Historical Statistics of the United States* (U.S. Government Printing Office, Washington, 1957), p. 9.

[120] Naturally, urban growth in one European country could affect migration from
another. For example, Irish emigrants came to British cities, Italians to French cities,
and Poles to German cities.

[121] Only 4.7 million Italians lived in towns of more than 50,000 inhabitants, and 2.5

others held that the urbanisation of western Germany explained the marked reduction in German emigration after the 1880s.[122]

The concept of the towns as a reservoir is essentially the way that the exponents of the North Atlantic long cycle saw the role of migration. They distinguished an eighteen to twenty-year cycle of urban growth on either side of the Atlantic. In one phase, urban growth was more rapid in the U.S.A. (and Canada), and immigration from Europe was high. In the other phase, urban growth was more rapid in western Europe, rural–urban migration was higher and emigration was low. The linking mechanism was capital movements, which created jobs in European towns in one phase, and in American towns in the other. There is some dispute about the exact nature of the dynamic mechanism which determined the swing, but some writers have favoured exogenous fluctuations in the rate of population growth.[123] This extremely important analysis is examined in detail in chapter 8. For the moment we will confine the discussion to the role of towns in the process of emigration.

Recent research is beginning to modify the view that the towns were an alternative destination for the essentially rural emigrants. It is known that towards the end of the nineteenth century, emigration from some of the urban areas of Scandinavia, Germany and Britain was proportionately higher than that from the rural areas and by the twentieth century this was probably true of many Italian towns.[124] But the precise nature of the relationship has only just begun to be

million in towns with 20–50,000 inhabitants in 1901. Only 1.4 million Irish lived in towns of more than 2,000 inhabitants in 1901. See L. M. Cullen, *An economic history of Ireland since 1660* (Batsford, 1972), p. 142.

[122] Walker, *Germany and the Emigration*, pp. 189–91. See also W. Köllman, 'The process of urbanisation in Germany at the height of the industrialisation period', *Journal of Contemporary History*, 4 (3), 1969, p. 61. It is interesting to note that the Irish government held this view as late as the 1950s. Following the report of the Emigration Commission of 1948, the Irish government attempted to foster industrialisation with the main aim of curbing emigration. They were largely successful in encouraging industrial growth but the rate of emigration failed to fall. See J. F. Meehan in B. Thomas (ed), *The economics of international migration*, p. 78.

[123] The long swing is particularly associated with the work of Abramovitz and Kuznets. See M. Abramovitz, 'The nature and significance of Kuznets' cycles', *Economic Development and Cultural Change*, 9, 1961, pp. 225–48. R. Easterlin, *Population, labour force and long swings in economic growth: the American experience* (N.B.E.R., Columbia University Press, New York, 1968). The first explicit discussion of British emigration in terms of long swings is in A. K. Cairncross, *Home and foreign investment, 1870–1913* (Cambridge University Press, 1953), chapters 4, 7 and 8. (This is based on much earlier work.) The concept was considerably refined and a large number of new variables added in Thomas, *Migration and economic growth* and Thomas, *Migration and urban development*. The two books replace a large number of articles.

[124] Semmingsen, 'Emigration from Scandinavia', p. 53. Hvidt, *Flight to America*, p. 41, 52.

explored. The most important work on this aspect of emigration has so far been carried out by Scandinavian scholars. This is partly because the data from these countries are much more informative. In Norway, Sweden and Denmark the emigration agents and shipowners were compelled to sign a contract with the emigrant which was subsequently lodged with the police. The passenger lists were formed from these contracts.[125] In Norway, for example, from 1867, lists were prepared by the police which gave the sex and age of all emigrants and whether their place of last residence was urban or rural. From 1876 the industries in which the males had worked were included.[126] In Sweden and Denmark the place of last residence can be checked with the manuscript census returns. The first conclusion that has emerged is that emigration from Danish and Norwegian towns was relatively higher than from the rural areas. That is, relative to the total population, more emigrants reported their place of last residence to have been a town than reported their place of last residence to have been a village. For example, 69,000 (44%) of the 156,000 emigrants who left Denmark between 1868 and 1900 came from Copenhagen, or another town. The mean urban population in this period was only 31% of the total population. Between 1900 and 1914, 47,000 (52%) of the 90,000 (adult) emigrants came from urban areas.[127] Over the whole period 1866–1915 Norwegian towns had higher emigration rates than the rural areas,[128] and in the period 1880–1910 emigration rates from Stockholm city and the urban areas of Sweden were only just below the emigration rates from the country provinces.[129]

[125] Hvidt, *Flight to America*, pp. 2–4. Lars-Goran Tederbrand, 'Sources for the history of Swedish emigration' in Rundblom and Norman, *From Sweden to America*, pp. 76–93 and Hvidt, 'Danish emigration prior to 1914', p. 158. For Sweden there is the additional source of the 'husförkorslangder' which gives details of removals from each parish.

[126] Although the occupation of about one-half of all Norwegian males was returned as 'domestic labourer'. This problem affects the British data. See chapter 3 below. The establishment of the demographic data base at the University of Umea will make record linkage much easier in Sweden. See J. Sundin, 'The demographic database at the University of Umea', pp. 251–9 in J. Sundin and E. Soderlund, (eds.) *Time, space and man* (Almqvist and Wiksell, Stockholm 1979).

[127] Hvidt, *Flight to America*, pp. 45–51. There was considerable variance between individual towns. The data make detailed analysis for the period after 1900 more difficult.

[128] Although 70% of the migrants came from the rural districts this was still less than their proportion of the total population. Semmingsen, 'Norwegian emigration', p. 156. J. E. Backer, 'Norwegian migration, 1856–1960', *International Migration* (Geneva), 4, 1966, pp. 172–85.

[129] Emigration rates from Swedish rural 'lön' (provinces) were 7.14, 4.04 and 4.36 per 1000 population in the decades 1880–90, 1890–1900 and 1900–10 respectively. Emigration rates from the urban lön were 6.46, 4.52 and 3.74 in the same decades. Sten Carlsson in Rundblom and Norman, *From Sweden to America*, p. 122. Emigration

The fact that many emigrants left from the urban areas does not tell us whether the urban emigrants were stage emigrants.[130] That is, were the emigrants whose last place of residence was given as an urban area, born in the urban area, or had they previously come there from a rural area? Data sets that provide both the place of last residence and the place of birth are rare, even in Scandinavia, but there is considerable direct and circumstantial evidence of the existence of this sort of stage migration. Ingrid Semmingsen showed that less than half of the emigrants from Bergen between 1875 and 1894 had been born there.[131] It is impossible to do the same calculation for Oslo, but Oslo emigrants were older, more likely to be married, and included more women and children than emigrants from rural areas – in other words, they had the characteristics of secondary emigrants. A general hypothesis of Scandinavian historians is that the developing Scandinavian cities exerted an initial attractive force on the surrounding countryside which tended to draw migrants towards them. In the long run, however, many of the rural–urban migrants went abroad.

These so-called 'urban influence fields' have been traced for Bergen, Oslo, Stockholm, Goteborg, Malmo, Norkopping, Helsinki, Tampere, Turku, and Copenhagen.[132] This way of looking at urban emigration is not mechanistic. All the writers point out that the rate of emigration

from Finnish towns between 1870 and 1914 was 3.1 persons per 1000 population p.a. compared with 2.8 persons from rural areas. But the urban areas were a very small proportion of total population (14%). Kero, *Migration from Finland*, p. 54.

[130] This is a particular use of the term 'stage' migrant. A rural emigrant could also be a 'stage' migrant if he had migrated from one rural area to another before emigrating. But for the sake of brevity, 'stage' migration refers to migration in the sequence rural–urban–overseas. The concept of stage migration is distinguished from 'chain' migration (discussed above) in that 'chain' migrants move along a path determined by the experience of previous migrants (frequently friends and relatives). Stage migrants merely move in a series of discrete stages. Stage migration can also be chain migration of course. The decision to emigrate, for example, may have been taken before a series of moves, or the decision to emigrate may only have emerged as a consequence of the migrant's experience during a subsequent stage (i.e. the decision of a rural-born migrant could have been affected by his experiences in a town). In practice, of course, it is often very difficult to discover the stage at which the key decision was taken. In South Haslingland (Sweden) for instance, the villagers who moved to the cities tended *not* to emigrate. But those who went to the small industrial towns did. See Bjorn Rondahl, *Emigration folk emflyttning och säsongarbete i att saguvorksdistrikt i sodra Haslingland, 1865–1910* (Sondia Historia Upsalusia 41, Almqvist and Wiksell, Stockholm, 1972), p. 269.

[131] Semmingsen, 'Norwegian emigration', pp. 156–7.

[132] Semmingsen, 'Norwegian emigration', p. 154. Hvidt, *Flight to America*, p. 58. Rundblom and Norman, *From Sweden to America*, pp. 134–6, Kero, *Migration from Finland*, p. 54. There were also 'urban influence fields' in the Ruhr. Köllman, 'Process of urbanisation in Germany', pp. 63–4.

from the individual rural areas in proximity to a great city was very varied. But the differential between urban emigration rates and those from the surrounding countryside can be explained by the process of stage migration. Fundamentally, the idea of the 'urban influence field' still implies that internal and overseas migration were substitutes for each other, and that the decision to migrate (irrespective of its direction) was rarely taken in one of the large cities. It tended to be taken in an environment that was not in the mainstream of the country's economic and social development. According to this view, urban emigration tended to be of two distinct types. One type was largely composed of people born in rural areas who had previously moved to a *developing* city like Stockholm, Oslo or Copenhagen. The other was composed of those who were born in a *declining* city like the old sailing ship ports of southern Norway and the small market towns of northern Jutland.[133]

Unfortunately, the nature of urban emigration remains elusive. It is now generally accepted by Scandinavian historians, for example, that many of the emigrants from the cities were stage emigrants who had been born in the rural areas. What is unknown, of course, is where the decision to emigrate was taken. If the rural–urban migrant had decided to emigrate before he came to the city then he was not a 'true' urban emigrant. He might, for example, have only lived in Oslo or Copenhagen long enough to earn his passage money. On the other hand, if the rural–urban migrant was converted to emigration when he was in the city, then the decision to emigrate must have been made in an urban environment. There are, of course, no data which would tell us the geographical distribution of the decision to emigrate, not least because the emigrant would probably not have been able to say how and where the actual decision was taken. But an adequate proxy would be the length of time that a rural–urban migrant had lived in the city before he emigrated. The precise length of time necessary for a potential emigrant to become urbanised is not obvious but it would be difficult to argue that a decision to emigrate taken after several years' residence in a city was not heavily affected by the urban environment. In this case, of course, the city would not be acting as a permanent or temporary reservoir for essential rural emigrants.

There has been little work so far on this aspect of stage emigration. The most important is a book by Nilsson, on emigration from Stock-

---

[133] Semmingsen, 'Emigration from Scandinavia', p. 52. Hvidt, *Flight to America*, pp. 64–5. Hvidt stresses the importance of towns that were not on the main railway lines.

holm in the years 1880–93. These were years when the rate of emigration was relatively high. Nilsson confirmed that up to three-quarters of Stockholm's emigrants in those years had been born outside the city.[134] But only one-fifth had lived in the city less than two years before emigrating, and nearly one-half had lived in Stockholm for more than five years.[135] Moreover, 40% of the emigrants who had previously migrated to Stockholm from outside had come from another town.[136] Hence, there is strong circumstantial evidence from this study that the decision to emigrate was taken in a city. In the case of Stockholm, urban emigration seems to have been qualitatively different from rural. In particular, internal migration and emigration would not be so much substitutes as complements.

X

In this chapter we have tried to identify the aspects of the history of European emigration before the First World War which are currently attracting the most scholarly attention. We have seen that emigration has come to be viewed as a complex process. Several explanations are now seen as rather unsatisfactory, even though the determinants of the fluctuations in the rate of emigration have proved to be susceptible to quantitative analysis. It has not been easy to isolate a set of variables (like differential population pressure) that would account for the relative incidence of emigration from different European countries – still less for the incidence of emigration from different regions of the same country.

The relative failure of the quantitative studies that use the nation–state as a unit to provide general explanations has shifted attention to the detailed (quantitative) studies of particular regions where emigration was common. Local and regional studies have been commonest in Scandinavia because the data are much better. A general theme of the recent work is the importance of the flow of information back to the part of the country from which the emigrants came. This

---

[134] Fred Nilsson, *Emigrationen från Stockholm*, p. 310. About 33,000 emigrants left Stockholm during the period 1880–93. This was about 11% of all Swedish emigration. Stockholm was not an emigration port. Her emigrants went via Bremen, Hamburg, Copenhagen and Goteberg.

[135] Nilsson, *Emigrationen från Stockholm*, Table 29, p. 317, 365. Tederbrand found that half of the rural–urban emigrants from the industrial towns of Vasternoerland in the period 1875–1913 had lived in a town for more than five years before emigrating. Tederbrand, *Vasternoerland och Nordamerika*, p. 308.

[136] Many of these emigrants had probably been born in rural areas. The stage migration was therefore: rural area – provincial town – Stockholm – overseas.

would explain why two outwardly similar regions could have very different emigration rates. There are several important issues raised by these detailed studies. The extent and significance of return migration. The transition from 'family' emigrants to 'individual' emigrants and the increase in the rate of return that accompanied it. And the effect of improvements in transport and communications on this and other characteristics of emigrants. That is, how far were the transport improvements an *exogenous* cause of emigration?

The other important issue of current concern is the role of the European cities in emigration. This is not simply a question of the proportion of emigrants who came from the rural or urban parts of the European countries – although this is obviously important. For example, how many of the urban emigrants had previously gone to the cities from the rural areas? This relates to the important question of whether internal migration in Europe (especially towards the cities), was a substitute for emigration because it removed the need for it; or whether it made emigration more likely because it created a taste for it. It might be mentioned at this point, that if it could be shown that most of the urban emigrants from a particular country could not have been born in the rural areas it would be a very interesting result. It would mean that the decision to emigrate was likely to have been taken in an environment that was at the centre of economic change and not in areas of the country that were being passed by.

The remainder of the book is an attempt to examine British emigration in the light of these issues, as far as it can be done from the existing data and from a large amount of new data which we have estimated.

3

The characteristics of British emigrants before 1914

I

Britain was one of the most important emigration countries in the late nineteenth and early twentieth centuries.[1] In the period of extensive European emigration up to the First World War, about 10 million or 20% of the emigrants came from Britain. British emigration was a relatively greater proportion of European emigration before 1900, since the very large movements from Italy and eastern Europe only began around that time. Table 2.1 shows that over the period 1851–1913, British emigration rates (i.e. total outflow per decade as a proportion of the mean decade population) were among the highest in Europe. We can also see from Table 2.1 that the large contribution of Britain to total European emigration was not merely a consequence of Britain being one of the very first countries of emigration. British emigration in the 1880s and early 1900s can be compared with the large-scale emigration at that time from other parts of Europe.[2] And,

---

[1] 'Britain' was of course technically not a country in this period but merely a name for two of the constituent parts of the United Kingdom. But Irish emigration was very different, and has to be treated separately from emigration from England, Wales and Scotland. (Although England and Scotland also had dissimilar emigration histories.) A difficulty is, that because the United Kingdom was the political unit some of the data are not sufficiently disaggregated until quite late in the period. For example, large numbers of Irish emigrants travelled *via* British ports, and the 'nationality' of Irish emigrants who had previously settled in Britain or whose parents had done so was sometimes ambiguous. In some of the literature the term 'British Isles' is used, probably to avoid the political implications of 'United Kingdom', but it is synonymous with it.

[2] Of course, there is an obvious objection that the great movements of the early twentieth century from eastern Europe were merely the first wave of even larger scale movements which did not occur because of the war and its political sequel. On the other hand, it is probable that the stage of mass emigration from Britain had been achieved in the 1850s but emigration was still hampered by the problem of the Atlantic crossing under sail.

if British emigrants came, in the main, from a few important *regions*, as they did from most of the other European countries, then some parts of Britain must have experienced rates of emigration that were comparable to those from the important emigration regions of continental Europe.[3]

It is not surprising that the first historians who surveyed the course of British emigration tended to assume that most emigrants left because of rural population pressure, the decline of rural industry and the effects of cheap American grain on rural incomes. The limited quantitative data that had been published made it extremely difficult to estimate the occupational structure and geographical origins of British emigrants. In the absence of good data, many of the writers assumed that British emigration had similar causes to emigration from other parts of Europe.[4] The best work of the earlier writers tended to be based on qualitative evidence, which was much more abundant for groups like the skilled artisans,[5] or on evidence which came from public bodies and was more concerned with the minority of emigrants who were assisted in some way.[6] The qualitative evidence said relatively little about the mass of emigrants, and could not overturn the view that British emigrants were predominantly rural. This view only began to be questioned through the exploitation of new data sources and the use of quantitative methods.[7] There are, however, still large gaps in our knowledge of the causes of British emigration.

What is surprising, is the tendency of the earlier writers to assume that the causes of British and European emigration were basically the same, when *a priori* we would expect the opposite. Britain and Ireland were the nearest countries to the New World and emigration from them had been virtually continuous in peacetime since the early eighteenth century. The British were the most important settlers in

---

[3] See Table 2.2 for a summary of emigration from the main regions of Europe for which there are adequate data. Several English counties achieved emigration rates (net of returns) comparable, for example, with some of the most emigration prone Italian provinces.

[4] For example, C. E. Snow, 'British emigration', pp. 239–60 in Ferenczi and Willcox, *International migrations*. W. A. Carrothers, *Emigration from the British Isles* (D. S. King, 1929), pp. 216–28. See chapter 2 for the current literature on emigration from the continent of Europe.

[5] For example, R. T. Berthoff, *British immigrants in industrial America* (Harvard University Press, Cambridge, Mass., 1953).

[6] For example, S. C. Johnson, *A history of emigration from the United Kingdom to North America, 1763–1912* (Routledge, 1913, reprinted Cass, 1966).

[7] In particular, the work of Charlotte Erickson on the American ships' lists and Brinley Thomas on the relation between investment and internal and overseas migration. This work is discussed in detail below.

all the regions of recent settlement outside Latin America. These regions were largely English speaking and had institutions comparable to those in Britain. In addition, Britain was always more urban and more industrialised than the other European countries of emigration. By 1901, less than 12% of the occupied population were in agriculture[8] compared, for example, with 37% in Germany and 58% in Sweden.[9] And the poorest workers in British agriculture did not own the land they worked and had no expectation of doing so.[10] On the other hand, as we have argued in chapter 2, the long run development of particular migration flows was probably a more important cause of emigration than changes in the relative economic circumstances in the gaining and losing countries. This presumably means that if British emigration *was* fundamentally different from continental European emigration, it is probably more likely to have been a consequence of the earlier contact between Britain and the important emigrant destinations than a consequence of the early industrialisation of Britain.[11] In other words, the assumption that the causes of British emigration were the same as the causes of European emigration may in one sense have been correct, but probably not because economic circumstances in the main emigration regions of Britain and Europe were similar.

II

It is very difficult to establish the character of British emigration in the nineteenth century from the published data.[12] Official British figures failed to distinguish emigrants from visitors, and British born passengers were not distinguished from Irish born. Before 1853, the data on the occupations of emigrants are seriously deficient and there are effectively no data available on the place of birth and the last

---

[8] 11.6% of the occupied male population were employed in agriculture, horticulture and fishing in 1901. B. R. Mitchell, *Abstract of British historical statistics* (Cambridge University Press, 1962), chapter 2, Table 60, p. 60.

[9] Mitchell, *European historical statistics*, Table C1, p. 156, 162.

[10] Not all the poor rural emigrants from the Continent were peasants – the Hungarians were often agricultural labourers, for example. But in effect few of the English can have been peasants in the European sense in the second half of the nineteenth century, although some of the Scots and Welsh could have been.

[11] Of course, it is also true that the British economy was affected by her superior contacts with the United States and other countries that were relatively rich in resources.

[12] The best collection of British emigration data is N. H. Carrier and J. R. Jeffery, *External migration: A study of the available statistics, 1815–1950*, General Register Office, Studies on Medical and Population Subjects No. 6 (HMSO, London 1953). See also P. A. M. Taylor, 'Emigration', pp. 59–98 in D. V. Glass and P. A. M. Taylor (eds.), *Population and emigration in 19th century Britain* (Irish University Press, Dublin, 1976).

residence of the emigrants. With one important exception,[13] these deficiencies cannot be remedied by reference to the immigration statistics of the receiving countries.

The Passenger Acts – the first of which was passed in 1803[14] – required the masters of outgoing emigrant ships to deposit a muster roll of their passengers and a continuous series of annual sailings from British ports exists from 1815.[15] When the Colonial Land and Emigration Commission was wound up in 1873, the Board of Trade became the responsible body. The initial purpose of collecting passenger statistics was to check the overcrowding of emigrant ships, rather than to measure emigration *per se*. Passengers on mail packets were not recorded until 1863, when it also became compulsory to record cabin passengers on emigrant ships, although some captains had been doing this voluntarily.[16] Ships carrying less than twenty passengers were excluded and the (relatively few) ships that sailed from the smaller ports were sometimes missed. It has been estimated that as many as 50% of British emigrants before the early 1850s were not counted. Coverage then improved markedly and was probably complete by the middle 1860s.[17] There is no information on returned migrants (i.e. inward sailings) until 1876. English, Welsh, Scots and Irish inward passengers were not shown separately until 1895.[18] The age, sex and marital condition of passengers was not given before 1877.[19] More seriously, the published British emigration statistics do not distinguish the nationality of passengers until 1853, so that emigrants from British ports before 1853 include both aliens and (more important) the Irish.[20] In the 1840s and early 1850s the majority of

[13] The returns of the ships' masters on arrival in the U.S.A. are available in the Library of Congress and have been used to great effect by Charlotte Erickson. Erickson, 'Who were?' There are also ships' lists available in Canada and Australia.

[14] For the history of the Passenger Acts see Oliver MacDonagh, *A Pattern of government growth: the Passenger Acts and their enforcement, 1800–1860*, (McGibbon and Kay, 1961), pp. 75–8, 212–19, 237–9, 293–303. See also Coleman, *Passage to America*.

[15] Estimates for the early years were published in the *33rd General Report of the Emigration Commissioners*, BPP 1877, XVIII, Appx. 1.

[16] It was often assumed, for example, that 'emigrant' was synonymous with 'steerage passenger'.

[17] The best discussion of the coverage of the Passenger Acts is in MacDonagh, *Pattern of government growth*.

[18] Carrier and Jeffery, *External migration*, Table B1, pp. 90–1. There was no official count of returns from the U.S.A. until 1907 but the unofficial count by the steamship companies 1868–1907 is generally supposed to be complete.

[19] Carrier and Jeffery, *External migration*, Table H1, p. 102.

[20] The nationality of about 20,000 emigrants was returned as 'not distinguished' in each year 1853–63. They were almost certainly aliens emigrating *via* British ports and travelling cabin class. The numbers in this category fell by about three-quarters when the Act of 1863 extended the regulations to include mail packets. See Thomas, *Migration and economic growth*, pp. 38–9.

the Irish emigrated via British ports (nearly all via Liverpool). When the country or origin of emigrants was first distinguished in 1853, 53.7% of U.K. born passengers from British ports were recorded as Irish. This was 82.6% of all Irish emigration in that year. It has often been assumed that this meant that up to 80% of all passengers from English ports between 1815 and 1853 were Irish.[21] This is based on a retrospective estimate published in 1864, that 90% of passengers from Liverpool between 1832 and 1853 were Irish.[22] This estimate was too large, or if it was correct, a very large number of English emigrants between 1825 and 1850 cannot have been counted at all. The estimate that 80% of all emigrants were Irish implies that outward movement to all destinations of English and Welsh born was only about 86,000 in the period. The English born population of the U.S.A. in 1850 was 279,000 and the Welsh born 30,000, which implies that at least 400,000 immigrants entered the United States, even if the bulk of them had arrived after 1840. In addition, a detailed examination of arrivals in the U.S.A. in five months of 1831 showed that only 25% of immigrants from British ports were Irish.[23] Even if we assume, for the sake of argument, that only 20% of passengers from English ports in 1825–34 were Irish, and that the proportion of Irish rose to 75% by 1845–53, this would imply that English and Welsh emigration was only 194,000 between 1825 and 1849. Since the American census of 1850 implies that English and Welsh immigration into the U.S.A. cannot have been less than 400,000, emigration of English and Welsh born to *all* destinations between 1825 and 1849 cannot have been less than 500,000 and could have been considerably more. But only 428,300 passengers were recorded as having left English ports in the period of which the majority were Irish, so it is clear that the early returns seriously undercount English emigrants.

The published returns of immigration into the United States which

[21] Most recently by Maldwyn Jones. Maldwyn Jones, 'The background to emigration from Great Britain in the nineteenth century', *Perspectives in American History*, 7, 1973, p. 27.

[22] *Twenty-fourth General Report of the Emigration Commissioners*, BPP, XVI, p. 13, quoted in Hansen, *Atlantic migration*, p. 183.

[23] Taken from Charlotte Erickson, 'Emigration from the British Isles', Table 1. The U.S. ships' lists show 8,258 arrivals from Britain into New York, Boston and Philadelphia in five months of 1831. Of those, 5,610 (67.9%) were English and Welsh, 529 (6.4%) were Scots and only 2,119 (25.7%) were Irish. Very few Irish came from London or Scottish ports. Professor Erickson's team are currently examining the ships' lists for 1841. (A sample of Liverpool passengers to New York in 1841 showed that about 53% were Irish.) I am grateful to Professor Erickson for allowing me to quote from an unpublished paper. She also showed that only 16% of emigrants from Liverpool in 1826–7 were Irish but there are few good ships' lists for that period. Erickson, 'Who were?' (1977).

start in 1820 are even less satisfactory than the British series.[24] Arrivals in the U.S.A. that were reported in the American statistics were between 5% and 15% less than outward sailings from the U.K. in each decade to the First World War.[25] This is partly because 'immigrant' was more strictly defined in the U.S.A.,[26] but in some of the early years the short fall between the American and the British series was spectacular.[27] Also, the component nationalities within the U.K. were not always properly specified in the American series, which can, therefore, only partially make up the deficiencies in the British data.[28] It can be shown, for example, that the apparent collapse of Welsh immigration into the U.S.A. after 1880 almost certainly did not occur. It was a consequence of the mis-reporting of the place of birth of immigrants in the American immigration statistics and in the census.

The most useful series of annual emigration from Britain is the gross outward movement of British born from British ports to non-European destinations, which is the basis of Figure 3.1 and Appendices 3 and 4. Outward sailings of British natives include members of the army, those on business trips and the outward movement of British born who were domiciled abroad. After 1912 these passengers were excluded.[29] But the outward passenger movement is the most consis-

---

[24] Summarised in Carrier and Jeffery, *External migration*, Table E (1), p. 93, and *Historical statistics of the USA* (American Government Printing Office 1957), Series C88–114, pp. 56–7 and 60–1. There is a good discussion of American immigration statistics in E. P. Hutchinson, 'Notes on immigration statistics of the United States', *Journal of the American Statistical Association*, 53, 1957, pp. 963–92.

[25] The short fall of arrivals in the U.S.A. is consistent, and hence not caused by the time lag between leaving the U.K. and arriving in the U.S.A. There is an important comparison of the classification of emigrants by nationality and by 'country from which sailing' in Carrier and Jeffery, *External migration*, Table 4, p. 42.

[26] The American series supposedly shows all alien 'passengers' until 1867. From then on it shows all alien immigrants to the U.S.A. but the precise definition of immigrant was occasionally changed. In fact, first class and cabin passengers were probably not counted before 1903. See Thomas, *Migration and economic growth*, p. 42.

[27] For example, in 1831 the British passenger series shows that 23,418 (English, Welsh, Irish and Scots) left for the U.S.A. The American series shows only 8,247 arrivals in the same period (strictly, in the 12 months ending 30 Sept. 1831). More seriously, Professor Erickson's analysis shows 8,258 British immigrants in the ships' list (from which the published American series was constructed) for five months of 1831 alone. The short fall in the American series must have been caused by shortage of staff or by inefficiency.

[28] Similar considerations apply to the immigration statistics of the other main destinations of British emigrants.

[29] This is why the sum of British 'emigration' to the U.S.A., Canada, and Australasia was smaller than their share of British overseas settlement. But the majority of British passengers to the rest of the world (i.e. Europe and the Far East) would not have regarded themselves as emigrants.

tent, has the merit of measuring all classes and avoids the problem of defining emigration.[30] Outward sailings of English and Scots net of inward sailings of English and Scots is the best proxy for total net emigration.

The published data are unsatisfactory for the analysis of the causes and characteristics of British emigration, because with one minor exception, there is virtually no published return (in either the British or overseas series) of the birth places of emigrants and the place of their last residence.[31] The data on emigrant occupations are also seriously deficient in both the British and the overseas series. The British series (which starts in 1854) did not distinguish between the constituent parts of the U.K. until 1877, when a separate return was made for Ireland.[32] Most important, emigrants were classified by occupation rather than by the industry in which they had worked. It is difficult to distinguish between migrants who had worked (in industry) in rural and urban areas, nor can we know how many of the carpenters, for example, had worked in a carpenter's shop or a shipyard. Nor can we tell the proportion of weavers who had worked in factories or at home. The most ambiguous occupation is 'labourer', which is, unfortunately, also the most common. Until the 1890s, about 50% of adult male emigrants from the U.K. were returned as 'general labourers'. A large number of these were presumably Irish but from the 1870s the number of British emigrants rose sharply and at least 30% of the general labourers must have been British.[33] Usually, less than 10% of adult male emigrants from Britain were returned as agricultural labourers. This classification is not used in the Irish series (which starts in 1877). It is not clear, therefore, what proportion of the general labourers were really agricultural labourers and what proportion of general labourers who were not agricultural labourers lived and worked in rural areas. The American series suffers from the same ambiguity. For example, in most years between 1875 (when the pub-

---

[30] The main problem of measuring 'emigration' is that it depended on the intention of the migrant at the point of departure. He may not have known this, and if he did he may have changed his mind.

[31] In a single return in 1841. Welsh born were never separated in the English data.

[32] Carrier and Jeffery, *External migration*, Tables 11–13, pp. 57–60. There are some problems in matching the Irish and British classification notably in the way those failing to give an occupation were tabulated.

[33] It is not clear what proportion of the Irish were labourers before 1877 because the Irish were not distinguished in the occupational tables before 1877. But between 1877 and 1920 about 80% of the Irish were returned as labourers. (Agricultural labourers were not distinguished in Ireland.) If the proportion of Irish who were labourers before 1877 was significantly lower than 80% then the proportion of British labourers must obviously have been higher.

lished series starts) and 1890, between 30% and 45% of all adult male English immigrants into the U.S.A. were returned as labourers and in some years the classification was abandoned.[34] The final problem is that no occupation was given for between 10% and 25% of adult male emigrants and for the majority of females.[35] The proportion with no occupation recorded is much less in the American series, but this may not mean the series is more accurate.

Since about 50% of British adult male emigrants were returned as either agricultural labourers, general labourers or having not stated an occupation, the occupational tables obviously do not resolve our uncertainty about what is likely to have been the dominant occupational group among the emigrants.

The problems which are posed by the statistical material partly explain the main trends in the literature. As we noticed before, the literature, until comparatively recently, has concentrated either on the development of emigration flows which could be examined from the surviving qualtitative evidence; or has explained the large scale movements by little more than *a priori* reasoning and guesswork. The earlier writers like C. E. Snow (in Ferenczi and Willcox) and M. R. Davie, who were concerned with the general case of European emigration, assumed from no evidence that British emigration must have been caused by virtually the same set of factors that caused the contemporary emigration from the continent of Europe.[36] This view was reaffirmed in 1953 by the influential United Nations publication, *The determinants and consequences of population trends*.[37]

For example, because the peaks of British emigration in the period 1815–50, occurred when conditions in Britain worsened, it was assumed that the emigrants were workers who had been adversely affected by poor harvests, high prices and industrial unemployment – i.e. they were poor labourers or workers in declining industries like handloom weaving.[38] The same assumption was made about the

[34] Relatively more labourers went to the United States.

[35] The majority of adult women were returned as unoccupied. In the early years 'married woman' and 'spinster' were counted as occupations. Even so, in most of the years before 1870 about 30% of all adult women were assumed to be neither 'occupied' nor 'married' nor 'spinsters'. After 1877 about 60% of adult women were returned as unoccupied which presumably included 'married women' and 'spinsters'.

[36] Snow, 'British emigration', in Ferenczi and Willcox, *International migrations*, pp. 240–50, and Davie, *World migration*. See chapter 2 for a discussion of the general causes of European emigration in the period.

[37] United Nations, *The determinants and consequences of population trends*, 'Population Studies', No. 17 (New York, 1953).

[38] Johnson, *History of emigration*, pp. 39–59. Helen I. Cowan, *British emigration to British North America*, revised edition (Toronto University Press, 1961), pp. 173–4. Ferenczi and Willcox, *International migrations*, vol. II, pp. 251–2.

emigrants in the 1880s. Carrothers, for example, drew a simple relationship between the agricultural depression and emigration. He argued that agriculture was depressed (which, in the main, it wasn't), emigration was at its highest rate in the nineteenth century, therefore the majority of the emigrants were from rural areas (and were probably agricultural labourers).[39]

A disproportionately large share of the surviving qualitative evidence has come from institutional sources – particularly the British and overseas government agencies. In consequence, much of the most informative work on British emigration has been written about the first half of the nineteenth century when both private and government emigration schemes were most important, and when the British government was concerned with conditions on emigrant sailing ships.[40] But in the whole period 1815–1914 only about 9% of British passengers travelled with a subsidy.[41] The majority of British emigrants must have made an individual (or family) decision, that was not directly related to any official inducements from Britain and overseas.[42] It was precisely when emigration increased because, among other things, conditions on emigrant ships improved with the transition from sail to steam in the 1860s, that the British government began to lose interest in it. The dominance of institutional evidence also explains the large literature that has been devoted to the settlement

[39] Carrothers was writing at a time when the years 1873–96 were thought to have been disastrous for British agriculture. This view has since been considerably modified. See T. W. Fletcher, 'The Great Depression in English agriculture, 1873–1896', *Economic History Review*, 1961, 13 (3), pp. 417–32. Carrothers, *Emigration from the British Isles*, pp. 227–30. See also M. Jones, *American immigration* (University of Chicago Press, 1960), p. 194.

[40] For example, W. S. Shepperson, *British emigration to North America* (Basil Blackwell, Oxford, 1957). Particular studies of British emigration policy are H. J. M. Johnston, *British emigration policy, 1815–1830. Shovelling out paupers* (Oxford University Press, 1972), F. M. Hutchins, *The colonial land and emigration commissioners* (University of Pennsylvania Press, Philadelphia, 1931).

[41] Probably less than 900,000 emigrants from Britain were supported by an institution of which about 350,000 travelled under various emigration schemes before 1873 (when the Colonial Land and Emigration Commission was wound up); between 50,000 and 100,000 were subsidised by trade unions of which 40,000 were agricultural labourers and about 450,000 were supported by Dominion governments, mainly after 1900. After 1918, the proportion of assisted passages was very much larger. W. D. Forsyth, *The myth of the open spaces* (Melbourne University Press, 1942), pp. 24–36; G. F. Plant, *Oversea settlement* (Oxford University Press, 1951), pp. 42–3; Davie, *World migration*, pp. 428–9, 433–4.

[42] This does not imply that most British emigrants made a decision to migrate *in vacuo*. It was shown in chapter 2 that many emigrants from the Continent of Europe relied on information (and sometimes encouragement) from returned migrants and from friends and relatives who were already abroad. There is little evidence about the sources of information that had been used by British emigrants.

and assimilation of British emigrants overseas.[43] Occasionally, it has
been possible to trace the migration of a very well defined (but unrepresentative) group – like the Mormons.[44] But usually, relatively
little can be traced from the institutional material about the British
background of emigrants. And finally, we know relatively little about
the experience of the greater part of British emigrants abroad because
the majority of British emigrants went to urban areas where there
were relatively few formal institutions to aid their settlement and
assimilation.

The emigrant letter has become an important way of avoiding some
of the bias in the institutional material. When the letters have been
arranged in series as, for example, has been done by Professor Erickson they are an important source because the exchange of letters was
one of the ways emigration developed.[45] When properly arranged,
a series of letters can give valuable insights into the causes of emigration from Britain, the information available to potential emigrants
and their mobility within the country to which they went. The main
problem in the analysis of emigrant letters is the degree to which
the surviving letters were a sample of all emigrant letters, and the
degree to which the writers of letters were a sample of all emigrants.[46]

A final bias is that more evidence has survived about those emigrants who were higher in the social and economic hierarchy. We
know more, for example, about farmers,[47] gentlemen and skilled
workers[48] than we do about building workers and agricultural
labourers. This is partly because there were relatively more migrants
of higher status in the early part of the period, partly because institutions like trade unions and companies[49] were more concerned with
the migration of skilled workers, and partly because the better off
left more records.

In conclusion, the literature on British emigration in the nineteenth

---

[43] For example, MacDonald, *Canada, immigration and colonisation, 1841–1903*.

[44] P. A. M. Taylor, *Expectations Westward*.

[45] Alan Conway, *The Welsh in America* (University of Wales Press, Cardiff, 1961). Erickson, *Invisible immigrants*. The problem remains that the letters show more about
the migrant experience *after* they had emigrated.

[46] An obvious issue is whether those emigrants who maintained their links with the
old country by writing home, for example, were those who had not been able to
assimilate or did not want to. See Erickson, *Invisible immigrants*, 1972, pp. 13–21.

[47] For example, Erickson, 'Agrarian myths'.

[48] Berthoff, *British immigrants in industrial America*, Erickson, *American industry and the
European immigrant*.

[49] For example, W. S. Shepperson, 'Industrial emigration in early Victorian Britain',
Journal of Economic History, 13 (2), 1953, pp. 179–92. Erickson, 'The encouragement
of emigration by British trade unions, 1850–1900', *Population Studies*, 3, 1949–50, pp.
248–73.

and early twentieth centuries has, until relatively recently, been biased towards the first half of the century, to organised migration and settlement, to the problem of assimilation, to the migration of entire families and to the skilled working class and middle class. The literature has been less informative about the background to emigration from Britain and its causes, about the temporary emigration of individuals and their rate of return, and about the experience of numerically the most important occupational groups. In other words, until recently the bulk of the literature has failed to examine British emigration when it was at its greatest relative and absolute importance – in particular the large flows of the 1880s and the early 1890s.

The most important contribution to British emigration history in recent years has been the analysis of the American ships' lists which were deposited by ships' masters as they landed in the United States, and which are now in the National Archives in Washington. (Most of the equivalent lists of outgoing passengers from Britain have been lost.) The American lists are an exceptionally rich source. All ships seem to have been covered.[50] The lists give the name, sex, age, occupation, and marital status of the immigrants and sometimes the European town of last residence. They list families in groups and distinguish those travelling alone. They have been very skilfully used by Charlotte Erickson[51] to analyse the occupations and other characteristics of British emigrants to the U.S.A. in the peak years of the 1880s and in the peak of 1831. The further analysis of the ships' lists offers the best way of extending our knowledge of British emigration to the U.S.A. But their bulk means that it will be a considerable time before they are fully exploited. The other important contribution has been by Brinley Thomas[52] who analysed the relationships between annual passenger movement from Britain and the continent and a set of economic variables of which the most important were British overseas and domestic investment. Following the earlier work of Cairncross he was able to manipulate the published census data in order to examine the relationship between the main flows of internal migration within Britain and emigration. This approach is capable

---

[50] See the remarkable book by Nils Olssen which identifies every Swedish immigrant to New York City 1820–50 and traces a large number of the immigrants in the Swedish records. Nils William Olssen, *Swedish passenger arrivals in New York City, 1820–1850*, (P. A. Norstedt and Soners Forlag, Stockholm, 1967), pp. xi–xvi.

[51] Erickson, 'Who were?' (1972) and 'Who were?' (1977). I am grateful to Professor Erickson for allowing me to quote from her unpublished paper.

[52] Thomas, *Migration and economic growth*, esp. chapters 7, 8 and 11 and Thomas, *Migration and urban development*.

of much more development and seems the only important alternative to the further analysis of the ships' lists.

III

This section reviews the evidence on the extent of emigration from Britain before the middle of the nineteenth century when the data are more abundant.[53] The most recent estimate of the number of emigrants is a by-product of the work of Wrigley and Schofield on the course of fertility and mortality. Their estimates suggest, for example, that net emigration from England in the seventeenth century was about 544,000.[54] This figure can only be tentative and it includes losses at sea, military deaths and, most important, net migration from England to Scotland and Ireland. Wrigley and Schofield's data can be compared with estimates of arrivals in the New World. The most recent – by Hank Gemery – suggests that about 378,000 left the British Isles for the New World between 1630 and 1700 (net of returns). Of these about 223,000 went to the Caribbean; 116,000 to the southern mainland colonies (principally Maryland and Virginia) and 39,000 went to the northern colonies.[55] The main problem is that Gemery's estimates include Irish and Scottish emigrants. It is thought that emigration from Ireland and Scotland to the mainland colonies was not very important before the eighteenth century. But it is likely that a large number of the emigrants to the West Indies in the seventeenth century were Irish.[56] It should also be pointed out that Gemery's figures are derived from estimates of the total population of the different colonies at different points in time, and from estimates of the natural increase in the intervening period. They must obviously be treated with caution.[57] On the other hand, independent estimates of

---

[53] The best summary of early English emigration, on which parts of this account are based, is Erickson, 'The English', pp. 315–36, in S. Thernstrom (ed.), *The Harvard encyclopaedia of American ethnic groups* (Harvard University Press, Cambridge, Mass., 1980). I am grateful to Professor Erickson for allowing me to see this paper in typescript and also to consult an unpublished paper which is more detailed. (The page references (if present) in subsequent footnotes refer to the *Harvard encyclopaedia*.)

[54] E. A. Wrigley and R. S. Schofield, *The population history of England, 1541–1871. A reconstruction* (Arnold, 1981), p. 219.

[55] H. A. Gemery, 'Emigration from the British Isles to the New World 1630–1700: inferences from colonial populations, in P. Uselding (ed.), *Research in Economic History*, 5, 1980, pp. 204–5.

[56] Erickson, 'The English', pp. 322–3.

[57] Obviously, any estimate of migration that depends on the residual between two point of time estimates is totally dependent on the quality of the data. In this case Gemery had no option but to estimate *all* the point of time population counts,

immigration into Virginia and Maryland, based on different data, broadly agree with Gemery. They show that 100,000 (net) entered these colonies between 1635 and 1705.[58] Most of these immigrants would have been English.

Emigration seems to have been relatively high in the middle years of the seventeenth century. Bridenbaugh estimated that about 80,000 left England in the so-called 'Great Migration' of 1628–42, of which 58,000 went to the New World.[59] But emigration rates in subsequent decades may have been higher. According to Wrigley and Schofield the peak losses probably occurred after 1640. This agrees with Gemery's estimate.[60] We can guess that the number of British emigrants in the seventeenth century was less than 500,000 net of a few returns – or on average less than 1 per 1,000 of the population each year. We can also guess that more than half of the emigrants left between about 1635 and 1665.

Wrigley and Schofield estimate that net emigration from England in the eighteenth century was about 519,000 persons. This would imply that compared with the previous century emigration rates had fallen but there are wide margins of error in the estimates. The qualitative evidence suggests that emigration from Britain was continuous in the eighteenth century except in the period of the European wars. The years following the wars (the 1720s, 1750s, 1760s and early 1770s and the years after 1815) all appear to have had above average emigration.[61] An important customs return for the period December 1773

mortality and fertility. A further problem is that Gemery assumes that 10% of emigrants to the West Indies died at sea and a further 10–15% died within one year of arrival. This is based on very fragmentary evidence – notably the experience of the white factors of the Royal African Company in West Africa, and the experience of the military in the nineteenth century. Gemery's assumptions about the level of mortality imply that immigration into the West Indies of 144,000 between 1630 and 1660 only resulted in an increase in population of 43,000. Gemery, 'Emigration from the British Isles to the New World', pp. 185, 197.

[58] Werthenbaker estimated that between 140,000 and 175,000 went to Virginia and Maryland between 1635 and 1705 but Craven's estimate for Virginian immigration reduces this. T. S. Werthenbaker, *The first Americans, 1607–1690. A history of American life*, Vol. II (Macmillan, New York, 1927), p. 26. W. F. Craven, *White, red and black: the seventeenth-century Virginian* (University Press of Virginia, Charlottesville, 1971), p. 16.

[59] Carl Bridenbaugh, *Vex'd and troubled Englishmen, 1590–1642* (Oxford University Press, 1968), p. 395. This flow ended with the declaration of the Commonwealth in 1649. Note that only 20,000 of the 'Puritans' went to New England.

[60] Wrigley and Schofield, *Population history of England*, pp. 219–20. Gemery, 'Emigration from the British Isles to the New World', p. 205.

[61] Erickson, 'The English', p. 323. About 350,000 are thought to have entered the U.S.A. in the eighteenth century from Europe and Africa, but this is only an educated guess. See J. Potter, 'The growth of population in America', in D. V. Glass and D. E. C. Eversley (eds.), *Population in history* (Arnold, 1965), pp. 664–5.

to April 1775 showed that about 6,000 had left, nearly all going to the American colonies.[62] This was a peak period, however, (which was the reason for government interest) and it is possible that English emigration was relatively no higher until 1815 when it rose sharply.[63] There does seem to have been a large outflow from Scotland in the third quarter of the eighteenth century; 25,000 are thought to have gone between 1763 and 1776.[64]

English (and Scots) emigration rose substantially after 1815. The large number of English emigrants is not apparent from the returns of outward passenger movement but these are deficient. As we pointed out, this is clear from the enumeration of English born in the United States' census. There were probably more than 500,000 net English emigrants between 1815 and 1850 and probably more than 100,000 Scots of which 80% may have gone to the U.S.A. (Wrigley and Schofield's data imply a net outward movement of about 621,000 English, and this was a period of substantial net migration to England from Scotland and Ireland.) Emigration again rose substantially in the 1850s and 1860s when there were about 1,200,000 outward bound passengers who were English and about 300,000 who were Scots (see Appendices 2–5). We can be fairly sure that the rate of return was low. (See chapter 5.) This means that there may have been as many English and Scots emigrants in the two decades of the 1850s and 1860s as in the whole of the seventeenth and eighteenth centuries.

IV

English and Welsh emigration rates fluctuated around a strong upward trend until the First World War and then fell. (See Figure 3.1.) We have seen that emigration (defined as outward passenger movement) was at a high level in 1853 when the data become reliable. Emigration peaked in 1854 when 91,000 left – a rate of 4.9 per 1,000

---

[62] Mildred Campbell, 'English emigration on the eve of the American Revolution', *American Historical Review*, 61, 1955, pp. 1–20. 76% of the emigrants went to Virginia and Maryland and 21% went to Pennsylvania. See also, G. R. Mellor, 'Emigration from the British Isles to the New World, 1765–1775', *History*, XL, 1955, pp. 68–83.

[63] It is sometimes said that 250,000 immigrants entered the U.S.A. between 1783 and 1815. About 100,000 are thought to have come from Ulster but how many came from Britain is not known. In fact the estimate is little more than a guess. See Hansen, *Atlantic migration*, pp. 77–8. Arrivals of British immigrants recorded in the American ships' lists may undercount passengers of course. There were only 50,000 English born recorded in the American census of 1810. See Erickson, 'The English', pp. 324–5.

[64] S. Donaldson, 'Scots', in S. Thermstrom (ed.), *The Harvard encyclopaedia of American ethnic groups*, p. 908.

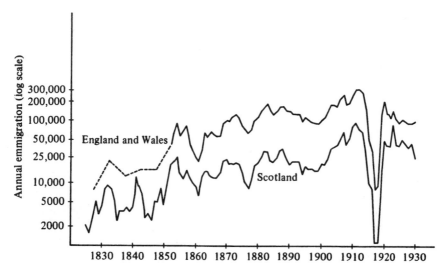

Figure 3.1 *Emigration (outward passenger movement) from Britain, 1825–1930*
Source: Appendices 2, 3, 4 and 5. English emigration before 1853 is assumed
to be 50% underestimated.

of the total population. Emigration then fell to a low of only 22,000
in 1861 (1.1 per 1,000) and rose slowly to a peak in the 1870s. Emigration in the 1870s was moderately high, averaging 97,000 p.a. (4.0 per
1,000) but from 1879 it began to rise rapidly, reached a peak of 183,000
(6.9 per 1,000) and continued at a high level until 1893. Nearly a quarter
of all emigration from England and Wales before 1930 occurred in
the fifteen years 1879–93. After the boom of 1879–93 emigration fell,
and in addition there seems to have been an exceptionally high rate
of return in the 1890s. (This is discussed below.) A second emigration
boom occurred after 1900. English and Welsh emigration had been
only 100,000 p.a. (about 3 per 1,000) in the 1890s but it rose to a
peak of 265,000 in 1907 (7.7 per 1,000) and to 315,000 (8.7 per 1,000)
in 1912. Nearly a third of all English emigration occurred in the so-
called 'Edwardian' period from 1900 to 1914. The peak year ever of
emigration from England and Wales was 1912, both when measured
in total numbers and as a proportion of the population. International
migration was effectively stopped by the First World War and there
was only one important year of English emigration afterwards (1920).
In the rest of the 1920s, English emigration rates reverted to the comparatively low levels of the 1850s and 1860s.

English emigration made an important contribution to the two key
periods of European emigration – the 1880s and the early twentieth

century but English emigration was also continuous and heavy over
a long period. English emigration fell below a rate of 3 per 1,000 in
only fourteen years between 1850 and 1914, and for the whole period
was among the highest in Europe.

The rate and fluctuations of Scottish emigration (i.e. emigration
from Scottish ports) can be seen from Figure 3.1 and Appendices 3 and
5. Appendix 3 shows gross Scottish emigration in the period 1825–53,
which is presumably underestimated but possibly by a lesser amount
than English emigration in the same period. Total overseas migration
from Scotland in the period 1853–1930 was 2.15 million compared
with 9.06 million from England and Wales. Hence, 19% of British
emigrants were Scots although Scotland contained only 13.7% of the
British population in 1853 and only 10.9% in 1930. The second important difference between Scots and English emigration was that Scots
emigration took place later. Half of the English emigration between
1853 and 1930 occurred before 1899 but it was not until 1906 that
half of Scottish emigration in the same period had taken place. Scots
emigration in the 1880s had been at an average rate of 7.1 per 1,000
(England Wales, 5.6 per 1,000) but the Scottish emigration grew faster
than English in the early twentieth century until it was running at
nearly twice the English rate. Between 1901 and 1914, 722,000 Scots
(11.2 per 1,000) left compared with 2.92 million English (6 per 1,000).
The final contrast with England was that heavy Scots emigration continued into the 1920s when the rate of Scottish emigration was nearly
as high as in the 1901–10 decade.

The demographic effects of emigration were very important in Scotland. In the 1881–90 decade, for example, Scots emigration was 54.1%
of the excess of births over deaths. In the 1901–30 period gross emigration was greater than Scottish natural increase in eleven years and
in five other years gross emigration was more than 75% of natural
increase. Over the whole period 1853–1930 Scottish overseas emigration was about 61% of its natural increase. England and Wales only
lost about 36%. These figures do not imply that the natural increase
of England and Scotland would have been 36% and 61% greater if
there had been no emigration (*ceteris paribus* and neglecting the effect
of emigrant age distribution). Return migration was common and
there was net immigration from continental Europe and Ireland.
Between 1895 and 1930 net overseas emigration from England and
Wales was 52.6% of gross overseas emigration (Appendix 4) and as
much as 65.3% of gross emigration from Scotland (Appendix 5).

The total effect of the net emigration of natives and of the net
immigration of foreigners is shown in Tables 3.1 and 3.2, where migra-

Table 3.1. *Net emigration. England and Wales, 1841–1930 (calculated from the census)*

	Net emigration (000s)	% of population	% of natural increase
1841–50	−81	0.5	3.7
1851–60	−327	1.7	12.8
1861–70	−206	1.0	7.2
1871–80	−164	0.7	4.7
1881–90	−601	2.3	16.5
1891–1900	−69	0.2	1.9
1901–10	−501	1.5	12.4
1911–20	−620	1.7	21.3
1921–30	−172	0.5	7.2

Table 3.2. *Net emigration. Scotland, 1861–1930 (calculated from the census)*

	Net emigration (000s)	% of population	% of natural increase
1861–70	−120	3.7	27.5
1871–80	−93	2.8	19.4
1881–90	−217	5.8	42.7
1891–1900	−53	1.3	10.6
1901–10	−254	5.7	46.8
1911–20	−239	5.0	57.2
1921–30	−392	8.0	104.2

Note: Scottish emigration includes net movement to England.
Source: Calculated from Carrier and Jeffery, *External migration*, Table 2, p. 14 and Mitchell, *Abstract of British historical statistics*, Tables 10 and 11, pp. 29–35. The totals for 1841–70 are adjusted for under-registration of births. See D. V. Glass, 'A note on the under-registration of births in the nineteenth century', *Population Studies*, 5, 1951–2, pp. 70–88. Net emigration includes net moves from England to Scotland and from Scotland to England. The total for 1911–20 excludes military deaths abroad.

tion is calculated from the natural increase between two census dates. The tables show that net emigration from England and Wales was only 21.3% of natural increase at its peak (1911–20), 16.5% in the 1881–90 decade and usually much less. In Scotland, net migration was 42.7% of natural increase in 1881–90, 46.8% in 1901–10, 57.2% in 1911–20 and 104.2% in 1921–30. Hence, Scottish population *fell* between 1921 and 1930 because of net emigration and migration to England. Scottish population probably fell in some individual years before the First World War when *net* overseas emigration exceeded natural increase (i.e. 1910–13). Over the whole period, Scottish emigration probably constituted a greater proportion of the natural increase of the population, than in any other European country except Norway and Ireland (where natural increase was exceptionally low). If England is counted as a foreign country Scottish emigration is in this regard only exceeded by Irish.[65]

The main destination of British 'emigrants' (i.e. passengers) can be seen from Tables 3.3 and 3.4. Table 3.3 shows that in the period 1861–1900, between 50% and 60% of all English and Welsh emigrants went to the U.S.A. The proportion was higher before 1853. The share of English emigrants going to Canada rose through the nineteenth century, but it was the destination of only 15% of passengers as late as 1891–1900, and some of the emigrants to Canada may have immediately crossed into the United States.[66] On the other hand, if these people had intended to stay in Canada when they departed from England they can be regarded as emigrants to Canada. Before 1850, it was cheaper to go to the U.S.A. via a Canadian port, although relatively few of the *English* seem to have done it. The share of English movement to Australasia was greater than to Canada in 1853–1900 (20% compared to 13%) and was exceptionally high in the 1850s which was the Gold Rush period.

After 1900, the U.S.A. ceased to be the dominant destination for English emigrants partly because Australia and Canada had become

[65] See M. W. Flinn (ed.), *Scottish population history from the seventeenth century to the 1930s* (Cambridge University Press, 1977), part 6, chapter 1. Flinn showed that net Scots outward migration (overseas) in 1835–1938 was 997,300 and that emigration in 1895–1938 was 43.7% of Scots natural increase. Norwegian emigration was 40% of natural increase, 1865–1914. He then assumed that the mortality of lifetime Scots migrants in England was two-thirds that of the English in the particular country where they resided. This assumption reflects migrant age distribution and is, in fact, taken from a paper of the author's subsequently modified. See D. E. Baines, 'The use of published census data in migration studies', in E. A. Wrigley (ed.), *Nineteenth-century society, essays in the use of quantitative data* (Cambridge University Press, 1972), pp. 319–28. Scots emigration to England and abroad would then be 54.6% of the natural increase. Flinn seems to have neglected the effect of English, Irish and foreign migration to Scotland.

[66] There was a particular advantage of emigrating to the U.S.A. *via* Canada in the early part of the century. The American Passenger Act of 1819 was much stricter than the British Act of 1823. This meant that ships sailing to Canadian ports could carry more passengers (in worse conditions) and were cheaper. In addition, the Canadian timber ships called at the smaller English ports which regular packets did not. But relatively few *English* emigrants took advantage of the cheaper passages, because they could afford to travel in more comfort. Three-quarters of the Irish travelled via Canada in the period 1825–50 because otherwise they could not afford to go.

Table 3.3. *Emigration (outward passenger movement) from England and Wales by destination, 1853–1930*

	To U.S.A. 000s %	To British North America 000s %	To Australasia 000s %	Other non-European destinations 000s %	To all non-European destinations 000s %
1853–60	195.7 (43.1)	30.3 (6.7)	218.5 (48.1)	9.9 (2.2)	454.4 (100)
1861–70	365.1 (60.3)	65.9 (10.9)	142.1 (23.5)	32.1 (5.3)	605.2 (100)
1871–80	549.8 (56.6)	126.4 (13.0)	200.4 (20.6)	94.0 (9.7)	970.6 (100)
1881–90	909.2 (58.7)	222.2 (14.3)	272.3 (17.6)	145.3 (9.4)	1549.0 (100)
1891–1900	600.3 (54.8)	159.8 (14.6)	103.2 (9.4)	232.6 (21.2)	1095.9 (100)
1901–10	649.7 (34.6)	623.6 (33.2)	187.8 (10.0)	414.4 (22.1)	1875.5 (100)
1911–20	288.2 (19.5)	652.1 (44.1)	304.5 (20.6)	234.3 (19.8)	1479.1 (100)
1921–30	153.7 (14.9)	345.1 (33.5)	312.3 (30.3)	218.1 (21.2)	1029.2 (100)
1853–1900	2620.1 (56.0)	604.6 (12.9)	936.5 (20.0)	413.9 (8.9)	4675.1 (100)
1901–1930	1091.6 (24.9)	1620.8 (37.0)	804.6 (18.4)	866.8 (19.8)	4383.8 (100)
Total 1853–1930	3711.7 (41.0)	2225.4 (24.6)	1741.1 (19.2)	1380.7 (15.2)	9058.9 (100)

Source: Calculated from Carrier and Jeffery, *External migration,* Table C(1), pp. 92–3 and Table D/F/G(1), pp. 95–6.

Table 3.4. Emigration (outward passenger movement) from Scotland by destination, 1853–1930

	To U.S.A. 000s %	To British North America 000s %	To Australasia 000s %	Other non-European destinations 000s %	To all non-European destinations 000s %
1853–60	35.1 (29.0)	28.4 (23.5)	54.6 (45.2)	2.8 (2.3)	120.9 (100)
1861–70	76.7 (51.8)	24.3 (16.4)	42.3 (28.5)	4.9 (3.3)	148.2 (100)
1871–80	88.1 (53.2)	25.8 (15.5)	41.1 (24.8)	10.7 (6.5)	165.7 (100)
1881–90	178.2 (64.8)	35.2 (12.8)	45.0 (16.4)	16.8 (6.1)	275.2 (100)
1891–1900	118.4 (63.7)	16.6 (8.9)	13.0 (7.0)	38.0 (20.4)	186.0 (100)
1901–10	187.6 (41.0)	169.6 (37.1)	31.1 (6.8)	69.2 (15.1)	457.5 (100)
1911–20	91.1 (26.0)	169.9 (48.6)	48.1 (13.7)	40.8 (11.7)	349.9 (100)
1921–30	157.4 (35.3)	161.6 (36.2)	85.8 (19.2)	41.5 (9.3)	446.3 (100)
1853–1900	496.5 (55.4)	130.3 (14.5)	196.0 (21.9)	73.2 (8.2)	896.0 (100)
1901–1930	436.1 (34.8)	501.1 (40.0)	165.0 (13.2)	151.5 (12.1)	1253.7 (100)
1853–1930	932.6 (43.4)	631.4 (29.4)	361.0 (16.8)	224.7 (10.4)	2149.7 (100)

Source: As for Table 3.3.

urbanised, and possibly because of mass immigration from southern and eastern Europe into the U.S.A. and because of Dominion settlement schemes. From 1901–30 less than 25% of English emigrants went to the U.S.A., but 37% went to Canada and 18% to Australasia. Emigration to Canada exceeded that to America in every year after 1905. So while the very large outflow of 1879–93 was dominated by emigration to the United States, the outflow of 1900–14 was not dominated by emigration to any one destination – although Canada was the single most important. In addition, in the early twentieth century a greater proportion of outward passengers went to destinations outside the U.S.A., Canada and Australasia – for example, to South Africa. In the period 1853–1900, 88.9% of all English passengers went to the U.S.A., Canada or Australasia. In 1901–30 those countries took only 80.3%. A larger proportion of outward passengers were not going to the emigrant destinations. This probably means that a larger proportion of outward passengers were not emigrants.

The destinations of Scottish passengers were not very different from those of English. The main difference was that the United States was becoming a more important destination for the Scots in the period 1853–1900 but a less important destination for the English. This is because until 1845 the Scots had been more likely to go to Canada.

V

There is little evidence of the geographical origins and the occupations of the early English emigrants. Two-thirds of a group of 2,155 who went to New England in the 1630s are known to have come from East Anglia, London and the Home counties and the West of England.[67] But this group is not representative. Until the third quarter of the eighteenth century, probably the majority of English emigrants travelled on free passages as indentured servants and were mainly young single males. The early emigrants to New England had travelled in family groups.

The main source of information about the characteristics of seventeenth and eighteenth-century emigrants is, therefore, the indentures. Galenson has recently analysed the surviving indentures of 20,657 persons from six groups who left at various times between 1654 and 1775. Only 3,810, or 18% of the indentured servants were female

[67] Charles E. Banks, 'English sources of emigration to the New England Colonies in the 17th century', *Proceedings of the Massachusetts Historical Society*, 60 (1927), pp. 366–72. Quoted in Erickson, 'The English', p. 322. The West of England and London had high emigration rates in the late nineteenth century, but not East Anglia.

and between 61% and 83% of the males in each group were aged 15–24.[68] Galenson's general conclusion about the occupational struc- ture is that *all* the main occupational groups of pre-industrial society were well represented. The indentured servants contained large numbers of farmers and artisans, as well as labourers and servants. Galenson takes this to mean that the social composition of the inden- tured servants was not very different to that of the country as a whole.[69] Galenson's views are rather controversial and conflict with previous interpretations of the same data which concluded that the majority of the indentured emigrants were relatively well off. For example, Mildred Campbell concluded from her analysis of two groups leaving Bristol in 1654–60 and 1684–6 that the majority were craftsmen, yeomen and farmers.[70] But the occupation of many emi- grants was not recorded. The important survey of about 6,000 emi- grants in 1773–5 is less ambiguous. Most occupations were recorded. The majority of the indentured servants were not poor and, in fact, were no poorer than those emigrants who paid their own fare. (About 60% of the adult males in this group travelled under indentures and about 30% financed themselves.)[71] Galenson holds that the 1773–5 group is unrepresentative. On the other hand, if they were a sample of all emigrants, it would imply that, in the main, poor people were not induced to emigrate because they could defray the cost of the passage by becoming indentured servants. Galenson holds that inden-

---

[68] D. W. Galenson, *White servitude in colonial America. An economic analysis* (Cambridge University Press, 1981), pp. 24, 28.

[69] Galenson, *White servitude*, pp. 47, 50.

[70] Mildred Campbell, 'Social origins of some early Americans', in J. M. Smith (ed.), *Seventeenth century America* (University of North Carolina Press, Chapel Hill, 1959), pp. 69–71. Quoted in Erickson, 'The English', p. 322. This list shows that of 36% of the indentured servants leaving Bristol for whom an occupation was given, 69% were yeomen and husbandmen and 22% were artisans and tradesmen. Galenson holds that the younger emigrants had no recorded occupation because they did not have one – i.e. they had no skill. The evidence on literacy in other listings seems to confirm this. Galenson, *White servitude*, pp. 52, 58. See, D. W. Galenson, '"Middling People" or "Common sort"? The social origins of some early Americans re-examined', *William and Mary Quarterly*, 3rd series, 35, 1978, pp. 499–524. M. Camp- bell, 'Response', in *ibid.*, pp. 524–40. S. Souden, 'Rogues, whores and vagabonds? Indentured servant emigrants to North America and the case of mid-seventeenth- century Bristol', *Social History*, III, 1978, pp. 23–38.

[71] Campbell, 'English emigration of the eve of the American Revolution', pp. 4–6. Occu- pations were recorded for 98% of adult males. 63% were tradesmen and craftsmen, 16% were farmers and only 11% were (urban and rural) labourers. Of the male emigrants, 59% travelled as indentured servants, 6% as redemptioners and 5% as convicts. (Redemptioners gave the master a note that their passage would be paid by relatives or friends on arrival, otherwise he could indenture them in the colony to defray the cost of the passage.)

tured servants – and by inference all emigrants – were of 'middling sort'. But he concedes that the skill level of indentured emigrants may have been higher in the eighteenth than in the seventeenth century. What does seem to be clear from this controversy, however, is that relatively few of the eighteenth-century emigrants can have been drawn from the ranks of the poor.

It is also noticeable that, as time went on, the indentured servants were less likely to have rural occupations and were more likely to come from urbanised parts of the country. For example, London was the most important origin of the 1773–5 group and the second most important was the industrial north. This change reflected the redistribution of the English population in the eighteenth century. It suggests (but no more), that many English emigrants in the period came from areas in the mainstream of economic change rather than from areas in which economic change was slower.

Indentured emigration ceased after 1780. But the scraps of evidence suggest that the character of English emigration changed little. Many of the emigrants to the United States after 1783 were skilled industrial workers who may or may not have transferred British technology to the U.S.A.[72] There were prohibitions on the emigration of artisans but they were easily evaded. (The existence of prohibitions could be taken as evidence that artisan emigration was taking place.) The evidence suggests that most English emigrants in the late eighteenth and very early nineteenth century were drawn from neither the urban poor nor the rural poor. (The characteristics of English emigrants after 1815 are discussed in Section VII.)

VI

Unlike the English, a large proportion of Scottish emigrants in the eighteenth century (and later) seem to have come from the poorest classes. Until the early nineteenth century Scottish emigrants probably

---

[72] There are many examples of English skilled workers in the U.S.A. in the early nineteenth century, but there is a controversy about the extent to which American industry relied on the transfer of technology. What is clear is that if there was technological transfer it must have depended on the migration of skilled workers, because there were no blueprints. For example, David Jeremy believes that the number of textile immigrants was insufficient to account for technological transfer to the American textile industries; that the English textile emigrants were mainly handloom weavers and that American technology was different to British. Hence, immigration of skilled British artisans cannot have been the reason for the growth of the American textile industry in the 1820s and after. D. Jeremy, *Transatlantic industrial revolution: the diffusion of textile technologies between Britain and America, 1790 to the 1830s* (Blackwell, Oxford, 1981), pp. 148–9, 256.

came mainly from the Highlands.[73] Population growth in the Highlands was rapid – which was particularly serious in a region with
primitive agriculture. The situation was not improved by the introduction of commercial cattle and sheep farming to the glens.[74] This does
not mean that population pressure was a sufficient cause of Highland
emigration, which does not seem to have been equally important in
all parts of the Highlands. Highland emigration was communal and
could not take place without the leadership of the tacksmen and the
approval of the lairds.[75] Highland emigration was not, strictly speaking, famine emigration because, unlike in Ireland, the emigration
tended to forestall serious pressure on the land. Hence, there were
no serious subsistence crises in the Highlands between the end of
the seventeenth century and 1847, when private charity was able to
take a great deal of the strain.[76] Highland emigration took place in
two phases. Between 1763 and 1779 about 25,000 are thought to have
gone, mainly from the west and the islands.[77] Between about 1780
and 1815 there seems to have been little permanent emigration
although harvest migration to the Lowlands and into foreign armies
continued. The fall in emigration is usually associated with several
important economic changes. The potato came to the Outer Isles in
the 1750s and was common in the Highlands by 1800. And the linen,

[73] Malcolm Gray pointed out, however, that the rural lowlands had twice the population
of the Highlands by the mid nineteenth century and must have produced more
emigrants. But unfortunately there is little direct evidence of Lowland emigration.
Gray's view rests on the changes in Lowland agriculture and the net migration losses
by Lowland parishes. It seems likely that many rural emigrants from Scotland before
1850 must have been Lowlanders but unfortunately, there is no way of knowing
what proportion of out-migrants from Lowland parishes went overseas. M. Gray,
'The social impact of agrarian change in the rural lowlands 1755–1875', *Perspectives
in American History*, 7, 1973, pp. 97–8. For the Highland economy and the Highland
migration see A. J. Youngson, *After the Forty-Five. The economic impact on the Scottish
Highlands* (Edinburgh University Press, 1973), chapters 5–7. Also, Flinn, *Scottish population history*, pp. 43 and J. D. Wood, 'Scottish migration overseas', *Scottish Geographical
Magazine*, December 1964, pp. 164–76.

[74] To be distinguished from the rearing of cattle and sheep on the hills which was
complementary to Highland agriculture.

[75] The tacksmen were effectively the agents of the landlords holding a tenancy which
they sublet to the crofters. The tacksmen might favour emigration simply because
it was the laird's policy. M. Adams suggested that they perceived a threat to their
way of life, but it is unclear how serious this was. M. Adams, 'The causes of the
Highland emigrations of 1783–1803', *Scottish Historical Review*, 17, 1920, pp. 73–89.

[76] See M. W. Flinn, 'Malthus, emigration and potatoes in the Scottish North West
1770–1870', pp. 47–64 in C. M. Cullen and T. C. Smout (eds.), *Comparative aspects
of Scottish and Irish economic and social history 1600–1900* (John Macdonald, Edinburgh,
1977).

[77] I. C. C. Graham, *Colonists from Scotland* (Cornell University Press, Ithaca, NY, 1956),
pp. 185–6. The customs return of 1774 listed 2,773 Scots emigrants and another
of 1775 lists 3,607. They were predominantly Highlanders; 64% were men.

kelp and fishing industries were introduced.[78] Fishing and kelp enabled the population to be moved from the central glens to the coast. But the linen industry moved to the Lowlands after 1800; the fishing could not compete with the large scale operations working out of the Clyde and the north east; and the removal of a protective tariff in 1815 destroyed the kelp industry.[79] At the same time, the Scots soldiers returned from the Napoleonic Wars; and the Lowland labour market was more difficult for the Highlanders to enter because of the immigration from Ireland which was nearer than the Highlands. Faced with the destruction of the new Highland economy the landlords began to favour emigration again and cleared more land for sheep. Most important, population growth accelerated after 1800.[80] The population of the six Highland counties grew at an annual rate of 0.7% in the period 1801–30, compared with 0.3% in the period 1775–1800.[81] But by 1841, emigration and movement to the Lowlands had been so large that the population of the Highland counties was no greater than it had been in 1801.[82] Between 1841 and 1861 the

[78] Kelp was a source of alkali fertiliser made by burning a particular seaweed. See Youngson, *After the Forty-Five*, pp. 125–44, for a description of the attempts to introduce new industries to the Highlands.

[79] The Highlanders who were moved to the west were not given enough good land to enable them to resume agriculture when the kelp industry collapsed. Since the landlords were rearing sheep and cattle in the glens there was little alternative to emigration.

[80] I.e. at a rate of 0.7% in 1801–30 despite heavy emigration compared with 0.3% in 1755–1801. Flinn thought the sharp acceleration in population growth after 1789 was caused by smallpox vaccination. (Innoculation was relatively unknown in the Highlands.) The total population of the six Highland counties (i.e. Argyle, Caithness, Inverness, Perth, Ross and Cromarty and Sutherland was approximately 337,000 at Webster's census in 1755, 382,000 in 1801 and 473,000 in 1831. In 1841 it was only 472,000. Flinn, *Scottish population history*, pp. 14–5. Youngson, *After the Forty-Five*, p. 161.

[81] Emigration rates were probably highest in the Western Isles. The population of the Western Isles grew from 19,000 in 1755 to 33,000 in 1811, i.e. at 1% p.a. compared with 0.3% p.a. for the whole of the Highlands. Well known emigration routes from the Western Isles were from Lewis and Skye to Nova Scotia and from S. Uist and Barra to Prince Edward Island.

[82] The suggestion by Gray and Kerr for example, that Highlanders ceased going to the Lowlands when the Irish began to arrive, is incorrect. Highland migration to the Lowlands continued although we do not know, of course, how large it would have been without the presence of the Irish. Possibly more important, the Highlanders had established emigration routes before the Irish arrived. See M. Gray, *The Highland economy 1750–1850* (Oliver and Boyd, Edinburgh, 1957), p. 183. B. M. Kerr, 'Irish seasonal migration to Great Britain 1800–1838', *Irish Historical Studies*, 3, 1942, pp. 365–80. T. M. Devine, 'Temporary migration and the Scottish Highlands in the nineteenth century', *Economic History Review*, 32 (3) 1979, pp. 344–59. For one example of Highland and Irish migration to the Lowlands see, R. D. Lobban, 'The Irish community in Greenock in the nineteenth century', *Irish Geography*, 6 (3), 1971, pp. 270–81.

Highland population fell by nearly 10%. This implies that up to a third[83] of the total population (i.e. 150,000) must have emigrated or gone to other parts of Britain. The annual rate of natural increase is unknown but it must have been about 1% in the period 1801–31. Even if natural increase was exceptionally low, out-migration from the Highlands to the Lowlands, England and overseas cannot have been less than 100,000 and may have been much more.[84] About 70% of Scottish emigrants were found to be from the north in an 1841 enumeration although this year may be exceptional.[85] Even so it is fairly clear that a large proportion of the Scottish emigrants in the late 1840s and the early 1850s were Highlanders.

Little is known about emigration from the Scottish Lowlands. There are scattered references to Lowland emigration in the eighteenth century (i.e. in the 1773–5 return) but there is no evidence that it was important before 1800. (Appendix 3 shows that (minimum) total sailings from Scottish ports were 130,000 between 1825 and 1850.) The gradual commercialisation of Lowland agriculture between 1790 and 1830 has been suggested as the cause of Lowland emigration.[86] The changes varied from one part of the Lowlands to another, but, in general, they made it more difficult for the cottier to obtain land, changed the agricultural labourer into a full-time employee and increased the share of pasture. On the arable, the demand for farm labour was partly met by the harvest migration of Irish and Highlanders. By the 1820s, there is some evidence of industrial emigrants from Scotland who are thought to have been handloom weavers.[87]

[83] The region of origin of 5,737 Scottish settlers in the U.S.A. from Colonial times to 1854 – all those that can be traced – showed that the emigrants were in the main not disproportionately likely to come from particular regions. The proportion of Highlanders and Lowlanders, for example, was not greatly different to the share of these regions in the Scottish population – 45% were from the Highlands which had one-third of the population. See S. Donaldson, *Scots*, p. 910. Flinn, *Scottish population history*, pp. 307–8; Flinn is doubtful that the famine increased mortality sharply. But he may have underestimated the effect of migration on births.

[84] The marriage rate (and hence natural increase) may have been low in the Highlands because of the sex ratio. In 1861, in the six Highland counties, only 41% of women aged 25–9 were married and 59.1% of those aged 30–4, compared with 54% and 68.9% in Scotland as a whole. Illegitimacy was low in the Highlands, but marital fertility was high. Flinn, *Scottish population history*, p. 37.

[85] The 1841 enumeration showed 8,572 emigrants in the first four months of 1841. Total Scottish emigration in that year was recorded as only 12,052. Appendix 3, *Census of Scotland 1841*, BPP 1843, XXII.

[86] Gray, 'Social impact of agrarian change', pp. 132–57. Gray is at pains to point out the great variation in Lowland agriculture, and the effect of the changes in different parts of Scotland. See also, D. F. MacDonald, *Scotland's shifting population, 1770–1850* (Jackson, Glasgow, 1937), pp. 23–31.

[87] A suggestion by Wood, among others. Wood, 'Scottish migration overseas', p. 169. Gray seems to imply the existence of 'urban influence fields' in Scotland at this

The relative importance of agricultural and industrial emigration is largely unknown but the usually accepted view is that Lowland emigration came from the poorer classes.

VII

We have already noted the tendency of many writers to regard the bulk of English emigrants in the period 1815–50 as extremely poor. The view was based on the comments of contemporaries and on the timing of English emigration. The exact extent of English emigration at the time cannot be stated with certainty, but there were peaks in 1819, 1827, the early 1830s and 1842. These were years of bad harvests, high prices and industrial depression, which would suggest that emigration at the peaks was largely composed of distressed agricultural labourers and rural and urban workers from industries with a high level of technological unemployment (like handloom weavers). The problem with this view is that it would predict high emigration rates, whereas emigration rates from England were modest. There were probably something over 500,000 English emigrants between 1815 and 1850 compared with over 2,000,000 Irish, one million of whom left before the Famine. A more sophisticated recent view is that distress did cause large scale migration in England, but it was internally towards the new industrial areas which acted as a safety valve. This could not have happened within Ireland.[88]

There were schemes to remove paupers from England overseas but they were quantitatively unimportant. Emigration under the New Poor Law averaged about 1,400 a year between 1835 and 1846 (when the scheme was wound up).[89] Data have survived giving the origins of Poor Law emigrants in the twenty-five months from June 1835 to July 1837 which was the peak period; 6,403 paupers were sent abroad of which the bulk came from the low wage agricultural counties of Norfolk (3,354) and Suffolk (1,083).[90]

time. He thinks that emigration from the more remote rural parishes was relatively higher than from those near the towns. But this is based only on net migration estimates. Gray, 'Social impact of agrarian change', p. 174.

[88] Jones, 'Background to emigration from Great Britain', p. 48. See also A. Redford, *Labour migration in England* (Manchester University Press, 1926, revised 1964), chapter 4.

[89] There had been some slight provision from individual parishes before the New Poor Law.

[90] The only other counties of importance were Kent (476), Sussex (404) and Wiltshire (372). Of the remaining counties, only Hampshire (182) and Middlesex (110) supplied more than 100 of the Poor Law emigrants. About 4,684 migrants were assisted to move internally under the same scheme, mainly to the Northern industrial counties.

The policy of the British government towards emigration had two aims; to relieve distress and to populate the colonies, the latter, partly as a counter attraction to the United States.[91] Emigration was encouraged in two ways; by giving free or reduced passages, grants of land and implements to individuals and by granting land in the colonies to speculators who made private arrangements to bring out settlers. All the schemes assumed that the emigrants had to be settled in agricultural communities for economic and political reasons. This attempt to freeze the economic and social structure of the colonies was a mistake. Total emigration under the various British government schemes which ran from 1846 to 1869 was about 339,000. This was only 7% of total emigration from England, Scotland and Ireland in the period. It was about 23% of emigration to Canada and Australia. However, it is possible that some of the assisted emigrants who went to Australia would have gone elsewhere had there been no assistance. There was also a considerable leakage of emigrants from Canada into the U.S.A. some of whom had presumably been assisted. We cannot assume that the early assistance schemes increased emigration by the number of emigrants who took advantage of the schemes.[92]

There are two important sources of quantitative data on the origins and characteristics of English emigrants in the period. The first is a special enumeration in the 1841 census, which gives the last county of residence of all the 9,501 English and Welsh emigrants in the six months from January to June 1841.[93] This return is summarised in Table 3.5. The highest emigration was from the West Riding of Yorkshire and the rural south and west. The southern counties[94] provided 17% of the emigrants and 27% came from the West Country.[95] These were counties in which agriculture had been depressed. But 24% of the emigrants came from Lancashire and the West Riding, that is, from places, which we can assume, were at the centre of economic change.[96]

Recent work on the passenger lists has shown that the bulk of

They came from the same counties. Significantly, the collapse of the scheme in 1837 was because of the industrial depression. See Redford, *Labour migration in England*, pp. 107–9.

[91] Taylor, 'Emigration', pp. 59–98, and Johnston, *Shovelling out paupers*, chapter 7.

[92] It is also thought that the later dominion schemes served in the main only to *divert* potential emigrants towards Canada and Australia.

[93] *Census of England and Wales*, 1841–1961. BPP, 1843, XXII.

[94] Kent, Surrey, Sussex, Hampshire, Dorset. The geographical distribution of emigrants may have been affected by heavy migration to Australia in 1841.

[95] Gloucestershire, Somerset, Wiltshire, Cornwall, Devon.

[96] In addition, 12% of the emigrants came from Wales and Monmouth.

Table 3.5. *Emigration from English counties, 1 January 1841–30 June 1841*
(in rank order)

	Number of emigrants	Annual rate per 1000 population
Yorkshire W.R.	944	62
Sussex	758	25
Cornwall	795	23
Cumberland	357	20
Monmouth	213	16
Somerset	671	15
Devon	736	14
Kent	652	12
Westmoreland	61	11
Dorset	177	10
Herefordshire	111	10
Cheshire	328	8
Lancashire	1362	8
Yorkshire E.R.	162	8
Yorkshire N.R.	153	8
Nottinghamshire	175	7
Gloucestershire	291	7
Total from England and Wales	9501	7

Source: Census of England and Wales, 1841.

English immigrants into the U.S.A. in 1827 and 1831 were probably not unskilled workers.[97] And in the main they did not come from declining industries. Professor Erickson analysed the previous occupations of the adult males among 6,100 immigrants who arrived in 1841, a year that she expected to be dominated by agricultural emigrants.[98] Table 3.6 summarises her findings. None of the adult male immigrants was returned as 'agricultural labourer' and only 9.5% of the English were returned as 'labourers', which places an upper limit on this group. About a quarter of the group had worked in agriculture in England, but they were farmers and not labourers. Professor Erickson divided the industrial workers in her group into pre-industrial craftsmen and workers in the industries which were modernising (e.g. the metal industries, engineering and textiles). Pre-industrial craftsmen

[97] Erickson, 'Emigration from the British Isles', pp. 186–7.
[98] This is not all of the English immigration into the U.S.A. in 1831. There are good ships' lists for New York arrivals for only five months which probably include 60% of the arrivals. The lists are complete for the ports of Philadelphia and Boston.

Table 3.6. *Occupations of English, Welsh and Scots immigrants into the U.S.A., 1831 (males aged 20 and over into New York, Philadelphia and Boston, 1831)*

Occupational class	English and Welsh (%)	Scots (%)
Agriculture	24.6	15.3
Labourer	9.5	17.3
Service	2.1	0.5
Pre-industrial craft	34.9	33.2
Industrial	16.5	15.8
Commerce and professional	12.4	17.8
	N = 1793	N = 202

Source: Erickson 'Who Were?' (1977), Table 14, p. 37. New York arrivals (1567) are for five months only.

made up 35% of the 1831 group. This is similar to the proportion in the late eighteenth-century evidence. Only 16% came from industries which were modernising. In the 1827 lists, 28% of the immigrants were pre-industrial craft workers and as we would expect handloom weavers formed the majority.[99] In other words, the majority of emigrants to the U.S.A. in 1827 and 1831 had worked in England at occupations which were wholly or partly insulated from the depressions in those years. There are also other characteristics that suggest that these emigrants were not 'pushed' out of England. The place of birth of 1,275 of the emigrants can be traced. Many of the farmers came from counties where agriculture was prosperous. Many of the handloom weavers came from large Lancashire towns where alternative employment was expanding, not from villages with no alternative save migration. Finally, three-quarters of the emigrants in the 1831 sample, including half of the adult males, travelled in family parties. Some 25% of the members of family parties were under fifteen, the same proportion as in the population of England and Wales.[100]

Assuming that Professor Erickson's conclusions will be confirmed by more research, we can be fairly sure that English (but not Scottish) emigrants in the first half of the nineteenth century were largely composed of people like farmers and skilled artisans who were capable

[99] According to Bythell, 1827 was the crisis year for cotton handloom weavers. D. Bythell, *The handloom weavers* (Cambridge University Press, 1969), p. 255.
[100] There are some difficulties with the analysis of family parties. Erickson, 'Emigration from the British Isles', p. 191.

of making a good living in England, but who were transferring a reasonably successful life-style from England to another country. Relatively few English emigrants seem to have come from a redundant occupation, a declining industry or rural poverty. (This may not have been true of the Welsh.)[101] This conclusion is partly confirmed by the experience of English immigrants in the U.S.A. In 1850, 45% of the English born were living in American states which had more than 50% of their population working in agriculture, and the evidence suggests that these English born immigrants in the U.S.A. were *farmers* and not agricultural labourers.[102] It is thought that some of these farmers had worked in industry before they left England. In addition, many of the industrial emigrants were involved in the transfer of British technology to the U.S.A. For example, in the 1830s and early 1840s, Staffordshire pottery workers moved a part of the industry to Trenton, New Jersey and to East Liverpool, Ohio and cotton workers moved from Lancashire to Fall River, Massachusetts.[103] An interesting speculation is that many English emigrants were able to avoid the economic and social changes that were associated with industrialisation in England by moving to the U.S.A. which was at an earlier stage of development.

VIII

The character of British emigration changed in the third quarter of the nineteenth century. In the first place, as can be seen in Figure 3.1, the rate of emigration was increasing. In the early 1850s, English (gross) emigration had averaged more than 4 persons in each 1,000 for three years (and possibly in one or two more).[104] Scottish emigration had averaged more than 7 per 1,000 for a similar period. These

[101] There is a commonly held view that Welsh emigrants in the first half of the century were probably small farmers and labourers and they were poor. In the eighteenth century they may have been better off and more like English rural emigrants. (This view is based on impressionistic evidence, however, which is in no way comparable to Professors Erickson's analysis of the occupation of English emigrants.) Some aspects of Welsh migration are discussed in chapter 10. A. Conway, 'Welsh emigration to the United States', *Perspectives in American History*, 7, 1973, pp. 177–271. See also A. H. Dodd, *The character of early Welsh emigration to the USA* (University of Wales Press, Cardiff, 1957).

[102] Erickson, 'Agrarian myths', pp. 62–3.

[103] Berthoff, *British immigrants in industrial America*, pp. 33–4, 76. H. Heaton, 'The industrial immigrant in the United States, 1783–1812', *Proceedings of the American Philosophical Society*, 95, 1951, pp. 519–27. See also, Jeremy, *Transatlantic industrial revolution*, pp. 148–9, 256.

[104] Emigration between 1815 and 1850 was underestimated but not by enough to deny the rapid acceleration in emigration rates after about 1850.

rates were not exceeded again before 1870–4. But in the fifteen years 1879–93 the rate of English emigration was consistently above 4 per 1,000 and Scottish emigration was consistently above 5 per 1,000. The long-term acceleration in the rate of emigration from Britain effectively implies that the emigrants were drawn from a wider range of occupations and possibly from a wider geographical area than in the early years.

The main changes in the occupations of emigrants (i.e. outward bound passengers) between 1854 and 1900 from the British Isles can be seen in Table 3.7. The table distinguishes between emigrants who had followed occupations in industries with rapid technical change (like textiles and engineering) and those where technology had changed relatively little (like shoemaking and tinsmithing).[105] The table must be read with extreme caution. For example, it is only possible to exclude Irish emigrants after 1877.[106] More important, the table only records the *occupations* of emigrants, not the industry in which the occupation was carried out. In particular, the proportion of labourers who were *agricultural* labourers, is unknown, as are the industries in which the other labourers had worked.[107] But it is possible to see the main trends in the occupations of adult male emigrants between 1854 and 1900 from this table.

The proportion of emigrants who were farmers fell, although there were always relatively more farmers among the emigrants than there were in the British labour force. The share of agricultural labourers rose. No more than 10% of the emigrants were agricultural labourers in the 1831 sample, when about 30% of the labour force were agricultural labourers. By the 1880s at the latest, emigrants returned as agricultural labourers had become *over*-represented (15.4% of the emigrants, 11.4% of the labour force).[108]

The dominant recorded occupation of emigrants was common labourer. In the 1850s, there were relatively more common labourers among British and Irish emigrants than there were in the labour force. But by the 1880s, there were four times as many British common

---

[105] This is essentially the same classification used by Professor Erickson for her paper on emigrants in the 1880s. See Erickson, 'Who were?' (1972), Appendix C, pp. 378–9.

[106] In 1877–80, 80% of the Irish were labourers, but the Irish data include many emigrants returned as skilled craftsmen.

[107] None of the Irish were returned as 'agricultural labourers', although the bulk of the Irish 'labourers' must have been agricultural. All 'agricultural labourers' so defined were assumed to be British, but this classification may not have been sufficient.

[108] This assumes that 80% of the labourers in the 1850s were Irish and that none of the British labourers was an agricultural labourer.

labourers as their share of the labour force. In this decade, at least a third of the adult male emigrants were common labourers (i.e. about 400,000) and at least a sixth were agricultural labourers (i.e. about 200,000).[109] The share of common labourers fell markedly in the 1890s, and continued to decline in the early twentieth century. White collar workers became relatively more important and by the 1870s they exceeded their share of the labour force.

In many ways, the occupations that were relatively under-represented among emigrants are more interesting. Over the period 1854–1900, relatively few emigrants came from the rapidly changing industries like textiles, iron and steel and engineering. Possibly more surprising, is that few of the emigrants had 'pre-industrial skills', like carpenters and locksmiths, and relatively, there were substantially fewer of them than there were in the labour force as a whole. There were, however, a large number of emigrants from at least two occupations where there had been relatively little technical change – those connected with the building industry and with mining. But if anything, they also tended to be under-represented overall – although as we will see this was not true at particular times.

In general, therefore, the main differences between the first and second half of the nineteenth century, were that in the latter period, a much large proportion of emigrants came from the lowest paid occupations (labourers and agricultural labourers, but apparently not domestic servants). The emigration of farmers, gentlemen and skilled craftsmen continued, but it was overshadowed after about 1850 by the emigration of other groups. Relatively few of the emigrants in the second half of the century were skilled craftsmen, whether from changing or unchanging industries.

It is not clear at what point British emigration changed in character – but there is some evidence of relatively heavy emigration of labourers in the years 1846–54.[110] The introduction of steamships into the British emigrant trade was probably the most important single influence, however. By 1870, virtually all British emigrants to the U.S.A. travelled by steamship compared with only 20% in 1862.[111] The cost of a passage

---

[109] This conclusion assumes that some of the 212,000 adult males whose occupations are not known were labourers.

[110] Of 848 English and Scottish immigrants arriving in New York 1846–54, whose occupations are known, 22.6% were labourers and 10.1% were in the building trades. This compares with only 10% in the 1830s. Erickson, 'Who were?' (1972), Table 6, p. 363.

[111] Carrothers, *Emigration from the British Isles*, pp. 213. Jones, *Background to emigration from Great Britain*, pp. 54–5. Cunard entered the emigrant trade in 1860. F. E. Hyde, *Cunard and the North Atlantic, 1840–1973. A history of shipping and financial management* (Macmillan, 1975), p. 59.

Table 3.7. Occupation of adult male passengers from the U.K., 1854–1900 and Great Britain, 1877–1900 (%)

Occupation	U.K. 1854–60	U.K. 1861–70	U.K. 1871–76	U.K. 1877–80	U.K. 1881–90	U.K. 1891–1900	G.B. 1877–80	G.B. 1881–90	G.B. 1891–1900
Agriculture									
(i) Farmers	12.3	8.2	6.0	7.1	5.5	4.9	8.3	5.4	5.2
(ii) Agricultural labourers	7.5	2.1	3.8	7.0	11.5	10.5	9.6	15.4	14.0
Labourers (N.O.S.)	48.9	59.4	47.1	39.5	45.2	31.8	24.6	32.4	15.2
Servants	0.5	0.4	0.4	0.3	0.4	0.8	0.3	0.3	0.9
Occupations with relatively little technical change									
(i) Building	7.6	4.0	4.5	4.6	4.5	3.9	5.0	5.2	4.6
(ii) Mining	4.3	6.4	4.0	3.6	4.1	5.8	4.8	5.4	7.7
(iii) Other pre-industrial skills	8.5	5.6	2.9	3.7	3.8	5.4	3.2	3.6	5.9
Occupations with relatively great technical change									
(i) Mechanics (N.O.S.)	—	—	11.5	8.3	6.4	6.9	10.7	8.5	9.0
(ii) Others	1.6	1.6	0.9	1.7	1.9	3.5	2.1	2.3	4.3
White collar	3.9	7.8	14.1	18.7	14.1	21.8	24.4	18.0	27.7
Other occupations	4.9	4.5	4.8	5.4	2.7	4.5	7.1	3.4	5.6
	100.0	100.0	100.0	100.0	100.0	100.0	100.0	100.0	100.0
Not stating an occupation	20.2	10.8	11.9	16.2	18.1	23.2	16.2	18.1	23.2
Total adult male emigrants (000s)	—	—	—	362.2	1502.3	980.0	276.3	1174.8	783.2

78

Definitions:

'Farmers'. All persons so defined.

'Agricultural labourers'. Persons defined as agricultural labourers, shepherds, and gardeners.

'Labourers'. All persons so defined.

'Servants'. All domestic servants, grooms and porters.

Occupations with relatively little technical change:

*'Building'. All builders, bricklayers, masons, plasterers, slaters, carpenters, brick and tile makers, painters, paper hangers, plumbers and glaziers.

'Mining'. All coal miners, other miners and quarrymen.

'Other pre-industrial skills'. Persons defined as skilled and all bakers and confectioners; blacksmiths, farriers; binders and stationers; boot and shoe makers; braziers, tinsmiths and whitesmiths; butchers and poulterers; cabinet makers and upholsterers; carvers and gilders; clock and watch makers; cyclemakers and trimmers; coopers; cutlers; engravers; hatters; jewellers and silversmiths; locksmiths and gunsmiths; millers and maltsters; mill workers; rope makers; saddle and harness makers; sail makers; sawyers; shopkeepers; shopmen and warehousemen; general smiths; sugar bakers and boilers; tailors; tallow chandlers and soap makers; tanners and carriers; wheelwrights and millwrights.

Occupations with relatively great technical change:

'Mechanics'. All persons so defined.

'Others'. All persons described as engineers; boiler makers;* spinners and weavers; dyers; shipwrights; turners; printers; woolcombers and sorters; engine drivers; railway servants.

'White collar'. All persons defined as clerks; gentlemen, professional men, merchants; students; schoolmasters; teachers; surveyors.

Other occupations. All persons returned as following an occupation not given above.

Notes: Occupations marked * only appear in the Irish series.

All agricultural labourers were assumed to be English since the category does not exist in the Irish series. The proportion of English and Irish 'labourers' who were agricultural labourers is unknown.

N.O.S. Not otherwise specified.

Source: Calculated from Carrier and Jeffery, *External migration*, Table 11, p. 57, Table 12, pp. 58–9, Table 13, p. 60, Table C(1), pp. 92–3, Table D/F/G(1), pp. 95–6; Table H(1), p. 102, Table 1(1), p. 104. See also Appendix C and D in Erickson, 'Who Were?' (1972), pp. 378–9. My table follows the categories used by Professor Erickson for the four years 1878, 1882, 1888 and 1897 but there are some differences. I have chosen to regard 'Mechanics' as having come from modernised industries. Nor have I attempted to distinguish services from industry. (Note that the criteria for distinguishing between emigrants who came from an industry with little technical change and those from changing industries is the change in the *industry* rather than the occupation. Hence, a wool sorter is in the latter category.)

from Liverpool to New York fell by about 40% between 1860 and the 1890s.[112] Even more important, the passage under steam was much quicker, which meant that the income forgone by the emigrants was less. But the introduction of steamships cannot have been the sole cause of the acceleration in British emigration which occurred before steamships were important. Nor can English emigration in the 1850s have been crisis migration, as it was in Ireland, parts of Germany and parts of Scotland. There was no famine in England. There is a strong possibility that large scale emigration from Britain developed into a mass movement and spread down the social scale before the great improvements in transport. In other words, had steam passages been available, the rate of British emigration in the late 1840s and early 1850s would presumably have been higher.

The second important change in the character of British emigration in the later nineteenth century, was that the rate of emigration of some groups seems to have become much more responsive to changes in opportunities in Britain and overseas. This implies that the rate of return increased (which it did). This was associated with an increase in the proportion of British emigrants going to the U.S.A. (Tables 3.3 and 3.4). The change in the character of British emigrants was first demonstrated by Charlotte Erickson in an important paper written in 1972.[113] Table 3.8, which is taken from Professor Erickson's paper, compares the occupational distribution of British emigrants (where it is known) in the low year of 1878, when there were only 83,000 emigrants, with the two most important years of the 1880s boom, 1882 and 1888, when there were respectively 195,000 and 207,000 emigrants, and with the low year of 1897 (111,000). The peak years of emigration correspond with peaks in the American trade cycle. The table shows that white-collar workers and skilled craftsmen seemed to have emigrated at a roughly constant rate. But when emigration was high, the bulk of the *additional* migrants seem to have been labourers. Less than 7,000 emigrants in the low year of 1878 were returned as labourers (both types) and just over 8,000 in the low year of 1897. When emigration was high (1882 and 1888) nearly 42,000 and 33,000 of the adult male emigrants whose occupation was known were labourers. In addition, if relatively few of the so-called 'labourers'

---

[112] Passage from Liverpool to New York cost £8.8.0 in 1860 and £6.6.0 in 1863. By the 1890s it had fallen to £5 and in the peak years of the 1880s competition had sometimes driven it as low as £4.4.0. The steamship crossed in about ten days pared with a sail passage which could take four to six weeks. Hyde, *Cunard and the North Atlantic*, p. 64.

[113] Erickson, 'Who were?' (1972).

Table 3.8. *Occupations of British adult male immigrants into the U.S.A. (where it is known) 1878, 1882, 1888, 1897*
(% share)

Occupation	1878 (Trough) 000s %		1882 (Peak) 000s %		1888 (Peak) 000s %		1897 (Trough) 000s %	
Farmers	2.8	(9.6)	1.8	(2.4)	6.0	(7.5)	2.5	(5.9)
Agricultural labourers	6.0	(20.9)	5.1	(7.0)	22.4	(28.1)	4.5	(10.5)
Labourers	0.8	(2.9)	36.8	(50.2)	10.4	(13.0)	3.7	(8.6)
Servants	0.1	(0.3)	0.2	(0.3)	0.8	(1.0)	0.9	(2.1)
Occupations with relatively little technical change								
Building	1.7	(6.0)	3.2	(4.4)	4.8	(6.0)	2.3	(5.4)
Mining	1.0	(3.6)	3.0	(4.1)	4.7	(5.9)	3.7	(8.6)
Other	0.4	(1.5)	1.0	(1.4)	2.2	(2.8)	1.4	(3.2)
Occupations with relatively great technical change								
Mechanics (N.O.S.)	3.1	(10.6)	5.7	(7.6)	10.0	(12.5)	3.7	(8.7)
Others	0.5	(1.6)	0.9	(1.2)	2.6	(3.2)	2.5	(5.8)
White collar	12.4	(43.0)	15.7	(21.4)	15.8	(19.8)	17.7	(41.1)
	28.8	(100.0)	73.4	(100.0)	79.7	(99.8)	42.9	(99.9)

Source: Adapted from Erickson, 'Who Were?' (1972), Table 9, p. 370. (See Table 3.7 for details of the classification.)

were agricultural labourers, then the bulk of the poorest emigrants
may have been urban labourers in 1882, but rural labourers in 1888.
(A problem is that 'agricultural labourer' may have been used as a
catch all term to describe rural emigrants from, say, Cornwall, where
there was a great deal of overlap between rural craftsmen, agricultural
labourers and farmers.)

Professor Erickson was able to show the occupations of the British
emigrants in more detail from the American ships' lists. The evidence
from the best lists (1885–8) is summarised in Table 3.9, which also
shows the occupations of a small group who were part of the great
migration of 1846–54. There are no comparable data on emigration
from Britain to other countries – with one exception.[114] On the other
hand, the U.S.A. was the most accessible destination, and probably
had the greatest range of employment opportunities. We can assume
that the majority of the emigrants who responded quickly to job opportunities overseas went to the U.S.A. Table 3.9 suggests that a large
percentage of British emigrants to New York were labourers in 1846–54
(compared with about 10% of immigrants on the 1831 list who were
labourers – Table 3.6). The 1885–8 lists, which include about 5% of
all adult male emigrants to the U.S.A., imply that nearly a third of
British emigrants were labourers. Relatively few emigrants in the 1880s
were craftsmen from either changing or unchanging industries, except
that there seems to have been an exceptional emigration of building
workers to the U.S.A. in 1885–8. In the 1880s, about 15% of the building labour force in New York State were said to be British seasonal
workers.[115] (The relation between emigration and the British building
cycle, which turned down in 1878 or thereabouts, is discussed in
chapter 8.)

Finally, the ships' lists suggest that the emigrants to the U.S.A.
in 1885–8 came mainly from urban areas, whereas the small sample
of 1846–54 came mainly from rural areas. In 1846–54, just over a quarter
of the emigrants in the sample came from towns of more than 20,000
population. At that time about a third of the British population lived
in large towns. But in 1885–8, urban dwellers were disproportionately
over-represented among emigrants to the U.S.A. Seventy-eight per
cent of the emigrants came from towns of more than 20,000 population
which contained only about half of the British population at this

---

[114] There is a study by Ross Duncan of emigration to Australia, 'Case studies in emigration. Cornwall, Gloucestershire and New South Wales, 1877–1886', *Economic History
Review*, 16 (2), 1963, pp. 272–89. The emigrants were all assisted.
[115] NY Bureau of Labour Statistics, 1885, New York, quoted in Erickson, 'The English'
(unpublished), p. 76–7.

Table 3.9. *Occupations of adult male immigrants from England and Scotland on New York ships' lists, 1846–54 and 1885–8*

	% of emigrants		% in occupation in Britain	
	1846–54	1885–8	1851	1881
Farmers	14.2	8.4	6.5	4.1
Agricultural labourers	0.5	1.1	20.4	11.4
Labourers	22.6	29.5	6.9	8.2
Servants	3.1	3.2	9.3	12.8
Occupations with relatively little technical change				
Building	10.1	18.1	7.4	9.1
Mining	5.2	8.0	5.2	6.4
Industrial	20.9	6.7	17.6	14.4
Occupations with relatively great technical change				
Mechanics (N.O.S.)	0.6	1.5	—	0.4
All others (mainly textiles and iron, engineering	17.3	8.1	16.0	19.2
White collar	5.6	15.6	10.5	14.1
Number of emigrants	848	8698	—	—
Number in occupation	—	—	6,625,000	8,893,000

Source: Adapted from Erickson, 'Who Were?' (1972), Table 6, p. 363. (See Table 3.7 for details of the classification.)

time.[116] Relatively more of the labourers came from the urban areas compared with better off emigrants. With the exception of building workers, the majority of urban emigrants were not skilled industrial workers but unskilled labourers, some of whom were probably connected with the building industry.[117] These data – which at the moment are all that we have – imply that at some time after the 1850s the large towns became the main source of British emigrants, and that this shift may have occurred *after* the acceleration in emigration rates and possibly after the introduction of steamships on the North Atlantic. A difficulty, however, is that urban labourers may have only gone in such large numbers in the years of heavy emigration. It is not known whether there was a trend towards more emigration of labourers or a series of emigration cycles, where urban labourers dominated the peaks.

A further problem, and one that cannot be examined from the published data nor from the ships' lists, is how many of the urban emigrants had come originally from the rural areas. The ships' lists give only the last place of residence, and we cannot tell if the urban emigrants had previously moved internally from rural areas to the towns before they went overseas. This raises a problem. Although the evidence from the ships' lists is very suggestive, it cannot overturn the view that the heavy emigration of the 1880s was caused by the problems of British agriculture or more accurately the problems of British rural society. The writers who thought that emigration in this period was determined by agricultural distress were mistaken, however, since they assumed that the rural emigrants went abroad *directly* from the rural areas.[118] But it is possible that the urban emigrants of the 1880s had previously moved to the towns in the seventies and the early eighties. To meet this point it is necessary to know the place of birth of the emigrants.

The proportion of emigrants travelling alone and the proportion of children is further evidence that the British emigrants had changed in character by the later nineteenth century. In the years 1875–1900, taken as a whole, about 21% of British emigrants were under fifteen, compared with 35% in the 1831 group. The greatest change was in

---

[116] Of the sample of 1846–54, 26.8% gave a town of more than 20,000 population as their last residence and 78.0% of the emigrants of 1885–8. At the 1851 census 35.0% of the population of Britain lived in large towns and 49.4% at the 1881 census. Principal towns are mainly municipal boroughs in 1851, but also include some conurbations where other definitions have been used. Principal towns in 1881 are urban sanitary districts.
[117] Erickson, 'Who were?' (1972), pp. 359–64.
[118] Erickson, 'Who were?' (1972), p. 371. Erickson, 'The English', p. 325–6.

the number of emigrants travelling alone. According to the 1885–8 lists, about eight times as many adult males crossed the Atlantic alone as travelled as part of a family group. In the 1846–54 lists there were less than two adult males for every one who was a part of a family group and in the 1831 lists about one half were part of a family group. It must be remembered that the crude ratio of female to male emigrants and of children to adults can be misleading. In the peak years of emigration in the 1880s, for example, the published data show that there were about two men for every woman emigrant. But the men were not necessarily attached to the women and children travelling on the same ship. The children and some of the women were probably joining a male relative who had gone ahead, but many of the women were probably single and travelling alone.

The proportion of British emigrants travelling on pre-paid fares is not known, but it is possible that remittances from overseas were unimportant, unlike in European or Irish emigration.[119] This was partly because the passage from Britain cost much less in real terms. A passage to the U.S.A. in the 1870s cost a British urban labourer about five or six weeks' wages. It cost a Swedish or German labourer at least three months' wages.[120] In addition, a second, and possibly more important, function of emigrant remittances to Ireland and to some continental countries was to subsidise the marginal farms of relatives. There were few marginal farms in England (although there were relatively more in Scotland and Wales).

We have already noted that there was relatively little direct aid to emigrants in the second half of the nineteenth century. Some skilled workers were financially aided to emigrate by their unions, a practice which seems to have started in the 1840s,[121] but it was rarely of more

---

[119] Government estimates of annual remittances from North America to the United Kingdom rose from about £500,000 p.a. in 1848–9 to more than £1,500,000 p.a. in 1852–4. They fell until the 1880s when annual remittances were again about £1,500,000 p.a. See Table 18, p. 167 in Schrier, *Ireland and the American emigration,* which is taken from the *Thirty-third General Report of the Emigration Commissioners 1872, HC 1873,* XVII, p. 78 and *Statistical Tables relating to emigration and immigration from and into the United Kingdom in the year 1887, and report to the Board of Trade thereon, HC 1888,* CVII, p. 18. Money orders sent from the U.S.A. to the U.K. totalled about £200,000 p.a. in the 1870s but rose to about £1,000,000 by the 1890s. See Table 19, Schrier, *Ireland and the American emigration,* p. 168 (taken from the *Annual reports* of the Postmaster General of the United States). The total amount including dollar bills sent in envelopes and via friends is obviously unknown. It is thought that the majority of the remittances to the U.K. went to Ireland.

[120] Steam passages from Liverpool to New York cost about £6 in the 1870s. An urban labourer in London and Lancashire made no more than £1 per week. Stockholm and Berlin labourers earned considerably less and passages were half as much again.

[121] See Shepperson, *British emigration to North America,* p. 184.

than local importance (for example, to aid victimised members).[122]
The attempt by the American Emigrant Company (1864) to recruit
skilled textile and iron workers was not very successful and ended
after two years.[123] Aid to unskilled emigrants was more important
but still small.[124] Joseph Arch claimed before the Richmond Commission (1881–2) that agricultural labourers and their families to a total
of 700,000 had been assisted to emigrate by his (short lived) union.
But he later retracted. The correct figure was probably 40–50,000 emigrants between 1872 and 1881.[125] Canadian emigration agents had
also been active among agricultural labourers but with the exception
of about 20,000 emigrants in 1868–71 were unable to induce adult
emigration to Canada.[126] In the late nineteenth century when (some)
emigrants were faced with a choice between assisted emigration to
rural Canada and unassisted emigration to urban America, it seems
that they virtually always chose the latter.

The rate of emigration to Australia was partly determined by the
supply of assisted passages, since the cost of emigration to Australia
was very high.[127] Assisted passages to Australia were rare after the
1860s, however, until just before the First World War. This was partly
the effect of the serious depression in Australia after 1893. Consequently, there was no shift of British emigrants towards Australia

[122] There has been some controversy whether union aid to their members to emigrate
was part of a long run strategy to reduce labour supply. See Erickson, 'The encouragement of emigration by British trade unions, 1850–1900', *Population studies*, 3, 1949–50,
pp. 248–73, and R. V. Clements, 'Trade Unions and emigration 1840–1880', *Population
Studies*, 9, 1955–6, pp. 167–80. See also H. L. Malchow, 'Trade unions and emigration
in late Victorian England: a national lobby for state aid', *Journal of British Studies*,
15 (2), 1976, pp. 92–116.

[123] Erickson, *American industry and the European immigrant*, pp. 17–23.

[124] There is some evidence that British immigrants in the U.S.A. used the recruiting
offices which had been set up in the ports of entry and at the main railway junctions
(like Chicago) in order to recruit unskilled labour primarily for railway construction.
But the British immigrants had made a decision to emigrate before they entered
these offices. Erickson, 'Who were?' (1977), p. 80.

[125] Assuming that each labourer was accompanied by three dependents. Pamela Horn,
'Agricultural trade unionism and emigration 1872–1881', *Historical Journal*, 15, 1,
1972, p. 97. For the disastrous Brazilian emigration scheme see P. Horn, 'Gloucester
and the Brazilian emigration movement 1872–73', *Transaction of the Bristol and Gloucester Antiquarian Society*, 89, 1970, pp. 167–74.

[126] About 80,000 children were sent to Canada between 1868 and 1925, but their emigration was largely financed in Britain. Joy Parr, *Labouring children: British immigrant
apprentices to Canada, 1869–1924* (Croom Helm, 1980), pp. 11, 40.

[127] Before the First World War the unassisted fare to Australia and New Zealand was
usually £12–£16 compared with £6–£8 to Canada and even less to the U.S.A. The
assisted fare to Australia was £2–£8. D. Pope, 'Empire migration to Canada, Australia
and New Zealand, 1910–1919', *Australian Economic Papers*, 11, 1968, p. 172.

in 1892–6, when the U.S.A. became less attractive. It appears that the lowest paid would only go to Australia at times when the U.S.A. was less attractive *and* assisted passages to Australia were readily available.[128]

We have been able to examine the occupations of the emigrants at particular times in the nineteenth century. An important feature was the great increase in the proportion of unskilled labourers. This feature and the parallel changes in the age and sex composition of the emigrants presumably means that by the 1880s at the latest, a large number of potential British emigrants were prepared to leave at short notice. They were probably predisposed to consider emigration, of course, but it appears that their immediate decision to emigrate depended on their appraisal of recent changes in the British economy and an economy overseas. This implies that there was a considerable flow of information, in particular from the United States, which attracted an increased proportion of the emigrants when emigration was at its peak. Curiously, there are few British emigrant letters extant for the late nineteenth century. This may reflect the random (and low) survival rate of letters, but (as Professor Erickson has surmised) it may mean that the letter was no longer the dominant source of information, and had been superseded by copies of American local newspapers which were available in England and by information from trade union sources.[129] In addition, the agencies in England that had been established by American railroads and state governments may have partly been used as sources of information. Finally, it is known that the rate of return to Britain was very high and we may surmise that many potential emigrants obtained information from returned migrants. But we have no way of estimating how important returned migrants were as a source of information.

---

[128] The issue is complicated because the periods of maximum assistance by the Australian state (and later Commonwealth) governments were all at periods of high employment. About 300,000 emigrants were assisted to go to Australia between 1909 and 1913. In the previous ten years none of the 1.3 million emigrants had been assisted. Total assisted passages in the period from the 1860s to the international depressions in 1929–33 were about 1.06 million to Australia, about 100,000 to Canada and about a quarter of a million to New Zealand. The great majority of assisted passages were granted after 1910. Davie, *World migration*, pp. 428–9, 433–4; Forsyth, *Myth of the open spaces*, p. 177; Plant, *Oversea settlement*, pp. 42–3.

[129] Erickson, 'The English' (unpublished), p. 79. In an article in the *Atlantic Monthly* of November 1894, it was claimed that the North of England had supported the Union in the Civil War because of the large circulation of (Northern) American newspapers, particularly in Lancashire and Yorkshire. J. M. Ludlow, 'The growth of American influence in England', *Atlantic Monthly*, 42, November, 1894, pp. 619–20. Quoted in M. Curti and K. Birr, 'The immigrant and the American image in Europe'.

IX

The main features of emigration from the continent of Europe in the hundred years before the First World War were discussed in chapter 2. British and European emigrants had many features in common, despite the fact that Britain had a long history of emigration and strong cultural and economic links with the countries of immigration. And although Britain was more industrialised than any country in Europe, emigrants had much in common with the emigrants from rural and less industrialised countries.

The evidence is sparse, but it appears that English (probably not Scottish) emigrants until the late 1840s, were not drawn from the poor. They tended to be farmers and craftsmen. They were probably not forced to emigrate by poverty nor by technological unemployment. (It appears that many emigrants in the early nineteenth century wished to become farmers.) They usually travelled in family parties and relatively few of them returned.

British emigration rates accelerated markedly in the late 1840s and 1850s, but (again with the exception of parts of Scotland) the heavy emigration was not because of a subsistence crisis as it was in Ireland or parts of Germany. By the 1880s, the character of British emigrants had changed. There had been a sharp increase in the proportion of labourers, a decrease in family emigration in favour of individual moves, and (as we shall see) a marked increase in the propensity to return. British emigration had become responsive to short run changes in economic opportunities at home and abroad, particularly to the American trade cycle. The U.S.A. became an even more important destination in the 1880s. Some of the characteristics of the British emigrants to the U.S.A. in the 1880s were similar to the so-called 'new immigrants' from southern and eastern Europe whom the Dillingham Commission (1911) considered to be inferior, that is, they were single, young, footloose, unskilled and had a high likelihood of returning home. Skilled emigrants continued to leave Britain, and the share of skilled emigrants increased after 1900 when emigration shifted towards Australia and Canada, but the British had probably entered the phase of 'new' immigration fifteen years before southern and eastern Europe. This was not a consequence of the British agricultural depression of the last quarter of the nineteenth century.

There are, of course, several other important issues that are raised in the European literature. Little has been said, so far, about the rate of return of British emigrants; the proportion of British emigrants who came from urban and from rural areas; the relation with internal migration and whether an appreciable number of British emigrants were stage emigrants.

The rate of return is discussed in chapter 5. Quite a lot is already known about it. For example, it is known that the returns to Britain were very high in the late nineteenth and early twentieth centuries. Chapter 5 also discusses the possible relationship between a high rate of return and outward movement. It also includes the author's new estimates of return migration in the 1860s and 1870s which show that return movement to Britain was already high before it was officially measured.

Very little is known, however, about the other issues. We can assume, that British emigration rates varied from one region to another as they seem to have done in many European countries. There is virtually no evidence, however, on the contribution of different regions to British emigration. This leaves a critical gap. It is not known how many of the emigrants in the second half of the century, came from the peripheral areas (both rural and urban) that economic change had passed by and which may have been suffering as a result, or how many of the emigrants came from the centre where economic change was rapid. The proportion of emigrants who came from urban and rural areas is also unknown, except for those that have so far been identified in the ships' lists for the 1880s and 1830s. And we do not know if the emigrants from the urban and industrial areas were stage migrants who had migrated there from a rural area, a less developed area, or an equally developed area.

The rest of this book attempts to throw some light on these questions. It is possible to estimate the place of birth of all English and Welsh emigrants between 1861–1900. (The method is discussed in the next chapter.) Chapters 6 and 7 show the place of birth of the emigrants in this period and (among other things) the relative contribution of urban and rural areas to English and Welsh emigration. Chapter 8 shows the relationship between internal migration and emigration – notably whether the movement from the rural areas to the urban areas was affected by changes in the rate of emigration and vice versa. In other words, was emigration a substitute for internal migration, or not? Chapter 9 contains an estimate of the maximum number of emigrants who could have been rural–urban stage emigrants. Finally, Welsh migration patterns are discussed in chapter 10.

4

The estimation of migration by county of birth[1]

I

This chapter describes the method used by the author to estimate the county of birth of English and Welsh emigrants in the late nineteenth century. It discusses the problems inherent in the data, the assumptions that were necessary and the degree of error in the final estimates. The chapter contains no sophisticated mathematics but it would be foolish to pretend that it makes easy (or even, interesting) reading. Any reader who is prepared to take the author's estimates largely on trust could read the next section which explains how they are derived in general terms and then proceed to chapters 5 to 10 which discuss how the new data affect our knowledge of English and Welsh migration history. It should be remembered, however, that almost all the conclusions of the book stand or fall by the accuracy of these estimates – although as will be explained they are sufficiently robust to stand a degree of error. In other words, the main conclusions of the book do not depend on the estimates being exceptionally accurate.

II

The method used to estimate the county of birth of the emigrants is, in theory, extremely simple. The first stage is to estimate the migration of *natives* out of a particular county, in a decade. That is, the movement of people who had been born in that county who left it

---

[1] Some of the problems raised in this chapter are discussed in two earlier papers; Baines, 'Use of published census data', and D. E. Baines, 'Birthplace statistics and the analysis of internal migration', pp. 146–64 in R. Lawton, (ed.), *British censuses of the nineteenth century* (Cass, 1978). The method discussed in this chapter is, however, considerably more refined.

for other counties or to go overseas. The second stage is to estimate the movement of these natives into all the other counties of England and Wales. The difference between the first estimate (the movement out of the county) and the second (the movement of natives of the county into the other counties) can only be the movement of natives of the county abroad in that decade.

This calculation can be expressed slightly more formally. The population of a county depends on the number of births, the number of deaths and the number of in and out-migrants (net migration). Net migration into and out of a county, in the period ($MIGqk^1$) can, therefore, be calculated by adding the natural increase to the initial population and subtracting the result from the final population – assuming only that the area of the county remains constant. That is:

$$MIGqk^1 = POPqi^2 - (POPqi^1 + Bqi^1 - Dqi^1)$$

where $POPqi^1$ and $POPqi^2$ are the total population of county i at the first and second census: Bqi^1 and Dqi^1 are birth and deaths respectively in the intervening decade and $MIGqk^1$ is net migration during the decade to other counties and abroad.[2] If $MIGqk^1$ is negative, there was net out-migration and if it is positive there was a net in-migration. This can be demonstrated by means of a simple example. We know that in the (hypothetical) county of Barsetshire the male population was 280,000 and 285,000 in 1861 and 1871 respectively. We also know that there were 90,400 births and 59,325 deaths in the decade – corresponding to a male birth rate of 16.0 per 1,000 (of the male and female population) and a death rate of 21.0 per 1,000. Hence, total out migration to all destinations ($MIGqk^1$) was:

$$MIGqk^1 = 285,000 - (280,000 + 90,400 - 59,325) = -26,075$$

Net migration of the *natives* of a county ($MIGik^1$) that is, of Barsetshire born from Barsetshire, can, in principle, be obtained in the same way, i.e.:

$$MIGik^1 = POPii^2 - (POPii^1 + Bii^1 - Dii^1)$$

[2] In the notation, the first letter in lower case is always the place of birth and the second the place of enumeration. i represents a particular county; j all other counties and o represents overseas; q is everywhere so that $i + j + o = q$ and k is everywhere except the particular county so that $j + o = k$. Therefore, POPqi is persons born in all counties and abroad, enumerated in county i (the total population). POP indicates a stock, a value at a point in time. B, D, IMIG and EMIG indicate a flow, a value throughout the time period. Therefore Dqi^1 represents deaths of all person (q) in county i during decade 1 and $MIGqk^1$ is migration of all persons to other counties and abroad (k) in decade 1. Decade 1 is the period between census 1 and census 2. This is written as 1861–70.

where $POPii^1$ and $POPii^2$ are the enumerated native populations (Barsetshire born enumerated in Barsetshire) and Dii^1 is native deaths in the decade. The deaths of natives in Barsetshire (Dii^1) is not known but native deaths must be all deaths in Barsetshire less migrant deaths, i.e.:

$$Dii^1 = Dqi^1 - Dki^1$$

Migrant deaths are not known at this stage. They have to be estimated. The method of estimating migrant deaths in a county is critical and is discussed in detail below. Native births in Barsetshire are, of course, the same thing as *all* the births in the county so that $Bqi^1 = Bii^1$. In our example, we know that 235,000 male natives of Barsetshire were living in Barsetshire in 1861 and 238,000 in 1871. Assume, for the moment, that we have been able to estimate the number of deaths of non-Barsetshire-born males who were living in Barsetshire in 1861–70 (10,649). We know that the total number of deaths was 59,325. Native deaths must, therefore, have been 59,325 – 10,649, i.e. 48,676. All births are natives, by definition, i.e. 90,400, hence native migration out of Barsetshire ($MIGik^1$) was:

$$MIGik^1 = 238,000 - (235,000 + 90,400 - 48,676) = -38,724$$

Native migration from Barsetshire ($MIGik^1$) is composed of two elements, net native migration to other counties ($IMIGij^1$) and net native emigration ($EMIGio^1$). If migrant deaths can be estimated, then net migration of Barsetshire born into other counties ($IMIGij^1$) is the difference between the population of Barsetshire born in the other counties at the first census ($POPij^1$), less deaths of Barsetshire born in other counties in the intervening decade (Dij^1), and the population of Barsetshire born in the other counties at the second census ($POPij^2$), i.e.:

$$IMIGij^1 = POPij^2 - (POPij^1 - Dij^1)$$

We estimated that 13,344 Barsetshire-born males had died in other English and Welsh counties between 1861 and 1871. Sixty-two thousand Barsetshire natives were enumerated in the other counties in 1861 and 75,000 in 1871. Hence, migration into the other counties ($IMIGij^1$) was:

$$IMIGij^1 = 75,000 - (62,000 - 13,344) = +26,344$$

Net native migration from county i ($MIGik$) less migration from county i into other counties ($IMIGij$) must be net native emigration

(EMIGio). Therefore:

$$EMIGio^1 = POPii^2 - POPii^1 + Bii^1 - (Dqi^1 - Dki^1) + POPij^2 - (POPij^1 - Dij^1)$$

We already know that 38,724 Barsetshire-born males left the county in the 1861–70 decade and 26,344 moved to other English and Welsh counties. Therefore, 12,380 must have gone overseas, i.e.:

$$MIGik^1 = -38,724$$
$$IMIGij^1 = +26,344$$
$$EMIGio^1 = -12,380$$

The net overseas migration and net internal migration of the natives of the fifty-two English and Welsh counties were calculated by this method for the four decades 1861–1900, distinguishing males and females.[3]

There are two main analytical problems and hence sources of error in the migration estimates. In the first place, the original data were not in immediately usable form. The enumeration units had to be made comparable between each decade and the units used for different purposes (such as vital registration and the census) had to be reconciled. Several important enumeration errors were discovered and corrected. Secondly, the derivation of a set of migrant death rates (Dji and Dij) raised several problems of historical judgement.

The assumptions necessary to solve these problems and the reliability of the estimates are discussed in the next section.

III

The main sources for this study are the enumeration of the 'Birthplaces of the People' from the *General Report* of the census and the *Annual Reports* and *Decennial Supplements* of the Registrar General. Birth places were always enumerated in counties although in some censuses the county of birth of the population of smaller units such as urban districts was given.

The birthplaces of the lifetime migrants in each county (POPki) were given only for individual English and Welsh counties, of which there were 53,[4] 'Scotland', 'Ireland' and 'overseas' (of which there were

[3] The data are only consistent for these four decades. Middlesex and London had to be combined because of enumeration errors. Hence, there were only fifty-two counties of birth.
[4] About 10% of the Welsh-born migrants returned their place of birth as 'Wales'. These were allocated among the Welsh counties in proportion to the contribution of those counties to the migrant population of the county in question, on the assumption

two categories). The county of birth of English migrants was not given in the Irish and Scottish censuses. Inter-county migration flows, can therefore only be estimated for English and Welsh counties. Unfortunately, the census used three different county units to enumerate the place of birth. In 1851, the *Registration* county of birth was given for the inhabitants of *Civil* (or so-called, Ancient) counties. In 1861–1901, the *Ancient* county of birth was given for the inhabitants of *Ancient* counties. In 1911, the Administrative county of birth was given for the inhabitants of *Administrative* counties.[5] There was no further question asked about the place of birth in the census – or any other measure of migration – until the census of 1951.

The distinction between the different county units used by the census is very simple. The Ancient county was the traditional county unit and often of very great antiquity.[6] The counties were still very fragmented at the beginning of the nineteenth century, but during the next fifty years most of the Ancient counties were consolidated into discrete units.[7] These units served for the early censuses but when the country had to be divided into small units for the beginning of vital registration in 1836, the Poor Law Unions of 1782 and 1834 had become the Registration districts. The Registration county was the sum of the Registration districts and it did not coincide with the Ancient county whose name it carried. For example, parts of the Registration district of Stockport (which was in the Registration county of Cheshire) were in the Ancient county of Lancashire. Similarly, part of the Registration district of Stourbridge (which was in the Registration county of Worcester) was in the Ancient county of Staffordshire.[8]

Finally, the Local Government reforms of 1888 created yet another unit, the Administrative county which was based on urban sanitary

that all the Welsh were equally unlikely to know their place of birth. When the county was in Wales, it was assumed that only those Welsh born outside that county would not know their county of birth. Welsh-born migrants remaining in Wales were far less likely to be returned as 'Wales' born than those in England. Some of the English born must have written 'England' as their county of birth but there was no provision for such a response in the tables of the earlier censuses. (About 1% of the English-born population wrote 'England' in 1911.)

5 A complete summary of the changes in the coverage of the census is contained in Interdepartmental Committee on Social and Economic Research, *Guides to official sources, No. 2 Census reports of Great Britain, 1801–1931* (HMSO, 1951). The place of birth enumerations are examined in some length in Baines, 'Birthplace statistics'.

6 Some were pre-Conquest principalities, old tribal areas and Danish administrative units. Others were effectives created in the nineteenth century.

7 In particular by the Counties (Detached Parts) Act of 1844.

8 A common problem was that the Poor Law Unions which formed the Registration districts were centred upon towns. Frequently these towns lay on rivers which divided ancient counties.

districts and the like.[9] In theory, it would have been possible to convert the 1911 and 1851 enumerations to Ancient county bases, but it was felt that it could not be done within an acceptable margin of error. This was very unfortunate because the 1901–10 decade had a higher rate of emigration than 1881–90, and, moreover, the emigration changed in direction. The problem was that a residual method of estimating migration (the only possible way of estimating migration from the census) is totally dependent on the quality of the data. If 1,000 natives of Devon who had not moved were enumerated in Cornwall at the second census, $POPii^2$ would decrease by 1,000 and $POPij^2$ would rise by the same amount. Other things being equal, net out-migration to all destinations ($MIGik^1$) would then be 1,000 too high, net migration into the other counties ($IMIGij^1$) would be 1,000 too low and Devon born net emigration ($EMIGio^1$) would be 2,000 too high.

The variance between Ancient and Administrative county boundaries in 1901 was often very large, as was the variation between Ancient and Registration counties in 1851 so that the possibility of serious errors of the kind mentioned above must also be large. The basic unit for the study had to be the Ancient county and the period had to be limited to 1861–1900.[10]

The geographical areas of the Ancient counties were almost, but not completely, consistent in the period 1861–1900. Some boundary adjustments were necessary but they rarely involved more than 1,000 persons. All the data were corrected to the area of the Ancient county as it was in 1891.[11] The assumption used when a small area was 'transferred' to create the county population within the borders of 1891, was that the losing population was a sample of the total population of the losing county. Hence, if the population of a county in 1881 was 1% less than it would be if it had been enumerated within the boundaries of 1891, then the native population was assumed also to be 1% less, i.e.:

$$\frac{POPqi \text{ (old area)}}{POPqi \text{ (new area)}} = \frac{POPij \text{ (old area)}}{POPij \text{ (new area)}}$$

A related problem is that the county of London did not exist as

---

[9] See V. D. Lipmann, *Local government areas, 1834–1945* (Blackwell, Oxford, 1949), chapter 3, and V. D. Lipmann 'The development of areas and boundary changes 1888–1939', in C. H. Wilson (ed.), *Essays on local government* (Blackwell, Oxford, 1948).

[10] A further problem is that the 1851 enumeration did not distinguish males and females.

[11] The correct total populations of the Ancient counties are in Mitchell, *Abstract of British historical statistics*, Table 7, pp. 20–3. There are some transcription errors in this table.

an administrative unit before 1888. The census defined 'London' as the 'metropolitan' parishes of the counties of Middlesex, Surrey and Kent.[12] This area was already built up in 1861 and subsequent sub-urban development in the London area occurred in the so-called *extra-metropolitan* parts of the counties and in Essex.

Finally, the corrected county of birth data were searched for enumeration errors. That is, for the misrecording of the county of birth from one census to another and hence the enumeration of part of the native population (POPii[1]) as part of the migrant population at the second census (POPji[2]) or vice versa.[13] A trend was fitted to the most important migrant populations (POPji) within each county (where they comprised more than 2,000 persons). Where a POPii or POPji showed a large deviation from the trend the equivalent native (POPii) or migrant (POPij) population of adjoining counties were checked to see if they exhibited a comparable deviation from trend. If, for example, the native population (POPii) of a particular county rose disproportionately fast between 1871 and 1881 and the native-born population of an adjoining county (x) enumerated within that county (POPxi) rose disproportionately slowly, then it was assumed that some migrants who were returned as such in 1871 were incorrectly returned as natives in 1881. In this case, POPii in 1881 was reduced and POPxi (and hence POPji) increased by the (one) value that would best fit the trend in the two populations.

Assume that the enumerated native population (POPii) of the county of South Riding was 25,000, 31,250, 37,763, 48,829 and 61,036 in 1861, 1871, 1881, 1891 and 1901 respectively, i.e. the native population was growing at a rate of 25%, 21%, 29% and 25% in each decade. In the same years 7,500, 9,000, 9,500, 12,960 and 15,552 natives of the adjoining county of Barsetshire were enumerated in South Riding, i.e. this group was growing at 20%, 6%, 36% and 20%. In this case we would assume that there had been an enumeration error. It is probable that some Barsetshire natives had been incorrectly returned as natives of South Riding in 1881. The probable extent of the mis-enumeration can be judged from the rate of growth of the relevant population. In this case, the effect of transferring 1,300 persons from

---

[12] POPqi, POPii, and POPii for London so defined are not always given in the census, but all the data exist to calculate it without error. In 1861 the individual parish popula-tions have to be summed. Some of the parishes were divided between two counties.

[13] One likely cause of such errors is the attribution of children's place of birth to that of their parents by the incorrect use of ditto marks in the enumerators' books. This was noticed in Sheffield by Tillot and in Glamorgan by one of my students. See P. M. Tillot, 'Sources of error in the 1851 and 1861 census' in Wrigley, *Nineteenth-century society*, p. 124.

the South Riding native population to the Barsetshire migrant population in 1881 is that the two groups would grow at a constant rate, 25% in each decade for the former and 20% for the latter. Therefore, we assumed that 1300 Barsetshire migrants had been incorrectly enumerated as South Riding natives.

The assumption on which this procedure is based, is that current migration makes a relatively unimportant contribution to the size of a lifetime migrant population compared to previous migration and the effects of mortality. Current migration into a county in a decade was only exceptionally more than one-third of the relevant total migrant population of the county at the beginning of the decade. Similarly, the size of a native population is far more dependent on fertility and mortality than on migration. It follows that the size of migrant and native populations could be fitted to a trend and large deviations from that trend must have been caused by exceptional fluctuations in migration or by enumeration errors. Fortunately, the number of presumed enumeration errors[14] discovered was extremely low (only 29 adjustments had to be made from nearly 1,000 cases). The major errors relate to London, where there was a serious confusion between London and Middlesex born; in Bristol where there was confusion between Gloucester and Somerset born, and in South Wales.[15]

The London area problem was met by combining London and Middlesex into one unit. The amended native London population comprised the native populations of London and Middlesex (POPii), plus the London-born population of Middlesex and the Middlesex-born population of London (POPij). The population that had been born in the other 51 counties (POPji) were combined, as were the London and Middlesex born population that were living in other parts of England and Wales (POPij). Finally, weighted birth and death rates were calculated.

Where presumed enumeration errors have been corrected the extent of the corrections and the effect of them are indicated in the estimates and in the conclusions drawn from them. In general, however, the county of birth data 1861–1901 stand up as a reliable source if handled with care.

The vital data present fewer problems than the census. Decade births and deaths could be converted from a Registration county base

[14] A few arithmetical errors in the published tables were also traced.
[15] The most important enumeration error in Glamorgan where about 7,600 male and 6,900 female migrants were returned as natives in 1871 leads to a very important result. See chapter 10.

to an Ancient county base with little problem.[16] This is because the published birth and death rates in the nineteenth century were merely total births and deaths divided by the population. These rates could, therefore, be applied to the mean Ancient county population ($POPqi^1 + POPqi^2 \div 2$) to obtain total births per decade (Bii^1) and total deaths (Dqi^1). (Of course, the total number of births and deaths in the county as a whole remains unchanged.) This procedure assumes that the vital characteristics of that part of the Ancient county which was not within the Registration county bearing the same name were identical with the vital characteristics of the Registration county.

The main problem with the vital data is the under-registration of births. The registration of births and deaths was made compulsory in 1837, but there were no penalties for failure to comply with the law until 1874. Death registration was assumed to have been complete in the period, but the Registrar General knew that many births were escaping registration.[17] Glass showed that at least 4% of all births were not registered in 1851–60 and 2% in 1861–70.[18] This gives only a global figure and it is quite possible that there were substantial differentials in the extent of under-registration, for example, between urban and rural counties.

There is an attempt to estimate the completeness of birth registration in individual English counties, by Teitelbaum.[19] He used a reverse survival method. That is, he applied survival ratios to each age group in the census population ($POPqi^2$) to estimate the size of the age group in $POPqi^1$ from which they were derived. If net migration and the survival ratios are known, a surplus of child survivors in $POPqi^2$ means that births were unregistered in the previous decade. Teitelbaum estimated that births were more than 3% under-registered in 9 of the 44 Registration Counties in 1861–70 and less than 1% under-registered in 8 counties. Mean under-registration in England and Wales was 1.9% in the 1860s and 0.6% in the 1870s. But it would have been incorrect to deduce from these estimates that, for the purposes of this study, the number of births in each county had to be individually adjusted. In the first place, Teitelbaum had to know the net migration

---

[16] Except that Wales comprised only two Registration counties. Vital data for Wales were calculated from individual Registration Districts.

[17] See D. Farr in *Census of England and Wales*, 1871, vol. IV, p. 55.

[18] By examining the changes in age structure. Assumptions were necessary about the extent of net emigration and its age distribution. Glass, 'Under-registration of births', pp. 70–88.

[19] M. S. Teitelbaum, 'Birth under-registration in the constituent counties of England and Wales 1841–1910', *Population Studies*, 28, 1974, pp. 329–43.

(MIGqi) from each county to know that the survivors in each age group had died and not migrated. But the net migration estimates are themselves dependant on the extent of under-registration. Incorrect allowance for migration could lead to relatively high errors.

Secondly, migration estimates are only affected by under-registration insofar as births are not recorded at all. Teitelbaum's explanation of a large part of the variance is that births (and registrations) often occurred in counties which were not the normal residence of the child's parents. He showed, for example, that births were over-registered in London, but under-registered in the neighbouring suburban counties. In these cases the births are not missed in the migration estimates since the child counts as a (very young) internal migrant. Teitelbaum's estimates do not lead to the conclusion that there was great variation in never-registered births between counties. In consequence differential under-registration was ignored and total births in 1861–70 were increased by 2% in all counties.

IV

The most important analytical difficulty in estimating inter-county migration flows is establishing a set of male and female lifetime migrant death rates ($\overline{Dij}$ and $\overline{Dji}$) for each county.[20] The death rate of lifetime migrants in a particular county depends on three factors – the age-specific mortality, the age distribution of current migrants (IMIGij) and the age distribution of lifetime migrants (POPij) who are the survivors of the previous current migrants. The age distributions of lifetime migrants depends on their previous age-specific mortality and on the rate of previous migration. The higher the rate of net in-migration and the lower the age-specific mortality the lower will be migrant deaths. The lower the rate of net in-migration and the higher the age-specific mortality the higher will be migrant deaths.

The single most important contribution to the number of lifetime migrant deaths in our method is the age distribution of current migrants. This is because an error in the assumption of the current migrant age distribution is cumulative, whereas an error in age-specific

---

[20] Fairly acceptable results were obtained in a preliminary paper by applying the same death rate for all lifetime migrant populations, that is, both POPji and POPij in each decade, assuming that the migrant mortality lay between 65% and 85% of the mortality of England and Wales in the same period. The error is lower, the nearer POPji approaches POPij. But even here, there is a considerable range of error since Dji could be at the lower end of the range and Dij at the higher. Since IMIGij is invariably greater than EMIGio, errors are relatively greater in EMIGio. There is no alternative to producing a migrant mortality rate for each POPij and POPji.

mortality and in the initial age distribution of lifetime migrants is not. It will be shown, below, that current migrants were young. If, for example, the assumed age-specific mortality of a migrant group was too high, then the method would generate more in-migrants which would lower the mean age of lifetime migrants and hence reduce migration in the next decade. Similarly, after about three decades the age distribution of lifetime migrants is determined far more by the ages of current migrants and by mortality than by the initial age distribution of the group. The relationship between the age distribution of current migrants and their mortality is demonstrated with the aid of a simple example later in this chapter.

The evidence that current migrants contained a disproportionate share of young adults is overwhelming. It is sometimes said that age is the only universally valid migration differential and that all others like sex, marital and social status and occupation are only valid under particular circumstances.[21] Migration involves a decision about investment on which younger people can expect a higher return. Perhaps a more important reason is that migration is often associated with particular stages in the life cycle, which most frequently occur among young adults – marriage and leaving the parental home for the first time. The youth of current migrants was a constant theme of the extensive nineteenth-century literature on rural depopulation.[22] Some care is necessary in the use of this evidence, however. It was largely based on impressions, and was often openly propagandist.[23] And a great deal of the nineteenth-century literature on rural–urban migration concentrated on agricultural labour which was only one of many occupations and not necessarily the most relevant.[24] The qualitative evidence is, however, complemented by a series of studies which examined the changing age structure of areas of heavy out-migration and demonstrated that the out-migrants must have been young.[25]

[21] For example, in D. S. Thomas, *Research memorandum on migration differentials* (New York, SSRC, No. 43 1938), pp. 160–7.

[22] See amongst a vast literature, J. R. Jefferies, *Hodge and his Masters* (reprinted, Faber, 1948). P. A. Graham, *The rural exodus* (Methuen, 1892) and the *Royal Commission on Labour, 1893–94*, XXXV and XXXVI which is quoted extensively in W. Hasbach, *History of the English agricultural labourer* (reprinted Cass, 1966).

[23] For example, Rider Haggard's attack on compulsory education in rural areas, because the Board Schools taught more than the potential agricultural labourers needed and induced them to go to the towns by widening their horizons. H. Rider Haggard, *Rural England* (Longmans, 1902), pp. 268–9.

[24] The single most important reason for out-migration in rural areas was probably the decline of rural industries and the growth of employment in the urban areas.

[25] A. L. Bowley, 'Rural population in England and Wales. A study of the changes in density, occupations and ages', *Journal of the Royal Statistical Society*, LXXVII (1914),

The introduction of various forms of continuous population register complemented by surveys in more recent years has enabled the age distribution of current migrants to be studied directly. In Britain and the U.S.A. (and in most western countries) the migration rate rises sharply from about the age of fifteen to a period in the mid-twenties.[26] In Hollingsworth's study of Scottish migration between 1939 and 1964 (based on national registration data and on the exchange of medical cards), 64.2 per 1,000 aged 15–19 and 78.8 per 1,000 aged 20–24 changed house annually, compared with 42.8 aged 10–14 and 51.6 aged 30–34. If Hollingsworth's age-specific migration rates are applied to the number of people in each age group in 1951 these data imply that 43.7% of a group of current migrants were aged 15–34 and 29.3% were under 15.[27] If the data are applied to the age distribution of 1881, then 45.2% of current migrants were aged 15–24 and 38.6% were under fifteen. It would be dangerous, however, to assume that twentieth century age-specific migration rates can be applied to the nineteenth century.

The education of children, housing and the care of aged parents were almost certainly less important influences in the decision to migrate in the late nineteenth century than they have become. For example, council tenants are at the moment relatively less mobile than owner-occupiers of the same age, but it is not clear whether this is because of the vested interest a council house represents, or whether it is because owner-occupiers tend to be in a higher socio-economic position.[28] In Britain, it appears that mobility is positively correlated with economic and social status.[29] If this were true in the late nine-

---

pp. 597–645. A. B. Hill, *Internal migration and its effects upon the death rates with special reference to the county of Essex* (Medical Research Council, 1925). G. H. Daniel, 'Labour migration and age composition', *Sociological Review* 30 (3) 1939, pp. 281–308. There is a good summary of the literature in J. Saville, *Rural depopulation in England and Wales 1851–1951* (Routledge, 1957), pp. 98–117.

[26] See T. H. Hollingsworth, *Migration. A study based on Scottish experience between 1939 and 1964* (Oliver and Boyd, Edinburgh, 1970), p. 90. A. Harris and R. Clausen, *Labour mobility in Great Britain 1953–1963* (Ministry of Labour and National Service, 1967). E. S. Lee and G. P. Barber, *Population Index*, 32, 1966, front cover. M. P. Newton and J. R. Jeffery, *Internal migration* (General Register Office. Studies on Medical and Population Subjects No. 5, HMSO, 1951). There is a short summary in T. H. Hollingsworth, 'Historical studies of migration', *Annales de Démographie Historique*, 1970 (Paris, 1971), pp. 87–91.

[27] Hollingsworth, *Migration*, pp. 88–91.

[28] See J. H. Johnson, J. Salt and P. A. Wood, *Housing and the migration of labour in England and Wales* (Saxon House, Farnborough, 1974) pp. 197–9, 201–3.

[29] D. Friedlander and R. J. Roshier, 'A study of internal migration in England and Wales, Part II. Recent internal movements'. *Population Studies*, 19, 1966, pp. 50–4. C. Jansen, 'Some sociological aspects of migration' in J. A. Jackson (ed.), *Migration* (Cambridge University Press, 1969), pp. 64, 69, 71.

teenth century, the number of children among current inter-county migrants would be affected by class differentials in fertility, which were widening by the 1880s.[30] There is no general evidence of the occupational distribution of late nineteenth-century migrants, although clearly the total number of white-collar workers in the general population from which the migrants were drawn was less than it is now. In addition, it can be argued that the superior migration rates of the higher socio-economic groups in contemporary Britain is a consequence of a particular type of recent economic growth. This is the position taken by F. Musgrove.[31] Musgrove argues that the social status of migrants has been relatively increasing since the early nineteenth century – although the evidence is rather thin. Another problem is that, according to some modern work, marriage appears to be a more important migration differential than age itself. Nineteenth-century qualitative evidence denies this; great stress was laid on the fact that the young migrants were single. Modern evidence of the age structure of current migrants must, therefore, be treated with caution.

Systematic evidence on the age distribution of lifetime migrants (POPij) is contained in the 1861, 1871 and 1911 censuses and from this it is possible to estimate the age distribution of the current migrants. In 1861 and 1871 the place of birth tables divided the lifetime migrants in each county into those 'under twenty' and 'over twenty'. In 1911, the complete age distribution was given for the lifetime migrants in most of the principle areas of in-migration. The age distribution of all migrants that had been born in four important areas of out-migration was also given.[32] In the main counties of in-migration, in 1861 and 1871, about 25% of the migrant population was under twenty compared with about 50% of the native population. The variation between counties was low.[33] In 1911, about 20% of the migrants were under twenty. This is broadly comparable with 1861 and 1871 allowing for falling mortality.

The first problem, therefore, was to estimate the age distribution of the current migrants (IMIGij) that is consistent with the observation

---

[30] D. V. Glass, *Population policies and movements in W. Europe* (Oxford University Press, 1940), p. 69.

[31] F. Musgrove, *The migratory élite* (Heinemann, 1963), pp. 10, 53–63.

[32] The POPkj of the counties of Carmarthen, Monmouth and of Birmingham, Bradford, Burton on Trent, Coventry, Hastings, Liverpool, Manchester, Middlesborough, London, Swindon, Aberdare and Rhondda. The age distribution of the POPji was given for London, Somerset, Huntingdon and Westmorland.

[33] 25.5% of the male lifetime migrant population were under 20 in the seventeen most important counties of in-migration ($\sigma = 6.7$) and 27.1% of the female ($\sigma = 2.7$).

Table 4.1. *Survivors of 1000 migrants aged 15–19, 1861–91*

1861	1871	1881	1891	
1000	1000	1000	1000	
	945	945	945	
		865	865	
			757	
			3567	under 20 = 28%

Note: The implied survival ratios are those of England and Wales in 1871–80.

that usually, about 25% of the lifetime migrants (POPij) were under twenty. Obviously, these young current migrants must have arrived within the last two decades. It is also clear that the majority of them must have arrived in the most recent decade. Any migrant who arrived after the middle of the first decade who was more than six years old would have been more than twenty years old at the end of the second decade (POPij[3]). The next question is how many of the young migrants were children as opposed to young people aged 15–19?

Young adults and young-middle-aged adults (ages 15–44) had relatively low mortality in this period. For example, if they had experienced the average mortality of England and Wales, at least 750 out of every 1,000 migrants aged 15–19 who arrived in a county in 1861 would have still been alive in 1891. If we include the survivors from a further 1,000 who arrived in 1871 and 1881 the total number of survivors in 1891 would have been 2,567 (Table 4.1). Hence, the 1,000 migrants aged 15–19 would have been 28% of the lifetime migrant population. But this assumes that there were no survivors from migration streams that arrived before 1861, which is highly improbable. If allowance is made for these survivors, the lifetime migrants aged under twenty would have been less than 25% of the total.

It is unlikely that the mortality experience of the lifetime migrants was significantly worse than that of natives. Hence, the fact that about 25% of lifetime migrants were under twenty is consistent with the assumption that the current migrants included some older people. This would have the effect of reducing the number of older migrant survivors and increasing the proportion of migrants who were under twenty. For example, if the current migrants in Table 4.1 had been aged 25–34, there would only have been 2,254 survivors in 1891 and the proportion of lifetime migrants over twenty would then have been

31%. It is also likely that these slightly older migrants were accompanied by children. The parents of these children must have been predominantly young (i.e. 25–34 at POPij^2). If the parents were older than this their families would probably be near complete. This is very unlikely if only 25% of the migrant populations were under twenty, since in the total population of England and Wales about 36% were under fifteen in the period.[34] It follows that there cannot have been many children, and their parents must have been young with incomplete families. (Children who were born subsequent to their parents' migration would be enumerated as natives, of course.)

We tested our assumptions of the age distribution of current migrants by trial and error. The age distribution that best meets the qualitative and quantitative criteria discussed above was comprised of 4% aged 0–4, 15% aged 5–14, 53% aged 15–24 (the unattached adults) and 28% aged 25–34 (the parents of the young children). Median age is 21. The population of children under five is low because they can only have arrived within the last five years of each decade. This age distribution is at POPij^2 which implies that the ages of *current* migrants were 4% aged 0–4, 34% aged 5–14, 51% aged 15–24 and 11% aged 25–34.[35] This appears unrealistically young, but it must be remembered that the age distribution of current migrants is *net of returns*. Return migrants were older than the first time migrants by definition. For example, if return migration was a third of outward, which is a realistic assumption, and 15%, 30%, 24%, 21% and 9% of the return migrants were aged 15–24, 25–34, 35–44, 45–54 and 55–64 respectively, then the age distribution of the first time migrants would be: 3% aged 0–4, 26% aged 5–14, 42% aged 15–24, 16% aged 25–34, 6% aged 35–44, 5% aged 45–54 and 2% aged 55–64.

The effect of our assumption of the age distribution of the current migrants can be demonstrated with the aid of a simple arithmetical model (Table 4.2). Table 4.2 is a stylised way of considering the experience of a group of lifetime migrants who were enumerated in the county of South Riding between 1851 and 1901. We have assumed

[34] This does not imply that migrants had smaller than average families. In the nineteenth century controlling families are thought to have avoided childbirth towards the end of the fecund period. But these children would be born after migration and would therefore be natives.

[35] The age distribution of current migrants is frequently confused with that of current migrants at the next census. This error occurs in D. Friedlander and D. J. Roshier, 'A study of internal migration in England and Wales, Part I', *Population Studies*, 19, 1966, pp. 239–79, H. A. Shannon, 'Migration and the growth of London 1841–1891', *Economic History Review*, 5, 1935, pp. 78–86 and B. Thomas, 'Migration into the Glamorganshire Coalfield 1861–1911', *Economica*, 30, 1930, pp. 275–94.

Table 4.2. A model lifetime migrant population, 1851–1901

Assumptions (i) The number of lifetime migrants was growing at 15% per decade. (ii) England and Wales, age-specific mortality

Ages	Current Migrants %	POPij 1851	s.r	S 1861	IMIGij 1861	POPij 1861	s.r	S 1871	IMIGij 1871	POPij 1871	s.r	S 1881	IMIGij 1881	POPij 1881	s.r	S 1891	IMIGij 1891	POPij 1891	s.r	S 1901	IMIGij 1901	POPij 1901
0–	4	20	.85	—	13	13	.88	—	15	15	.89	—	17	17	.92	—	20	20	.93	—	23	23
5–	15	100	.93	17	50	67	.95	11	57	68	.96	13	66	79	.97	16	74	90	.97	19	84	103
15–	53	230	.91	93	176	269	.92	64	200	264	.93	65	233	298	.94	77	263	340	.95	87	298	385
25–	28	190	.88	209	93	302	.90	247	106	353	.90	246	123	369	.91	280	139	419	.92	323	157	480
35–	—	180	.85	167	—	167	.85	272	—	272	.85	318	—	318	.86	336	—	336	.86	385	—	385
45–	—	140	.77	153	—	153	.78	142	—	142	.77	231	—	231	.77	273	—	273	.78	289	—	289
55–	—	90	.64	108	—	108	.63	119	—	119	.62	109	—	109	.61	178	—	178	.61	213	—	213
65–	—	40	.32	58	—	58	.38	68	—	68	.38	74	—	74	.37	66	—	66	.36	109	—	109
75–	—	10		13	—	13		22	—	22		26	—	26		27	—	27		24	—	24
	100	1000		818	332	1150		945	378	1323		1082	439	1521		1253	496	1749		1449	562	2011
Migrant deaths					14				16				17				15				16	

	1851–60	1861–70	1871–80	1881–90	1891–1900
Total IMIGij	346	394	456	511	578
Total deaths (Dij)	196	221	258	283	316
Population at risk (POPij)	1075	1237	1422	1635	1880
Implied migrant death rate	18.6 per 1000*	17.7 per 1000*	18.1 per 1000	17.3 per 1000	16.9 per 1000

*Not used to determine migrant death rate because they are affected by the choice of age distribution in POPij[1]
s.r: Probability of surviving from POPij to POPij[2]
S: Survivors from POPij to POPij[2]

that the number of lifetime migrants in South Riding grew at 15% per decade or 75% between 1861 and 1900. In England and Wales, 66 of the 104 (POPij) migrant groups (i.e. 52 counties and 2 sexes) and 44 (POPji) migrant groups increased between 50% and 99% in those years. In other words, 15% per decade was a typical rate at which the lifetime migrant groups grew in the period 1861–1900.

It is also assumed (for the moment) that 2% of the lifetime migrants enumerated in South Riding in 1851 were aged 0–4, 10% were aged 5–14, 23% were aged 15–24, 19% were aged 25–34, 18% were aged 35–44, 14% were aged 45–54, 9% were aged 55–64, 4% were aged 65–74 and 1% were over 75. This is a realistic assumption of the age distribution of a migrant group into which migrants had been moving for some time. Our assumption about the initial age distribution, it should be noted, is similar to the age distribution of 1901 generated by the model, which is our own estimate of the effect of fifty years migration.

Columns 4, 8, 12, 16 and 20 are survival ratios which show the probability of the lifetime migrants living until the next census. Hence, the 20 lifetime migrants aged 0–4 in 1851 (column 3) had a 0.85 chance of surviving until 1861 (column 5) which means that 17 were still alive to be enumerated in 1861. Similarly, the 100 lifetime migrants aged 5–14 had a 0.93 chance of surviving until 1861 and 93 did so. The survival ratios were derived from the age-specific mortality recorded in the relevant Registrar General's *Decennial Supplements*.[36] The level of age-specific mortality does not affect our test of the effect of our assumptions of the age distribution of current migrants as long as the ratio of mortality at one age to another remains the same. This is discussed below.

Table 4.2 should be read as follows. In 1851, 1,000 lifetime migrants (POPij) were enumerated in South Riding (column 3). We estimate that 818 of the migrants were still alive in 1861 (column 5). But 1,150 lifetime migrants were enumerated in 1861. (The lifetime migrant population in this model is assumed to grow at 15% per decade.) Hence, 332 migrants (1,150–818) must have arrived between 1851 and 1861 – plus the in-migrants who arrived after 1851 but died before 1861. Now, we have assumed that 4% of these migrants were aged 0–4, 15% were aged 5–14, 53% were aged 15–24, and 28% were aged 25–34. The 1,150 lifetime migrants in 1861 (column 7), would then

[36] *Decennial Supplement* to *33rd Annual Report*, 1872, XVII; 44th, 1884–5, XVII; 55th, 1895, XXIII and 1897, XXI: 65th, 1905, Cd 2618, Cd2619, XVIII. Reference had also to be made to the *Annual Reports* to obtain vital data for individual Welsh counties.

Table 4.3. *Age distribution of current migrants at POPij²*
(net of returns)

	Assumed age distribution (AD_1) %	Older age distribution (AD_2) %
0–4	4	4
5–14	15	15
15–24	53	33
25–34	28	25
35–44		15
45–54		8

comprise 13 persons aged 0–4, 67 aged 5–14, 269 aged 15–24, etc. We can now apply the survivorship ratios of 1861–70 (column 8) to this group, which implies that there were 945 survivors in 1871. In 1871, 1,323 migrants were enumerated. Hence, there were 378 migrants into South Riding in 1861–70, 439 in 1871–80, 496 in 1881–90 and 562 in 1891–1900 (Columns 10, 14, 18 and 22 respectively). We ignore the decades 1851–60 and 1861–70 because the estimates of current migration are too dependant on the assumptions made about the initial age distribution of the migrant group (column 3). In other words we assume that in-migration had occurred before 1851.

According to our model, there were 456 migrants in the decade 1871–80 (including those who died before 1881). If the migrants had arrived at a constant rate the average population at risk would have been $(1,323 + 1,521) \div 2 = 1,422$. There were 258 migrant deaths (column 14). Hence, the assumption that the age distribution of current migrants was as in column 2 implies that the death rate of the migrant group was 18.1 per 1,000 in 1871–80, 17.3 per 1,000 in 1881–90 and 16.8 per 1,000 in 1891–1900 if age-specific mortality was the same as in England and Wales.

It is difficult to conceive that the current migrants could have been younger. But they could have been older, for at least some part of the forty years 1861–1900. Our oldest conceivable age distribution of current migrants is given in Table 4.3 where it is contrasted with the one that best agrees with the available quantitative and qualitative data.

If AD_2 is substituted for AD_1 in our model the death rate of the migrant group would be 19.8 per 1,000, 20.0 per 1,000 and 20.1 per 1,000 in 1871–80, 1881–90 and 1891–1900 respectively – i.e. between 8 and 16% higher. The effect of this would be to increase the estimate of in-migration (IMIGij) by between 5% and 10%. This differential is identical at different levels of age-specific mortality. If the number of lifetime migrants was growing at 25% per decade (as in some of the industrial counties) then AD_2 would imply that migrant deaths were between 6% and 25% higher. This would increase the estimates of in-migration (IMIGij) by between 3% and 9%. Now AD_2 can only have occurred in isolated decades, if at all, because, as was argued above, it is logically impossible in the long run. Current migrants can only have been as old as AD_2 for individual decades. Since it is logically impossible for AD_1 to have been lower, the maximum error must lie in the lower half of the range.

We assumed, therefore, that errors caused by an incorrect assumption of the age distribution of current migrants were only exceptionally likely to affect our estimates of in-migration (IMIGij) by much more than 5%.

V

The second problem involved in the calculation of a set of lifetime migrant death rates is to establish the age-specific mortality of male and female migrants. Age-specific mortality is a less important cause of error than the age distribution of current migrants because the estimate of the number of migrants (IMIGij) in any decade depends on the number of migrant deaths (Dij). If Dij^1 were too high, $IMIGij^1$ is too high. Since migrants are young, $POPij^2$ will be too young and mortality will be reduced. Hence, errors in age-specific mortality are self-correcting. In a county where the POPij was growing at 15% per decade, an upward error of 10% in age-specific mortality would increase migrant deaths (Dji) by between 5% and 10% and in-migration (IMIGij) by between 3% and 6%. For the reasons stated above the error is lower the higher the rate of in-migration. If the county grew at 25% per decade an over-estimate of age-specific mortality of 10% would increase Dji between 7% and 8% which would increase IMIGij between 2% and 3%. This is a low degree of error but not low enough to justify the application of the same age-specific mortality to all the lifetime migrant groups.[37] Age-specific mortality was as high

---

[37] An early unpublished paper produced fairly acceptable results for differential emigration but the possible errors were too large to allow a sufficiently detailed analysis of the relation between emigration and internal migration. See D. E. Baines, 'Emigration and internal migration in England and Wales 1861–1901', Paper given at the MSSB/SSRC conference on New Economic History, Harvard University, 10–12 September 1973.

as 25% above the mean rate in England and Wales (in Lancashire) and as low as 30% below (in Huntingdon, Wiltshire and Dorset). The very high variance in age-specific mortality between counties is concealed by the crude death rates because the counties with the highest age-specific mortality had the largest proportion of their population in the young age groups.[38] Nor is the variance in age-specific mortality only a consequence of variations in infant mortality. If this were true, the effect of differential mortality between counties would be much less important, because the migrants were relatively unaffected by infant mortality, particularly in the first three months when disproportionate numbers of infant deaths occurred.

The mortality experience of lifetime migrants must obviously have been related to that of the natives in the counties to which they had moved. The problem is to establish by precisely how much. General mortality in the counties of heavy in-migration (London and Lancashire, for example) was weighted by the experience of the poorest groups, who were both particularly susceptible to disease and who had high fertility.

For the purposes of argument we can distinguish two important influences on the mortality of lifetime migrants. One relates to the environment which many of them encountered in the large towns which were the most important destinations. We can call this influence 'nurture'. The other relates to the effect of their up-bringing which could have been outside the large towns or in the rural areas. This can be called 'nature'. There is no evidence that migrants were disproportionately susceptible to urban diseases; indeed the weight of contemporary opinion was that they were healthier than the natives of the large towns to which they went. Nor is there any evidence that migrants were at the bottom on the urban socio-economic hierarchy. In fact, it is possible that migrant selection favoured the relatively better off or those who would become better off. Most lifetime migrants would probably not fall to the bottom of urban society and their age-specific mortality was possibly less than that of natives.

The effect of the environment on the death rate of lifetime migrants (i.e. the 'nurture' assumption) was estimated by applying the age standardised mortality in the counties in which the lifetime migrants were living. For example, in 1881–90, 40% of the lifetime migrants (POPij) who had been born in Barsetshire were living in London, 20% were in Staffordshire, 10% in Warwickshire and 30% in the rest

---

[38] In 1881, for example, the unweighted mean of male crude death rates was 18.80 per 1,000, $\sigma = 1.56$. If the county populations had identical age distributions, the unweighted mean death rate would have been 17.90 per 1,000, $\sigma = 2.43$.

of England and Wales. Age standardised mortality in those counties was 23.2 per 1,000, 21.3 per 1,000, 20.4 per 1,000 and 20.0 per 1,000 respectively. The weighted lifetime migrant death rate of Barsetshire natives in 1881–90 ($\overline{\text{Dij}}$) was, therefore, 21.6 per 1,000. We assumed that the 1881–90 value bore the same relation to the England and Wales death rate in the other decades. Similarly, we assumed that the mortality level of lifetime migrants in Barsetshire (POPji) must be the age standardised mortality of Barsetshire itself (17.6 per 1,000). We established the mortality level for each of the 104 lifetime migrant groups (POPij and POPji) for both males and females.

The 'nurture' assumption gave us an upper limit of migrant mortality. The lower limit, the 'nature' assumption, was assumed to be the mean mortality of England and Wales. This was the most realistic lower limit of migrant mortality because migrant mortality would not be as low as mortality in the rural areas – which in any case were not the source of all internal migrants. In theory, the 'nature' mortality would be an upper limit if the migrants from an urban county were distributed among rural counties. This did not occur, however. We can assume that the mortality of each lifetime migrant group must lie between the rate calculated on the 'nature' and the 'nurture' assumptions.[39]

We have shown how we estimated the age distribution of current migrants and the mortality levels appropriate to the migrant groups. It remains to show how we allowed for the rate of in-migration. In the period 1861–1900, the lifetime migrant populations grew at a rate which varied between −2% per decade (the male POPji of Montgomery) and 42% per decade (the female POPij of Essex). Since we had estimated the age distribution of current migrants and their mortality, we could use the rate of growth of the migrant groups to estimate a set of migrant death rates ($\overline{\text{Dij}}$ and $\overline{\text{Dji}}$).[40] If the age distribution of current migrants is assumed to be fixed, the relation between the rate of growth of the migrant groups can be reduced to a set of linear equations based on Table 4.2 and similar tables which used different assumptions. For example, we estimated that the lifetime migrants who had been born in Barsetshire had a mortality level of 21.6 per 1,000, on the 'nurture' assumption. Their numbers grew 94% between 1861 and 1901. The relationship appropriate to that level of mortality

---

[39] If the final migration estimate was adjusted, however, the adjustment had to imply a level of migrant mortality that lay *between* the 'nature' and the 'nurture' assumptions.
[40] Only Dji refer to one county. Dij are deaths in all the destinations of lifetime migrants from country i in England and Wales.

(in 1881–90) is given by:

$$y = 29.71 - 6.45 \log 94$$

when y is the death rate of the migrant population. Hence, the upper limit of the migrant death rate in 1881–90 is 17.0 per 1,000. Similarly, the lower limit of the death rate of Barsetshire born in other counties in 1881–90 (the 'nature' assumption) is given by:

$$y = 28.58 - 6.23 \log 94$$

Hence, the lower limit of the Barsetshire migrant death rate in 1881–90 is 16.3 per 1,000. It will be remembered that the lower limit of migrant mortality is that of England and Wales. We assumed that the 'true' death rate must lie between these limits and we, therefore, took the mean value. We assumed that the migrant death rates bore the same relationship to the England and Wales death rates in each decade. The final migrant death rate for natives of Barsetshire is:

$$[(17.0 \times 23.4 \div 20.0) + (16.3 \times 23.4 \div 20.0)] \div 2 \text{ i.e. } 19.48 \text{ per } 1,000$$

By an identical process we estimated the death rate of the lifetime migrants living in Barsetshire in 1861–70 (23.15 per 1,000). It was then a simple matter to find the actual number of deaths and therefore the number of migrants who moved to the other counties and overseas.

It is important to remember that our estimates of migrant death rates are entirely consistent with the total recorded deaths in the returns of the Registrar General. Our estimates, in effect, reallocate the total number of deaths in each county between natives and non-natives. The total number of deaths in England and Wales remains the same.

Our method, in effect, makes assumptions about only two of the determinants of migrant deaths – the age structure of the current migrants and the level of age-specific mortality. The third determinant of migrant deaths is the age structure of the lifetime migrants at the beginning of the period under consideration. It was not necessary to know this, however. The simple migration models (Table 4.2) which were used to determine the relationship between the rate of in-migration and migrant deaths on various assumptions start with a lifetime migrant population with a hypothetical (but realistic) age distribution. But only the estimate of migrant deaths in the last three decades (1871–1900) was used as a basis of the estimates of the 'true' migrant death rate. This procedure eliminated any errors from an incorrect choice of age distribution in POPij[1] at the cost of assuming that the

age structure of current migrants was constant, and that the relationship between the mortality at different ages in the various counties
of England and Wales was the same as in England and Wales as
a whole. That is, a five year old was twice as likely to die in the
decade as a twenty year old in all counties irrespective of the level
of mortality.[41]

The disadvantage of this method of estimating migrant deaths is
that it fails to take account of exceptional events. In an individual
decade, the rate of in-migration or the characteristics of current
migrants could diverge sharply from the mean rate or mean characteristics. This would affect migrant deaths in that decade and subsequently. But as long as our assumptions of the mean characteristics
are sound, the effect of exceptional changes on the level of in-migration
(IMIGij) is limited, because current migrants are a relatively small
proportion of all lifetime migrants. Further errors could occur if the
characteristics of age-specific migrant mortality diverged in one decade
from the characteristics of all mortality in the county by more or less
than the average divergence. This is thought to be unlikely in the
short run. The advantage of our method of estimating migrant deaths
is that it avoids cumulative errors. In any case, it does not follow,
for example, that even if the initial age distribution of all POPij and
POPji were known, and Dij could be calculated for each decade, that
errors would be avoided. In the first place, variations in the age distribution of current migrants are not known. More important, Dij^2 would
be dependent on the estimate of Dij^1. This could introduce serious
cumulative errors which our method largely avoids. Similarly, the
attempt to estimate each IMIGij into individual counties – which would
require 5,408 individual calculations for each decade – would not
increase the accuracy of the estimates. If the same assumptions about
age distribution and mortality were used for each migrant group, there
would be no point in calculating inter-county flows to estimate emigration. If separate assumptions were used for each flow, the possibility
of error would have been large.

We have already seen that the main source of error in migrant deaths
(Dij) is error in the age distribution of current migrants (IMIGij). If
the current migrants were exceptionally old in one decade, an upward
error in Dij would be generated which could exceptionally reach 10%
after several decades. This would increase in-migration by between
3% and 9% depending on the other assumptions. The greatest relative

---

[41] It is important to remember that Dij includes deaths of migrants who arrived within
the decade. The population at risk is $POPij^1 + POPij^2 \div 2$, so that the implied migrant
death rates are constructed in the same way as nineteenth-century crude rates.

Table 4.4. *Native migration from Barsetshire, 1861–70*
(000s and as a % of the total native population in England
and Wales)

IMIG	26,344 ± 667	8.6% ± 0.2%	
EMIG	12,380 ± 1199	4.1% ± 0.4%	

effect of error in current migrant age distribution occurs when in-migration is low. The effects of errors in age-specific mortality are at their greatest when in-migration is high. At their maximum these could also lead to an error of 10% in Dij. But if our assumptions of mean migrant mortality and the age distribution are correct, it follows that the bulk of the error can only occur in one decade. The main effect of errors in mortality occurs when in-migration is high and the main effect of errors in migrant age distribution occurs when in-migration is low. The greatest effect of the two sources of error cannot occur simultaneously. Similarly, if the age distribution of IMIGij was too old and their mortality too low, then errors would tend to cancel out. We can be fairly sure that errors caused by deviations in age-specific mortality from its mean level and deviations in the age distribution of current migrants from their mean level, are very unlikely to change Dij in any one county by as much as 10% in any one decade and the more likely range is much less.

All the migration estimates in this study (which we set out in detail in Appendix I) are given within a range which corresponds to a presumed error of ±5% in migrant death rates. In our example, we estimated that the death rate ($\overline{Dij}$) of male Barsetshire-born migrants in 1861–70 was 19.48 per 1,000 and that the death rate of lifetime migrants in Barsetshire was 23.15 per 1,000. POPij[1] and POPij[2] were 62,000 and 75,000 respectively. Migrant deaths (Dij) were therefore:

$$\frac{(62,000 + 75,000)}{(2 \times 1,000)} \times 19.48 \times 10 = 13,344$$

Our final estimate of the migration of Barsetshire born into other counties (IMIGij) was +26,344. Similarly, deaths of lifetime migrants in Barsetshire (Dji) were 10,649, which meant that native deaths were 48,676. (Dii = Dqi − Dji). This gave us a final estimate of natives out-migration (MIGik) of −38,724. If our estimate of migrant deaths is subject to an error of ±5%, the Dij would lie between 14,011 and 12,677. Similarly Dji would lie between 11,181 and 10,117. In turn, this means that MIGik lies between −39,256 and −38,192, and IMIGij lies between +27,011 and +25,677. EMIGio = MIGik − IMIGij. Hence

the number of Barsetshire-born emigrants in 1861–70 must lie between
−11,181 and −13,579.

No conclusions are drawn about native migration from any of the
counties that are not robust enough to withstand non-compensating
errors of 5% in the death rate of the lifetime migrants in other counties
and in the death rate of lifetime migrants in the county. Errors of
more than 5% can only have occurred in particular decades and in
individual counties. It follows, therefore, that when we consider
migration over several decades or aggregate migration from several
counties, the estimates are more robust.[42]

VI

There is a relatively easy way of checking our estimates of emigration
and internal migration and, hence, our assumptions about the age
distribution of the migrants and their mortality. The sum of our estimates of the emigration by the natives of each of the fifty-two counties
of England and Wales must be an estimate of the total emigration
of natives of England and Wales. It is possible to estimate this value
independently. Net emigration of *all* persons from England and Wales
in any one decade must be the difference between the total population
at the beginning and end of the decade plus the natural increase,
i.e.:

$EMIGqo^1 = POPqe^2 - (POPqe^1 + Bee^1 - Dqe^1)$, where q is everywhere and e is England and Wales.

Now by the same method we can estimate net movement into England
and Wales by natives of other countries, i.e.:

$IMIGoe^1 = POPoe^1 - (POPoe^2 - Doe^1)$ where o is overseas. (All
those born in England and Wales must be natives, of course.)[43]

$EMIGqo^1 - IMIGoe^1$ must be net migration overseas of English and
Welsh natives ($EMIGeo^1$) which is the sum of the natives of all the
counties ($\Sigma EMIGio^1$).

The net movement of 'overseas' born (i.e. Scots, Irish, colonials

---

[42] This is actually an idealised description of the method used by the author. For com-
puting reasons it was necessary to generate the final migration estimates on a series
of assumptions about the probable mortality of the migrants *before* the correct assumptions of the lifetime migrant death rate were determined. The true values were then
chosen from the most appropriate death rate.

[43] This is the only way of estimating total emigration from England and Wales, net
of returns. Returned migrants to Britain were only distinguished after 1876 and they
include Scots and Irish. Returned migrants to England and Wales were not distinguished until 1895. See chapter 5.

Table 4.5. *Net emigration of 'overseas' born into England and Wales, 1861–1900 (000s)*

Born in		1861–70	1871–80	1881–90	1891–1900
Ireland	males	+ 73.1	+ 90.9	+ 12.5	+ 47.5
	females	+ 75.0	+ 72.3	+ 19.3	+ 33.3
Scotland	males	+ 41.9	+ 42.6	+ 36.6	+ 44.2
	females	+ 39.6	+ 40.8	+ 36.6	+ 37.8
Island in the British seas	males	+ 4.8	+ 4.0	+ 2.6	+ 5.4
	females	+ 6.6	+ 4.6	+ 3.3	+ 5.1
Colonies	males	+ 12.6	+ 16.7	+ 13.3	+ 17.2
	females	+ 15.8	+ 18.6	+ 17.1	+ 22.3
Foreign countries	males	+ 28.9	+ 35.8	+ 49.7	+ 84.1
	females	+ 28.4	+ 23.3	+ 37.0	+ 60.1
Total (including 'at sea')	males	+161.7	+191.1	+114.9	+198.4
	females	+165.7	+160.6	+113.3	+158.6

Note: see text for method of estimation.

and foreigners) into England and Wales was calculated in exactly the same way as the net movement into England and Welsh counties (IMIGij). The age distribution of current migrants from overseas was assumed to be identical to that of English and Welsh-born current migrants except in the case of colonial born where the age distribution of current migrants at POPij[2] was assumed to be 8% aged 0–4, 24% aged 5–14, 40% aged 15–24 and 28% aged 25–34. This is consistent with the percentage that were aged under 20 at the 1861 and 1871 census. Presumably a large proportion of colonial born were at school.[44] The age-specific mortality of the 'overseas' born was assumed to be entirely determined by conditions in the county of residence (The 'nurture' assumption).[45] The estimates of net movement of 'overseas' born into England and Wales are given in Table 4.5.

[44] There was a greater proportion of boys than girls under twenty among the 'colonial' born.

[45] The estimated mortality of the Irish in England and Wales, for example, may have been affected by their previous experience of low mortality in Ireland, but it was still above the mean level of the English counties in which they had settled.

Migration in a mature economy

Table 4.6. *Net native emigration from England and Wales, 1861–1900*
(000s)

		(1) EMIGio	(2) IMIGoe	(3) EMIGqo(1)	(4) EMIGqo (2)
1861–70	males	−321.8	−161.7	−160.1	−161.9
	females	−223.8	−165.9	− 57.9	− 46.2
1871–80	males	−346.2	−191.1	−155.1	−115.5
	females	−236.2	−160.6	− 75.7	− 43.9
1881–90	males	−561.4	−114.9	−446.5	−409.43
	females	−352.5	−113.7	−238.8	−210.0
1891–1900	males	−320.8	−198.4	−122.4	−125.1
	females	−108.2	−158.6	+ 50.3	+ 71.5

Key: (1) EMIGio sum of estimates of net emigration of natives of each of the
52 counties
(2) IMIGoe net movement of overseas born into England and Wales
(3) EMIGqo (1) implied net emigration of all persons from England and
Wales (EMIGio–IMIGoe)
(4) EMIGqo (2) direct estimate of net emigration

Table 4.6 shows the comparison between the two methods of estimating total native emigration and should be read as follows. In
1861–70, the sum of the county estimates show that 321,800 male
emigrants left England and Wales net of returns (ΣEMIGio). We also
estimated that 161,700 who had not been born in England and Wales
entered the country, net of returns (IMIGoe). Hence, net emigration
of natives and non natives was 160,100 (EMIGqo). We can also calculate EMIGqo directly, in which case it is estimated to have been 161,900
(EMIGqo(2)).[46]

If we assumed that the direct estimate of emigration (EMIGqo(2))
was completely accurate it would imply errors in the original estimates, as shown in Table 4.7. The correspondence is generally good.
Obviously, it would be possible to adjust our estimate of emigration
from each county so that the total equalled the amount implied by
the direct measure.[47] But this operation would be spurious since it

[46] Emigration from England and Wales by all of these measures includes movement
to Ireland and Scotland.
[47] It is also possible that the direct estimates of EMIGko could be faulty. There is an
alternative estimate in Carrier and Jeffery, *External migration*, p. 14 which is slightly
different to the author's. (*Footnote cont. next page.*)

Table 4.7. *Implied error in net native emigration. (000s) (adjustment
necessary to equalise estimates of ΣEMIGio)*

	1861–70	1871–80	1881–90	1891–1900
males	+ 1.8 (0.6%)	−39.6 (11.4%)	−37.2 (6.6%)	+ 2.7 (0.8%)
females	−11.7 (5.2%)	−31.8 (13.4%)	−28.8 (8.2%)	−21.2 (19.6%)

would assume that there were no errors in the estimation of migration
into England and Wales of the people who had been born outside.
This estimate depends on assumptions about the age structure and
mortality of overseas-born migrants – a group about which much less
is known than English and Welsh born migrants. In addition, the
apparently high percentage errors in the estimates of female emigration (17.7% in 1871–80 and 19.6% in 1881–90) are based on the
differences between very low estimates (see Table 4.6). However, it
is fairly clear that some of the errors in 1871–80 and 1881–90 must
have been caused by an incorrect estimate of migrant deaths (Dij)
as opposed to an incorrect estimate of the deaths in England and
Wales of foreign born. We assume this was the case when the implied
error exceeded 20,000 males and females. Hence, only the 1870s and
1880s estimates were adjusted and by the minimum amount that is
likely to have been caused by an error in Dij. Presumably, the error
was caused by an error in our estimate of migrant deaths (Dij) which
was itself caused by an assumption about the age of current migrants
that was too low or by an assumption about age-specific mortality
that was too low.

We reduced the emigration estimates (EMIGio) for each county by
6% in 1871–80 and by 3% in 1881–90. The criteria adopted for allocating
the correction between each county was that (a) no alteration to EMI-
Gio was allowed that implied an increase in migrant deaths of more
than 10%. And notwithstanding (a) no alteration to the level of emigration was allowed that implied that migrant deaths (Dij and Dji)
were not within the upper and lower limits determined by the 'nature'
and 'nurture' assumptions. And (c) the relative error in Dji and Dij
was the same.
[47] *(contd.)*

	1861–70	1871–80	1881–90	1891–1900
Direct estimate of EMIGko (persons)	208,000	159,000	619,000	54,000
Estimate by Carrier and Jeffrey (persons)	206,000	164,000	601,000	69,000

The procedure can best be demonstrated by means of an example. We estimated that native emigration from Barsetshire in 1871–80 was as follows:

MIGik   35,392 ±   538
IMIGij   30,345 ±   767
EMIGio   5,047 ± 1,305

$\overline{\text{Dij}}$ and $\overline{\text{Dji}}$ were 18.6 1,000 and 22.0 1,000 respectively. Our test suggests that EMIG is 6% too high. This was assumed to be because we had estimated an insufficient number of migrant and/or native deaths. Dij was too low and Dji was too high. If Dij (Barsetshire-born deaths in other counties) was too low, it would have the effect of reducing IMIG and increasing EMIG. If Dji (migrant deaths in Barsetshire) were too low it would increase native deaths (Dii) which would reduce MIG. (It will be remembered that native deaths in Barsetshire are all deaths less migrant deaths.)

If EMIG was 6% too high, the 'true' EMIG would be 5,047 − 303 = 4,744, i.e. there were 303 additional deaths. We assumed that the implied error in Dij and Dji was proportionately the same. Therefore we distributed the 303 additional deaths in the ratio of Dij to Dji. This means that if EMIG was 6% too high, Dij was 178 too low and Dji was 125 too high. The amended Dij was 15,523 and the amended Dji was 10,642. The new migration estimates were as follows:

MIGik   35,267 ±   532
IMIGij   30,523 ±   776
EMIGio   4,744 ± 1,308

Finally, we tested whether the new values implied reasonable levels of $\overline{\text{Dij}}$ and $\overline{\text{Dji}}$. The implied $\overline{\text{Dji}}$ was 21.9 per 1,000 compared with the original level of 22.0 per 1,000. Similarly, the new $\overline{\text{Dij}}$ was 18.8 per 1,000 compared with 18.6 per 1,000. These were also between our upper and lower limits of migrant death rates based on the 'nature' and 'nurture' assumptions. Hence, the new estimates were consistent with our previous assumptions. For example, Dij would not have been increased by more than 370 because that would have implied a migrant death of more than 19.0 per 1,000 which is the limiting 'nurture' assumption.

VII

It is important to make clear exactly what our estimates of native migration show. In the estimates presented in Appendix I, a migrant is assumed only to have moved between two of three places – his native county, all other English or Welsh counties and overseas. Unless he remained abroad until after the next census or died abroad, he does not count as an emigrant. All movements are net of returns. When a Suffolk-born emigrant returned home, he masked an outward move by a Suffolk-born emigrant. If a Suffolk-born migrant moved to Lincolnshire and then emigrated in the next decade, he counted as a Suffolk-born emigrant since the Suffolk-born $POPji^2$ had fallen compared with $POPij^1$. If he returned to Essex in the next decade, he masked the emigration of a Suffolk-born man, since the Suffolk-born $POPij^3$ was greater than $POPij^2$. What the method shows is the net effect of each decade of migration not the actual flows.

A related problem is that all emigrants are classified by their county of birth rather than by their county of last residence. This raises difficulties but the county of birth is important, and it is critical, for example, to an understanding of the relationship between urban growth and emigration. The only other way of systematically examining the origin of English emigrants, the ships' lists, give the last permanent residence of the emigrants. It is possible to use the ships' lists to show, for example, that the emigrants of the 1880s came from urban areas, but not if they had originally come from rural areas.[48] In any case, the place of an emigrant's last residence may or may not be conceptually important. If a Devon-born man went to Manchester, and was converted to emigration while he was there, then Manchester is in a real sense the origin of his emigration. But if he left Devon with the full intention of emigrating then he was an emigrant who came from Devon no matter how long he lived in Manchester. Reality probably lay somewhere between. Many of the emigrants probably did not know what their original intentions had been. For this reason it is difficult to know the size of the population at risk, when we calculate migration rates. It is misleading to use the mean total population of the county of birth. (This problem is discussed below.)

The problem of the 'origins' of the migrants is far more serious in a study of inter-county flows. The internal moves that we actually observe are a much smaller proportion of total moves than observed emigration is of all emigration. Migration rates are normally high for short periods and for small areas. In addition, the direction of internal moves is concealed unless only one move took place per decade. Hence, a study of inter-county flows offers little guide to the total rate of internal migration. Nor are the moves that are actually observed

---

[48] Erickson 'Who were?' (1972).

Table 4.8. *Emigration (outward passenger movement) from England and Wales by decade, 1861–1900 (000s)*

	Sailings	Highest year	Lowest year
1861–70	605	105	22
1871–80	971	123	72
1881–90	1549	183	126
1891–1900	1096	138	87

likely to be a sample of the moves that occurred. Rural–urban moves were more likely to be permanent than urban–rural moves. Therefore, a study of internal migration based on the method discussed in this chapter would overstate the rural–urban movement that occurred compared with movement between urban counties. For these reasons, no attempt was made to calculate inter-county flows.

The county is not an ideal unit of measurement because English and Welsh counties varied greatly in both area and population. The important variable is the population of a county, not the geographical area. For example, if the spread of information was an important factor it would probably be related to population density. The actual size of the county would be less important since the distances involved were not great. But some of the counties did not even contain a large town. A migrant from those counties who went to the nearest large town would cross a county boundary. This is probably one reason why the smaller counties tended to have high internal migration rates. But county size *per se* could not be the explanation for high *emigration* rates. A more serious difficulty is that the larger counties had a much more varied occupational structure, and were therefore much more difficult to classify. A large number of emigrants from the industrial county of Yorkshire could have been rural, for example.

The enforced division into census decades is not ideal. The census decades did not exactly correspond with fluctuations in the rate of emigration. Outward sailings peaked in 1873, 1883, 1888 and 1895, that is in three of the four decades. But the 1880s was a decade of consistently higher emigration than the other decades (see Table 4.8). Moreover, when account is taken of returns, the rate of English and Welsh-born emigration was very varied. It was 2.4% in the 1860s, 2.1% in the 1870s, 3.1% in the 1880s and 1.3% in the 1890s.[49] The decades do, therefore, correspond with periods of historical interest.

[49] Excluding 'emigration' to Scotland and Ireland.

Finally, the emigration estimates include the net migration of English born to Scotland and Ireland. There are no data on the birth places of English and Welsh migrants in Scotland. Net migration to Scotland of English and Welsh born between 1861 and 1900 was 140,000 and migration to Ireland was 75,000. This was only 9% of all 'emigration' but it cannot be assumed that it was equally important from every county. It is possible, however, to estimate migration to Scotland from the northern counties where it was of greatest relative importance.

We can assume that migration from the northern counties to Scotland had the characteristics of internal migration rather than of emigration. There is no reason to think that a migrant who moved from, say, Northumberland to Scotland was significantly different to one who went to another part of England and Wales. In particular, we would expect the sex ratio of migrants to Scotland to be the same as that of internal migrants rather than that of emigrants. Appendix 6 compares the sex ratio of emigrants and internal migrants from Northumberland, Durham, Cumberland and Westmorland with emigrants from other parts of England and Wales and emigrants from England and Wales as a whole. The sex ratio of the internal migrants from the northern counties (i.e. those who went to other English and Welsh counties) was the same as migrants from London, Glamorgan and the West of England. Between 50% and 53% of the internal migrants were women. Similarly, 36% of emigrants from Durham and Westmorland were women which compares with 37% from England and Wales as a whole. But 42% of the emigrants from Northumberland and Cumberland were women which was exceptionally high. This is probably because many of the 'emigrants' were internal migrants who were going to Scotland. If we assume that the migrants to Scotland had the same sex ratio as those who went to other parts of England we can distinguish the 'emigrants' who went to Scotland. For example, 24,700 male and 17,700 female emigrants left Northumberland for Scotland and overseas between 1861 and 1900. It was assumed that 50% of those who went to Scotland and 37% of those who went overseas were female. If these assumptions are correct, that is if Northumberland internal migrants were similar to those in England and Wales as a whole then about 7,000 males and 7,000 females must have gone to Scotland. This leaves about 17,700 males and 10,700 females who must have gone overseas, about 63% of whom were male and 37% female. Similarly, it can be shown that about 14,000 'emigrants' from Cumberland went to Scotland. Hence, about 28,000 or 20% of the English emigrants who went to

Scotland came from the two border counties of Northumberland and Cumberland. But there is no evidence to suggest that a dispropor- tionate number of the emigrants from Westmorland and Durham went to Scotland. These two counties were the nearest to the border after Cumberland and Northumberland.

VIII

The presentation of the migration estimates presents some problems. We have seen that the migrants are classified by their county of *birth*. The population at risk, therefore, was the total native population. In any one decade, for example, the Barsetshire-born emigrants were drawn from the native population of Barsetshire plus the Barsetshire born living in other counties. Barsetshire-born emigration, therefore, is expressed as a percentage of the mean Barsetshire-born population in each decade.

The difficulty arises when we attempt to estimate the proportion of the Barsetshire-born population who emigrated over the whole period. This is obviously not the same as the mean rate of emigration in each decade, because the Barsetshire-born population at risk for the forty years was not the sum of the population in each decade but a much smaller number. We can obtain a proxy for the total number at risk by assuming that emigration was only considered by those aged 15–24. (Strictly, those aged 10–19 at the beginning of each decade.) Since an individual can only be aged 15–24 in one ten-year period in his lifetime, the sum of the Barsetshire born aged 15–24 in each decade is the sum of all Barsetshire born aged 15–24 over the whole period. Obviously, emigrants were not confined to those aged 15–24, and if we assume that these were the only population at risk, the rate of emigration would be overstated. But if the number of emigrants is deflated by the numbers in the age group who were most likely to consider it we have a very useful tool which shows the relative importance of emigration in each of the counties.

It is relatively easy to estimate the proportion of the native popula- tion of a county who were aged 15–24. Table 4.2 shows that in a lifetime migrant population growing at 15% per decade (which was a typical rate), the migrant population aged 15–24 would be about 19% of the population at all times. This ratio is not affected by the level of mortality as long as the relationships between the mortality of each age group remained fixed. We assume for the purposes of this rather rough and ready estimate that those aged 15–24 were 19% of all migrant groups. Hence, the Barsetshire-born population at risk of emigration in 1861–70 was 19% of the Barsetshire born in other counties aged 10–19 in 1861, plus the population of the county of Barsetshire aged 10–19 in 1861, less 19% of the lifetime migrants living in Barsetshire in 1861. Table 6.3 shows emigration from the English and Welsh counties as a proportion of their population aged 15–24.

IX

There have been very few attempts to use the nineteenth-century county of birth data to examine late nineteenth-century migration and none have attempted to examine emigration. The most comprehensive study is by Friedlander and Roshier.[50] They used a method similar to that used by the author to estimate migrant deaths (Dij). A set of lifetime inter-county migration streams was derived for all fifty-two counties for each decade 1851–1911 and for the forty-year period 1911–1951. (There was no place of birth enumeration in 1921 and 1931.) Each internal migration stream (IMIGij) entered into the calculation of the next lifetime migrant population (POPij) and hence all the streams were dependent on the experience of the previous decade. There was obviously a strong possibility of cumulative error. The study is very unsatisfactory. The main weaknesses are that it does not show true inter-county migration, the assumption of the age distribution of current migrants is obviously incorrect, the mortality of current migrants is ignored, and the assumed age-specific mortality takes no account of local conditions. Most important, there is no appreciation of the boundary problems.

We have already seen that a migrant who moved from Hertfordshire to Buckinghamshire and then to London, counts as if he made a single move to London. Friedlander and Roshier derived internal migration indices which measured all internal inter-county flows, as if no secondary or tertiary moves had occurred. There was no provision for emigration. Nor can the observed migrant moves be taken as a sample of all moves because, as we discussed above, this method is bound to overstate rural–urban migration. Secondly, Friedlander and Roshier assume that the age distribution of current migrants at POPij[2] was 34% aged 0–9, 15% aged 10–19, 28% aged 20–29, and 23% aged 30–39. Their current migrant group clearly contains too many children. This age distribution implies that over 40% of current migrants were children under 10 (*net of returns*). Yet only 25% of the total population of England and Wales were under 10 years old in 1861. Similarly,

---

[50] Friedlander and Roshier, 'Internal migration in England and Wales'.

there are too many children in their assumption of the initial lifetime migrant population – 26% under 10 and too few aged 10–19. Friedlander and Roshier justify these assumptions on the grounds that when the age distributions are projected from 1851 to 1911 the resulting age distribution is virtually the same as the published distribution in 1911. But this procedure is spurious, because there is more than one possible solution. Almost all assumptions of the initial age distribution of lifetime migrants will predict the final age distribution, because eventually POPij becomes dependent only upon age-specific mortality and the assumed age structure of current migrants. But, as we have seen, the implied rate of in-migration depends critically upon the assumptions that have been made about mortality and age distribution. The question is not whether a hypothetical lifetime migrant system can generate a particular age distribution, but whether the assumptions in the model are reasonable.

Friedlander and Roshier used a common set of survivorship factors to reduce the lifetime migrant populations. These were based on the mean mortality in England and Wales. Their estimate of migrant deaths was therefore too low for the main counties of in-migration and too high for the main counties of out-migration. The effect is to reduce the calculated in-migration into the urban and industrial counties, and to increase out-migration from the rural counties. (If migrant deaths (Dki) were too high in rural areas then native deaths (Dii) would be understated and out-migration (MIGik) would be too high.)

In general, their assumptions about the age distribution of the migrants and their mortality tend to underestimate migrant deaths. For example, deaths that occurred to current migrants – those that occurred between their arrival and POPii^2 – are ignored. The net effect is that migrant deaths must be understated by at least 20% in some decades which means that internal migration (by their definition) must be at least 10–15% underestimated.

There is, however, a much more serious criticism of these estimates. Friedlander and Roshier neglected to adjust their raw data to standard units. Some of the data they used are expressed in Registration counties (1851), some in Ancient counties (1861–1901) and some in Administrative counties (1911). As we have seen, the counties were not coterminous and their populations could very by as much as 10%. This is a very serious problem in migration studies which depend on a residual method. If, for example, the boundary of a county was redrawn because of an administrative change then an apparent migration would occur, since some people would be enumerated in the second census in a different county without having moved. There is also an attempt to predict migration between 1911 and 1951, by inserting a guess of the lifetime migrant populations in 1931. This has no historical validity.

There have been no other works as wide ranging as that of Friedlander and Roshier. Brinley Thomas[51] was the first to use the county of birth data in this way. He estimated migration into Glamorgan between 1861 and 1911 by county of birth. Current migrants were assumed to be aged 15–24 and lifetime migrants 35–44 in 1861.[52] The POPij[1] of each county of origin was reduced by the mortality of the 35–44 age group, and the survivors of POPij[1] were reduced by the mortality of the 45–54 age group, and the survivors of IMIGij[1] by the mortality of the 25–44 age group. This process was repeated until the 1901–11 decade. H. A. Shannon used the same method to show flows by county of birth into London, except that he assumed that the lifetime migrant population was aged 35–44 in 1851, because migration to London was of longer standing.[53] There are very few other studies of the published data and none show any novel analytical features. Recent studies that include material on internal migration have concentrated on the (unpublished) census enumerators' books.[54] This source has the inestimable advantage that the place of birth can be directly correlated with age, marital condition and occupation. But the amount of data so far has limited the scale of the studies with one important exception.[55] In addition, unpublished census data are protected by the 100 year rule, so no work on the years after 1881 has so far been possible.

[51] Thomas, 'Migration into the Glamorganshire coalfield'.
[52] In fact he assumed that the current migrants were aged 15–24 at the time of the *second* census.
[53] Shannon, 'Migration and the growth of London'.
[54] For example, M. Anderson, *Family Structure in nineteenth-century Lancashire* (Cambridge University Press, 1971). W. A. Armstrong, *Stability and change in an English county town. A social study of York 1801–1851* (Cambridge University Press, 1974).
[55] A group at Edinburgh University has been working on a 2% sample of the 1851 census.

5

Return migration to Britain, 1860–1914

I

Return migration to continental Europe has attracted a good deal of attention. The main issues in the literature were discussed in chapter 2 and there is little point in repeating them *in extenso*. It is generally assumed that more than a quarter of the emigrants who left Europe between 1815 and 1914 returned to their native country. The rate of return to most continental European countries increased markedly some time about the turn of the century. In the years before the First World War returns to most countries seem to have been at least a third of outward movement.[1] The highest rate of return was probably to Italy. A recent estimate suggests that 58% of Italian emigrants to the U.S.A. in the seven years after 1907–8 returned home before the First World War.[2] Returns from South America were comparable.

The experience of returned migrants has been seen as an important factor in the decision to emigrate. In some cases, the material condition of those who had gone overseas and returned was so superior to the condition of those who had stayed behind, that it led to an immediate increase in emigration.[3] But in the long run, the importance of returned migrants seems to have been more subtle. They gave potential emigrants a source of detailed information about, for example, employment opportunities in overseas countries, and the

---

[1] This is the usually accepted (educated) guess. See Gould, 'European inter-continental emigration', p. 606.

[2] This estimate is the difference between alien departures from the United States in the seven years 1907/8 to 1913/14 and alien arrivals in the years 1904/5 to 1910/11. Gould, 'Return migration from the U.S.A.', p. 86. Some of the emigrants were arriving for the second time, of course. Return migration rates from the U.S.A. to Italy were much lower before the early twentieth century.

[3] For example in the 'American fever' in Norway and Sweden in the 1860s. Semmingsen, 'Emigration and the image of America', pp. 26–54.

way was open for a considerable increase in the rate of emigration. As far as is known, potential emigrants relied far more for their information on personal contacts from returned migrants and from emigrant letters than on the advertisements of shipping companies and employment agencies.[4] This presumably means that the bulk of the emigrants who returned to Europe could not have been failures. There is relatively little direct evidence on this point, but it is difficult to see how the number of emigrants leaving Europe could have continued to rise, if the advice they had received from those who returned had told them not to leave.

It must be remembered that many of the emigrants who returned to Europe had decided to do so *before* they left.[5] (Even so, some of these so-called 'temporary' emigrants stayed overseas for several years.)[6] Temporary emigration seems to have been particularly common from Italy and the Balkans.[7] Its growth was associated with the great improvement in international passenger transport that occurred at the end of the nineteenth century. The growth of temporary emigration was also connected with the growth of large urban centres like New York, São Paulo and Buenos Aires where the demand for labour in industry and services was frequently buoyant. It is doubtful, however, if the changes in the international economy were a sufficient cause of the growth of temporary emigration in the early twentieth century. Temporary migration between different parts of Europe was common long before the great growth of international migration, and many of the temporary migrants who went overseas in the later nineteenth century came from regions that were already important sources of temporary migrants to other parts of Europe. There seems to have been considerable regional (or possibly local) variation in the rate of temporary emigration as there was in the rate of 'permanent' emigration.[8] This was probably also because the flow of information was an important factor.

[4] See Curti and Birr, 'Immigrants and the American image', pp. 212–13.

[5] Gould showed that the rate of return to European countries from the U.S.A. in the years before the First World War was positively correlated with the proportion of returned males among the returned migrants. This could only mean that the intention to remain in the U.S.A. at the time of emigration largely determined the rate of return. Gould, 'Return migration from the U.S.A.', p. 64.

[6] Of returned migrants from the U.S.A. between 1908 and 1914, 77% had been there less than five years. Gould, 'Return migration from the U.S.A.', p. 57.

[7] See Palairet, 'The "New" migration and the newest' and Gould, 'Return migration from the U.S.A.'.

[8] The agricultural migrants to South America came from the Po Valley as did other harvesters who went to other parts of Europe. The bulk of the emigrants to the United States came from southern Italy. Hence, the north Italian emigrants were

II

We would not necessarily expect that return migration to Britain was comparable with return migration to the continental European countries. For example, some young men in southern Europe went overseas for short periods, in order to maintain their relatives on marginal farms. By the late nineteenth century this was rarely necessary in Britain. On the other hand, we can assume that British emigrants had made the transition from family emigration (where people went to settle), to individual emigration (where they were likely to return), as early as any country in north and north-west Europe, and before large scale emigration *of any sort* had started from south and south-east Europe.[9] By the 1880s at the latest, large numbers of British people seem to have been willing to go overseas at relatively short notice. [10] Their rapid response implies that they had access to abundant and accurate information which is what we would expect. By the late nineteenth century, Britain had a highly urbanised and literate population; and her links with the countries of immigration were both exceptionally close and long-standing. We would expect that Britain had a high rate of return migration before it occurred in most, if not all, other countries.

At some point in the late nineteenth century, the rate of return of British citizens to Britain did increase markedly. We can show that over the period of about fifty years that ended with the First World War inward passenger movement averaged about 45% of outward movement.[11] This implies that returned *emigrants* could not have been very much less than 40% of the number of outward emigrants. It

more likely to work in agriculture abroad and the south Italians were more likely to work in industry. This distinction became less marked before the First World War as more northerners went to the U.S.A., although it was never the dominant destination for them. See Gould,'Return migration from the U.S.A.', pp. 69–71.

[9] There was no substantial period of 'family' emigration from south and south-east Europe. See chapter 2.

[10] And the occupations of the emigrants changed. When emigration was at its peak in the 1880s the dominant occupation was unskilled labourer, but there were relatively fewer labourers when emigration was relatively low. See Table 3.8.

[11] That is, the inward passenger movement to Britain was on average 45% of outward passenger movement in the same year. It is usually assumed that Italy had the highest rate of return just before the First World War and Gould estimated that 57.9% of the 1904/5 to 1910/11 emigrants to the U.S.A., returned before the First World War. But return migration to Italy only reached that rate just before the war. The official Italian data show that returns were 42.3% of outward movement in 1892–6, 30.9% in 1897–1901, 37.9% in 1902–6, 72.6% in 1907–11 and 64.9% in 1912–15. The problem is that Gould's estimate and the official data should *exclude* businessmen and travellers, whereas the British data do not. See Foerster, *Italian emigration of our times*, p. 529. Gould , 'Return migration from the U.S.A.', p. 86.

Table 5.1. *Inward passenger movement to Britain from extra-European countries as a % of outward movement, 1876–1914*

	Outward sailings (000s)	(i) % return	(ii) % return	(iii) % return
1876	83.5	65.2	85.5	
1877	72.4	67.1	88.3	
1878	83.4	48.6	65.8	
1879	123.0	23.1	30.8	
1880	133.9	20.7	35.1	
1876–80	496.2	38.8	55.8	
1881	166.8	21.7	31.5	
1882	195.2	19.6	28.0	
1883	214.4	23.1	34.4	
1884	169.6	37.7	53.9	
1885	147.6	41.2	57.9	
1886	171.6	34.3	46.6	
1887	206.6	30.4	42.2	
1888	206.8	33.6	45.5	
1889	188.9	40.6	54.6	
1890	160.6	50.2	68.2	
1881–90	1824.1	32.5	45.5	
1891	160.0	47.1	64.4	
1892	157.0	46.6	62.3	
1893	156.7	48.9	65.2	
1894	114.0	75.8	103.8	
1891–94	587.7	53.1	71.7	
1895	130.8			63.6
1896	119.7			67.7
1897	110.8			69.5
1898	106.2			68.6
1899	103.5			78.5
1900	122.9			63.5
1895–1900	694.0			68.2
1901	132.5			61.0
1902	163.5			51.4
1903	214.4			43.2
1904	213.2			54.0
1905	211.9			47.5
1906	272.9			40.1
1907	331.6			40.5
1908	219.3			60.1

(*cont. next page*)

Table 5.1 (*contd.*)

	Outward sailings (000s)	(i) % return	(ii) % return	(iii) % return
1909	238.4			47.4
1910	335.4			37.0
1901–10	2333.0			46.5
1911	391.5			37.1
1912	387.1			27.5
1913	345.0			23.1
1914	184.0			52.6
1911–14	1307.6			32.7

Source: Calculated from Carrier and Jeffery, *External migration*, Table B(1), pp. 90–1, and Table C(1), pp. 92–3. Before 1895, Irish passengers entering Britain from overseas were assumed to be British. In column (i) we have assumed that the Irish and British were equally likely to return to Britain. In column (ii) we have assumed that there were *no* Irish among the returned passengers who were returned as British. The true return rate of British passengers lies between these two limits. British returned passengers were properly distinguished from Irish after 1895, which is the basis of column (iii).

is doubtful if any other European country had a comparable rate of return in this fifty-year period.[12]

The data do not exist to enable us to calculate the true rate of return migration. Inward passengers to Britain were first counted in 1870, but aliens were not distinguished from British born before 1876, and the Irish not before 1895. More seriously, the total of inward passengers recorded in any one year included four different types of traveller – each one of whom could be returning for the first time, or for a second or third time. Firstly, inward passengers include those travelling on business, with whom we can include military men and their families; secondly, British citizens domiciled abroad and visiting Britain; thirdly, 'temporary' emigrants who had left Britain with the express purpose of returning after a relatively fixed period and finally 'lifetime' emigrants who had decided to return to Britain. In practice the borderline between the groups might be blurred – particularly the distinction between 'temporary' and 'lifetime' emigrants – but conceptually the groups are distinct. The original decision to leave the

[12] See footnote 13 for the basis of this (very crude) estimate. See the criticims of several quantitative studies of British emigration in chapter 2.

country, made by a member of each group, was of a different order. There is no easy way of distinguishing between travellers, temporary emigrants and permanent emigrants before 1912 when 'emigrant' was more strictly defined. Our guess that *emigrant* returns in the fifty years before 1914 were little under 40% of gross emigration is based on the number of non-emigrant returns first recorded in 1912. Unfortunately, the 1912 data are far from satisfactory.[13] The best proxy for annual British emigration we have is gross outward passenger movement. The best proxy for annual net emigration, is therefore annual gross outward movement less gross inward movement (when it is available). But it must be remembered that the annual total of gross outward and inward movement, included people who would not have been classed as emigrants, some of whom were travelling to and from countries (like India) which were never considered as emigrant destinations. Unfortunately, much of the literature on British emigration has treated emigration and gross outward movement as if it were the same.[14]

Total passenger arrivals in Britain from extra-European countries in the years 1895–1914 (when we have total inward passenger move-

---

[13] 'Emigrant' was more strictly defined from 1 April 1912; outward and inward movement was given for the last nine months of 1912 by both definitions. On the old definition there were 305,647 departures and 84,052 arrivals (a rate of return of 27.5%). On the new definition, there were 296,894 departures and 57,183 arrivals (a return rate of 19.2%). The new data imply, however, that there were 26,869 returning passengers who were not emigrants and only 8,753 outward-bound passengers who were not emigrants. In the long run, outward and inward non-emigrants passengers must be equal, by definition (except insofar as some died abroad). We must assume, therefore, that outward-bound emigrants were less strictly defined than inward bound. If we assume that the number of outward and inward-bound travellers and businessmen were equal, then returns were 20.5% of outward movement in the last nine months of 1912. (Unfortunately, 1912 was a period of exceptional emigration.) The 1912 data suggests that non-emigrant passengers were about 36,000. Since there is no reason to expect great fluctuations in the number of non-emigrants but probably an upward trend, we could assume that 36,000 was about the maximum number of non-emigrant passengers. Assuming that there were about 15,000 non-emigrant passengers per year in the 1880s and that they increased by about 35% per decade, this would imply that emigrant returns were about 35% in the 1880s; about 60% in the 1890s; about 40% in 1901–10 and about 20% in 1911–14. This implies that 39% of all emigrants from Britain before the First World War returned. But these estimates are extremely speculative. See Carrier and Jeffery, *External migration*, Table C1, p. 93.

[14] Although returns to Britain seem to have been something under a half of outward passenger movement there is hardly any evidence available about the characteristics and composition of return migrants and it is hardly mentioned in the literature. Virtually the only work, by Shepperson, is concerned with the decision to return from the United States to Britain of a few well known (and relatively well off) emigrants. W. S. Shepperson, *Emigration and disenchantment* (University of Oklahoma Press, 1966).

ment), were nearly 2 million, compared with outward sailings of 4¼ million. That is, returns were about 47% of English and Welsh outward movement and 39.3% of Scots.[15] The rate of return before 1895 is less clear, because the Irish were not distinguished. Table 5.1 shows inward sailings as a percentage of outward sailing between 1876 and 1895 calculated on two assumptions; (a) that the ratio of inward to outward sailings was the same for British and Irish (column (i)) and (b) that *all* inward sailings were British and that no Irish returned. We know that the rate of Irish returns was very low, and less than the British. British returns as a proportion of outward sailings must lie between the values in column (i) and column (ii). Table 5.1 shows that returns in the 19 years before 1895, cannot have been much less than in the period after 1895 – about 45% of outward sailings.

The rate of return in the 1860s and 1870s, can be estimated from the net emigration of English and Welsh natives from England and Wales. This value depends on the estimation of the mortality of life-time internal migrants within England Wales. The method, which cannot be applied to Scotland, is described in detail in chapter 4. The results are shown in Table 5.2. Emigration of English and Welsh born, net of returns to England and Wales, was found to be about 492,000 in 1861–70 and about 487,000 in 1871–80. This implies that returns to England and Wales were about 19% of outward sailings in the 1860s, and about 50% in the 1870s. The great increase in the rate of return presumably must have occurred towards the end of the 1860s or at the very beginning of the 1870s. The 1860s was the decade when steamships came to dominate the North Atlantic passenger trade. This conclusion can be confirmed by comparing the growth in the size of the English-born population in the countries which were taking large numbers of British immigrants. For example, the English (and Welsh) born population of the U.S.A. rose by 155,000 in the 1860s, when gross outward passenger movement from England to the U.S.A. was 310,000 (Table 5.3). This is consistent with a relatively low rate of return (taking the deaths of emigrants in the U.S.A. into account). On the other hand, in the 1870s, when more than half a million English people entered the U.S.A., the English-born population rose by not much more than 100,000, and in the 1900s, when

---

[15] Strictly speaking the rate of return in 1895–1914 was not 45.9% because the returning travellers and returning emigrants were not drawn from the same population as the outgoing travellers and emigrants, some of whom had left before 1895. Nor do we know the proportion of outward and return migrants who were moving for the second time. (This also applies to the Italian data.)

Table 5.2. *Returns of natives to England and Wales, 1861–1900 (minimum estimates)*

		(i) Gross outward passenger movement (000s)	(ii) Net emigration English and Welsh born (000s)	(iii) Gross inward passengers (minimum returns) (000s)	(iv) % returns (i/iii × 100)
1861–70	persons	605.2	491.9	113.3	19
1871–80	males	645.1	294.1	351.0	54
	females	326.5	193.1	133.4	41
	persons	971.6	487.2	484.4	50
1881–90	males	1002.2	505.5	496.7	50
	females	546.8	305.6	241.2	44
	persons	1549.0	811.1	737.9	48
1891–1900	males	678.4	292.8	385.6	57
	females	417.5	78.1	339.4	81
	persons	1095.9	370.9	725.0	66

Source: Gross outward passenger movement from Appendix 4. Net emigration of natives from Appendix 1. (See chapter 4.) Net emigration includes net movement to Europe, gross outward passenger movement does not. Inclusion of movement to Europe would increase the rate of return. The number of male and female passengers in 1871–80 assumes that the sex ratio in 1871–80 was the same as in 1877–80.

133

Table 5.3. *Emigration from England and Wales to the U.S.A., 1850–1929.*
English- and Welsh-born population in the U.S.A., 1850–1930

	Total outward passenger movement to the U.S.A. 000s		English and Welsh born in U.S.A. 000s	Change since previous census 000s
1850–59	386.3	1850	308.5	—
1860–69	309.7	1860	477.4	+ 168.9
1870–79	549.2	1870	629.6	+ 155.2
1880–89	891.7	1880	747.5	+ 117.9
1890–99	637.2	1890	1009.2	+ 261.7
1900–09	637.0	1900	934.1	− 75.1
1910–19	310.0	1910	960.2	+ 26.1
1920–29	184.2	1920	880.9	− 79.3
		1930	869.8	− 11.1

Source: Historical statistics of the United States, Table C228–95, pp. 117–18. Carrier and Jeffery, *External Migration,* Table D/F/G, (1), pp. 95–6. Outward migration for 1850–3 is an estimate – see Appendix 2. Outward migration is total outward passenger movement to 1912 and total outward movement of emigrants thereafter.

more than 600,000 sailed from England to the U.S.A., the English-born population rose by less than 30,000.

It is important to remember that we are concerned with changes in *the trend* of return migration. For example, it is known that return migration from the U.S.A. was as much as a third of outward sailings between 1858 and 1861.[16] But outward passenger movement to the U.S.A. in 1858–61 was less than 50,000. If the returned migrants of 1858–61 had gone to the U.S.A. in the previous four years (1854–7) then only 8% of them could have returned. Similarly, it is obvious that part of the explanation for the increase in returns in the 1870s is that there were serious depressions in the U.S.A. But the point is, that after the 1860s the long run rate of return was always high, *irrespective of economic conditions in the U.S.A.*

The very high rate of return movement from America to England was not unique. For example, between 1901 and 1915 nearly 1.3 million people entered Australia, virtually all of whom were British, and 1.1 million left it. And over the whole period 1853–1920, 1.4 million persons went to New Zealand and nearly a million returned. But between

---

[16] *22nd Report of the Emigration Commissioners,* 1862, BPP XXII, 1862 quoted in Jones, 'Background to emigration from Great Britain', p. 24.

1853 and 1880 returns from New Zealand were only 36% of the 444,000 outward sailings, whereas, between 1881 and 1920 returns were 82% of the one million outward sailings.[17] The break corresponds to developments in transport on the New Zealand route. It must be remembered, however, that many of the returned passengers had not been emigrants.

III

We are now in a position to say a little more about return migration in the period 1861–1900. Our new estimates of English and Welsh emigration show that about the same number of emigrants left the country (net of returns) in the decade 1861–70, as in the decade 1871–80 – allowing for the margin of error in the estimates. This means the number of emigrants was a smaller proportion of the population in the 1870s than in the 1860s. Male emigration, net of returns, cannot have been less than 2.8% of the mean population in the 1860s, and female emigration cannot have been less than 1.8%. In the 1870s, male emigration cannot have been more than 2.7% and female cannot have been more than 1.7%. In contrast, outward passenger movement of natives of England and Wales was much higher in the 1870s (4.0%) than in the 1860s (2.8%).[18] The higher rate of outward passenger movement in the 1870s is usually thought to have been a consequence of the change from sail to steam on the North Atlantic which took place over the decade of the 1860s. In the 1870s, virtually all transatlantic migrants travelled by steam ship. It is obvious that the easier passage under steam must have increased the rate of emigration (*ceteris paribus*).[19] But, partly because of the years of depression in the U.S.A., the early effect of the steamship seems to have been to induce relatively more emigrants to return to England and Wales than were induced to leave. We can see this from Table 5.2. The table compares net outward movement from the United Kingdom of natives of England and Wales, with outward sailings of English and Welsh to extra-European destinations.[20] We do not know outward sailings from England

[17] These data include all passenger arrivals and departures. A recent estimate of emigration to New Zealand shows 227,000 net arrivals for the whole period 1875–1911. Migration to New Zealand was only 5,500 net in the period 1881–1911 when there was a net movement of about 33,000 from New Zealand to Australia. J. M. Gander, 'New Zealand net migration in the latter part of the nineteenth century', *Australian Economic History Review*, 19 (2), Sept 1979, pp. 151–68. Davie, *World migration*, p. 434.
[18] The proportion of females before 1877 is not known.
[19] There is, for example, also the matter of the American Civil War in the early 1860s.
[20] That is, it is the sum of our estimates of net migration of the natives of the fifty-two English and Welsh counties, *less* net movement of English and Welsh-born into Scotland and Ireland.

to European destinations, but the rate of return from Europe was higher than from overseas because few of the passengers were emigrants. Hence, Table 5.2 underestimates the rate of return from outside Europe. It is clear that the rate of return migration must have increased between 1861–70 and 1871–80 by much more than the rate of outward migration. Outward passenger-movement rose from 605,000 in the 1860s to 871,000 in the 1870s – i.e. by about 44%. But *inward* sailings must have risen by more than 400% (from about 110,000 in the 1860s, to about 480,000). Therefore, the rate of *permanent* emigration in the 1870s, was lower than in the 1860s, although the rate of outward passenger movement was more than 40% higher. This result is commensurate with what is known about the British and American economies in the 1860s and 1870s. For example, the rate of increase of American railway mileage rose in every year in 1861–71, but fell from 1871 to 1875.[21] British building activity seems to have fallen from 1863–71, and risen from 1871–7.[22] In other words, the estimate that net emigration was relatively lower in the 1870s than it was in the 1860s, fits rather better into the idea of a North Atlantic long cycle than does the rate of outward passenger movement in the two decades. On the other hand, it is very difficult to draw conclusions about cycles from emigration data which are decade averages.

The evidence for a British building cycle is not very conclusive however, and the idea of a North Atlantic cycle is not universally accepted. (These matters are dealt with in chapter 7.) There is an additional complication. If the introduction of steamships was the cause of the increase in the rate of return migration to England, it follows that some of the returning migrants may have returned in the 1860s had steam passages been available. For these emigrants, their decision to return would have related to conditions in the 1860s, not to conditions in the 1870s.

Table 5.2 also shows the very interesting pattern of return movement in the four decades 1861–1900. Returns were only 19% of outward passenger movement in the 1860s. In the 1870s, there were half as many inward passengers as there were outward and in the 1880s, inward passengers were 48% of outward. The 1880s was a period of heavy emigration when we would expect that the rate of return would fall. But there was little difference between the 1870s and the 1880s in this respect. We can assume that the number of

[21] Thomas, *Migration and economic growth*, p. 92.
[22] Thomas, *Migration and economic growth*, pp. 103, 175. J. Parry Lewis, *Building cycles and Britain's growth* (Macmillan, 1965), pp. 194–200. Parry Lewis put the peak of house-building outside London and South Wales in 1876.

businessmen and travellers was increasing on trend but hardly by enough to explain the rise in inward passengers from about 480,000 in the 1870s to about 740,000 in the 1880s. The only explanation is, either, that there was a considerable increase in the number of temporary migrants in the 1880s, or, that very large numbers of the emigrants of the 1870s returned in the 1880s despite the high level of outward movement. The former seems more likely. An increase in the number of temporary emigrants would tend to confirm Professor Erickson's view that there was a large increase in the number and proportion of unskilled workers (in particular, building workers) in those years in the 1880s when emigration was at a peak.[23]

Finally, Table 5.2 shows that women were less likely to return than men in the 1870s and 1880s (and probably in the 1860s). The female rate of return was increasing, however, which was presumably because the proportion of life-time emigrants travelling in families was falling. But in the 1890s, inward female movement was about 80% of outward movement. This was a much higher rate of return that that of men which was also very high, (57%).[24] We would expect the non-migrants to include a disproportionate share of men, so that the exceptional inward movement of women in the 1890s must have been returning female emigrants – some of whom must have gone in the 1880s. This suggests that a relatively larger proportion of the women emigrants in the 1880s ultimately returned to England and Wales than did the male emigrants. The majority of the temporary emigrants of the 1880s were probably men. But women were probably more likely to be temporary migrants. In other words, in the 1880s, a large proportion of women emigrants seem to have been prepared to emigrate for a short time, even though as a whole women were less likely to emigrate than men.

Finally, we can examine the relation between the annual movement and returns. Figure 5.1 (which is based on Table 5.1) shows that the number of return migrants was more stable than outward sailings. This is partly because non-emigrants were nearly equally represented in inward and outward movement, by definition. Hence, non-emigrants were a larger proportion of inward movement. We might expect that the periods when outward sailings were increasing (i.e. 1877–83, 1885–7, 1899–1903, 1905–7 and 1908–11) were periods when returns were small and falling, and that return migration was greater in the

---

[23] Erickson, 'Who were?' (1972). The composition of British emigrants in this period is discussed at length in chapter 3.

[24] If anything, the net movement of female natives of England and Wales was *overstated*. Hence, the rate of return is, if anything, understated.

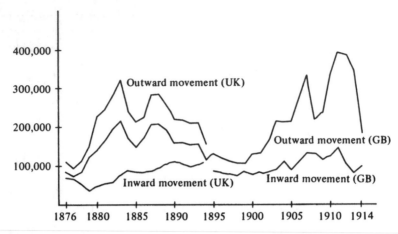

Figure 5.1 *Outward and inward passenger movement, 1876–1914*
Source: Table 3.1, Carrier and Jeffery, *External Migration*, Table C (1), pp. 92–3
and Table D/F/9.

intervening years when emigration was falling. This would imply that
the emigrants who went in the early years of a boom remained abroad
until conditions deteriorated, and only then began to return. This
view is intuitively satisfying but it is not supported by the evidence.
Outward and inward movement rose and fell in unison in all but
eight years between 1876 and 1914. In periods when emigration rose,
returns *rose*, either simultaneously or with a very short time lag.[25]
In years when emigration was falling, returns were sometimes
increasing, particularly in the 1890s, but there is no obvious pattern
of an alternating cycle of emigration and returns.

IV

The pattern of return movement suggests a hypothesis that within
the mass of British passengers there were several distinct flows. This
hypothesis can be expressed in economic terms but it is not implied
that the decision to emigrate was solely governed by economic considerations. In the first place, large numbers of passengers were not

[25] Inward passenger movement increased in nineteen of the twenty-three years when
outward movement increased between 1876 and 1914. It failed to rise in thirteen
of the seventeen years when outward movement failed to rise. There were only
eight years when inward movement increased and outward movement fell or vice
versa. The amplitude of the fluctuations would be greater if non-emigrants could
be excluded.

emigrants. Secondly, we can assume that some emigrants returned after a very short stay even though economic conditions favoured remaining abroad. They may have decided to do this *before* they left Britain. These emigrants could be described as restless; people who tended to solve short-term social and economic difficulties by moving on.[26] It is also possible that some emigrants returned to Britain when it was generally unfavourable to do so because prospects in a *particular* overseas industry or region had deteriorated although conditions in the economy as a whole had not. This would be economically rational behaviour. Many of the additional return migrants in the years when we observe that emigration was increasing could have been in this category. A different, and more obvious, category of emigrant must have consisted of people who remained abroad until they were disillusioned, until economic conditions in say, the United States, worsened relative to economic conditions in Britain. Some of these emigrants had probably always expected to return but some may not have. Presumably, many of the returning migrants of the 1890s had remained abroad for some time because the 1880s had been particularly good in the United States, Australia and Canada. On the other hand, we must remember that the majority of British emigrants never returned, even if they had intended to.

The great increase in the rate of return was almost certainly caused by the improvement in transport and communications. We have mentioned the introduction of steamships on the North Atlantic in the 1860s. This had two effects. Initially it meant that the number of emigrants returning to Britain increased markedly when economic conditions in the receiving countries deteriorated. This is part of the reason for the high rate of return in the 1870s. But in the long run, the relative ease of travel – on the North Atlantic in particular – meant that an increasing number of English emigrants who had no intention of settling overseas left with the specific intention of returning. In effect, it was becoming relatively easy *to return*, which meant that the decision to go could be taken more lightly. The effect of overseas depressions still led to an increase in returns – as in the 1890s. But the fluctuation in the rate of returns was much less than in outward movement. In addition, inward and outward movement tended to rise and fall together. We take this to mean that, *in the long run* the returning migrants induced more people to emigrate than to stay at home. The shift to what has been called 'individual' emigration

---

[26] See R. C. Taylor, 'Migration and motivation. A study of determinants and types', pp. 99–133, in J. A. Jackson (ed.), *Migration* (Cambridge University Press, 1969).

appears to have occurred earlier in Britain than in other countries. Our estimates suggest that not much less than 40% of English emigrants in the fifty years before the First World War, returned. This was almost certainly much higher than the rate of return to any other country in this period.

6

The birthplace of English and Welsh emigrants, 1861–1900

I

One feature of European emigration before the First World War that has attracted considerable scholarly interest is the marked variance in emigration rates from the different regions of European countries. For example, someone living in the Italian province of Calabria in the early twentieth century was six times more likely to emigrate overseas than someone living in Tuscany.[1] Broadly similar differences in regional emigration rates have been observed in the Scandinavian countries, Germany and Austria–Hungary at various times in the late nineteenth and early twentieth centuries.

The discovery of considerable variance in emigration rates between the different parts of European countries raised some very important issues. There have been attempts to relate regional emigration rates to the economic and social features of the individual regions. But there does not seem to be a simple set of economic and social characteristics that would explain why many emigrants left one area and few left another.[2] For example, research in Scandinavia has shown that emigration rates from urban areas were frequently higher than from rural areas.[3] This has cast some doubt on the view of most of the earlier writers that the bulk of European emigration before the

---

[1] Emigration from Calabria was the equivalent of 368 persons in every 1000 between 1902 and 1913. Tuscany lost only 52 per 1000. (The majority of the emigrants from Calabria returned, of course.) See J. S. Macdonald, 'Agrarian organisation, migration and labour militancy in rural Italy', *Economic History Review*, 16, 1963, p. 62.

[2] Gould pointed out, for example, that most quantitative analyses could not predict emigration rates by reference to a set of economic and social variables more accurately than a single regression of the previous year's emigration on the current years. Gould, 'European inter-continental emigration', p. 658. See chapter 2 and the references cited there.

[3] Semmingsen, 'Norwegian emigration', p. 156. Hvidt, *Flight to America*, pp. 45–51.

First World War was related to problems within rural society – in particular population pressure and the effect of industrialisation on rural industries. The reason, of course, that emigration rates are difficult to predict from the condition of the areas from which the emigrants came is because emigration seems partly to have been dependent on the flow of information from abroad. The information available to a prospective emigrant – from letters and from the experience of those emigrants who had returned – would tend to rise as the rate of emigration rose. Once an initial emigration had occurred, an area might continue to experience relatively high emigration *irrespective of economic or social circumstances*. This well known phenomenon is usually called chain migration.

It is also possible that many European emigrants were stage migrants. The idea of stage migration rests on two observations. Firstly, that it was easier for migrants to move in short stops. And secondly, that each move made it relatively easier for migrants to make a subsequent move. Part of the explanation for the relatively high emigration rates from some Scandinavian cities, for example, is because some of these emigrants had come from outside the city. In other words, urban emigration was high because the emigrants included people of two kinds; those who had been born in the city, plus those born outside the city for whom the city was a stage in their emigration.[4]

With one important exception there are no quantitative studies which show those areas of Britain from which the bulk of the emigrants came.[5] Obviously, our view of British emigration in the nineteenth century would be very different if, for example, it could be shown that the bulk of the emigrants came from those parts of the country that were at the centre of industrial change (say, the industrial towns) rather than from those parts of the country which were not (say, the more remote rural areas). Most accounts have either avoided quantitative statements on the provenance of British emigrants or have been based on guesswork. For example, the very influential view of the nature of British emigration before the First World War which is based on the writings of Professor Brinley Thomas rests on an implicit assumption, that all the emigrants came from the rural areas –

---

[4] Semmingsen, 'Norwegian emigration', pp. 156–7. Hvidt, *Flight to America*, p. 58. Rundblom and Norman, *From Sweden to America*, pp. 144–6. There are several other examples. See chapter 2, and footnote 132.
[5] Erickson, 'Who were?' (1972). Professor Erickson's work is discussed in detail in chapter 3.

for which there was no quantitative evidence.[6] The main quantitative contribution has been made by Professor Charlotte Erickson. We discussed her work in detail in chapter 3. In brief, she was able to show that in the 1880s, the majority of British emigrants probably came from the urban areas. (They were also largely unskilled.) This does not seem to have been the case in the late 1840s, but the point at which British emigrants began to resemble a sample of the total population is not clear. Nor is it clear whether the dominance of urban emigrants was related to the very heavy emigration in the 1880s or whether a break in the trend had occurred at some earlier date. Professor Erickson's work is based on the place of last residence of the emigrants. Hence, it is not known, for example, if the urban emigrants which she has identified had made a previous move from the countryside, which appears to have been quite common in Scandinavia.

Our estimates of the place of birth of all English and Welsh emigrants in the last forty years of the nineteenth century make it possible to examine the geographical origins of the bulk of emigrants for the first time. This chapter and chapter 7 discuss the implication of our estimates. We are able to show with some certainty, for example, the proportion of emigrants who had been born in urban and in rural areas. This chapter also contains an attempt to relate the rate of emigration from each county to a set of variables that are designed to capture economic and social conditions in that county. We will also make some preliminary observations about the relationship between internal migration and emigration and the extent of stage emigration.

II

Our estimates of the county of birth of all English and Welsh emigrants between 1861 and 1900 enable us to answer several important questions with varying degrees of certainty. The first is simply the number of emigrants who were born in urban and rural counties. This is shown in Table 6.1, which can be taken as an accurate summary of the contribution of different parts of the country and of the urban and rural counties to total emigration.[7] The most striking feature is the very

[6] Thomas, *Migration and economic growth*, pp. 124–5. Professor Thomas's work is discussed in detail in chapter 8.
[7] Table 6.1 and all other tables are drawn from the detailed migration estimates set out in Appendix 1. The significance of our assumptions can easily be seen in Appendix 1 which shows the effect of errors of 5% in migrant mortality on our estimates of internal and overseas migration from the counties. It was explained in chapter 4 that the key variables are the deaths that we ascribe to, say, Devon-born lifetime migrants in other counties (POPij) and to lifetime migrants in Devon (POPji). The

Table 6.1. *English and Welsh emigrants (net of returns) born in urban and rural counties, 1861–1900*

	Males 000s	Females 000s	Total 000s	% of all emigrants
1. *Urban 1*				
(a) London and Middlesex	243.2	176.5	419.7	17.9
(b) Lancashire	149.0	89.9	238.9	10.2
(c) Warwickshire and Staffordshire	104.9	66.1	171.0	7.3
	497.1	332.5	829.6	35.3
2. *Urban 2 (with significant rural parts)*				
(a) Yorkshire, Durham, Northumberland, Cheshire, Nottinghamshire, Gloucestershire and Leicestershire	275.7	171.5	447.2	19.0
(b) S.E. suburban/rural	133.6	54.1	187.7	8.0
(c) Industrial Wales	52.0	32.1	84.1	3.6
	461.3	257.7	719.0	30.6
3. *Rural*				
(a) West of England	210.7	112.4	323.1	13.8
(b) East of England	88.2	39.9	128.1	5.5
(c) South Midlands	65.7	24.0	89.7	3.8
(d) Rural Wales and borders	99.4	56.8	156.2	6.7
(e) Other rural	62.5	40.5	103.0	4.4
	526.9	273.6	800.5	34.1
Total emigration	1484.9	863.8	2348.7	100.0

Key: 2(b) South-East suburban/rural: Essex, Kent, Surrey, Hampshire, Sussex.

2(c) Industrial Wales: Glamorgan and Monmouth.

3(a) West of England: Wiltshire, Dorset, Devonshire, Cornwall, Somerset.

3(b) East of England: Huntingdonshire, Cambridgeshire, Suffolk, Norfolk, Lincolnshire, Rutland.

3(c) South Midlands: Northamptonshire, Bedfordshire, Buckinghamshire, Hertfordshire, Oxfordshire, Berkshire.

3(d) Rural Wales and Borders: All Wales except Glamorgan and Monmouth plus Shropshire and Herefordshire.

3(e) Other Rural: All other counties (Derbyshire, Worcestershire, Cumberland, Westmorland).

Notes: For definitions of urban 1, urban 2, and rural see text. Surrey is included in 2(b) although its mean urban population was only 33.5%. Emigration to Scotland and Ireland is included, except from Cumberland and Northumberland. The percentages may not add up to 100 due to rounding.

large number of emigrants who were born in urban counties. England and Wales lost (net of returns) about 2⅜ million emigrants in the forty years. Of those, over 800,000 (i.e. about 35%) had been born in London, Lancashire and the West Midlands, and over 500,000 (nearly 25%) had been born in other counties which would be considered urban and industrial. Less than a third of all emigrants in the last forty years of the nineteenth century had been born in the rural counties of the south west, East Anglia, the Midlands and Wales. The most important rural area in emigration was the West of England. A third of a million emigrants came from the five counties of Cornwall, Devon, Somerset, Dorset and Wiltshire. This was nearly 14% of all emigration from England and Wales and nearly a half of all emigration from the counties that were predominantly rural.

It is obvious, however, that the relative contribution of 'urban' and 'rural' counties depends on the definitions that are adopted. For example, it does not follow that emigrants from the so-called 'urban' counties came from the urban parts of those counties. We defined the urban part of a county as a continuous built up area containing at least 20,000 people. The proportion of the population of each county that was living in urban areas of more than 20,000 people was calculated from cartographic evidence and did not depend, for example, on the urban areas having the status of a municipal borough or urban district.[8] A population of 20,000 is a commonly used bench mark in urban studies and is designed to distinguish the smaller market towns from towns with a relatively wide range of occupations and with a

---

number of migrant deaths depends mainly on the assumption of the age-specific mortality of current migrants and, to a lesser extent, on the assumptions of the age-specific mortality of lifetime migrants. In most counties an error of 5% in migrant deaths in each decade represents the difference between our assumption that the current migrants – net of returns – had a median age of about 18 and that only 13% were 25 or over; and an assumption that the median age was about 25 and that 38% were 25 or over. Alternatively a 5% error would represent an over or under-estimate of the age-specific mortality of lifetime migrants of about 10% in each decade; or a combination of the two errors. If both errors were present they would partially net out. All our conclusions are sufficiently robust to withstand systematic non-compensated errors of this magnitude. In other words, as long as the age structure of current migrants was within the range mentioned above and mortality was within 10% of our estimate, then none of our conclusions can be falsified by errors in migrant mortality. The exception to this is in our estimates of the total emigration from the counties. In this case we assume that most errors net out over four decades.

[8] A series of contiguous villages with a population of 20,000 or more was counted as an urban area. A small town that adjoined a town in another county was counted as an urban part of the county if the total population of the two adjoining towns exceeded 20,000.

different cultural and visual environment.[9] By this definition, all the population of Cornwall lived in rural areas throughout the period,[10] and 68% of the population of Leicestershire were rural in the 1860s and 49% in the 1890s. London, Lancashire and the West Midlands were highly urbanised as early as 1861–70. The rural population of London (including Middlesex) Lancashire, Warwickshire and Staffordshire was only 5%, 32%, 34% and 48%, respectively, of the total population in the 1860s, and this had fallen to 3%, 14%, 21% and 27% by the 1890s. We can be fairly sure that the majority of emigrants born in London, the West Midlands and Lancashire had been brought up in an urban environment. Hence in Table 6.1 these counties are designated as 'urban 1'. We can be less sure about the emigrants from the other urban counties. Thirty-seven per cent of the population of Yorkshire,[11] 42% of Northumberland and 44% of Durham and Gloucestershire were still living in communities of less than 20,000 in 1891–1900. A similar problem arises with the counties of Essex, Surrey and Kent, which included parts of the London conurbation, and other substantial towns, but about a half of their population remained rural, by our definition, in the 1890s. We cannot say with certainty whether the emigrants from these counties were more likely to have been urban than rural born. These counties were designed 'urban 2'. Our definition of a 'rural' county was that the mean urban population was less than 35% over the period as a whole. (Most were substantially less.)[12] The bulk of the emigrants from rural counties must have been born in the rural areas. Some had no continuous urban areas of more than 20,000 and in most of the others the urban population was a very small proportion of the total before the 1890s which was the decade with the lowest emigration.

It is important to remember that 'rural' is not the same thing as 'agricultural'. The large emigration flows from rural counties were not paralleled by large falls in the numbers working in agriculture (see Appendix 7). In addition, most mining villages were not part of an urban community of 20,000 or more people. Hence, large

---

[9] See C. M. Law, 'The growth of urban population in England and Wales 1801–1911', *Transactions of the Institute of British Geographers*, 41, 1967, pp. 125–43.

[10] Although the combined population of the towns of Redruth and Camborne, for example, exceeded 20,000 after 1871, the two towns were separated by open country. Hence, by our definition the population lived in two small communities of less than 20,000, rather than in a single community of more than 20,000.

[11] For example, the census did not distinguish between those born in the East Riding and those born in the West Riding.

[12] The sum of the urban population in each of the four decades was less than 35% of the sum of the total population of the county in each of four decades.

numbers of the rural-born emigrants from Glamorgan and Durham, for example, could have been miners.

Stage emigration adds a complication. We cannot tell from the data in Table 6.1 how many of those born in rural counties had moved to an urban county before going abroad. We can of course discount the possibility that substantial numbers of those born in urban counties emigrated from rural areas.[13]

There seems little doubt that the majority of English emigrants in the last forty years of the nineteenth century came from towns. At least one-third, and probably a half of all emigrants must have been *born* in urban areas. (There is a more precise estimate in chapter 9.) They had presumably spent most of their lives in towns and cities – although not necessarily the one in which they were born. In addition, there were probably fairly large numbers of urban emigrants who had been born in the rural parts of the industrial counties or in the rural counties. The probable extent of rural–urban stage emigration will be quantified in chapter 9. But it is obvious from this preliminary display of our estimates that English and Welsh emigration in the later nineteenth century cannot have been a consequence of agricultural distress. The estimates also cast serious doubt on the idea that the growth of towns in England and Wales was a safety valve which reduced emigration. This view is usually taken to mean that migrants from the rural areas went to the towns rather than emigrate.[14] But the majority of decisions to emigrate seem to have been made in the urban parts of the country. Hence, migration to the towns is unlikely to have been a substitute for emigration.

III

Common sense might have led us to expect that the urban counties were the most important source of late nineteenth-century emigrants. London, Warwickshire, Staffordshire and Lancashire in which about 35% of English and Welsh emigrants had been born, contained over 31% of the population in 1861 and nearly 34% in 1901. But, as we have seen, until relatively recently the bulk of the literature assumed that most British emigrants had been born in rural areas. The implica-

[13] Only 9% of the natives of the six most urbanised counties (those with 60% or more of their population in urban areas containing at least 20,000 people) were living in the other forty-six counties in 1901. 57.9% of those who had been born in one of the twenty-four most rural counties (less than 25% urban) were living in the other twenty-eight counties of England and Wales. In fact, the urban county born POPji was proportionately lower than the rural county born POPji in *all* counties.

[14] See, for example, Jones, *Background to emigration from Great Britain*, pp. 45–6, 60–2.

tions of this view are absurd. The urban areas (by our definition of 'urban') contained 44% of the population in 1861 and 56% in 1901. If the bulk of the emigrants (for the sake of argument, two-thirds) *had* been born in the rural counties, then the mean emigration rate from the rural counties would have been three times as high as from the urban counties. This would mean that no less than 14% of the total rural population must have emigrated *net of returns* in the period 1861–1900, in addition to any net internal migration. In fact, we shall see that natives of urban counties were on average only marginally less likely to emigrate than natives of rural counties. Many rural counties had emigration rates below the average for England and Wales, and several highly urbanised counties had emigration rates considerably above the national average. Finally, if we include the rural–urban stage emigrants, it is likely that emigration from urban counties was relatively greater than from rural.

Our estimates show the migration of natives of each county. The population of each county at risk is, therefore, the sum of natives of the county living in that county (POPii) and those living in other counties in England and Wales (POPij). The numerator of the Devon emigration rate, for example, includes emigrants from, say, Glamorgan who had been born in Devon and excludes emigrants from Devon who were born in Cornwall. The difficulty is that the age structure, the occupational structure and the other characteristics of the Devon-born in other counties are unknown. We know only the demographic and economic situation within the county of Devon itself. But the Devon-born emigrants who left from another county may have been unaffected by conditions in Devon at the moment of emigration. The practical problems are not too serious, however. In the first place, Devon-born emigrants from Glamorgan must have been affected by conditions in Glamorgan for a shorter period of their lives than emigrants who went directly from Devon and conditions in Glamorgan were irrelevant to a stage emigrant who had decided to emigrate before he left Devon.

It is very important to deflate native emigration by the total native population at risk. For example, the population within the geographical area of the county of Devon was smaller than the population from which Devon-born emigrants were drawn. This was true of all the rural counties. Conversely, relatively fewer natives of urban counties were living outside those counties but there were relatively more rural in-migrants. The population at risk in urban counties was smaller than the total population of the urban counties. If we deflated by the total population, emigration from rural counties would be overstated relative to emigration from urban counties. The true population at risk is clearly the total native population (POPii + POPij) but it must be remembered that it is possible that many rural-born emigrants did not leave from their county of birth.

The rate of emigration is the number of emigrants (or internal migrants) expressed as a percentage of the mid-decade population of natives of that county in England and Wales. (This is effectively the same thing as a mean annual emigration rate for each 1,000 of the native population.) When we wish to show the mean rate of emigration of natives of a county for the whole period 1861–1900, the total number of emigrants is expressed as a percentage of the sum of the mid-decade populations in each decade. This is the mean rate of emigration weighted by the population in each decade. It is also important to show the total number of people at risk of emigrating in the four decades. The sum of the natives of Devon who were enumerated in each decade is obviously far larger than the total number of individual natives of Devon who were alive during the forty years 1861–1900. An easy way of solving this problem is to assume that each individual only considered emigration between the ages of 15–24. The stock of 15–24 year olds in each decade would then be a proxy for the population at risk.[15] Obviously, many emigrants were not aged 15–24, but the stock of 15–24 year old provides a convenient bench mark with which to judge the relative importance of emigration from the different counties over the whole period. It also makes it clear that high rates of emigration could only be achieved if the emigrants were drawn from a wide range of age groups.

There were very wide variations in the rate of emigration from English and Welsh counties (they can most easily be seen in Figures 6.1 and 6.2). Emigration of male natives of Cornwall, Brecon, Herefordshire and Pembroke averaged more than 5% of their population in each decade. This was equivalent to about a quarter or more of their young adult males.[16] Yet male emigration from Bedfordshire, Derbyshire, Gloucestershire and Leicestershire averaged 1.5% or less which was equivalent to less than 8% of young adults. The variation in emigration rates was equally large for female emigration. Brecon and Cornwall lost the equivalent of a quarter of their female young adults

---

[15] We need to know the stock of 15–24 year olds who were natives of each county and living within the whole of England and Wales, which is not the same thing as the stock of 15–24 year olds enumerated in each county. The method of estimation is described in chapter 4.

[16] I.e. the sum of male natives aged 15–24 in the period. Emigration from Pembroke was 23.3% of its male population aged 15–24.

Migration in a mature economy

Table 6.2. *Emigration by natives of English and Welsh counties (net of returns), 1861–1900 (% of total native population born in each county). Weighted mean of rate in each of four decades*

Males	%	Females	%
Cornwall	10.5	Brecon	5.4
Brecon	5.9	Cornwall	5.3
Herefordshire	5.2	Monmouth	3.6
Pembroke	5.1	Montgomery	3.3
Monmouth	4.9	Huntingdon	2.9
Montgomery	4,8	Herefordshire	2.8
Durham	4.3	Pembroke	2.8
Westmorland	4.3	London and Middlesex	2.5
Devon	4.2	Merioneth	2.4
Glamorgan	4.2	Westmorland	2.4
Somerset	4.2	Durham	2.3
London and Middlesex	3.9	Cheshire	2.2
Merioneth	3.8	Glamorgan	2.2
Dorset	3.8	Somerset	2.1
Cumberland (5.0)	3.5	Staffordshire	2.1
Huntingdonshire	3.5	Worcestershire	2.1
Staffordshire	3.5	Cumberland (3.4)	2.0
Cardigan	3.4	Nottinghamshire	2.0
Cheshire	3.4	Devon	1.9
Hampshire	3.4	Radnor	1.9
Caernarvon	3.3	Cardigan	1.8
Anglesey	3.2	Carmarthen	1.8
Rutland	3.2	Rutland	1.8
Shropshire	3.2	Warwickshire	1.8
Worcestershire	3.2	Dorset	1.7
Buckinghamshire	3.1	Shropshire	1.7
Wiltshire	3.1	Buckinghamshire	1.5
Carmarthen	2.8	Lancashire	1.5
Kent	2.8	Northamptonshire	1.5
Northamptonshire	2.8	Sussex	1.5
Nottinghamshire	2.8	Flint	1.4
Suffolk	2.8	Hampshire	1.4
Warwickshire	2.8	Suffolk	1.4
Flint	2.7	Surrey	1.4
Lancashire	2.7	Wiltshire	1.3
Oxfordshire	2.6	Yorkshire	1.3
Lincolnshire	2.5	Northumberland (2.0)	1.2
Radnor	2.5	Lincolnshire	1.1
Berkshire	2.4	Anglesey	1.0
Essex	2.4	Derbyshire	1.0
Sussex	2.3	Oxfordshire	1.0
Northumberland (2.9)	2.1	Bedfordshire	0.9
Norfolk	2.1	Gloucestershire	0.8

Table 6.2. (contd)

Males	%	Females	%
Yorkshire	2.1	Kent	0.8
Cambridgeshire	2.0	Hertfordshire	0.7
Hertfordshire	1.9	Leicestershire	0.7
Denbigh	1.8	Norfolk	0.7
Surrey	1.6	Caernarvon	0.6
Derbyshire	1.5	Denbigh	0.4
Gloucestershire	1.5	Essex	0.3
Leicestershire	1.4	Cambridgeshire	0.2
Bedfordshire	1.3	Berkshire	0
England and Wales	3.1	England and Wales	1.7

Note: Emigration rates from Northumberland and Cumberland exclude estimated emigration to Scotland. Values in brackets include emigration to Scotland from these counties. See chapter 4.
Source: Appendix 1.

but five counties may have lost as few as 2%.[17] The mean emigration rate in each decade for the English and Welsh as a whole was about 3.1% for males and 1.7% for females. This rate of emigration is the equivalent of 12.1% of the young adult population (15.4% of the males and 8.9% of the females). About 37% of .all emigrants were female.[18]

It must be emphasised that our estimates of native emigration which are displayed in Tables 6.2 and 6.3 are *net of returns* to England and Wales. Just over 2¼ million natives of England and Wales went overseas and did not return between 1861 and 1900. In the same period about 4½ million English and Welsh passengers left UK ports for overseas destinations. This means that there were somewhat under 2 million inward passengers.[19] Not all inward and outward passengers can be classed as emigrants, but with the exception of the 1860s, when inward movement was low, the number of returned emigrants cannot have been much less than 40% of outward emigration.[20] Hence, *on average,*

[17] Some of the values for female emigration are very small and less reliance can be placed on them.
[18] The unweighted mean rates of emigration by county of birth are normally distributed. For males, $\bar{x} = 3.28\%$, $\sigma = 1.46\%$, for females $\bar{x} = 1.78\%$, $\sigma = 1.08\%$.
[19] Between 1861 and 1900, 2,349,000 persons left England and Wales (net of returns). Of these, 112,000 went to Scotland and 75,000 went to Ireland. Persons who returned for the second time masked two outward emigrants.
[20] Table 5.2. Return migration is discussed in detail in chapter 5.

Table 6.3. *Emigration by natives of English and Welsh counties (net of returns), 1861–1900 as a % of those aged 15–24*

Males	%	Females	%
Cornwall	44.8	Brecon	26.4
Brecon	28.1	Cornwall	26.2
Herefordshire	25.0	Monmouth	17.6
Monmouth	24.7	Montgomery	16.3
Pembroke	23.3	Huntingdonshire	14.6
Montgomery	22.4	London and Middlesex	14.6
Durham	22.2	Herefordshire	14.3
Glamorgan	22.1	Pembroke	13.6
Westmorland	21.6	Merioneth	12.5
London and Middlesex	20.7	Durham	12.1
Devon	20.1	Westmorland	12.0
Somerset	19.5	Cheshire	11.6
Merioneth	18.5	Glamorgan	11.6
Dorset	18.3	Worcestershire	11.0
Cumberland	17.4	Somerset	10.6
Staffordshire	17.4	Staffordshire	10.6
Cheshire	17.3	Nottinghamshire	10.5
Hampshire	17.0	Cumberland	10.3
Huntingdonshire	16.3	Devon	9.9
Caernarvon	15.7	Radnor	9.3
Shropshire	15.7	Warwickshire	9.3
Worcestershire	15.7	Rutland	9.1
Anglesey	15.2	Cardigan	9.0
Wiltshire	14.8	Dorset	8.9
Buckinghamshire	14.7	Carmarthen	8.8
Rutland	14.6	Shropshire	8.6
Nottinghamshire	14.5	Lancashire	8.1
Warwickshire	14.1	Sussex	8.1
Cardigan	14.1	Anglesey	7.9
Kent	14.0	Surrey	7.9
Lancashire	13.7	Northamptonshire	7.8
Northamptonshire	13.7	Buckinghamshire	7.7
Suffolk	13.5	Hampshire	7.4
Oxfordshire	12.7	Suffolk	7.3
Carmarthen	12.6	Wiltshire	6.9
Flint	12.6	Flint	6.8
Lincolnshire	12.3	Yorkshire	6.5
Berkshire	12.0	Northumberland	6.3
Essex	11.9	Lincolnshire	5.6
Radnor	11.9	Oxfordshire	5.3
Sussex	11.2	Derbyshire	5.1
Northumberland	10.5	Bedfordshire	4.3
Yorkshire	10.5	Gloucestershire	4.1
Norfolk	10.0	Kent	4.0

Table 6.3. *(contd)*

Males	%	Females	%
Cambridgeshire	9.5	Leicestershire	3.9
Denbigh	8.6	Norfolk	3.9
Surrey	8.0	Caernarvon	2.9
Derbyshire	7.5	Denbigh	2.0
Gloucestershire	7.5	Essex	1.2
Leicestershire	7.3	Cambridgeshire	1.0
Bedfordshire	6.5	Hertfordshire	0.4
Hertfordshire	5.0	Berkshire	0.1
England and Wales	15.4	England and Wales	8.9

Source: Appendix 1.

our estimates of emigration from the English and Welsh counties, net of returns, understate gross emigration by something under 40%.

We have chosen to assume that net emigration was a sample of gross emigration. That is, we assume, for the purposes of this study, that all natives of English and Welsh counties were equally likely to return to England and Wales. There is little direct evidence to substantiate the view that net emigration rates and the rate of return were positively correlated, although, for example, it is known that returns to Cornwall were very high.[21] Cornwall had, by far, the highest rate of net emigration. Our assumption on the relation between outward and return emigration is based on the idea that the flow of information was an important component in the decision to emigrate, which seems to be a reasonable conclusion from a reading of the European literature. We also assume that there were no substantial parts of England and Wales that remained virtually ignorant of emigration after 1860. In other words, for the moment, we assume that there was virtually no 'blind' emigration. We will, however, be able to show that it is a reasonable assumption. The evidence is discussed in chapter 7.

On the other hand, it is possible that our estimates fail properly to capture temporary emigration. The apparently high net emigration rates from some counties may be because their natives had a low propensity to return. In that case, the rate of return to the other coun-

---

[21] John Rowe, *Cornwall in the age of the Industrial Revolution* (Liverpool University Press, 1953), pp. 321–2, 325–6. Returning emigrants to Cornwall were said to have held up the price of farms in the agricultural depression of the 1880s. P. J. Parry, *British farming in the Great Depression, 1870–1914* (David and Charles, Newton Abbot, 1974), p. 63.

ties which had relatively low net emigration, must have been cor-
respondingly higher. But we think that it is more reasonable to assume
that temporary and permanent emigration were complements rather
than substitutes. Hence, our estimates of emigration from English
and Welsh counties can be read in two ways. Firstly, they give as
accurate an estimate of permanent emigration as we think is possible.
Secondly, they may give an accurate estimate of temporary emigration
as well.

The counties with the highest emigration rates – taking the period
1861–1900 as a whole – can be seen in Tables 6.2 and 6.3.[22] Table
6.2 shows the mean value of the rate of emigration in each of the
four decades. Table 6.3 shows the number of emigrants as a proportion
of those aged 15–24. This table can be read as a proxy for the proportion
of the total population of each county who emigrated in the period.
The correspondence between the two series is very close.[23] This is
not surprising since the proportion of the natives of each county that
were aged 15–24 was very similar. (For our purposes, it is immaterial
whether tne natives were located in their county of birth or in another
county, of course.)[24]

It is clear from the maps (Figures 6.1 and 6.2 which are based on
the tables), that the rate of emigration showed a marked geographical
pattern. Emigration rates rose from east to west. Imagine a line from
halfway along the Scottish border to halfway along the south coast.
Twenty-five counties would be to the east and twenty-seven to the
west. (Derby, Warwickshire, Oxfordshire, Berkshire and Hampshire
would all be to the east.) If we count rural Wales as one county,[25]
no less than fourteen of the (now) seventeen western counties had
male emigration rates above the national average of 3.1% per decade.
Twelve had female emigration rates above the national average of
1.7% per decade. Emigration from England and Wales was 15.4% of
the total male population at risk and 8.9% of the female. Male emigration rates were above the national average in only five of the twenty-

[22] To avoid tedious repetition it is not always stressed that the emigration rates refer
to natives of the county living within the whole of England and Wales.
[23] The rank order correlation between the two series is 0.985 for males and 0.986 for
females.
[24] This is not strictly true. The most important urban counties had very much larger
numbers of young in-migrants, than of young out-migrants. The young in-migrants
produced large numbers of children. This means that a relatively high proportion
of the native-born population of these counties were children, and a relatively smaller
proportion were young adults. Hence, emigrants from the main urban counties
(London, Warwickshire and Lancashire) were a larger proportion of their native
young adults than of their total native populations.
[25] Because it was composed of an excessive number of small counties.

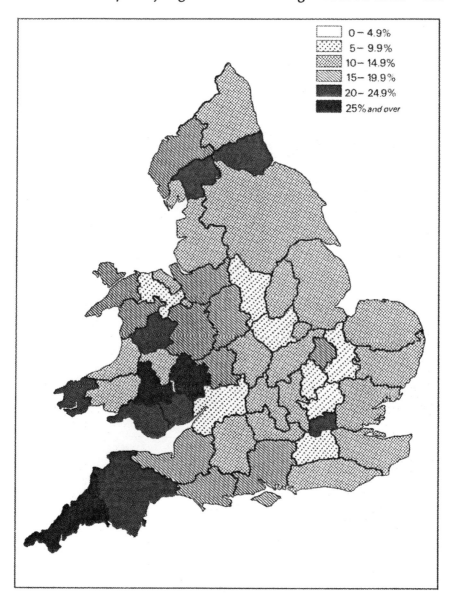

Figure 6.1 *Emigration by male natives of English and Welsh counties (net of returns), 1861–1900 as a % of those aged 15–24*

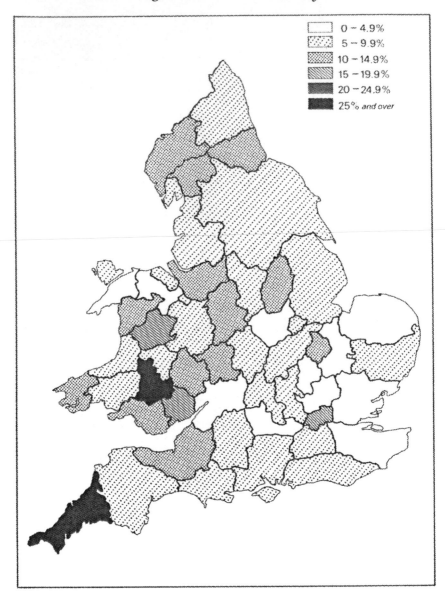

Figure 6.2 *Emigration by female natives of English and Welsh counties (net of returns), 1861–1900 as a % of those aged 15–24*

five eastern counties and female rates were above in only six. We will show that the marked geographical pattern was not a consequence of the distribution of urban and rural counties or of their relative size, and was probably not, therefore, some other differential in disguise. We will also discuss the extent to which the high emigration rates from the western counties occurred because they were nearer to the North Atlantic or because they were further from London.

There were seven main regions[26] where emigration rates were significantly above the mean rate from England and Wales. The regions with relatively high emigration can be seen in Table 6.4. They were, the West of England, rural Wales and the borders, Cumberland and Westmorland and perhaps surprisingly, industrial South Wales, County Durham and London. Emigration rates were below the mean from the Home Counties, the South East, East Anglia, the East Midlands, Lancashire and Yorkshire. Emigration from the rural western counties of Dorset, Devon, Cornwall and Somerset was exceptionally high – although emigration from Wiltshire (the other county of the traditional West of England) was below the mean rate.[27] But 294,000 natives of the other four western counties went overseas (and did not return) between 1861 and 1900. This was nearly a quarter of all males at risk and nearly an eighth of all females. Cornwall alone lost 118,500 people, the equivalent of over 40% of its young adult males and over 25% of its young adult females. Some went to Scotland, however.[28] Assuming that the rate of return to Cornwall was about the same as to England and Wales as a whole, gross emigration must have been about 20% of the male Cornish-born population in each decade and about 10% of the female. This is not as high as from the famous regions of Italy, some of which achieved emigration rates of 30% or more per decade, but it must be remembered that mass emigration from Italy lasted for not much more than twenty years.[29]

[26] A region is defined as a group of contiguous counties all of which have comparable emigration rates. This condition is relaxed for rural Wales where the counties are very small and the migration flows contain only small numbers of emigrants.

[27] Only 12.8% of the population of the West of England lived in urban areas in 1861–70 and 22.1% in 1891–1900 – mostly in Plymouth and the southern suburbs of Bristol.

[28] There are known to have been many Cornish miners in the Scottish coal mines. See A. J. Youngson Brown, 'Trade union policy in the Scots coalfields, 1855–1885', *Economic History Review*, 2nd series, 6, 1953–4, p. 38.

[29] Emigration from the Abruzzi, the Basilicata and Calabria was between 34% and 37% of the total population in the years 1902–13. But the rate of return migration in this period probably exceeded 50%. Hence, the famous Italian emigration regions were losing about 15% of their population overseas net of returns over a period of less than twenty years, compared with Cornwall which was losing at the rate of about 8% net of returns, over a period of forty years. MacDonald, 'Emigration differentials in rural Italy, pp. 55–72. Foerster, *Italian emigration of our times*, p. 529.

Table 6.4. *English and Welsh emigrants (net of returns) born in urban and rural counties, 1861–1900 (mean % of native population and % of native total young adult population)*

	(A)		(B)	
	Males %	Females %	Males %	Females %
1. *Urban 1*				
(a) London and Middlesex	3.9	2.5	20.7	14.6
(b) Lancashire	2.7	1.5	13.7	8.1
(c) Warwickshire and Staffordshire	3.2	1.9	16.0	10.1
2. *Urban 2 (with significant rural parts)*				
(a) Yorkshire, Durham, Northumberland, Cheshire, Nottinghamshire, Gloucestershire and Leicestershire	2.5	1.5	12.4	7.5
(b) South East suburban/rural	2.6	1.0	12.9	5.4
(c) Industrial Wales	4.5	2.6	23.0	13.7
3. *Rural*				
(a) West of England	5.1	2.4	23.6	12.6
(b) East of England	2.4	1.0	11.8	5.4
(c) South Midlands	2.4	0.9	11.1	4.4
(d) Rural Wales and Borders	3.6	1.9	16.3	9.3
(e) Other rural	3.0	2.0	13.3	8.7
All urban	3.0	1.7	15.0	9.1
All rural	3.4	1.7	16.0	8.5
England and Wales	3.1	1.7	15.4	8.9

Notes:
(A) Number of emigrants as a % of total native population born in each county. Weighted mean of rate in each of four decades.
(B) Number of emigrants as a % of natives aged 15–24 in whole period 1861–1900.
Source: For further notes see Appendix 1 and Table 6.1.

Cornwall was probably an emigration region comparable with any in Europe.

It is not difficult to find reasons why emigration from Cornwall was so high. Part of the emigration was obviously connected with the decline of copper and tin mining after the crisis of 1866.[30] There was considerable movement to the Welsh and Lanarkshire coalfields, where Cornish miners had gone in earlier depressions. But there is evidence to suggest that the Cornish miners were more likely to emigrate than move to another part of Britain. This was partly parochialism and partly because 'the Cornish could not live without the mines'.[31] This normally meant hard-rock mining in which they had important skills. Our migration estimates confirm this view. Emigration from Cornwall was particularly heavy in the 1860s and 1870s and Cornwall was the only English county where there were more lifetime male emigrants than lifetime internal migrants.[32] But even in the 1860s and 1870s it is unlikely that more than half the Cornish emigrants had been dependent on mining. Rowe estimated that 120,000 people depended on mining at its peak and that the mining labour force of about 40,000 fell by half in the two decades.[33] This presumably means that Cornish emigration would have been substantial without the miners and comparable to that from Devon. On the other hand, most of the links that made it easy for the Cornish to emigrate may have been dependent on the earlier emigration of Cornish miners which was common in the 1850s. The course of Cornish emigration raises two important questions – the degree to which emigration from Cornwall was determined by features that were unique to Cornwall or by features that also occurred in other counties; and the importance of information in the decision to emigrate.

Emigration rates from rural Wales were not as high as from the West of England but were above the English average. We should not place too much emphasis on the rate of emigration from individual rural Welsh counties because some of the flows were very small and the percentage error is large. There is also a suspicion of enumeration errors, for example, between Caernarvon and Anglesey. If we consider

---

[30] Rowe estimated that about 11,400 jobs were lost in eighteen months or about 30% of the labour force. J. Rowe, *Cornwall in the age of the Industrial Revolution* (Liverpool University Press, 1953), p. 378.

[31] Rowe, *Cornwall in the age of the Industrial Revolution*, p. 326.

[32] Cornwall lost (net of returns) 44.7% of the male population at risk (15–24) but only 29.7% to other English and Welsh counties, 26.2% of the female population at risk went overseas compared with 35.4% who moved internally.

[33] About 3,000 displaced miners were absorbed into the china clay industry.

rural Wales as a whole it had an average male emigration rate of 3.4% (about 1 in 6) and a female rate of 1.9% (about 1 in 11). Most writers of Welsh emigration have assumed that emigration from Wales was low in the late nineteenth century. Maldwyn Jones, for example, thought it 'virtually ceased' after 1880.[34] Rural Welsh emigration is sometimes thought to have been low because the rural Welsh preferred to move to industrial Wales. We now know that the rural Welsh were more likely to emigrate than the English, but, much more suprisingly, the Welsh who had been born in the urban parts of Wales were even more likely to emigrate than the rural Welsh. Glamorgan lost, on average, 4.2% of its male population each decade and 2.2% of its females. This was equivalent to about 22% of its young male adults and about 12% of young adult females. This was one of the highest emigration rates from any county – urban or rural. Emigration from Monmouth was even greater but Monmouth was not highly urbanised and the emigrants could have come from the rural parts of the county.[35] Hence, it is not clear whether the Monmouth emigrants were similar to those from the adjacent county of Glamorgan who must have included many miners and industrial workers; or whether they were more similar to emigrants from the rural border counties. Shropshire and Herefordshire lost a total of 41,000 emigrants which was proportionately more than from rural Wales.

Some of the emigrants who had been born in rural counties may have left from the urban areas. For example, some of the Herefordshire and Shropshire-born emigrants may have migrated to the Black Country or the Potteries before they went overseas. The extent of rural–urban stage emigration is very difficult to estimate from data which merely show lifetime changes in residence, but our estimates (chapter 9) suggest that this kind of stage emigration may not have been important in England and Wales. We we are able to show that natives of the rural counties to the south and east of Birmingham were possibly less likely to emigrate than those born in the West Midlands (Worcestershire, Staffordshire and Warwickshire). This phenomenon is even more obvious in the South East where none of the rural counties that surrounded London had a native emigration rate as high as natives of London itself. And we have already seen

---

[34] Jones, *Background to emigration from Great Britain*, p. 77.
[35] Only 19% of the Monmouthshire population were living in urban areas (more than 20,000 population) in 1861–70 and 38% in 1891–1900. It must be remembered that most mining communities in Monmouth were rural. The urban population of Glamorgan was 44% and 67% of the total population in the two decades.

that Glamorgan natives were more likely to emigrate than people who had been born in the Welsh rural counties.

Emigration was high from the four northern counties with the exception of Northumberland. Cumberland and Westmorland had no towns of any size, were remote from the industrial areas and Cumberland (and possibly Westmorland) had overseas contacts via the Cumberland and north Lancashire ports. They were rather similar to Devon and Cornwall. Cumberland lost emigrants at an average rate of 3.5% of males and 2.0% of females in each decade. This was the equivalent of losing about 17% of its young adults males and about 10% of its females. Mean emigration from Westmorland was 4.3% of males and 2.4% of females in each decade or about 22% and 12% of the population at risk.

More surprising, is that there seems to have been exceptionally heavy emigration from County Durham. In the forty years 1861–1900, 92,000 Durham-born emigrants (net of returns) left. This would have been about 22% of young adult males and about 12% of young adult females. (A mean rate of 4.3% and 2.3% of the total native population in each decade.) The two counties whose economies were most dominated by coal exports (Durham and Glamorgan) had the highest emigration rates of all industrial and urban counties.

Our estimate of Durham emigration does not seem to have been influenced by migration to Scotland – which was relatively near, of course. The method that was used to eliminate excess 'emigration' to Scotland from the four northern counties was discussed in chapter 4. It depends on an analysis of the migrant sex-ratios of the counties. Our conclusions were that 14,000 of the lifetime 'emigrants' from Cumberland and a similar number from Westmorland went to Scotland but that lifetime migration from Durham (and Westmorland) to Scotland was no greater than the average rate from other English and Welsh counties. It is possible that there was a considerable temporary migration from Durham to Scotland but this cannot affect our estimates of Durham born emigration unless the temporary migrants were living in Scotland on the night of the English census. The bulk of long stay emigrants from County Durham must have gone overseas.[36]

The other industrial and urban county with a high propensity to emigrate was London.[37] We have already noted that 16% of the male

[36] There were very few lifetime Durham-born migrants living in other counties and we can assume that most emigrants left from County Durham itself.
[37] We have already noted that London had to be combined with Middlesex. But only 5% of the combined population of London and Middlesex were living outside the built up area in 1861–1900 and only 3% in 1891–1900.

emigrants between 1861 and 1900 had been born in London and no less than 20% of all females. On average London was sending 3.9% of its natives overseas each decade (net of returns) and 2.5% of its females. Put another way, natives of London were about 50% more likely to emigrate than the natives of other counties. London lost the equivalent of just under 18% of the population at risk compared with just over 11% of the population elsewhere. It is possible that Londoners were more likely to go to Australia and that London provided a relatively large share of Australian immigrants. There is some slight evidence in the Australian data for this conjecture.[38] The majority of emigrant ships to Australia sailed from London while emigrant ships from London to other countries were rare.

The very heavy emigration from London is even more startling because emigration from the surrounding counties was exceptionally low. Beyond the partly suburban counties of Surrey, Kent and Essex, the whole area to the west and north and East Anglia was largely dependent on agriculture and had only a small urban population. Earnings were relatively low. Migration to London from the ten southeast rural counties of Sussex, Berkshire, Hertfordshire, Buckinghamshire, Huntingdon, Oxfordshire, Bedfordshire, Cambridgeshire, Suffolk and Norfolk was high and particularly high for women. On average 314,000 natives of these counties were living in London of which 183,000 (58%) were female.[39] This was 9.4% and 12.5% of the male and female population that had been born in the rural southeastern counties. But these people do not seem to have acquired the emigration habits of the native Londoners. Only 109,700 male and 41,800 female natives of the rural counties emigrated, either from their own county, from London, or from another county. This would only have been 11.0% of male young adults and only 5.0% of female, compared with 20.7% and 14.6% of young Londoners.

IV

There were about five males for every three female emigrants from England and Wales between 1861 and 1900. Females were 36.8% of all emigrants net of returns. By the 1860s England and Wales had passed the stage when most emigration occurred in family groups, although the male dominance was not as great as it was among Italian emigrants, of course.[40]

---

[38] Duncan, 'Late nineteenth-century migration into New South Wales'.
[39] I.e. the median population in the period 1861–1900.
[40] See Erickson, 'The English', p. 326. Of all Italian emigrants between 1876 and 1914 81% were male. Ferenczi and Willcox, *International migrations*, p. 820.

Table 6.5. *Male and female emigration, 1861–1900 (net of returns)*

Born in	% of emigrants	
	Male	Female
London and Middlesex	57.9	42.1
Lancashire	62.4	37.6
Warwickshire and Staffordshire	61.3	38.7
All highly urbanised (Urban 1)	59.9	40.1
Yorkshire, Durham, Northumberland, Cheshire, Nottinghamshire, Gloucestershire and Leicestershire	61.7	38.3
S.E. suburban/rural	71.2	28.8
Industrial Wales	61.8	38.2
All less urbanised (Urban 2)	64.2	35.8
West of England	65.2	34.8
East of England	68.9	31.1
South Midlands	73.2	26.8
Rural Wales and Borders	63.6	36.4
Other rural	60.7	39.3
All rural	65.8	34.2
England and Wales	63.2	36.8

We would expect that male and female emigration rates from the same county were positively correlated, if only because a proportion of emigrants must have travelled in families. There were no counties which had very high or low emigration rates for one sex only.[41] Female emigrants were between 30% and 44% of all emigrants in thirty-nine of the fifty-two counties, in five they were more than 45% and in eight they were less than 30%.[42] We must, however, be careful about the sex ratio among emigrants from some of the small rural counties. If we ignore the eight counties where total female emigration in 1861–1900 was less than 1500 persons, the female emigration was between 30% and 44% of all emigration from all but six counties. There was, however, an important difference between urban and rural counties, which is shown in Table 6.5. On average, the percentage

[41] The rate of male emigration from each county in each decade was regressed on female emigration rates. $R^2 = 0.63$ and 0.55 for first differences.
[42] Rutland, Radnor, Cambridgeshire, Hertfordshire, Berkshire, Denbigh, Caernarvon and Anglesey.

of females among the emigrants who had been born in the four most urbanised counties was about 40%. In the rural counties it was only just over 34%. The percentage of females was also higher among emigrants from the 'less urbanised' counties. The sex ratio[43] was higher than the mean ratio from England and Wales as a whole from all four of the highly urbanised counties (the highest was London with 42.1%) and in seven of the other fourteen urban counties. Curiously, the share of female emigrants was low from Glamorgan and Durham. Only 34.8% of emigrants from Glamorgan and 35.7% from Durham were female despite the relative shortage of jobs for women in the mining counties. On the other hand, only ten of the twenty-seven rural counties, where female emigration exceeded 1500, had an above average emigrant sex ratio. The share of women emigrants was low in all the West of England counties except Cornwall, in all the eastern counties except Huntingdon and in all the South Midland counties except Bedfordshire. Worcestershire (41.2%) and Derbyshire (39.5%) were the only important rural counties with more than 39.0% of their emigrants female. The proportion of women emigrants was also relatively low from all the Welsh counties where emigration exceeded 1500 except two, as it was from the border counties of Herefordshire and Shropshire.

It is clear from the distribution of the emigrant sex ratio that the proportion of females was not related to the rate of emigration. The ratio was low for example in the West of England and in the rural counties on the Scottish and Welsh borders which had high emigration and also low in the eastern counties and the South Midlands both of which had low emigration. On the other hand the female ratio was high in London which had above average emigration but also high in other urban counties which produced few emigrants.

Another possibility is that the relatively large proportion of women among urban emigrants and the low proportion among rural was a consequence of changes in the nature of emigration. The tentative conclusion of Charlotte Erickson's work (which we discussed in chapter 3), was that in the first half of the nineteenth century a relatively large number of British emigrants seem to have come from areas that were little changed by industrialisation, and that they went permanently. But at some point in the second half of the century, a new kind of emigrant seems to have appeared who was more likely to return and who was less likely to travel with a family party. This was probably connected with the introduction of steamships on the

---

[43] The higher the sex ratio the greater the proportion of women to men.

North Atlantic in the 1860s and we now know that return migration increased sharply in the 1870s. When Professor Erickson examined the origins of British emigrants in the 1880s she found that they came mainly from places where economic change had been rapid.[44] We might think that the sex ratio of the emigrants from rural and urban counties reflected these changes in some way. In this case we would expect that the emigrants from the rural areas included a larger proportion of women. If the character of emigration from the rural areas had not changed as rapidly as the emigration from the urban areas, rural emigration would have contained more families who intended to settle abroad and hence more women.[45] But we have seen that rural emigrants contained a larger proportion of men. In fact, taking England and Wales as a whole, women emigrants do not seem to have been much less likely to return than men in any decade.[46]

Women who had been born in the rural areas may have been less likely to emigrate because of the greater attraction of domestic service in the urban areas. A woman who had been born in London, for example, was less likely to see domestic service as an escape. It was probably less attractive than the factory. Domestic service had 'unsocial hours' and demanded deference – although by women's standards the wages of domestic servants were relatively high.[47] And country girls were often preferrred as servants. In either case domestic service offered no escape for urban-born women which could explain why women formed a larger share of the emigration from urban counties. It may also explain why almost one in seven of the London-born population who were at risk emigrated but only one in twenty of those who had been born in the ten surrounding rural counties, even though a large proportion of the latter were actually living in London. If female emigration was affected by the relative attractiveness of domestic service, we might expect that internal migration and emigra-

---

[44] See in particular, Erickson, 'Who were?' (1977), Erickson, 'Who were?' (1972), pp. 360, 364.

[45] The low female sex ratio among rural emigrants would be consistent with the emigration of large numbers of (male) single adults from the cities, if a substantial proportion of rural-born emigrants had moved to the towns before emigrating. It will be shown in chapter 9, however, that this cannot have been the case.

[46] Returns were 41% of outward-bound women in 1871–80, 44% in 1881–90 and 81% in 1891–1900. Male returns were 54%, 50% and 57% respectively. Since, presumably, a large proportion of non-emigrant passengers were male, the proportion of women emigrants who returned cannot have been much less than men. See Table 5.2.

[47] For descriptions of the female labour market see D. Baines, 'The labour market 1860–1914', pp. 144–74, in R. Floud and D. McCloskey (eds.), *The economic history of Britain since 1700* (Cambridge University Press, 1981), and P. G. Hall, *The industries of London since 1861* (Hutchinson, 1962), pp. 60–1, 118.

tion from the rural counties would be negatively correlated. We did find that female internal migration and emigration were substitutes (i.e. were negatively correlated) but the relationship was not strong enough to confirm our hypothesis that the possibility of finding jobs in the towns reduced female emigration from rural areas.[48]

V

In this section we will examine the relationship between the economic and social character of the counties of England and Wales and the rate of emigration from the counties. We will discuss, among other things, the possible effect of the extent of urbanisation in the counties, the degree of literacy, the occupational structure, the level of income and the existence of population pressure. There are many other features of economic and social life that may have influenced the rate of emigration but, unfortunately, there is very little systematic information available. We also know virtually nothing about the non material factors which affected the propensity to emigrate. We cannot assume that potential emigrants based their decision on the factors that we know about, or only on material factors. All we can do is to try and establish the relative influence of the material factors about which we do have some information.

We are faced with an immediate difficulty. We know only the conditions in the county of birth of an emigrant, which was not necessarily the county from which he left. And even if we knew the exact extent of stage emigration, we would still not be able to distinguish between those stage emigrants whose decision to emigrate was taken in the county from which they left (and was, therefore, affected by conditions there) and those who had already decided to emigrate when they were still living in their native county. This was a distinction which many stage emigrants could not have made at the time. On the other hand, we can assume that the (adult) stage emigrants *were* affected by conditions in their native country at the point when they left it.

The first possible explanation of differential emigration rates is technical. This is that emigration rates from the very small counties may have been biased by their size. We have already seen in chapter 4 that the county is not an ideal unit. They varied greatly in population size and the smaller counties had relatively high emigration rates. Seven of the nine counties which had a total native population of

---

[48] See Appendix 7. The problem was that the internal migration variable is correlated with the lagged dependent variable which was not significant.

less than 100,000 persons (six of which were in Wales) had native emigration rates (both male and female) above the mean for England and Wales.[49] This could be caused by errors in the estimates. The emigration estimates are the residual of net native outflow to all destinations and net native movement into all the other counties. The degree of error in the estimates is greater the smaller the emigration flow. On the other hand, we would expect most of these errors to net out over the period as a whole. And over the period as a whole the (weighted) mean emigration rates from the small counties remain high. High emigration from small counties could, of course, have been caused by real factors. One factor is simply that a county with a small population is unlikely to include a large town, which might have provided an alternative destination for its migrants. But as we have seen, a simple, rural/urban division does not explain differential emigration rates. However, high emigration from a small rural county could be explained in another way. Emigration could have depended on a flow of information built up from the experience of friends and relatives. In this case the level of emigration may have been very different between neighbouring villages. The small counties like Rutland and Radnor which had high emigration rates might have contained more emigration-prone communities. If the distribution of these communities was random, we would expect the variance of emigration rates from the small counties to have been greater than that from the larger. But this was not the case.[50] We can be fairly sure, therefore, that emigration rates from the small rural counties were not likely to have been disproportionately affected by errors in the estimates.

When we attempt to assess the relative importance of the factors that affected the decision to emigrate, we are faced with a problem. If the decision to emigrate was rational – which, of course, we are assuming – then a prospective emigrant considered his circumstances at home in the light of his expectation of improved circumstances in another country. This means, of course, that the frequent distinction in the literature between 'push' factors and 'pull' factors is unrealistic.[51] The problem is that we do not know the destination of emigrants from individual counties. We are forced to make the unrealistic

[49] The counties were Huntingdon, Rutland, Westmorland, Brecon, Radnor, Montgomery, Flint, Merioneth and Anglesey. Emigration from seven of these counties was relatively higher than from England and Wales as a whole by both measures of the rate of emigration.

[50] The unweighted emigration rate per 100 persons per decade from the small counties was 3.77 for males ($\sigma = 1.02$) and 2.50 ($\sigma = 1.22$) for females. For England and Wales as a whole it was 3.12 ($\sigma = 1.52$) for males and 1.58 ($\sigma = 0.94$) for females.

[51] This point is made by Gould, 'European inter-continental emigration', p. 633.

assumption that all English and Welsh emigrants had the same expectations, and that their decision to emigrate can be explained by evidence that only relates to England and Wales.

An obvious hypothesis is that people chose to emigrate because there were insufficient jobs available. There are several aspects to this. In the first place there was a demographic effect. The supply of young people may have been too high and some may have decided to emigrate. We might expect this to partially explain emigration from the rural counties. Fertility was fairly high in rural counties and infant mortality was low. With no out-migration, real incomes in some rural counties might have fallen. But we could find no relationship between the rate of emigration from rural counties and fertility. For example, five of the ten counties with the highest fertility had mean emigration rates above that for England and Wales and six had female rates above average. However, all but one of the counties that had both high fertility and high emigration were *urban*. (Not suprisingly, three of these were mining counties.) Only two of the five rural counties with high fertility had above average emigration. On the other hand, six of the eight rural counties with the lowest fertility had above average male emigration and five had above average female.[52]

The level of age-specific fertility is not, however, a satisfactory way of measuring the number of new entrants to the labour market which affected the job prospects of young adults. The number of young adults entering the labour market was also determined by their mortality history and by the rate of net migration. We can test whether the rate of emigration was a consequence of an excess of young adults in the labour market from the proportion of young adults in the population of each county. It is clear, however, that there was no significant variation in the proportion of the native population in each county living within England and Wales who were aged 15–24. We can see from a comparison of Table 6.2 and Table 6.3 that county emigration

[52] The emigration rates used were the (weighted) mean of the rate in each decade as a percentage of the total native population. In this case it would obviously be inappropriate to express the number of emigrants as a proportion of the 15–24 age group. The G.R.R. was taken from a well-known paper by Glass. D. V. Glass, 'Changes in fertility in England and Wales', in L. Hogben (ed.), *Political arithmetic* (Allen and Unwin, 1938), pp. 180–1. The counties with the highest age-specific fertility were, in descending rank order, Monmouth, Glamorgan, Durham, Derbyshire, Staffordshire, Brecon, Lincolnshire, Northumberland, Denbigh and Flint. These all had a G.R.R. above 2.350 per 1000 in 1861 and in 1881 and were still among the counties with the highest fertility in 1911. The counties with the lowest G.R.R., in descending rank order were Cardigan, Surrey, Devon, Westmorland, Sussex, Caernarvon, Hertfordshire, Somerset, Berkshire, Lancashire, Kent and Dorset. These all had a G.R.R. that was never above 2.350 per 1000 and all twelve were in the lowest sixteen in 1911.

rates of the total native population and emigration rates of the young adult population are highly correlated.[53] The young adult native population *includes* any person who may have gone to another county because they found it difficult to obtain (adequate) jobs in their native county. A better proxy for the supply of young adults to the labour market would be the relative size of the total young adult population. We found, however, no evidence in our model that emigration rates were related to the proportion of the population of the counties that were aged 15–24.[54]

A second possibility is that the propensity to emigrate was affected by the level of wages. We would expect that a fall in the level of wages in a particular county, or more realistically, a relatively slow rate of increase, would lead to an increase in the rate of emigration. This would presumably be a sign that the demand for labour was relatively low. There is no adequate series of county wage rates in the main occupations, but it is possible to use the earnings of agricultural labourers as a proxy for all unskilled wages. This is because agricultural wages near the towns had to reflect the wages of the unskilled urban workers.[55]

On the other hand, the structure of occupations in the counties might have had an effect on emigration rates. In other words, we might expect that counties where there were rather few jobs outside agriculture would have a less attractive labour market than counties with a range of occupations. We would expect that a fall in the proportion of the population engaged in agriculture would be associated with a rise in the rate of emigration.[56] We would also expect that

[53] For example, the rank order correlation between the two series was 0.985 for males and 0.986 for females.

[54] In the best specification, the coefficient of the 'age' variable was not significant for female emigration, and both coefficients had an unexpected sign (that is that an increase in the proportion in the young adult age groups was associated with a decrease in the rate of emigration). See Appendix 7.

[55] The wage levels are taken from E. H. Hunt, *Regional wage variations in Britain 1850–1914* (Clarendon Press, Oxford, 1973), pp. 62–3. This book contains an extensive discussion on the practical and theoretical issues involved in the construction of a county wage index. Dr Hunt points out, for example, that the cost of living was in general lower in towns, so that the real differential between rural and urban incomes was, if anything, greater than the nominal difference. Dr Hunt's earnings series is heavily dependent on Bowley's estimates of 1867 and 1897–8 which he subjected to a rigorous scrutiny without, however, being able significantly to improve them. Dr Hunt's estimates provide agricultural wage levels for each county at two points – 1868 and 1897–8. These were used for the two decades 1861–70 and 1891–1900 and the data for the two intervening decades were interpolated. We assumed that wages increased at a constant rate in the two intervening decades.

[56] The proportion of the county population engaged in agriculture was taken from C. H. Lee, ed., *British regional employment statistics, 1841–1971* (Cambridge University

the range of jobs available would be greater in the urban areas, and that emigration would be higher from the rural areas. But, as we have already noted, there was no simple relationship between the degree of urbanisation of a county and the propensity of its natives to emigrate. On average, rural-born males were only about 7% more likely to emigrate than urban born and rural-born females were about 6% *less* likely to emigrate[57] (Table 6.4). Males had a higher than average propensity to emigrate in seven of the eighteen urban counties and fifteen of the thirty-four rural counties. Female emigration was similar.[58]

Unfortunately, within the context of our model, the proportion of the population living in urban areas in each decade, the proportion of the population that were engaged in agricultural occupations and the earnings of agricultural labourers were not significantly related to the rate of emigration from the counties.[59]

Our inability to find a relationship between a set of variables that are intended to capture the nature of the labour market in which potential emigrants had to find a job does not, of course, prove that potential emigrants did not consider material factors. Nor, of course, does it prove that the difference in emigration rates from English and Welsh counties is inexplicable.

It may be that great differences in the propensity to emigrate from the different counties were because the potential emigrants were not equally aware of the opportunities that were available to them overseas. This could be simply because some counties had been losing large numbers of emigrants in past decades. There is no direct way of measuring the amount of information available to prospective emigrants. But the distance from the emigration ports, the extent of literacy and the rate of emigration in previous decades can be used as proxies.

The distance from the two emigration ports, London and Liverpool, cannot have been an important factor. The principal town of nearly

Press, 1979). The data for the number of women in agricultural occupations are rather poor and we used the proportion of males as an independent variable in the female migration equations.

[57] Emigration in the period 1861–1900 was the equivalent of 16.0% of the total young adult males in rural counties and 8.5% of females compared with 15.0% of urban young adult males and 9.1% of females.

[58] Females had a higher than average propensity to emigrate from eight out of eighteen, and sixteen out of thirty-four rural counties.

[59] The main problem was that the fit of the equation which contained only these and similar variables was very poor. Nor were the variables all significant and some had unexpected signs. See Appendix 7 for a full description of the model used and the results.

every county was within 180 miles of one or both of these ports – an easy rail journey. The regions furthest from the emigration ports were South Wales and the West of England, both of which had exceptionally high emigration. This may have been because, before the steamships took over the emigrant trades, emigrants took passage from a large number of small ports, like Falmouth, and we would expect that the emigrants continued to leave, even if they had subsequently had to go *via* Liverpool. We would also expect that the inhabitants of the seaports were more informed about the emigrant destinations, whether the ports handled emigrants or not. Total emigration from coastal counties (that is counties containing a seaport capable of taking an ocean-going sailing vessel) was about 12% higher than emigration from inland counties (Table 6.6). Overall, emigration rates rose from east to west and emigration from the western coastal counties was about 9% higher than from the eastern coastal counties. Thirteen of the eighteen western coastal counties had male emigration rates above the mean for England and Wales compared with only three of the twelve eastern coastal counties.[60] But more important, Table 6.6 shows that natives of *inland* counties in the western half of the country were on average more likely to emigrate than natives of coastal counties in the eastern half of the country. And, finally the inclusion of a dummy to capture the presence or absence of a seaport did not improve the performance of our model. In other words, we can find no evidence that, taken as a whole, the population living in the vicinity of the ports were more likely to emigrate.[61]

The only comprehensive data available on the level of literacy in the counties in the last forty years of the nineteenth century is the ability to sign the marriage register. This is a very crude index of literacy which some experts have dismissed,[62] but it does have the merit of testing the ability to sign by the age group which was most likely to consider emigration. We would expect that the more literate the county population, the more informed they were about the (detailed) benefits to be gained by emigration. We would also expect potential emigrants in England and Wales to be better informed than their counterparts in continental Europe. It is thought that the British were more likely to rely on newspapers while on the continent poten-

---

[60] Eleven of the western coastal counties had mean female emigration rates above the mean level for England and Wales and only three of the eastern counties.

[61] It is also worth noting that natives of Lancashire which contained by far the most important emigrant port were about a third less likely to emigrate than natives of other western coastal counties.

[62] See, for example, the discussion in R. S. Schofield, 'Dimensions of illiteracy 1750–1850', *Explorations in Economic History*, 10 (4), 1973, pp. 440–1.

Table 6.6. *Emigration by natives of coastal and inland counties, 1861–1900 (net of returns). (% of total native population aged 15–24.)*

29 coastal counties		18 western	11 eastern
Males	16.1	17.4	15.1
Females	9.2	9.9	8.8
23 inland counties		10 western	13 eastern
Males	13.5	16.0	11.5
Females	7.9	9.9	6.2
England and Wales			
Males	15.4		
Females	8.9		

Notes:
Eastern counties: Northumberland, Durham, Yorkshire, Nottinghamshire, Leicestershire, Warwickshire, Oxfordshire, Berkshire, Hampshire and all counties to the east.
Western counties: Cumberland, Westmorland, Lancashire, Cheshire, Staffordshire, Worcestershire, Wiltshire, Dorset and all counties to the west.
Source: Appendix 1.

tial emigrants seem to have gained more information from letters (which were sometimes read aloud).[63] We did not find, however, that in our model the extent of literacy was a significant explanation of differential emigration rates (see Appendix 7).

Our migration model is described in detail in Appendix 7.[64] The dependent variable was the rate of migration (expressed as a proportion of the total native population) in each decade. This gave us fifty-two observations of male county emigration rates in each of four decades – 208 in all, and a further 208 observations of female emigration. Similarly, we had 208 observations of the rate of movement out of each county into all other counties for both males and females. The dependent variables were as follows: the proportion of the male and female population of each county who were aged 15–24; the proportion of the male population working in agriculture; the proportion of all males and females who signed the marriage register with a mark; the level of male agricultural wages; the proportion of the county population living in an urban area containing more than 20,000 per-

[63] Erickson, 'The English', p. 79.
[64] Most of the work on the model was undertaken by Dr Mary Morgan. The description of the model and the results discussed here are taken from her paper which is given in full in Appendix 7.

sons and the rate of migration (both overseas and to other counties) in the previous decade. The form of the model was therefore:

Net migration = $F(B_1$ age + B_2 agriculture + B_3 literacy + B_4 wages

$$+ B_5 \text{ urban} + B_6 \text{ migration})$$

We expected that emigration would be related to the number of people in the young adult groups and in the urban areas but to the *change* in the numbers in agriculture, literacy and wages since the previous decade. We expected that emigration would be positively correlated with the proportion of young adults, changes in literacy and the rate of emigration in the previous decade. We expected that emigration would be negatively correlated with changes in the proportion in agriculture and changes in the level of wages. We had no expectation of the effect of living in urban areas on emigration.

It is important to remember that emigration from the English and Welsh counties did not start in 1861. Some of the influences that affected the decision to emigrate were not new. For example, any flow of information is likely to have been cumulative. Potential emigrants could have been affected by the experience of previous emigrants who had left before 1861. Similarly, the effect of changes in the level of wages depended partly on the level of wages in 1861 and possibly on changes that had occurred before then. We could not, of course, assume that all the counties had the same economic and social characteristics in 1861. We were, however, able to proxy the effect of the past history of each county by the use of a dummy variable. Another difficulty is that there may have been factors in particular decades that are not captured by the variables, and which affected emigration from different counties. These factors could be overseas, for example, a mining boom or they could be domestic, for example, some political change. These effects were proxied by a second set of dummy variables.

The models were estimated by covariance analysis. The method used was to compare the most restricted model with the least restricted model. The most restricted model explained the rate of emigration from each county in each decade only with the variables which attempted to capture the condition of the labour market and the flow of information available to those people who were considering emigrating, that is all the variables which we detailed above. The least restrictive model included in addition the time and county dummies. The relation between the most and least restrictive models would tell us the relative importance of, for example, the extent of literacy and the level of wages on the decision to emigrate.

When the model was estimated, we found virtually no evidence that the rate of emigration from the counties was related to variables like the level of wages or the extent of literacy.[65] The fit of the equation was considerably improved by the addition of the dummy variables. The most restricted model of male and female emigration had an $\bar{r}^2$ of 0.1644 and 0.1681 respectively. This was improved to 0.5755 and 0.3193 by the inclusion of dummy variables.

Even in the least restricted model some of the coefficients were not significant or had wrong (i.e. unexpected) signs. In the 'best' explanation of female emigration, neither the proportion of young adults, the proportion literate, the level of wages nor the extent of urbanisation were significant and the proportion in agricultural occupations had an unexpected sign. All these variables together explained very little of the variance in emigration rates between counties.

On the other hand, the lagged dependent variable (the rate of emigration in the previous decade) was significant and had the expected sign. We took this to imply that chain migration was occurring. Further evidence for this was that male and female emigration rates were positively associated. This was not independent of the other variables, however. In other words, some circumstances would lead to an outflow of both male and female emigrants. Other circumstances would lead to an outflow with relatively more male emigrants or relatively more females. This may merely mean that some circumstances induced families to emigrate. Unfortunately we do not know what determined the sex balance of emigrants because most of the factors were captured only by the dummy variables.

Finally, our variables were quite successful in explaining migration from the counties into all the other counties. (At least, as far as it can be measured by this method.) The internal migration models have quite high R^2. The proportion of the population in agriculture and in urban areas was significant, and had the expected sign, as was the previous rate of internal migration, even in the most restricted model. The inclusion of time and county dummy variables further increased the degree of explanation and also increased the significance of the explanatory variables. In other words, internal migration from the counties can partly be explained by reference to their economic

---

[65] The model was not sensitive to the precise values of the emigration flows in each decade. For example, if the emigration rates were deflated by the total population in the county (as were the dependent variables) this would increase the apparent importance of emigration from the rural counties; but it made virtually no difference to the results.

circumstances, but unfortunately we have not been able to explain emigration in this way.

VI

Some tentative conclusions about the causes of emigration from England and Wales in the last forty years of the nineteenth century can be given. The highest emigration rates occurred from the rural counties of the West of England, Wales, Cumberland and Westmorland; and from the urban counties of London, Durham, South Wales and the West Midlands. East Anglia, Lincolnshire, the Home Counties, Lancashire, Yorkshire and the East Midlands produced few emigrants relative to their population. The majority of the emigrants had not been born in rural counties and emigration rates from rural counties were only marginally higher than from urban counties. If we include those emigrants from urban counties who had been born in rural counties, emigration rates from urban counties may have exceeded those from rural counties.

Our general interpretation of the results of the emigration model was as follows. It is fairly clear that the distribution of emigrants between the English and Welsh counties was not random, and that there was a pattern in the incidence of emigration. This conclusion is based on the fact that the dummy variables improved the fit of the equations. (It is also obvious from Figures 6.1 and 6.2.) Unfortunately, the pattern cannot be explained by the variables that were designed to capture the local economy and the situation in the labour market that the potenial emigrants were facing. In other words, the environment of some counties seems to have induced relatively more of their natives to emigrate, but we do not know the particular features of the environment that had influenced the emigrants.

Counties that had lost relatively large numbers of emigrants in one decade tended to lose relatively large numbers in the next decade, but this was not universally true. This may have been because an important change in the economic and social environment in an individual county was affecting the flow of emigrants.

The reason that we failed to explain differential emigration with variables that were designed to capture the condition of the labour market is probably one of four. In the first place, the emigration rate from a county may conceal great variations in the propensity to emigrate from different parts of that county. This could have been because there were local variations in, say, employment opportunities. In this case, we could only explain differential emigration if we had data tnat referred to individual communities, or perhaps to individual families. Our present data are inadequate. If the decision to emigrate depended on local factors it would also mean that potential internal migrants were much more widely spread through the counties than potential emigrants. (This is because our variables were successful at predicting internal migration.)

Another reason for the inability of our model to predict differential emigration rates is that the availability of information may have varied considerably. Our data on the information flow are not very satisfactory, to say the least. People in some areas could have been totally ignorant of the possibility of emigration and could not, therefore, have considered it. But it is unlikely that there were very many parts of the country that were totally ignorant of emigration. It is more likely that some people had a vague notion of emigration while others had a much more detailed and sophisticated understanding of the benefits they could gain from it. This view is supported by the wide fluctuations in the annual rate of emigration, which suggest that the emigrants were aware of the most favourable time to leave. In chapter 7, we examine emigration from individual counties in the 1880s, which was a decade when emigration should have been particularly attractive. We found that emigration rose from most counties which previously had relatively low emigration. This does not suggest that there were many parts of the country where information was scarce.

The third possible explanation is that information was fairly readily available in all counties, but the *threshold* which would induce an individual to emigrate was different. For example, a similar reduction in the number of jobs in agriculture (other things being equal) may have led relatively more people to emigrate from Devon than from Norfolk. Unfortunately, we do not know what were the factors that influenced this decision.

The final reason why we cannot explain differential emigration may be because internal migration may have been a substitute for emigration. The counties which lost relatively fewer emigrants may have been sending relatively more people to other parts of England and Wales. This proposition is examined in detail in chapter 8. We found that the relation between overseas and internal movement was rather limited.

We suspect that the answer to the question why more people went from some counties than from others was partly because there were special circumstances in particular villages and (parts of) towns and partly because the quality of hard information about emigration was very varied – although few people were ignorant about it. In short we think that our evidence is consistent with the view that emigrants were heavily dependent on the experience of people who had gone before. This may mean that emigration tended to run in families.

7

English and Welsh emigrants in the 1880s and 1890s

I

The relatively high rate of emigration from Britain in the 1880s has, not unnaturally, attracted considerable scholarly attention. It used to be a common view, for example, that it was the consequence of an agricultural depression and that the fall in the rate of emigration in the 1890s was because agriculture revived.[1] This issue was examined by Charlotte Erickson in a well-known paper.[2] She was able to show that the majority of British emigrants to the U.S.A. in the 1880s had previously lived in urban areas. She also showed that large numbers of the emigrants were unskilled workers. Professor Erickson's findings suggest that an agricultural depression was not the main cause of the emigration, but they do not prove it. Among other things, we need to know where the emigrants had been born. If the condition of agriculture was related to the rate of emigration we would expect that the number of rural-born emigrants increased in the 1880s and decreased in the 1890s.

The course of emigration in the 1880s is part of a wider issue. We can assume that more people emigrated in the 1880s because the net benefits of emigration were greater in that decade than in other decades. But were these emigrants more likely to have come from those counties from which emigration had been high or from those counties where it had been low?

The answer to this question will provide some important clues about the significance of the flow of information. If the additional emigrants of the 1880s came from the counties with no recent tradition of emigration, it would be likely that many areas of the country were aware

[1] For example, Jones, *American immigration*, p. 194.
[2] Erickson, 'Who were?' (1972).

178

of the possibilities of emigration but that some people required a relatively larger stimulus than others. If, on the other hand, the additional emigrants of the 1880s came from the counties which had been losing emigrants heavily in the 1860s and 1870s the result could be interpreted in two ways. It could mean that the information flow was relatively limited or it might possibly mean that people in some counties knew about the benefits of emigration but those benefits were still below their emigration threshold.

II

It is not difficult to show that emigration must have been exceptionally attractive in the 1880s. The rate of emigration was greater in the 1880s than in any other decade in the nineteenth century from every north and west European country with a history of substantial emigration.[3] The near simultaneous increase in emigration in the 1880s suggests that there were some powerful attractive forces in the overseas countries of immigration.

It has long been known that the timing of immigration into the United States in the late nineteenth century was closely related to the trade cycle.[4] The 1880s was a period of considerable prosperity in the United States. The two cyclical peaks (for example, in railroad construction) of 1882 and 1887 were separated by only a relatively minor downturn. On the other hand, the panic of 1893 was followed by a very serious depression and immigration fell markedly. Australia and Argentina also enjoyed rapid growth in the 1880s, and high rates of immigration, followed by serious depressions in the 1890s when immigration collapsed.[5] It has also been possible to link the rate of

---

[3] See Table 2.1. This table shows emigration from the main European countries expressed as the annual average in each decade from 1851–60 to 1901–10. Obviously, the precise emigration rates are very sensitive to the time periods chosen, but England and Wales, Norway, Sweden, Denmark, Switzerland, Germany and the Netherlands all had relatively higher emigration in 1881–90 than in any other decade. This was also true of Belgian and French emigration although the total number of emigrants was very low from these countries. The only countries where emigration in another decade exceeded that in 1881–90 were Scotland, where it was higher in 1901–10 and those countries where emigration in the third quarter of the nineteenth century had been very low. These were the countries of southern and eastern Europe, notably Italy, Portugal, Spain, Finland and Austria–Hungary.

[4] See Jerome, *Migration and business cycles*, p. 208.

[5] There were about 381,000 net arrivals into Australia in the 1880s, compared with 193,000 in the 1870s and only 23,000 in the 1890s. There were 638,000 net arrivals into Argentina in the 1880s compared with 86,000 in the 1870s and 319,000 in the 1890s. These data are calculated from Ferenczi and Willcox, *International migrations*, pp. 540, 542, 907, 947.

emigration with fluctuations within Europe as well as overseas, in Sweden, for example.[6]

The most influential work on the timing of emigration has followed the discovery of 'long swings' of eighteen to twenty years' duration in investment in Britain and the U.S.A.[7] (This issue is merely summarised here. It is discussed in detail in chapter 8.) 'Long swings' are thought to have occurred in 'population sensitive' investment such as housing and railways, the timing of which alternated in Britain and America. The peaks of the American cycle corresponded with peaks in the cycle of emigration and the peaks in the British cycle corresponded with troughs in the emigration cycle. An important linking mechanism was the long run fluctuations in the level of British home and overseas investment. According to Professor Brinley Thomas, with whom much of this work is associated, the British building cycle peaked in 1877, fell to 1887 and peaked again in 1899. The American cycle went from a trough in 1878 to a peak in 1890. This meant that throughout most of the 1880s, the rate at which new jobs were created in Britain was slowing down but the rate of job creation in the U.S.A. was increasing. The opposite was true in the 1890s. Emigration from Britain to the U.S.A. would be very attractive in the 1880s and very unattractive in the 1890s.

III

Our examination of emigration from England and Wales in the peak decade 1881–90 and the decade of low emigration in 1891–1900 is subject to some reservations. In the first place, the decades do not exactly correspond to turning points in the annual rate of emigration. The decades do roughly correspond to important phases of emigration, however. The decade 1881–90 captures the bulk of the years of extremely heavy emigration of 1879–91, and the decade 1891–1900 captures most of the years of low emigration which were 1894–1901.[8] In any case, the data on annual emigration are subject to a largely unknown degree of error. The only proxy for annual emigration is the recorded number of outward bound passengers. We can show that *inward* passenger movement must have been about a half of

---

[6] Thomas, *Swedish population movements*, pp. 166–9.

[7] See Thomas, *Migration and economic growth*, and *Migration and urban development*.

[8] Outward passenger movement peaked in 1873, 1883, 1888 and 1895. In the 1880s, annual movement was always between 183,000 and 126,000. This compares with a minimum of 72,000 and a maximum of 123,000 in the 1870s and 87,000 and 138,000 in the 1890s. See Appendix 4.

outward in the last three decades of the nineteenth century,[9] but we do not know the annual rate of return. It is possible that the apparent fluctuations in the number of emigrants were countervailed by variations in the annual number of returned migrants or in the movement of people who were not migrants.

A second difficulty is that our estimates of the level of emigration in a decade are subject to estimation error. This does not affect the estimates of the mean level of emigration for the forty years 1861–1900, because it is legitimate to assume that most of the errors in the deaths of lifetime migrants would net out over the whole period. But in any one decade, the emigration of the natives of a particular county could only be estimated within limits determined by an error of ±5% in lifetime migrant deaths.[10] The estimate of the long run age structure of current migrants (the key assumption) cannot be seriously wrong, but, obviously, in any one decade the current migrants who had been born in a particular county could have been exceptionally young or exceptionally old. Similarly, the mortality experienced by a particular group of lifetime migrants in any one decade, may have deviated substantially from the trend of lifetime migrant mortality over the forty years appropriate to that particular group.

We can be fairly sure, however, that our estimates of total emigration of English and Welsh natives in each decade are subject to less error than the sum of the emigration from the constituent counties. It is extremely unlikely that the current migration flows from the whole of England and Wales in any one decade were on average exceptionally young or exceptionally old or that the majority of lifetime migrant groups were subject to exceptional mortality. Finally, any undetected errors caused by the misenumeration of lifetime migrants in the census net out when we sum the emigration from the fifty-two counties.

---

[9] See Table 5.2 and the discussion of return emigration in chapter 5.

[10] It may be convenient to restate the significance of the limits in our estimates. The precise effect of an error in the lifetime migrant deaths of ±5% in any one county depends on the rate at which in-migration was occurring, but in most counties it would be the equivalent of an error of about ±10% in the implied age-specific mortality of lifetime migrants. Since migrant mortality must approximate that of the entire county population errors from this source are unlikely to be large. Alternatively, an error in migrant deaths of ±5% corresponds to the most probable effect of an error in the age distribution of current migrants. If we compare the youngest conceivable age distribution of current migrants (net of returns) with the oldest conceivable the effect could be to reduce the implied lifetime migrant death rate by about 10%. But the true range of error must be much less. It must also be remembered that the maximum effect of an error in the age-specific mortality of migrants cannot occur simultaneously with the maximum effect of the age distribution of current migrants. It is reasonable to assume, therefore, that the great majority of our estimates of migrant mortality lie within a range of error of ±5%. See chapter 4.

It seems reasonable to assume that about half of the errors that occur in each estimate of emigration from the individual counties would net out if we summed the county estimates in each decade. Hence, we assume that our decade estimates for the whole of England and Wales are correct to about ±2½% in lifetime migrant deaths.

IV

Something under 500,000 or about 2.4% of the native population of England and Wales emigrated (net of returns) in the 1860s. Emigration was at about the same level in the 1870s (2.1% of the native population) but rose sharply in 1881–90 when over 800,000 emigrants or 3.1% of the native population left the country, and did not return. In the 1890s, however, net native emigration fell to less than 400,000 people which was only 1.3% of the native population, and by far the lowest rate in any of the four decades.

We cannot be precisely sure of the proportion of female emigrants because of estimation errors, but they must have been between 36% and 42% of all emigrants in the 1860s, 1870s and 1880s. In the 1890s, however, the share of females fell markedly and they may have been less than 25% of all emigrants.[11] The number of male and female emigrants in each decade is shown in Table 7.1 and the percentage of females in Table 7.2. The estimates in these tables *exclude* migration to Scotland and Ireland. The total number of English and Welsh emigrants which is shown in these tables is, therefore, about 200,000 (or about 9%) less than our estimates of the sum of emigration from the individual counties.[12]

The relative importance of the urban and rural parts of the country in each decade is shown in Table 7.3. The contribution of the rural counties is summarised in Table 7.4. It is clear that the condition of agriculture cannot have been the dominant cause of the rise in the number of emigrants in the 1880s and the fall in the 1890s. Table 7.4 shows that when emigration was high in the 1880s, the proportion of emigrants who had been born in rural counties was *lower* than it had been in the 1870s. When emigration slowed down in the 1890s

[11] This may seem surprising, but it is more likely that our estimate of female emigration in the 1890s is an *overestimate*. See Table 4.5. The low rate of net female emigration in the 1890s is almost certainly a consequence of an exceptionally high rate of return. See Table 5.2.

[12] The estimate of 200,000 'emigrants' to Scotland and Ireland excludes those known to have gone from Cumberland and Northumberland. See chapter 4.

Table 7.1. *Net native emigration from England and Wales, decades, 1861–1900*

	1861–70		1871–80		1881–90		1891–1900	
	000s	%	000s	%	000s	%	000s	%
Males	291.6 ± 15.4	(2.9 ± 0.1)	294.1 ± 16.7	(2.6 ± 0.1)	505.5 ± 17.3	(4.0 ± 0.1)	292.8 ± 18.8	(2.1 ± 0.1)
Females	200.3 ± 14.8	(1.9 ± 0.1)	193.1 ± 16.0	(1.6 ± 0.1)	305.6 ± 17.8	(2.3 ± 0.1)	78.1 ± 19.1	(0.5 ± 0.1)

Note: Excludes migration to Scotland and Ireland.
Source: Appendix 1.

183

Table 7.2. *Female % of all emigrants*
(net of returns), 1861–1900

	%
1861–70	38–44
1871–80	36–42
1881–90	37–38
1891–1900	16–26

Note: The exact proportion of female
emigrants is not known because of the
range of error in the estimates. In 1861–70,
for example, male emigration must have
been between 276,000 and 307,000 and
female emigration between 185,500 and
215,000.
Source: Table 7.1.

the proportion of emigrants who had been born in rural counties was
almost certainly higher. Between 1871–80 and 1881–90 the number
of emigrants who were natives of rural counties increased by between
43,000 and 100,000 whereas the number of emigrants who had been
born in urban counties increased by between 193,000 and 320,000.
When agriculture improved in the 1890s, the number of rural-born
emigrants fell by only 89,000–150,000, but the number of urban-born
emigrants fell by between 240,000 and 396,000.[13] These results confirm
the work of Charlotte Erickson who was the first to show that most
of the emigrants in the 1880s came from the urban areas.[14] In addition,
it is now clear that most of the emigrants of the 1880s must have
been *born* in the urban counties. They were not rural-born people
who had been living in an urban county.

It is important to remember that the heavy fall in the number of

---

[13] It is unlikely that a disproportionate number of emigrants in the 1880s came from
the rural parts of urban counties. Fluctuations in emigration from the highly urbanised
counties (London, Warwickshire, Staffordshire and Lancashire) were very similar
to fluctuations in emigration from the less urbanised counties like Cheshire and
Leicestershire. The number of emigrants who had been born in the four most urbanised counties rose from the 1870s to the 1880s by between 95,000 and 181,000.
It is likely, therefore, that the observed increase in the number of urban emigrants
in the 1880s reflects changes in the number of emigrants who were born in urban
areas; rather than a disproportionate increase in the number of emigrants who had
been born in the rural parts of urban counties.
[14] Erickson, 'Who were?' (1973), pp. 360–1.

emigrants from the rural counties in the 1890s was not because there was a shortfall in the number of young adults in their populations. This explanation is obviously plausible. Emigrants and internal migrants were heavily weighted with young adults.[15] It is possible that continuous out-migration from the rural counties could have reduced the proportion of young adults in the population. In particular, it could have reduced the birth rate so that the pool of prospective emigrants was smaller. In other words, the children of the rural migrants were born in an urban county or overseas.

We cannot test this proposition directly, because we do not know the number of emigrants who left from the rural counties, only those who had been born in rural counties. But it is clear that there was no shortfall in the total number of young adults in England and Wales who had been born in rural counties. We described a technique for estimating the native population of a county who were aged 15–24 in chapter 4. These estimates are summarised in Table 7.5. This table shows that there must have been a continuous increase in the number of 15–24-year-olds who had been born in the rural counties – from about 1,470,000 in the 1860s to about 1,778,000 in the 1890s. In particular, there were *more* rural-born young adults living in England and Wales in the 1890s than there had been in the 1880s despite heavy emigration in that decade. In the 1880s, the emigrants who had been born in rural counties were between 15% and 17% of their young adult population. But in the 1890s the emigrants were only between 7.6% and 9.4% of the same group (Table 7.6). This can be taken to mean that only about half the rural-born young adults chose to emigrate in the 1890s than had done so in the 1880s, or that it would have been possible for twice as many rural-born emigrants to have left the country in the 1890s without digging any deeper into the older age groups.

An objection to this conclusion, is that large numbers of the rural emigrants may have been stage emigrants, who left from an urban county to which they had previously moved. If this were the case, it would have been possible for the population at risk in the rural counties to have been falling, when it was rising in the country as a whole.

This cannot have been the case, however. In the first place we know from the census that there was no fall in either the number or the proportion of young adults in the rural counties up to the

---

[15] The contemporary and current literature is discussed in chapter 4.

Table 7.3. *Net native emigration by regions and by urban and rural counties, 1861–1900 (000s)*

Born in		1861–70	1871–80	1881–90	1891–1900
Urban 1	M	100.5 ± 10.0	101.4 ± 10.0	177.9 ± 10.3	117.3 ± 11.0
	F	92.7 ± 9.0	81.4 ± 10.3	117.9 ± 10.8	40.5 ± 11.6
Urban 2 less urbanised	M	58.5 ± 6.0	46.0 ± 7.1	112.7 ± 7.1	58.5 ± 8.3
	F	43.1 ± 5.7	33.2 ± 6.2	75.4 ± 10.7	17.1 ± 7.7
S.E. suburban/rural	M	20.7 ± 3.6	29.8 ± 4.0	54.4 ± 4.5	28.7 ± 5.3
	F	10.0 ± 3.3	15.4 ± 3.8	26.0 ± 4.7	2.7 ± 5.0
Industrial Wales	M	17.9 ± 0.9	13.0 ± 0.9	13.2 ± 1.1	7.9 ± 1.3
	F	14.1 ± 0.7	11.7 ± 0.8	8.3 ± 0.9	+2.0 ± 1.1
Rural West of England	M	52.1 ± 2.4	57.9 ± 2.9	60.0 ± 2.9	40.7 ± 2.8
	F	23.5 ± 2.6	36.4 ± 2.7	31.8 ± 3.1	20.7 ± 3.3
East of England	M	17.5 ± 1.8	16.0 ± 2.3	35.1 ± 2.4	19.6 ± 2.2
	F	7.0 ± 2.1	12.4 ± 2.2	14.2 ± 2.5	6.3 ± 2.6
South Midlands	M	12.1 ± 1.8	22.4 ± 2.1	14.3 ± 2.2	16.9 ± 2.4
	F	— ± 2.2	11.3 ± 2.3	9.5 ± 2.5	3.2 ± 2.8
Rural Wales and Borders	M	26.7 ± 2.2	20.5 ± 2.2	36.4 ± 2.2	15.8 ± 2.4
	F	18.0 ± 2.0	5.0 ± 2.0	22.7 ± 2.2	11.1 ± 2.2

Other rural	M	12.1 ± 1.7	11.0 ± 1.8	27.7 ± 1.9	11.7 ± 1.9
	F	11.8 ± 1.6	5.5 ± 1.7	18.5 ± 1.8	4.7 ± 2.0
All urban 1	M	100.5 ± 10.0	101.4 ± 10.0	177.9 ± 10.3	117.3 ± 11.0
	F	92.7 ± 9.0	81.4 ± 2.2	117.9 ± 10.8	40.5 ± 11.6
All urban 2	M	97.1 ± 5.3	88.8 ± 6.0	180.3 ± 6.4	95.1 ± 7.5
	F	67.2 ± 7.4	60.3 ± 8.2	112.4 ± 9.6	17.8 ± 10.5
All rural	M	120.5 ± 5.0	127.8 ± 5.7	173.5 ± 5.8	104.7 ± 5.9
	F	60.3 ± 8.0	70.6 ± 8.4	96.7 ± 9.3	46.0 ± 9.8

Key:
Urban 1. London and Middlesex, Lancashire, Warwickshire, and Staffordshire.
Urban 2. Less urbanised. Yorkshire, Durham, Northumberland, Cheshire, Nottinghamshire, Gloucestershire, Leicestershire.
S.E. suburban/rural. Essex, Kent, Surrey, Hampshire, Sussex.
Industrial Wales. Monmouth and Glamorgan.
West of England. Wiltshire, Dorset, Devonshire, Cornwall, Somerset.
East of England. Huntingdonshire, Cambridgeshire, Suffolk, Norfolk, Lincolnshire, Rutland.
South Midlands. Northamptonshire, Bedfordshire, Buckinghamshire, Hertfordshire, Oxfordshire, Berkshire.
Rural Wales and Borders. All Wales except Glamorgan and Monmouth plus Herefordshire and Shropshire.
Other rural. All other counties (Derbyshire, Cumberland, Westmorland, Worcestershire).
Notes: Includes migration to Scotland and Ireland, except from Northumberland and Cumberland. For the definition of urban and rural counties, see chapter 6. (In the counties that were designated 'urban' the mean population living in urban areas containing more than 20,000 persons was at least 35%, except in Surrey, where it was 33.5%.)
Source: Appendix 1.

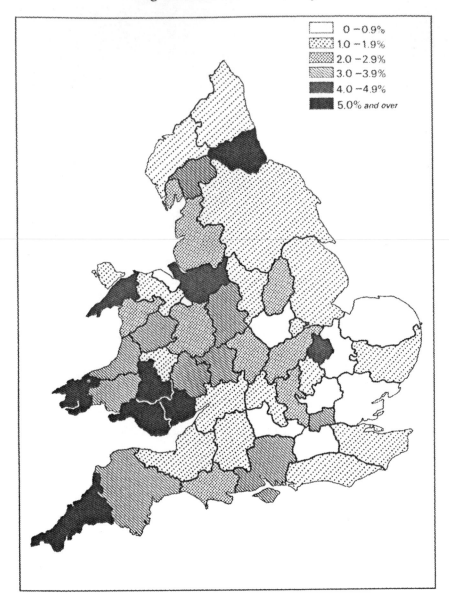

Figure 7.1 *Native emigration from English and Welsh counties (net of returns), decades, 1861–1900 as a % of total native population (mid-range estimates), 1861–70*

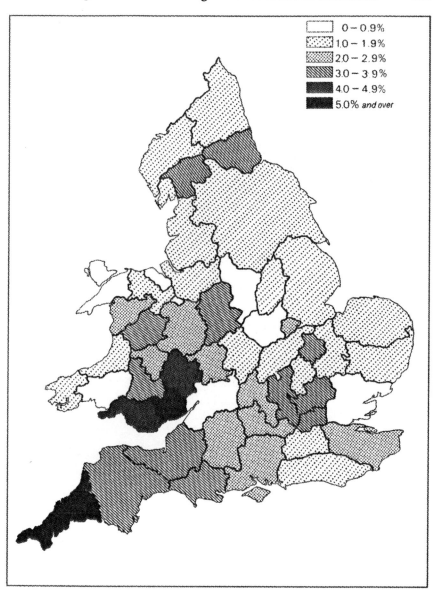

Figure 7.2 *1871–80*

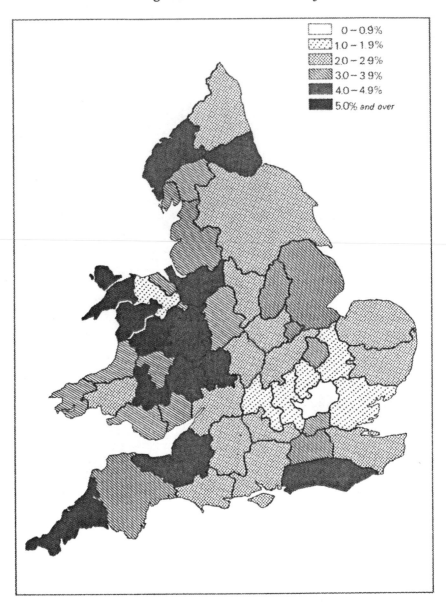

Figure 7.3 *1881–90*

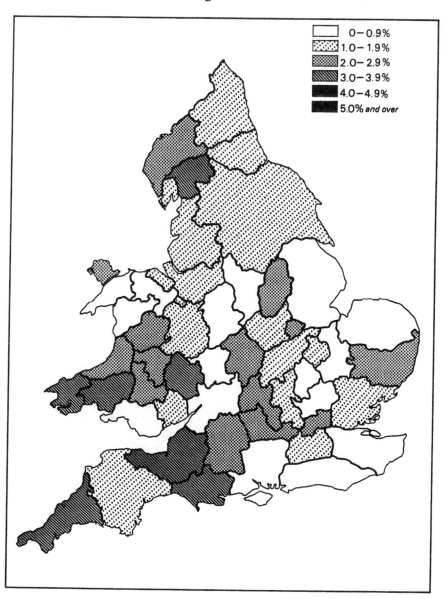

Figure 7.4 *1891–1900*

Table 7.4. *Emigration (net of returns) by natives of rural counties,*
1861–1900

	000s	% of all emigrants
1861–70	167.8–193.8	31.1–36.0
1871–80	184.3–212.5	34.8–40.1
1881–90	255.1–285.3	29.7–33.2
1891–1900	135.0–166.4	32.0–39.5

Note: The exact percentage of emigrants who were born in the rural counties
is not known because of the degree of error in the estimates.
Source: Tables 6.1 and 7.3.

Table 7.5. *Natives of rural counties aged 15–24 living in England and Wales*
(000s)

	1861–70	1871–80	1881–90	1891–1900
Males	736.1	781.8	849.8	893.2
Females	733.1	772.9	832.1	884.6
	1469.2	1554.7	1681.9	1777.8

Source: Appendix 1 and Table 7.3. See chapter 4 for the method of estimating
the percentage of the native population of each county that were aged 15–24.

Table 7.6. *Net emigration by natives of rural counties as a % of those aged*
15–24 (% of mid-decade population)

1861–70	1871–80	1881–90	1891–1900
11.4–13.2	11.9–13.7	15.2–17.0	7.6–9.4

Source: Appendix 1.

1890s.[16] Secondly, we have been able to estimate from the census
that the population who had been born in the rural counties and who
were living in the urban counties was too small to have provided

[16] For example, the proportion of young adults (15–34) *increased* in all but three of
the thirty-four rural counties between 1861–70 and 1891–1900. Nor were there any
significant differences between the proportion of the rural and urban populations
that were aged 15–34. In 1861–70, only three of the eighteen urban counties had
more than 34.0% of the population in this age group and no rural county had less
than 29.0%. In 1891–1900 there were only two rural counties with less than 30%
and only four urban counties with over 36%. We must remember that the proportion

Table 7.7. *Proportion of female emigrants (net of returns) who were born in urban and rural counties in each decade, 1861–1900·*

Born in	1861–70 %	1871–80 %	1881–90 %	1891–1900 %
Urban 1	47–48	39–50	36–43	18–33
Urban 2	40–42	36–45	36–41	1–25
Rural	32–36	32–39	33–39	26–37
All counties (England and Wales)	38–44	36–42	37–38	16–26

Source: Appendix 1. For the definition of urban and rural counties see Table 7.3.

a large proportion of the rural-born emigrants.[17] For example, it can be shown that even if a rural–urban move doubled the propensity to emigrate, the number of emigrants from urban areas who had been born in rural counties *or in the rural parts of urban counties* would still be less than 39% of all the rural-born emigrants. This result, which is an absolute maximum estimate, means that more than 60% of rural-born emigrants must have gone *direct* from a rural area. This estimate reinforces our view that the decline in the number of rural-born emigrants in the 1890s cannot have been a consequence of changes in the age structure of the population of the rural counties.

V

There appears to have been some important trends in the sex composition of emigrants in the last four decades of the nineteenth century. Table 7.7 shows that the share of female emigrants was very similar in 1861–70, 1871–80 and 1881–90. Again, it is impossible to be precise because of estimation errors, but between 36% and 44% of all emigrants in these decades were female. But in the 1890s no more than 26% were female and the percentage may have been as low as 16%.

The reason for the change in sex ratio was that the proportion of females among urban emigrants was probably falling in the 1880s and suffered a decisive fall in the 1890s. Table 7.7 shows the proportion

of young adults in the total population of a rural county underestimates the proportion of young adults in the total native population (the population at risk) because there were more young natives of a rural county living in other counties (POPji) than there were young natives of other counties living in the rural county (POPji).

[17] See Table 9. The method used to estimate the maximum number of state emigrants who had been born in rural counties is discussed in detail in chapter 9.

Table 7.8. *Proportion of emigrants (net of returns) in each decade who were born in urban counties, 1861–1900*

	1861–70 %	1871–80 %	1881–90 %	1891–1900 %
Males	60–64	57–62	66–68	64–69
Females	70–74	63–70	68–73	47–64

Source: Appendix 1. For the definition of urban counties see Table 7.3.

of female emigrants from the four highly urbanised counties (London, Lancashire, Staffordshire and Warwickshire), from the less urbanised counties and from the rural counties. The share of females from the highly urbanised counties fell from 47%–48% in the 1860s to only 36%–43% in the 1880s. It is not clear when this fall occurred but it is probable that it was between the 1870s and 1880s. What is clear, is that there was a decisive fall in the share of female emigrants from the highly urbanised counties in the 1890s. In the 1860s, nearly a half of the emigrants from the highly urbanised counties were female. In the 1890s, on the other hand, between a third and a fifth of these emigrants were female.

The sex composition of emigrants from the less urbanised counties was not dissimilar. The proportion of females was roughly constant in the first three decades (36% to 45%), but fell markedly in the 1890s, when less than 25% of their emigrants were female. In the 1860s, between 70% and 74% of all female emigrants had been born in urban counties but by the 1890s only 47% to 64% had been born in urban counties (Table 7.8).

It is tempting to explain the fall in the proportion of female emigrants from the urban counties as a consequence of a shift from 'family' to 'individual' emigration.[18] In other words, the reason that there were relatively large numbers of female emigrants in the 1860s was because they were part of family parties. But in the 1880s and 1890s, there was an increase in the number of men travelling alone. This change in the nature of emigration could have occurred later in the rural counties, so that the proportion of female emigrants from rural counties remained relatively higher than from urban counties. This is unlikely to be the explanation, however. In the 1880s, for example, the probable fall in the share of females among urban emigrants occurred

[18] See chapter 3. The best summary of the character of the English emigrants is Erickson, 'The English'. This only covers emigration to the U.S.A. of course.

at a time when the total number of female emigrants was *rising*. This would imply either an increase in family emigration or an increase in the number of female emigrants travelling alone. A more plausible explanation is that the transition from family to individual emigration occurred at roughly the same time for men and women and that the sharp rise in the rate of female emigration from urban counties in the 1880s and the fall in the 1890s was because women were becoming more involved in emigration as individuals rather than as members of family parties. The great fall in the share of women in net emigration in the 1890s is most likely to have been a consequence of an increase in their rate of return. This would mean that women who left in the 1880s were more likely to return in the 1890s than were men who left in the 1880s.

VI

The idea that there was a 'transition' in the character of English and Welsh emigration is a very important one.[19] Simply stated, the emigrants in the early part of the century could loosely be described as 'settlers'. They travelled as families and were unlikely to return to England. It is also thought that the early emigrants had above average incomes. It is possible that the motive for emigration was to improve a particular life style or to maintain a life style that was threatened by economic change at home. But it is fairly clear that in the second half of the century English emigrants became increasingly willing to go abroad for a short term advantage. Obviously, the number of people who were prepared to emigrate for a short period and then to return was greater than the number who were prepared to settle abroad. So the increase in the flow of information from abroad and the fall in the cost of transport, was associated with an increase in the rate of emigration and in the rate of return. The implication of this view is that in the years when emigration was at a peak, the emigrants were nearer to a sample of the whole population than in the years when emigration was relatively low. They were also more likely to go to the U.S.A. We know from Professor Erickson's work that there were relatively more urban labourers among the emigrants in the 1880s than in her sample from the early years of the century.[20]

Our estimates also suggest that there were relatively more urban emigrants in the 1880s. Table 7.4 shows that about 35% to 40% of

[19] See Erickson, 'The English', p. 326.
[20] Erickson, 'Who were?' (1972), pp. 360–1 and 'Emigration from the British Isles'.

all emigrants in the 1870s had been born in rural counties compared with about 30% to 33% in the 1880s and 32% to 40% in the 1890s. In other words, about 60% to 65% of all emigrants had been born in urban counties in the 1870s. This rose to 67% to 70% in the 1880s when emigration was at its peak. But urban-born emigrants were still 60% to 68% of all emigrants in the 1890s even though emigration had fallen to an extremely low level. The estimates may be misleading, however. In the first place, they are not corrected for the population at risk. Since the urban population of England and Wales was increasing, correcting for the population at risk would, for example, reduce the proportion of urban emigrants in the 1890s relative to the 1880s. Secondly, our estimates show only the *county of birth* of the emigrants and, for example, may conceal heavy emigration from the urban areas in the 1880s of people who had been born in rural areas.

There is another issue which is related to the spread of information. If the flow of information was greater to those areas from which emigration had been high for some time, we would expect that in the years when emigration was particularly attractive, a relatively large number of (short-term) emigrants would leave those counties. If this view is correct we would expect the additional emigrants of the 1880s to have come, not necessarily from the urban counties, but from those counties – urban and rural – where the tradition of emigration was high. On the other hand, information could have spread easily to most parts of the country. In this case, in the years when emigration was most attractive we would expect the additional migrants to have come from a wide range of counties and not just those with a history of high emigration.

It is, of course, obvious that the rate of emigration from a county in a particular decade was partly determined by factors that were unique to that county – like the decline of a particular industry. We cannot infer from the timing of emigration from a particular county that it was determined by the immediate attractiveness of overseas countries. On the other hand, it is only in the case of the smallest counties that local factors would be likely to be so important.

It is also necessary to distinguish between the factors that determined the propensity to emigrate and those that determined when the emigration occurred. For example, the decline of a local industry might have made people more likely to emigrate, but they would be less likely to do so if they knew, for example, that the labour market in the U.S.A. was very tight. But if, subsequently, they discovered that the labour market was buoyant, it could tip the balance in favour of emigration. It is clear that the timing of emigration must have been heavily influenced by short run conditions in overseas countries.[21] We also know that the great variation in emigration rates from English and Welsh counties could not be explained by changes in the structure of employment, and wages, or population pressure[22] (see chapter 6 and Appendix 7). This probably means, either that some areas of the country were substantially better informed about the benefits of emigration than others, or that there was no shortage of information but that the degree of response to it was very varied. We would not expect, for example, that two builder's labourers with identical incomes would have the same response to a newspaper report of a shortage of builder's labourers in New York.

The relative importance of the 'information flow' effect and the 'threshold effect' can be tested by comparing the contribution of individual counties to the heavy emigration in the 1880s. Our conclusions about the flow of information would probably depend on whether we found that the additional emigrants came from the traditional counties of emigration or from counties where emigration had previously been low.

VII

This section examines the contribution of the urban counties to emigration in the individual decades and particularly in the peak decade of the 1880s. An important initial observation is that Londoners may not have been more likely to emigrate in the 1880s than they were in the 1870s[23] and that emigration from industrial South Wales definitely fell. At the same time, emigration from some important rural counties rose. There was a marked increase in the rate of emigration in the 1880s from the other urban counties but this was from a low level. Hence, not all the counties where emigration increased in the 1880s were urban, and not all the counties where emigration failed to increase were rural.

The proportion of all emigration between 1861 and 1900 that

---

[21] Jerome, *Migration and business cycles*, p. 208. Thomas, *Swedish population movements*, pp. 166–9. This issue is discussed in chapter 2.

[22] The detailed results are set out in Appendix 7.

[23] Our data are insufficiently precise for us to be sure that London-born emigration rose in the 1880s or not. The male emigration rate was 4.0% ± 0.5% in the 1870s and 4.7% ± 0.4% in the 1880s. Female emigration was 3.2% ± 0.5% and 2.9% ± 0.4% respectively. Compared to the majority of urban counties this change in emigration rates is very low. Many of the urban counties that 'peaked' in the 1880s had an increase in emigration rates of two or three percentage points, net of estimation errors.

occurred in each decade, is summarised in Table 7.9.[24] The data have been corrected for the population at risk. Table 7.9 assumes that the total native populations of the regions grew at the same rate and that the total native populations had the same relative size as in 1861–70.

Table 7.9 shows that there was considerable variation in the share of total emigration from each region that occurred in the 1880s. The English urban counties (excluding London) lost about 40% of their total emigration in this decade. But only about 30% of London emigration occurred in that decade and only 20% of emigration from industrial South Wales. There was a similar contrast between the rural counties. Less than 30% of total emigration from the rural west took place in the 1880s, but probably 36% of emigration from the rural east.

The fluctuations in the rate of emigration from urban counties were probably related to its rate. For example, between 3.5% and 4.5% of male Londoners emigrated (net of returns) in the 1870s and 4.3% to 5.1% in the 1880s. Male emigration from the suburban south-east counties (Surrey, Essex, Kent, Sussex and Hampshire) was 2.2% to 2.8% of their native population in the 1870s and 3.7% to 4.3% in the 1880s. Hence, the propensity to emigrate of male natives of these counties rose by at least a third and could have nearly doubled. But

[24] It is important to remember that our estimates are net of return emigrants and exclude temporary migrants. It is possible, for example, that there was relatively more temporary emigration from urban counties. In this case, our estimates of net native emigration from urban counties would include a smaller proportion of gross emigration. This might have been particularly true of the 1880s, for example, when it is known that large numbers of building workers left the industrial cities. On the other hand returns to England and Wales in the last three decades of the nineteenth century were very high – 54% of outward passenger movement. But this is unlikely to bias our results against the implied number of gross emigrants from urban counties too seriously. Only about 31% of the population lived in rural counties over the period as a whole. If, for the sake of argument, *none* of the returned migrants had been born in rural counties then 78% of outward passengers who had been born in urban counties must have returned. So, unless we assume that the rural born were *more* likely to return, the rate of return to urban counties must lie between 54% (equal chance of return) and 78% (no rural returns). However, it is obvious that some of the rural born must have returned, so that the true rate of return to urban counties must lie within this range. There is also some evidence that argues against an exceptionally high rate of return of urban born. We know that emigration from London (net of returns) may not have risen in the 1880s and that emigration from South Wales definitely fell. It is difficult to see how this could have been caused by an exceptional increase in the rate of return at a time when emigration from most other urban counties was rising. It seems more probable that our implicit assumption that there was not a great deal of variance between return emigration rates to urban and rural counties in the 1880s is correct. Return migration is discussed in detail in chapter 5.

Table 7.9. *Proportion of the total emigration (net of returns) from each region, per decade, 1861–1900 (corrected for the population at risk)*

		1861–70 %	1871–80 %	1881–90 %	1891–1900 %
Urban					
London	M	24.8 ± 4.3	25.5 ± 3.3	30.4 ± 2.6	19.6 ± 2.4
	F	33.4 ± 4.4	29.3 ± 4.2	27.0 ± 3.6	10.2 ± 3.3
Lancashire, Warwickshire, Staffordshire and all other industrial counties	M	27.3 ± 2.5	18.6 ± 2.4	36.5 ± 2.2	17.6 ± 2.2
	F	33.1 ± 3.8	20.8 ± 3.6	38.0 ± 3.4	8.0 ± 3.2
South East suburban counties	M	19.0 ± 3.3	24.2 ± 3.2	38.9 ± 3.2	17.9 ± 3.3
	F	23.0 ± 7.4	29.4 ± 7.2	43.7 ± 7.8	3.9 ± 7.3
Industrial Wales	M	43.8 ± 2.2	25.5 ± 1.7	20.9 ± 1.7	9.9 ± 1.5
	F	52.2 ± 2.7	33.4 ± 2.2	19.0 ± 1.9	(+4.6 ± 2.5)
Rural					
West of England	M	25.7 ± 1.2	27.7 ± 1.4	28.1 ± 1.4	18.4 ± 1.3
	F	21.8 ± 2.3	32.6 ± 2.4	27.9 ± 2.6	17.6 ± 2.8
East of England	M	21.5 ± 2.6	19.6 ± 2.8	38.3 ± 2.6	20.5 ± 2.3
	F	19.0 ± 5.8	31.6 ± 5.5	34.6 ± 6.0	14.8 ± 6.0
South Midlands	M	20.5 ± 3.0	35.1 ± 3.3	21.0 ± 3.2	23.4 ± 3.3
	F	— ± 10.6	49.6 ± 10.2	38.6 ± 10.2	11.9 ± 10.6
Rural Wales and Borders	M	27.7 ± 2.3	21.2 ± 2.2	35.9 ± 2.2	15.2 ± 2.3
	F	33.2 ± 3.7	9.0 ± 3.5	39.0 ± 3.9	18.8 ± 3.7
Other rural	M	23.8 ± 2.9	19.0 ± 2.7	30.0 ± 2.6	17.3 ± 2.3
	F	33.4 ± 3.9	15.3 ± 3.5	39.2 ± 3.5	12.2 ± 3.5
England and Wales	M	25.7 ± 11.2	22.7 ± 1.2	33.5 ± 1.1	18.0 ± 1.1
	F	30.0 ± 2.0	25.4 ± 1.9	34.5 ± 1.9	10.0 ± 1.8

Source: Appendix 1. For definition see Table 7.3.

the propensity of Londoners to emigrate could not have risen by much more than a third and may have fallen. Even so, Londoners were more likely to emigrate in the 1880s than natives of the surrounding counties. In other words, in the South East, the greatest additional pressures to emigrate were found in those counties where the tradition of emigration had not been strong.

This seems to have been generally true of all the urban counties. London-born emigration was more than a third higher than the average for England and Wales and exceeded the mean rate in every decade. It fell little if at all in the 1870s, rose little if at all in the 1880s and fell less than average in the 1890s (Table 7.9). Consequently, London emigration was relatively high in the 1870s and 1890s when emigration as a whole was relatively low. A particular feature of London emigration was that female emigration was exceptionally high in the 1860s and 1870s. Nearly a half of London emigration in those decades was female, which was between a fifth and a quarter of all female emigration from England and Wales. The rate of emigration from industrial South Wales over the whole period (3.5%) was nearly half as high again as it was from England and Wales (2.4%) but the pattern of emigration was quite different. It fell in every decade, and by the 1890s was substantially below the rate for England and Wales. Again, the proportion of female emigrants was also relatively large in the early decades (over 40%) but unlike London, male emigration was also exceptional. It is worth noting at this point, that the relatively large share of female emigrants from South Wales in the 1860s and 1870s is unlikely to have been simply a reflection of the lack of opportunity for women in the heavy industries. County Durham (the other area dominated by coal and iron) experienced high emigration, but the number of females was if anything relatively low. And the proportion of females was exceptionally high from London which had the most buoyant female labour market. We are left with the intriguing fact that the two urban regions where female emigration was relatively the most important were the least responsive to the signals that drew so many urban emigrants overseas in the 1880s.

Male and female emigration definitely rose from all eleven other urban counties in the 1880s, except male emigration from Staffordshire, and fell in the 1890s from every county except Warwickshire (i.e. – our lowest estimate of the rate of emigration in the 1880s is higher than our highest estimate in the 1870s; this means in effect that emigration increased in the 1880s by more than one percentage point except for Staffordshire-born males). The pattern from the southeast (suburban) counties was similar. Emigration definitely rose in the 1880s from all the five south east counties except Surrey and Essex (the latter for females only). Male emigration fell from every county in the 1890s and female emigration in Hampshire, Kent and Sussex. About 40% of total emigration from those counties (holding population constant) occurred in the 1880s compared with no more than 30% of total London emigration (Table 7.9).

With one exception, the urban counties where emigration may not have risen in the 1880s had relatively *high* emigration rates for the period as a whole. On the other hand, most of the counties from which emigration definitely peaked in the 1880s had relatively *low* emigration rates both in the 1880s and over the whole period. Table 7.10 shows this pattern. Monmouth, London, Glamorgan and Hampshire had mean emigration rates above the average for urban counties (12.0% of the 15–24-year-old age group). But their greatest emigration probably did not occur in the 1880s. Only one county (Surrey) which did not have peak emigration in the 1880s had relatively low emigration overall. But of the thirteen urban counties which did have peak emigration in the 1880s only four had relatively high emigration and nine were below the mean for all urban counties in the four decades.[25]

The implications of this pattern of emigration are discussed below. At this point, however, it is worth noting that the pattern of emigration from London and South Wales fits the fluctuations in the urban building cycle quite well. If we assume that the attractiveness of overseas destinations was greater in the 1880s than in the other three decades, then the failure of the natives of London and South Wales to respond to that stimulus could have been because of a counter-attraction at home. The counter-attraction could have been a high level of building activity. Building activity in most of the English provincial towns seems to have peaked in 1876 and 1878 and was at a low level through most of the 1880s.[26] On the other hand, building in London did not peak until the early 1880s[27] and remained at a high level in that decade. And building may have been increasing in South Wales in the 1880s.[28]

It seems probable that most of the urban counties whose emigration peaked in the 1880s did not have a strong tradition of (recent) emigra-

---

[25] The Spearman rank order correlation between average emigration rates from urban counties from 1861–1900 and the proportionate (second difference) increase in emigration between 1871–80 and 1881–90 is −0.5955. (This is significant at the 5% level.) We used the mid-point estimates of county emigration rates.

[26] Parry Lewis, *Building cycles and Britain's growth*, pp. 164–85.

[27] S. B. Saul, 'Housebuilding in England, 1890–1914', *Economic History Review*, 15, 1962, p. 134.

[28] J. H. Richards and J. Parry Lewis, 'Housebuilding in the South Wales coalfield 1851–1913', *Manchester School*, 24, 1956, p. 295.

Table 7.10. *Peak emigration in the 1880s and the mean emigration rate,
1861–1900. Natives of urban counties (Number of emigrants as a % of the
native population aged 15–24, 1861–1900)*

Counties from which emigration peaked in the 1880s (%)		Counties from which emigration failed to peak in the 1880s (%)	
		Monmouth	21.0
		London	17.9
Durham	17.1		
		Glamorgan	16.8
Cheshire	14.4		
Staffordshire	14.0		
Nottinghamshire	12.5		
		Hampshire	12.2
Warwickshire	11.6		
Lancashire	10.9		
Sussex	9.7		
Kent	9.0		
Yorkshire	8.4		
Northumberland	8.4		
		Surrey	7.9
Essex	6.7		
Gloucestershire	5.8		
Leicestershire	5.6		
All urban counties	12.0		
All English and Welsh counties	12.1		

Note: Emigration 'peaked' in the 1880s, if the lowest estimate of the rate of
emigration in that decade exceeded the highest estimate of the other decades.

tion. In the 1870s, about 43% (±5%) of all urban emigration came
from the eleven urban counties where emigration was clearly below
the average for England and Wales in that decade. Those counties
were Surrey, Essex, Sussex, Gloucestershire, Warwickshire, Leicestershire, Nottinghamshire, Cheshire, Lancashire, Yorkshire and Northumberland. In the 1880s, these same counties produced 58% (±5%)
of all urban emigrants. In other words the seven urban counties where
emigration had been relatively high in the 1870s, produced between
40,000 and 80,000 additional emigrants in the 1880s whereas the urban
counties where emigration had been relatively low, produced 165,000
to 235,000 additional emigrants. For every additional emigrant that
left the high emigration urban counties in the 1880s, between two
and six left a county where there had been relatively little recent emigration. Of course, some emigrants may have been born in the rural

parts of those counties. But it seems probable that natives of the majority of the urban counties including Lancashire, Yorkshire and the suburban south east had a relatively high emigration threshold. They would only emigrate when the incentive was particularly high.

VIII

It is more difficult to analyse the fluctuations in the rate of emigration from the rural counties. It seems that many of the urban-born emigrants in the 1880s came from counties which produced relatively few emigrants in the other three decades. But we can see in Table 7.11 that this was unlikely to have been true of the rural counties.[29] Emigration from thirteen of the thirty-four rural counties definitely peaked in the 1880s. Of these thirteen counties, nine had emigration rates for the period as a whole that were lower than the weighted mean rate from the rural counties as a whole.[30] But twelve of the twenty-one rural counties from which emigration failed to peak also had relatively low emigration rates for the period as a whole.

This result could be misleading, however. Our definition that emigration from a county peaked in the 1880s is that our lowest estimate of the rate of emigration in the 1880s exceeded our highest estimate in the other three decades.[31] The number of emigrants from some of the rural counties was very small. This means that the margin of error in our estimates is relatively large. (In the case of many of the small counties, for example, we cannot be sure that the rate of emigration peaked in the 1880s unless it was more than 1.5 percentage points above its highest levels in the other decades.) There is also the possibility that there are some (small) uncorrected boundary changes – notably in rural Wales. To account for these problems, we could eliminate the three English counties that had a population of less than 100,000 in 1901 (Huntingdon, Rutland and Westmorland) and combine the rural Welsh counties. This leaves twenty English counties and rural Wales. Emigration from eight of these, including rural Wales, peaked in the 1880s. Five produced relatively few emi-

---

[29] The Spearman rank order correlation between average emigration rates from rural counties from 1861–1900 and the proportionate increase in the rate of emigration between 1871–80 and 1881–90 is 0.0038.

[30] The weighted mean emigration rate from the rural counties was the equivalent of 12.3% of the 15–24 age group.

[31] It will be remembered that our estimates of the rate of emigration from individual counties are between limits imposed by errors of ±5% in the death rate of lifetime internal migrants who had been born in that county. The cause of possible errors is discussed in footnote 5 above and in detail in chapter 4.

Table 7.11. *Peak emigration in the 1880s and the mean emigration rate, 1861–1900. Natives of rural counties (Number of emigrants as a % of the native population aged 15–24, 1861–1900)*

Counties from which emigration peaked in the 1880s (%)		Counties from which emigration failed to peak in the 1880s (%)	
		Cornwall	35.4
Brecon	27.2		
		Herefordshire	19.7
Montgomery	19.4		
		Pembroke	18.3
		Westmorland	16.8
Merioneth	15.5		
		Huntingdonshire	15.4
		Somerset	15.1
		Devon	15.0
Cumberland	13.9		
		Dorset	13.6
Worcestershire	13.3		
Shropshire	12.1		
		Cardigan	12.1
		Rutland	12.0
		Buckinghamshire	11.3
		Wiltshire	10.9
		Northamptonshire	10.8
		Carmarthen	10.7
		Radnor	10.6
Suffolk	10.4		
Flint	9.8		
Caernarvon	9.3		
		Oxfordshire	9.0
Lincolnshire	8.9		
Anglesey	8.0		
Norfolk	7.0		
Derbyshire	6.3		
		Berkshire	6.1
		Denbigh	5.4
		Bedfordshire	5.4
		Cambridgeshire	5.3
		Hertfordshire	2.8
All rural counties	12.3		
All English and Welsh counties	12.1		
All rural Welsh counties	12.8		

Note: see Table 7.10.

grants for the period as a whole. But seven of the thirteen counties that failed to peak in the 1880s also had relatively low emigration rates. There does not seem, therefore, to have been any relation between the overall level of emigration from rural counties and their rate of emigration in the 1880s. The additional rural-born emigrants of the 1880s do not seem to have come from counties where the tradition of emigration was low.

There do seem to have been some important geographical patterns in rural emigration, however. Emigration from counties in rural Wales and the East of England was more likely to peak in the 1880s than emigration from counties in the West of England and the South Midlands. For example, more than 35% of emigration from rural Wales and the Borders between 1861 and 1900 occurred in the 1880s, but less than 30% from the West and South Midlands. (These proportions are corrected for the population at risk.) Emigration rose from the majority of the rural Welsh counties in the 1880s and fell in virtually all in the 1890s.

IX

This chapter has examined the birthplaces of English and Welsh emigrants in the last four decades of the nineteenth century. We have paid particular attention to the origins of the emigrants in the 1880s when emigration was at a very high level. The changes in the geographical origins of emigrants also provide some clues about the extent of information available to prospective emigrants, and, therefore, some clues about the decision to emigrate.

Our first conclusion was that the heavy emigration in the 1880s cannot have been caused by an agricultural depression. The number of rural-county-born emigrants in the 1880s increased by no more than 100,000 and possibly by much less. But there were at least 200,000 additional emigrants who had been born in the urban counties and there may have been more than 300,000. We can also show that the majority of the additional emigrants of the 1880s cannot have been stage emigrants – at least they cannot have been born in a rural county and have emigrated from an urban county.

The additional emigrants of the 1880s came from a wide range of counties – both urban and rural. But most of the urban counties which normally had relatively low emigration lost emigrants at a much higher rate in the 1880s. These included the important counties of Lancashire, Cheshire, Yorkshire, Warwickshire, Northumberland and Nottinghamshire, which meant that a greater share of the emigrants had been born in urban counties in that decade. Between 60% and 65% of all emigrants had been born in urban counties in the 1870s. This rose to between 67% and 70%.[32] The share in the 1880s would have been higher if the (already high) emigration from London had risen significantly and if emigration from South Wales had not fallen. London and South Wales were areas from which emigration had been relatively heavy in the 1870s. The distinctive pattern of emigration from these areas is consistent with the idea that the building cycle in London and South Wales was distinct from that in the country as a whole.

The fall in the number of emigrants from the rural counties in the 1890s was not because there was a shortfall of young adults which had been caused by continuous out-migration. The number of rural-born young adults increased in each successive decade[33] and age-specific emigration rates from rural counties in the 1890s were probably not much more than half their level in the 1880s. But emigration from the urban counties (taken as a whole) fell even more in the 1890s.[34] Hence, the fall in the number of emigrants in the 1890s could not have been caused by an agricultural revival.

Emigration rates from the majority of English and Welsh counties increased in the 1880s and were usually higher than in any other decade of the period. Emigration in the 1880s was at its peak rate from at least twenty-six of the fifty-two counties and it was definitely lower than in the 1860s, 1870s and 1890s in only six counties. The increase in emigration in the 1880s was not, of course, confined to England and Wales. The rate of emigration rose from virtually every country in northern and western Europe. We take this to mean that there were powerful attractive forces in the countries of immigration, although there may also have been particular forces operating within the European countries.[35]

Emigration seems to have been exceptionally attractive in the 1880s. We can start from an assumption, therefore, that if other things were equal, emigration would have peaked from every English and Welsh

[32] The share of urban and rural emigrants is corrected for the population at risk.
[33] Nor is it true that the young adult rural-born population was disproportionately concentrated in urban counties. The age structure of the rural counties only changed marginally between 1861–70 and 1891–1900.
[34] The fall in urban emigration in the 1890s was largely because of a fall in female emigration from urban counties. This was probably because there was an increase in the rate of female return.
[35] The increase of emigration from England and Wales in the 1880s was associated with an increase in the proportion of emigrants going to the U.S.A. This presumably means that there were fewer 'settlers' in the 1880s and more individual emigrants who were prepared to emigrate for a short time.

county in that decade. If emigration from a particular county did not peak in the 1880s it was presumably for one of two reasons. Either many of the county's inhabitants had not received any signal that told them about the advantages of emigration; or they were well informed about some overseas countries but some countervailing influences made emigration relatively less attractive.

There is an obvious objection to this hypothesis. Changes in the rate of emigration from a county may have been exclusively related to changes in the social and economic structure of the county itself.[36] In that case we would not be able to distinguish between the response to the flow of information and changes within England and Wales. It will be remembered, however, that after exhaustive testing, we could find no relationship between changes in native emigration rates from the counties and a set of demographic, social and economic variables which were designed to capture the conditions within the counties themselves, although it is possible that local conditions were important in individual cases. (The analysis is discussed in detail in Appendix 7.)

Our failure to explain the variance in county emigration rates is open to several possible interpretations but it seems plausible that the flow of information must have been an important variable. It was also clear that emigration rates from the counties were related to those in previous decades, which means that there must have been some long run (or historical) causes of emigration at work. We have used the device of an 'emigration threshold'. The emigration threshold denotes the amount of emigration from each county that would have occurred in each decade assuming that overseas conditions remained constant. In other words, we regarded the propensity to emigrate in each decade as a consequence of historical factors, which, naturally, included the rate of emigration in previous decades. This device

[36] Another possible objection is that the rural-born migrants may have been stage emigrants whose decision to emigrate was taken in an urban environment. This issue is discussed in detail in chapter 9. Our main conclusion was that rural–urban stage emigration could not have been very important in England and Wales. There were two main reasons for believing this. In the first place the lifetime migrant populations of the urban counties that had been born in rural counties were too small to have produced more than a third of rural county emigrants – even if we assumed that a rural–urban move *doubled* the propensity to emigrate. Secondly, the timing of rural-born emigration suggests that the majority went directly overseas. For example, there was a considerable increase in the rate of emigration of natives of many counties with large migrant populations in London. But there was no increase in the proportion of London-born emigrants. If the rural-born emigrants were stage migrants whose decision to emigrate was based on the conditions in London, why did the same conditions not induce more Londoners to emigrate? Similarly, rural Welsh-born emigration rose in the 1880s but emigration of natives of industrial South Wales fell.

enabled us to assume, for the purposes of argument, that the *timing* of emigration was largely determined by the attractiveness of overseas countries. This depended, in turn, on the amount and quality of information that was available to potential emigrants, and was, therefore, partly a consequence of the history of emigration from the country.

Broadly speaking, the emigration history of most counties in the last four decades of the nineteenth century falls into one of four models depending on their emigration in the 1860s and 1870s and their response to the favourable emigration conditions in the 1880s. The four models are as follows: counties where emigration was low (compared to England and Wales as a whole) in the 1860s and 1870s and remained low in the 1880s; counties where emigration had been low but increased markedly in the 1880s; counties where emigration was high in the 1880s but not significantly higher than in previous decades; and counties with a history of high emigration but where it increased markedly in the 1880s. The four models may imply rather different things about the flow of information.

Our categories must be regarded as rather tentative because the degree of error in our estimates make it impossible to be absolutely sure of the pattern of emigration from some of the counties in the 1860s and 1870s. A county was only regarded as having 'peak' emigration in the 1880s if our lowest possible estimate of its native emigration rate in that decade exceeded our highest estimate in the 1860s, 1870s and 1890s. A county was normally regarded as having a relatively high long run emigration rate if it was the equivalent of at least 15% of the 15–24 age group and a relatively low rate if it was the equivalent of 9% or less. (English and Welsh emigrants in the whole period 1861–1900 were 12% of the 15–24 age group.) The emigration history of twelve counties did not easily fit one of our four models and these counties could not be considered. Our models include only forty counties or 86% of all emigrants.[37]

The majority of emigrants in the last forty years of the nineteenth century came from counties where the rate of emigration increased markedly in the 1880s. And the majority of *these* emigrants came from counties which had relatively low emigration in the 1860s and 1870s. (Even in the 1880s, most of these counties were losing emigrants at a lower rate than England and Wales as a whole.) This

[37] We were not able to consider the counties of Hampshire, Dorset, Wiltshire, Suffolk, Northamptonshire, Rutland, Worcestershire, Warwickshire, Carmarthen, Cardigan and Caernarvon. The main reason was that their emigration rates were not dissimilar to the national average and, hence they could not be regarded, either, as having relatively high or relatively low emigration.

group included the urban counties of Lancashire, Yorkshire, Nottinghamshire, Gloucestershire, Leicestershire and Northumberland; the South East (partly suburban) counties of Kent, Surrey, Sussex and Essex; and the rural counties of Norfolk, Lincolnshire, Derbyshire, Cumberland, Shropshire, Flint, Radnor, Merioneth and Anglesey. Thirteen of the counties had a long run emigration rate below 9% of the 15–24 age group. Four (Sussex, Lancashire, Flint and Radnor) had slightly higher rates and two (Nottingham and Cumberland) had moderately high long run emigration.[38] All these six counties had relatively low emigration in the 1860s and 1870s but relatively high emigration in the 1880s. About 35% of all emigrants came from the nineteen counties and between 40% and 46% of all emigrants in the 1880s.

It is not clear whether the low rate of emigration in the 1860s was because the emigration threshold of most people living in these counties was high or because only a few people had adequate knowledge. We can assume that by the 1880s most potential emigrants were well informed, because if they were not, emigration would have been unlikely to increase markedly in that decade. It is possible that the amount of information increased exogenously in the 1880s, so that many people became aware of emigration at a time when it was particularly favourable. But it is difficult to believe that large numbers of the inhabitants of the large northern and midland cities which included, for example, many Irish immigrants, were unaware of the benefits of emigration before the 1880s. It is possible, however, that many natives of the rural counties, Lincolnshire and Norfolk, for example, were badly informed about emigration before the 1880s.

There were a few counties where emigration increased markedly in the 1880s but from a relatively high level. They included the industrial counties of Durham, Staffordshire and Cheshire and the rural Welsh counties of Montgomery, Pembroke and Brecon. In addition, it is likely that emigration from Somerset and Westmorland increased substantially in the 1880s but the estimates lay just outside our range of error. We can assume that many natives of these counties had been quite well informed about emigration *before* the 1880s. We can also assume that the emigrants who went in the 1880s had received some powerful signals from overseas. About 17% of all emigrants came from these counties and a similar proportion in the 1880s. To this group we could add the other two West Midlands counties

---

[38] Long run emigration rates from Lancashire and Sussex were 10.9% and 9.7%. The rest were substantially lower.

(Worcestershire and Warwickshire) both of which had substantially increased emigration but neither of which had particularly high or particularly low emigration.[39]

This means that between 59% and 69% of all emigrants in the 1880s came from counties where there had been a substantial increase in the rate of emigration. We can take this to mean that most of the emigrants in the 1880s had made a decision to emigrate which was based on some sort of signal that they were receiving. We can also be fairly sure that an important reason why emigration was lower in the 1860s and 1870s than in the 1880s was not lack of information, but because many potential emigrants chose to stay at home. This must have been true of many people living in the counties where emigration was high, like Durham, Cheshire and Staffordshire and it was probably also true of people in many other counties including Yorkshire and Warwickshire.

The other important group of counties were those where the rate of emigration in the 1880s was high but probably no higher than it had been in the 1860s and 1870s. (In some counties emigration fell.)[40] These counties were losing emigrants continuously in the 1860s and 1870s and at a relatively high rate, and we can assume that most of the emigrants were well informed. This group included London, the industrial counties of South Wales and the rural counties of Devon, Cornwall and Herefordshire. About 32% of all emigrants came from these counties of which more than half came from London alone.

A plausible explanation of the distinct pattern of emigration from these counties is that some strong countervailing forces were either increasing the rate of emigration in the 1860s and 1870s or reducing it in the 1880s. We have already referred to the fluctuations in building activity in London and South Wales which do not seem to have matched the building cycle in other urban areas.[41] Employment in this important sector in London and South Wales may have been increasing in the 1880s at a much faster rate than elsewhere. Similarly, emigration from Devon and Cornwall in the late 1860s and early 1870s was obviously related to the catastrophic collapse of copper mining. It is worth pointing out, however, that only about half of the Cornish

[39] Both counties had relatively high emigration in the 1860s and 1880s. The long run emigration rates were 11.6% of the young adult age group for Warwickshire and 13.3% for Worcestershire.

[40] Emigration definitely fell from Cornwall and Glamorgan in the 1880s and probably fell in Monmouth and Herefordshire. London emigration was probably the same as in the 1870s.

[41] Thomas, *Migration and urban development*, pp. 26–37.

emigrants and a much smaller proportion of the Devonian emigrants in these decades can have been connected with mining.[42] In other words, Devon and Cornwall were likely to have had high emigration even if there had been no depression in mining.

There is also a possible general explanation of the distinctive pattern of emigration from London, South Wales, the West of England and Herefordshire. We could conjecture that a part of their population had a low emigration threshold but that was *very low*. Emigration was always high from certain villages and parts of towns – which may mean it was high among certain families. Emigration was even more attractive in the 1880s, but it was not possible for it to increase because it could not have been much higher in previous decades. There were few emigrants from the rest of the population in the 1880s because their emigration threshold was too high.

This explanation is thought to be less likely than the idea that powerful countervailing forces – like the building cycle or the collapse of copper mining – may have increased emigration in the 1860s and 1870s and reduced it in the 1880s. If there had been no mining collapse in the West of England, for example, emigration would probably have peaked in the 1880s as it did from most other counties. If this is correct, it presumably means that potential emigrants from these counties made a decision on the *timing* of emigration in the same way that potential emigrants made a decision in the counties from which emigration peaked in the 1880s.

There are very few counties from which emigration was consistently low. They were Hertfordshire, Oxfordshire and Denbigh. Emigration from these counties was virtually always below the national average,[43] there was no peak in the 1880s and none lost more than the equivalent of 9% of their young adult population. It is possible that the emigration threshold in these counties was exceptionally high. That is, that quite a few people had considered emigration and rejected it – even in the 1880s. But these counties were all part of relatively remote rural regions where, for example, agricultural earnings were very low.[44] This is consistent with our view that these people had insufficient

---

[42] Rowe, *Cornwall in the age of the Industrial Revolution*, pp. 321–2, 325–8. There is some discussion of this point in chapter 6.

[43] Hertfordshire and Oxfordshire had relatively higher emigration in the 1870s but the numbers involved are very small.

[44] As late as 1898, the weekly agricultural labourer's wage in one of these counties (Oxfordshire) was only about 14s. 8d. per week and in another (Berkshire) was about 15s. 1d. Wages were between 16s. 1d. and 16s. 5d. in three of the other counties and 16s. 9d. in Denbigh. The average for England and Wales was about 17s. 2½d. E. H. Hunt, *Regional wage variations*, pp. 61–4.

information available to them to be able to consider emigration. Only 2% of emigrants came from these counties.

It is often suggested that emigration in the late nineteenth century was a marginal activity. The emigrants are often assumed largely to have been composed of people who did not come from places that were at the centre of economic change and who had been failing to benefit from many of the changes that were occurring in the rest of the economy. Another view is that the emigrants had little real knowledge about their destination beyond the fact that it was prefer-able to their part of England or Wales. Our examination of the pattern of emigration in the 1880s suggests that, in the main, both of these views are incorrect. The emigrants were no more likely to come from marginal parts of the country. In addition, when conditions overseas made emigration particularly attractive, there was a large increase in emigration from many industrial counties. This can only mean that the potential emigrants were well informed about their possible desti-nations. Most emigrants were not taking part in a 'flight to America'. Far more of them had the information and ability to weigh up the gains and losses of emigration.

IX

There was no simple reason (like an agricultural depression) for the increase of emigration in the 1880s. The additional emigrants came from a wide range of counties which suggests that the timing of emi-gration was related to something that was happening overseas. Our analysis of the pattern of emigration in the four decades suggests that at least 80% of all emigrants in the 1880s came from counties where the decision to emigrate seems to have been taken by people who had enough information to weigh up the advantages and dis-advantages. The emigration pattern also suggests that potential emi-grants in most of the large urban counties were well informed as early as the 1860s and this may also be true of many of the rural counties. Only a few rural counties had an emigration pattern that suggests that information was scarce.

8

Emigration and urban growth

I

The relation between urban growth and emigration has been an important issue in the literature on European emigration. Migration to the cities and emigration have often been thought of as substitutes because a potential emigrant had the option of moving to a city within his own country. The implication of this view is that (if other things remained equal) emigration would fall as a country became more urbanised.[1] It has been argued, for example, that the fall in the rate of emigration from Germany after the 1880s was because the eastern German emigrants were increasingly diverted to the industrial areas of western Germany.[2] It has also been argued that the high rate of emigration from Ireland and Italy in the same period was because there was little urban development.[3]

It is obvious that emigration must have been affected by urban growth and by modern industrial development. But it is not obvious that in most European countries there was a simple trade-off between rural–urban migration and emigration. The idea of a trade-off assumes that the emigrants came from the rural areas and is not dissimilar from a commonly expressed view that the emigrants came from those areas where there was no industrialisation.[4] But there are many coun-

[1] By the late nineteenth century the countries of immigration were becoming urbanised. There were rarely sufficient jobs created in the rural areas to absorb all the European immigrants. The European emigrant was faced with an implied choice of a move to an overseas city or a city in his own country.
[2] Walker, *Germany and the Emigration*, pp. 189–91. Köllman, 'The process of urbanisation in Germany', p. 61.
[3] See J. F. Meehan, 'Eire', in Thomas, *Economics of international investment*, p. 78.
[4] In general, the extent of urbanisation or industrialisation does not predict emigration rates from European countries very well. See chapter 2.

tries where urban growth does not seem to have inhibited emigration. Emigration rates from the urban areas of European countries were often high and sometimes higher than from the rural areas.[5] This was true of England and Wales in the late nineteenth century where there was hardly any difference between the propensity to emigrate of natives of urban and rural counties.[6] In addition, emigration from England and Wales *increased* as the country became more urban and industrial.

We would expect that urban growth affected emigration to a greater extent in Britain than in other countries. The country was more urbanised and there were few rural areas far from an important town. But it is not obvious whether we would expect urban growth to *increase* or *decrease* emigration. Urban growth could have increased the rate of emigration because the towns were nearer to the centre of economic change and closer to the important trade and shipping routes. Consequently, as the towns grew, people living in them became more informed about overseas countries and possibly acquired more contacts that were important to emigration. We have estimated that about one-third of all English and Welsh emigrants between 1861 and 1900 had been born in London, Lancashire and the West Midlands, which supports this view. It is also possible that migration to the towns, of itself, made subsequent emigration more likely.

On the other hand, urban growth may have inhibited emigration because it increased the options available to potential emigrants. Those living in rural areas, for example, could choose to go to an urban area. In some periods a move to another part of the country would possibly be more attractive than emigration. In this case, we would expect internal and overseas migration rates to be negatively correlated and to move inversely when we compare one decade with another. If the decision to emigrate was not related to what was happening in other parts of England and Wales, either because the internal migrants and the emigrants were drawn from different groups of people, or because emigration and internal migration were not seen as alternatives; we would expect the relevant migration rates to be positively correlated.

---

[5] Emigration from Danish and Norwegian cities is known to have been relatively higher than from the rural areas. See Semmingsen, 'Emigration from Scandinavia', p. 53. Semmingsen, 'Norwegian emigration', p. 156. Hvidt, *Flight to America*, pp. 45–51.

[6] Between 1861 and 1900 the urban counties lost the equivalent of 15.0% of their male native population aged 15–24 and 9.1% of their female population. The rural counties lost 16.0% and 8.5% respectively.

II

Potential English and Welsh migrants in the later nineteenth century were faced with an exceptional choice of destinations. The country had six important industrial regions, for example, London, Lancashire, the West Midlands, South Wales, Teeside and the West Riding, each of which had a distinctive industrial structure, and several second rank industrial areas like the Potteries and Humberside. There were also many industrial towns located within the rural counties (like Luton, Swindon and Lincoln). Lastly, agriculture in England and Wales was also very diverse and there were always some areas where agriculture (or horticulture) was expanding.

Potential European migrants were faced with a much easier decision than the English and Welsh. The smaller towns were less industrial and less diversified than their English counterparts and in many countries there were only a few important urban centres. In extreme cases like Finland or Denmark internal migration was dominated by only one city.[7]

This is not meant to imply that English and Welsh emigrants had considered migration to a range of towns and rejected it. Migrants could move along relatively well trodden paths and an Englishman did not need detailed information about every English region in order to benefit from migration. But we can assume that, between them, the entire population of a county would know a great deal about the rest of England and Wales. For example, a native of Rutland was enumerated in every English county in 1861 and in every Welsh county except Cardigan and Brecon.[8] The native population of Rutland at that time was only 16,400. English migrants were faced with a more complex decision than those on the continent of Europe. This does not mean that the English migrant could be more easily satisfied without leaving the country. If this was true, the rate of emigration from England and Wales would have been the lowest in Europe. In fact, it was one of the highest (Table 2.1). The English were faced with a greater range of alternatives to emigration, but because England (and therefore most of its potential emigrants) was urban and industrial, their expectations were higher.

Table 8.1 shows, in summary form, the extent and the main direction of internal migration. The data are based on the work of T. A. Welton who calculated the net balance of migration in every continuously

---

[7] See Hvidt, *Flight to America*, pp. 127–33; Kero, *Migration from Finland*, pp. 54–5.
[8] I am indebted to Dr E. H. Hunt for this information.

built up area for the period 1881–1901.[9] The rural areas are the
residuals. A. K. Cairncross extended the Welton calculations to create
a series including each decade 1841–1911.[10] The Welton/Cairncross
estimates were an important contribution, because the real boundaries
of the built up areas did not match the local government boundaries.
The county is a particularly unsatisfactory unit for the analysis of
internal migration. The counties varied greatly in population and area,
and the small ones were more homogeneous than the large. Both
Lancashire and Yorkshire, for example, included a large rural sector.
The county boundaries also divided urban areas like Bristol and Manchester in an arbitrary way. The Welton/Cairncross estimates show
that the rural areas lost more than 4.5 million migrants (internally
and abroad) in seventy years. This loss was nearly as large as their
total natural increase – despite high fertility – so that the population
of the rural areas rose less than 13% in 1841–1911 when the population
of England and Wales more than doubled. Heavy out-migration from
rural areas was continuous and universal which means that it is extremely unlikely that there is a single explanation for it. Agriculture
began to shed labour in the 1850s, and between 1851 and 1911 the
agricultural labour force was reduced by 708,000 of which the bulk
were agricultural labourers. But obviously, the bulk of the rural out-
migrants cannot have been agricultural labourers. Other causes of
rural out-migration are the decline of rural handicraft industry, the
urban demand for domestic servants and the serious housing problem
in many rural areas.[11] Migration from the rural areas fell in the 1890s.
This was largely caused by the spread of towns into rural areas and
by the recovery of British agriculture from the so-called 'Great Depres-

[9] An extremely onerous task. T. A. Welton, *England's recent progress: an investigation of the statistics of migration, mortality etc. in the twenty years from 1881–1901, as indicating tendencies towards the growth and decay of particular communities* (Chapman and Hall, 1911).

[10] A. K. Cairncross, 'Internal migration in Victorian England', *Manchester School*, 17 (1), 1949, pp. 67–87, reprinted in his *Home and foreign investment*. Cairncross's estimates only exist in summary form. The working papers were lost in the Second World War.

[11] See J. Saville, *Rural depopulation* and R. Lawton, 'Rural depopulation in nineteenth-century Britain', pp. 227–55 in R. W. Steel and R. Lawton, (eds.), *Liverpool essays in geography* (Longmans, 1967), R. Lawton, 'Population changes in England and Wales in the late nineteenth century: an analysis of trends by registration districts', *Trans-actions of the Institute of British Geographers*, 44, 1968, pp. 55–74. There was an enormous contemporary literature. Among the better works are Bowley, 'Rural population in England and Wales', Graham, *The rural exodus*, Hasbach, *The English agricultural labourer*, pp. 343–50, which quotes extensively from the *Royal Commission on Labour*, 1893, and M. Ogle, 'The alleged depopulation of the rural districts of England, 1851–1881', *Journal of the Royal Statistical Society*, 70, 1889, pp. 205–40.

Table 8.1. *Population growth and migration, England and Wales, 1841–1911. (000s)*

	Population 1841	Population 1911	Natural increase	Migration (net)	Migration × 100 Natural increase	POP 1911 × 100 POP 1841
Greater London	2,262	7,315	3,802	+1,251	31.9	324
8 Largest N. towns[a]	1,551	5,192	2,747	+893	32.5	335
9 Colliery districts	1,320	5,334	3,363	+650	19.3	404
Textile towns	1,387	3,182	1,706	+90	5.3	230
Rural districts N.	2,426	2,875	2,093	−1,644	−78.6	119
Rural districts S.	3,740	4,086	3,209	−2,863	−89.2	110
England and Wales	15,914	36,070	21,336	−1,210	−5.7	227

Note: [a] Manchester, Liverpool, Birmingham, Leeds, Sheffield, Leicester, Hull, Nottingham.
Source: Cairncross, *Internal migration in Victorian England*, pp. 82–6.

217

sion'. It is not true that the fall in the *rate* of rural depopulation in the 1890s was because previous migration had removed the parents of potential migrants. Age-specific migration rates fell. This important point is discussed in chapter 7.

Another reason for the high rate of internal migration in the late nineteenth century was related to the demand for labour in industry and services.[12] Between 1851 and 1911 employment in iron and steel and engineering grew by 910,000 and employment in mining grew by 784,000.[13] By the early twentieth century industry was probably more concentrated (on the coalfields) than at any time before or since.[14] Hence, migration towards the largest industrial towns was substantial. Manchester, Liverpool, Birmingham, Leeds, Sheffield, Leicester, Hull and Nottingham gained 893,000 migrants, net of returns, between 1841 and 1911 (Table 8.1). The colliery districts gained 650,000 migrants in the same period. The single most important destination was London, which gained 1.25 million net migrants between 1841–1911. London was the main destination because it had the greatest expansion in commercial and domestic services. Thirty-five per cent of the increase in the number employed in these occupations between 1851 and 1911 occurred in London and the Home Counties. In addition, London had the greatest range of occupations and other attractions.[15] The position of London among British cities was rather like the position of the U.S.A. among the countries of immigration.[16]

[12] It must be remembered that many present day barriers to migration were much less important in the nineteenth century. There was a free (rented) housing market and outside the skilled trades (which were decreasing in relative importance), the trades unions were unable to restrict entry into most occupations. Most potential migrants would probably not have been seriously deterred by the problem of aged relatives because there were relatively few of them, and more children to look after them. Nor would they have been deterred by the problems of educating children.

[13] The data on the numbers employed in the main occupational groups are taken from Hunt, *Regional wage variations*, and from his unpublished London Ph.D. thesis with the same title.

[14] A. J. Brown, *The framework of regional economics in the United Kingdom* (NIESR, Cambridge University Press, 1972), pp. 105–8.

[15] London had been the dominant destination of migrants since before the Industrial Revolution. See J. Patten, *Rural–urban migration in pre-industrial England* (Oxford University, School of Geography, Research Papers No. 6, 1973).

[16] The two main immigrant groups went to London and the large towns. Of the 750,000 Irish in Britain in 1851, half were living in London, Glasgow, Manchester and Liverpool. In 1911 these four cities still held about half of the 550,000 Irish. The east European Jews were even more heavily concentrated. In 1911 about three-quarters of them were in London. Total Irish migration between 1841 and 1911 was about 1,000,000 net of returns of which about 600,000 had arrived by 1861. Migration from eastern Europe was more than 120,000 almost all of it coming after 1881. See J. A. Jackson, *The Irish in modern Britain* (Routledge, 1963), chapter 1 and J. E. Handley, *The Irish in modern Scotland* (Cork University Press, 1947). L. D. Gartner, *The Jewish*

Internal migration was not the main cause of population growth in the cities. About three-quarters of their population growth was from natural increase (Table 8.1). This estimate is rather misleading, however. It assumes that the birth and death rate of migrants and natives were identical. If allowance is made for migrant age structure, then migration caused about 40% of population growth and natural increase 60%. The contribution of migration to population growth in the coalfields, where marital fertility was high, was even less. Eighty-four per cent of the growth was caused by natural increase, or about two-thirds if allowance is made for migration. On the other hand, the slow growth of population in rural areas was a consequence of out-migration.[17]

It is important at this stage to make clear how the migration flows that we are discussing were calculated. Internal migration was calculated by subtracting the population at the first census from the population at the second census and adding the inter-censal natural increase. Assuming the boundaries are held constant and registration was complete, this method cannot be faulted. But the method only shows the net effect of a decade of migration, not the migration itself. This method only measures one movement per decade per migrant unless he returned before the next census when he would be missed altogether. Inward movement masks outward movement. Emigration (and immigration) are included. Hence, the arrival of an Irishman in Liverpool, for example, masked the internal migration or emigration of a Liverpool resident.

A final problem is that all measures of net migration by this method – which is usually called the residual method – obviously only measure net movement across the boundaries of the area. But within a large urban area there were far more opportunities available to a potential migrant than within a village or market town.[18] The residual method does not measure all migration, only a proportion. But the method captures a larger sample of rural–urban moves than urban–urban moves. Rural–urban migration is relatively overstated and we cannot infer from the higher net migration rates out of the rural areas that their migrants had made less individual moves.[19]

---

immigrant in England, 1870–1914 (Wayne State University Press, Detroit, 1960). A method of estimating total Irish immigration is described in chapter 4.

[17] See Baines, 'The labour market, 1860–1914', pp. 156–9.

[18] The concept of 'intervening opportunities' was developed by Stouffer. S. A. Stouffer, 'Intervening opportunities. A theory relating mobility and distance', *American Sociological Review*, 5, 1940, pp. 845–67.

[19] It is possible that rural migrants tended to move for longer distances than urban but our view that rural migration is overstated relative to urban does not depend

III

The most influential work on the relation between internal migration
in Britain and emigration is by Brinley Thomas. It appeared between
1954 and 1973, although some of the ideas go back to his earliest
work in the 1930s.[20] Thomas's main aim was to establish the existence
of a close relationship between the growth of the British and American
economies and to expose what to him was the inadequacy of American
centred models. Migration formed only a part – but a vital one –
of the work. Professor Thomas's starting point was the concept of
population sensitive investment first developed by S. Kuznets in
1930.[21] Thomas demonstrated the existence of cycles of 18–20 years
duration in the growth of American railway mileage and in residential
construction between 1847 and 1914, which peaked in 1856, 1871,
1882/7 and 1910. The building/railroad cycle was highly correlated
with fluctuations in migration into the U.S.A. and with fluctuations
in capital imports.[22] (The turning point in American immigration preceded the turning point in American railroad construction before
1871 but followed it thereafter.) Professor Thomas did not deny that
immigration was sensitive to the American trade cycle – which is

on this. It is known that many migrants only moved for short distances probably
because they depended on local information networks. The dominance of short distance moves which was one of Ravenstein's famous 'laws of migration' can be seen
from the enumeration of the county of birth in the census from 1851 to 1911. Ravenstein's most important article was E. G. Ravenstein, 'The laws of migration', *Journal
of the Royal Statistical Society*, 48, 1885, pp. 167–235. Redford, *Labour migration in England*, Shannon, 'Migration and the growth of London', H. C. Darby, 'The movement
of population to and from Cambridgeshire 1851–61', *Geographical Journal*, 101 (3),
1943, pp. 118–25, all use the place of birth data from the census to show the predomi-
nance of short distance moves. The importance of short distance moves does not
mean that there was no overall pattern of migration in the country. The migrants
either made a second move or they 'displaced' others who moved to another (and
possibly larger) town. In practice, however, it is not easy to distinguish between
'second movers' and those who were 'displaced'. See Michael Anderson, 'Urban
migration into nineteenth-century Lancashire: some insights into two competing
hypotheses', pp. 131–44 in M. Drake, *Historical demography. Problems and projects* (Open
University, 1974).

[20] The most important work is the first edition of his book, *Migration and economic
growth*. Thomas, 'Migration and international investment', pp. 3–16, and B. Thomas,
'Long swings in international migration and capital formation', *Bulletin of the International Statistical Institute, Proceedings of the 34th Session*, 40, book 1, Toronto, 1964,
pp. 398–412. Several of his papers are reprinted in the second edition of *Migration
and economic growth*. Professor Thomas answered several of his critics in *Migration
and urban development*.

[21] Kuznets, *Secular movements in production and prices*. For a later statement see
S. Kuznets, 'Long swings in the growth of population and related variables'. *Proceedings of the American Philosophical Society*, 102 (1), 1958, pp. 25–52.

[22] Thomas, *Migration and economic growth*, pp. 92, 175.

obvious from a glance at the rate of annual emigration from Britain. But the short term fluctuations were subsumed within an 18–20 year long swing. Immigration was a key factor in the American cycle. High immigration followed investment in railways after 1871, and was to a construction boom which in turn increased the demand for funds.[23] This increased the rate of return on British capital exports to the United States. Immigration continued to grow until the return on railway and housing investment fell. Thomas thought that in the earlier years (i.e. the 1850s and 1860s) the migration cycle was caused by a long cycle of births, but this is debatable.[24] As the British economy became more sophisticated the mechanism was not population pressure *per se*, but the influence of the birth cycle on the building cycle.

A. K. Cairncross and others had shown that residential construction was an important component of total British investment; that housebuilding was possibly a substitute for overseas investment, and that fluctuations in housebuilding were largely unrelated to the trade cycle.[25] This led to the idea of a distinct building cycle, of which J. Parry Lewis was the most well known exponent.[26] The idea of a building cycle starts from the proposition that housebuilding was speculative.[27] To builders, the most important signal of unsatisfied demand was rising rents. Rising rents led to a building boom until the real price of housing fell (i.e. until rents were seen to be falling). Construction then fell, but the market was in excess supply in the medium run. The dynamic factor was the rate of family formation. A high rate of family formation was a consequence of high birth rates twenty or so years before and each period of rapid family formation would produce an echo effect a generation later. According to Parry Lewis, the British building cycle peaked in 1878 and in 1896, that is, building activity was at a very low level when emigration peaked in 1883 and 1888 but was at a high level in the 1890s when emigration was falling.

Professor Thomas's view is that the American and British building cycle alternated (Table 8.2). In the upswing in Britain when rents were rising, investment in housing and transport improvements was

[23] Ibid., pp. 177–8.
[24] Ibid., p. 116.
[25] Cairncross, *Home and foreign investment*, pp. 209–21; B. Weber, 'A new index of residential construction, 1838–1950', *Scottish Journal of Political Economy*, 2, 1955, pp. 104–32; E. W. Cooney, 'Long waves in building in the British economy in the nineteenth century', *Economic History Review*, 13 (2), 1960, p. 257.
[26] Parry Lewis, *Building cycles and Britain's growth*, pp. 164–85, and J. Parry Lewis, 'Growth and inverse cycles: a two-country model', *Economic Journal*, 74, 1964, pp. 109–18.
[27] Largely because houses were durable and replacement could be deferred and because their purchase and construction depended on credit.

Table 8.2. *Peaks and troughs of American and British building cycles,*
1847–1920

Peak G.B.	Peak U.S.A.	Trough G.B.	Trough U.S.A.
1863	1853	1855	1864
1877	1871	1871	1878
1899	1890	1887	1900
1920	1909	1912	1918

Source: Adapted from Thomas, *Migration and economic growth,* p. 175.

rising. Hence, demand for labour increased in British towns which drew internal migrants from the rural areas. When the British building boom entered the downswing, domestic investment fell and overseas investment rose. The building cycle in America rose, drawing British capital to the U.S.A. and creating jobs which were partly filled by emigrants from Britain. Emigration reduced the pressure on housing, and rents began to fall. According to Professor Thomas the North Atlantic building cycle was a migration cycle in disguise. He argued that in the 1880s, for example, internal migration in Britain was falling and emigration was rising, but domestic investment and building were falling. By the 1890s internal migration was rising and 'capital outlay showed a sharp upswing, with emigration falling off rapidly to a very low point at the end of the decade'.[28]

Brinley Thomas's argument about the fluctuations in internal migration was largely based on the Welton/Cairncross estimates of which the important part is summarised in Table 8.3. His reading of the Welton/Cairncross data can be seen from the following passage.

The rate of industrialisation was at its height in the decade 1841–51 when three-quarters of a million people were absorbed by the urban centres, while net emigration was only 81,000. The contribution from the countryside was barely sufficient to appease the vast appetite of the growing industrial areas. The next ten years saw a further large gain by the towns amounting to nearly two-thirds of a million people; but by now the flood from the countryside was so great that not even the expanding home industry could cope with it, and one-third of a million people sought a living abroad. During the next two decades, the sixties and seventies, the net gain of the towns totalled

[28] Thomas, *Migration and economic growth,* p. 128. Glamorgan was an important exception to this pattern. Since most of the output of Glamorgan was exported, the 'Atlantic economy' model would predict that internal migration into Glamorgan was high when British capital exports were high (i.e. in the 1880s) and emigration was high when British domestic investment was high (i.e. in the 1870s). This important issue is discussed in detail in chapter 10.

Table 8.3. *Gains (+) and losses (−) by migration from towns and colliery districts and from rural areas in England and Wales, 1841–1911 (000s)*

	Towns and colliery districts	Rural areas	Net emigration
1841–50	+742.3	−443.2	−299.1
1851–60	+620.3	−742.6	−122.3
1861–70	+623.5	−683.0	−59.6
1871–80	+689.2	−837.5	−148.3
1881–90	+228.1	−845.4	−617.4
1891–1900	+606.0	−666.4	−60.4
1901–10	−207.1	−294.9	−502.0

Note: Net emigration is the residual and is therefore slightly different from the estimates in Carrier and Jeffery, *External migration*, which are used in chapter 3. Emigration includes movement to Scotland and Ireland. Two minor arithmetical errors have been corrected.
Source: Thomas, *Migration and economic growth*, p. 124. Taken from Cairncross, *Home and foreign investment*, p. 70.

one and a third million people . . . Emigration settled down to a comparative low level as industry absorbed three-quarters of the rural exodus. From the seventies to the end of the period the inverse relation from decade to decade is striking. The rate of internal migration in the eighties fell to 9 per 1,000 while the rate of emigration rose to 23 per 1,000; in the nineties internal migration went up to 21 per 1,000 and emigration fell to 2 per 1,000 . . . the decade 1901–11 actually registered a net loss for the industrial sector, whereas the outward balance of emigration reached 501,000 or 15 per 1,000 of the population.[29]

The quotation shows that Brinley Thomas saw the rural areas as the origin of all migrants before 1900 (i.e. the net origins). Migrants were drawn either to the towns or overseas, depending on the relative rate of overseas and domestic investment. In fact, the Welton/Cairncross data are ambivalent. For example, according to Welton/Cairncross the rural areas lost 838,000 people in 1871–80 and the urban areas gained 689,000 (Table 8.3).[30] In 1881–90, the rural areas lost 845,000 and the urban areas gained 228,000. Brinley Thomas assumed

[29] Thomas, *Migration and economic growth*, pp. 124–5. The migration rates are net migration per 1,000 of the total population of England and Wales at the beginning of the decade.
[30] In the first edition of his book, Brinley Thomas's argument was based on the original Welton/Cairncross estimates which we summarised in Table 8.3. In the second edition he marginally modified the amount of migration to the 'colliery districts'. He estimated that 834,000 had left the rural areas in the 1870s and 220,000 entered the urban areas. In the 1880s, 837,000 left the rural areas and 220,000 entered the urban. Thomas, *Migration and economic growth*, Table 145.

Table 8.4. *Net internal migration and emigration in England and Wales,*
1881–90 and 1891–1900 (000s)

A. Brinley Thomas interpretation

1871–80

	Rural areas		Urban areas
To urban areas	−689.2	From rural areas	+689.2
To overseas	−148.3	To overseas	0
	−837.5		+689.2

1881–90

	Rural areas		Urban areas
To urban areas	−228.1	From rural areas	+228.1
To overseas	−617.4	To overseas	0
	−845.4		+228.1

B. Alternative explanation

1871–80

	Rural areas		Urban areas
To urban areas	−837.5	From rural areas	+837.5
To overseas	0	To overseas	−148.3
	−837.5		+689.2

1881–90

	Rural areas		Urban areas
To urban areas	−845.4	From rural areas	+845.4
To overseas	0	To overseas	−617.4
	−845.4		+228.1

Source: Table 8.3.

that this meant that rural–urban migration was very high and rural
emigration was low in the 1870s, and that rural–urban migration was
low and rural emigration was high in the 1880s. In fact, these data
are consistent with several explanations of the source of the emigrants.
In particular, the data are consistent with low emigration from the
urban areas in the 1870s and high *urban* emigration in the 1880s.

Table 8.4 makes the ambivalence of the Welton/Cairncross data
clear. If, like Brinley Thomas, one starts with an implicit assumption
that the source of all emigrants was the rural areas it follows that
the difference between the outflow from the rural areas and the inflow

into the urban must be the number of net rural migrants – 148,000 in the 1870s and 617,000 in the 1880s. But it is possible, for example, that in the 1870s all the 838,000 rural out-migrants went to the towns and the 148,000 emigrants came not from the rural areas but from the towns. This would still leave 689,000 net urban arrivals. Similarly, 845,000 could have gone to the towns in the 1880s, the towns could have lost 617,000 overseas and gained only 228,000 net migrants. It is obviously unrealistic to assume that all emigrants came from the towns but no more so than assuming that they all came from the rural areas.

We now know, of course, that the rural areas cannot have been the main source of English and Welsh emigrants between 1861 and 1900. More than a third of all emigrants had been born in the highly urbanised counties of London, Lancashire and the West Midlands another third in the other counties which could be described as urban (Table 6.1). We have also been able to show that there were at least two additional emigrants in the 1880s who had been born in urban counties for each additional emigrant who had been born in a rural county.[31]

In chapter 9 we have made a tentative attempt to adjust our estimates of the place of birth of the emigrants to estimates which show the places from which the rural emigrants left. We also attempted to estimate how many emigrants came from the rural parts of urban counties. This exercise is subject to quite a large margin of error, but between 1861 and 1900 at least a half and possibly two-thirds of all emigrants were likely to have left from a town which contained at least 20,000 people.[32] (The latter is a much more strict definition of 'urban' than that used by Welton/Cairncross.)[33] Hence, the internal

---

[31] In the 1880s, there were 43,000 – 100,000 more rural-county-born emigrants than in the 1870s, but there were 195,000–320,000 more urban-county-born. About 35–40% of all emigrants were rural in the 1870s but only 30–35% in the 1880s. This means that relatively few urban emigrants of the 1880s can have been born in rural counties and have moved to the urban counties in the 1870s. (This would also be consistent with the Welton/Cairncross data.)

[32] This estimate assumes that people living in the rural areas of urban counties had the same propensity to emigrate as those living in the urban parts. The estimate that two-thirds of all emigrants left from an urban area assumes that persons who had moved to the urban areas from the rural parts doubled their propensity to emigrate. The estimate that a half of all emigrants came from urban areas assumes that rural–urban migrants were no more likely to emigrate than if they had remained in rural areas. See chapter 9.

[33] In the Welton/Cairncross estimates the definition of urban area is largely political. It includes municipal boroughs, urban districts and also colliery villages even when they were not local authority areas. The rural areas were residuals. Our definition of urban depends on cartographical evidence and excludes all discrete built-up areas with less than 20,000 persons.

migration leg of the 'Atlantic economy' collapses. The towns could not in the main have acted like reservoirs which sometimes absorbed the outflow from the rural areas and sometimes failed to.

There have been several other important theoretical and empirical objections to the Brinley Thomas thesis. There is some doubt if the North Atlantic cycle is a true cycle or merely an empirical observation. A true cycle needs an internal dynamic which changes the downturn into an upturn without an external shock. The weakness of the Brinley Thomas thesis is that it has proved very difficult to show empirically that the birth/family formation cycle existed, and hence the nature of the linking mechanism.[34] This does not affect his analysis of the relation between emigration and urban growth, however. More serious objections to the building cycle/migration mechanism were raised by Habakkuk and Saul.[35] Habakkuk was the first person to regard the inverse relationship between emigration and internal migration as unproven. He conjectured that when the data became available they might show, for example, that migration to the towns did not fall in the 1880s.[36] Both Habakkuk and Saul held that the empirical evidence did not suggest the existence of a national building cycle but a set of local cycles with no common pattern. In particular, building activity in London was still increasing in the late 1870s and early 1880s when it was declining in the provinces. (Saul also thought that the decline in many provincial cities occurred in 1876 not 1878.) Moreover, the fall in housebuilding in the 1880s did not, of itself, suggest the existence of a national building cycle.[37] Professor Thomas countered this criticism with a new set of estimates of migration into the main towns that were calculated by a survival method. He compared the migration series with a new building series based on the inhabited house duty.[38] But the degree of error inherent in his calculations of in-migration was large. Also he had to admit that London and South Wales did not fit into a national building cycle. We should probably retain some scepticism about the existence of a British build-

---

[34] Some commentators have thought that the mechanism was autonomous movements in the balance of payments. See, for example, J. G. Williamson, *American growth and the balance of payments, 1820–1913* (University of North Carolina Press, Chapel Hill, 1964), and J. G. Williamson, 'The long swing: comparison and interaction between the British and American balance of payments', *Journal of Economic History*, 22 (1), 1962, pp. 21–46.

[35] H. J. Habakkuk, 'Fluctuations in housebuilding in Britain and the United States in the twentieth century', *Journal of Economic History*, 22, 1962, pp. 198–230; S. B. Saul, 'Housebuilding in England 1890–1914', pp. 119–37.

[36] Habakkuk, 'Fluctuations in housebuilding', p. 217.

[37] Saul, 'Housebuilding in England', p. 134.

[38] Thomas, *Migration and urban growth*, Appendix B, pp. 45–54.

ing cycle. Finally there remains the fundamental issue of the statistical technique used to measure the long swing. The main data (investment, immigration, capital flows, construction) do not suggest a long swing as they stand. They have to be fitted to a trend which is parabolic in form and around which there is considerable deviation.

IV

We now know that the main pattern of emigration in England and Wales was not a continuous outflow from the rural areas which (depending on their relative attractiveness) either went to the towns or overseas. This does not mean that emigration and rural–urban migration were unrelated, however. We can be sure that virtually all potential emigrants were aware that they could move to a town or city. But we do not know how close were the decision to emigrate and the decision to move internally. In the first place, a migration decision depended on the behaviour of other people in the area. If emigration increased from a rural area, someone who had been considering internal migration might have been persuaded to go abroad, or not to move at all, or to be confirmed in his decision to move internally. It is possible that the behaviour of one member of a family affected the decision of others.[39] For example, the decision of a brother to emigrate may have helped persuade his sister to move to London. But in addition to the behaviour of other people, the decision to migrate depended on the previous migration experience of the person concerned.

This section examines long run emigration and internal migration rates from the rural counties. Natives of those counties where emigration was high may have been relatively less likely to move to another part of England and Wales than natives of counties where emigration was low. In effect, emigration could have been high from some counties because internal migration was low.

We are forced to use the rural counties as proxies for the rural areas – which excludes the rural parts of the urbanised counties. Even the rural counties were not homogeneous – in some, for example, the migrants could go to the nearest town without leaving the county at all – but this is not too serious. The population at risk of migrating in each county is the total native population living within England and Wales. Hence, our measure of internal migration is the number of moves (net of returns) across the border of each county made by

---

[39] In fact, we could find no significant relationship between male emigration and female internal migration from the same rural county. See chapter 7.

natives of that county excluding moves overseas. We avoid double counting the population at risk (i.e. of counting the same person in more than one decade) by expressing total migration as a proportion of the native population aged 15–24, in the period 1861–1900.[40] (For comparison, Table 8.6 shows internal migration as a percentage of the mean total native population in each decade.) There is some double counting of migrants who left the counties in one decade and emigrated in the next. This can be shown to be low, however.[41]

Tables 8.5 and 8.6 show the long run migration rates for each rural county in the period 1861–1900. We explained in chapter 4 that most misenumeration and estimation errors net out over the whole period. We can, therefore, take the tables as an accurate summary of the variation in migration rates. A glance at the tables shows that there was no simple inverse relationship between long run emigration rates from the rural counties and internal migration.[42] In the forty years after 1861, the rural counties lost about 12.6% of their population by migration in each decade (net of returns). About 10% of the population went to other counties and about 2.6% went overseas. This was the

[40] See chapter 4, for the method of estimating the native population aged 15–24.

[41] In any one decade, a migrant can only have moved to another county or abroad. But if a migrant moved from, say, Cardigan to Glamorgan in 1878 and then emigrated in 1882 he would be included in the estimates of internal migration of Cardigan natives in 1871–80 and in the estimates of Cardigan emigrants in 1881–90. The sum of emigration and internal migration from Cardigan in 1861–1900 would be overestimated by an amount which depended on the extent of stage emigration. It is possible to estimate the probable maximum extent of rural–urban stage emigration by a method which is discussed in detail in chapter 9. It was estimated that stage emigration from rural counties varied from 20–50% of all emigration. But the total outward movement from a county is only overestimated by stage emigration captured by the census, which depends on the mean period that stage emigrants lived away from their native county. The extent of double counting is given by the relationship $[(\overline{SEMIG}\text{Io} \times \overline{P}) \div 10]$ where $\overline{P}$ is the mean stay of rural migrants in urban counties in years and SEMIGio is the rate of stage emigration as a percentage of the total native population. Assuming that $\overline{P}$ was not more than five years, the double counting of total movement could only have been as high as 1% in four counties (and only for males). There must have been stage emigration from all counties, and hence double counting of total movement. The range in three-quarters of the counties lay between 0.8% and 0.4%. The relative incidence of stage emigration cannot therefore have seriously affected the estimates of total outward movement in the period.

[42] The rank order correlations of internal and overseas migration rates as a percentage of the population (ages 15–24) are −0.166 (males) and −0.193 (females). If we deflate by the total native population the rank order correlation is −0.20 (males) and −0.21 (females). None of the results are significant at the 5% level. In the migration model which is reported in Appendix 7, we included all counties. We found that there was no significant relation between male internal and overseas migration rates. There was some relation between female internal and overseas migration but it was highly correlated with the lagged dependent variable – the migration rate in the previous decade.

equivalent of 62.1% of their young adult population, 12.3% of which emigrated and 49.8% of which went to other English and Welsh counties. (Unless otherwise specified we will use the total native population aged 15–24 as a proxy for the total population at risk.) We examined those counties where either the emigrants or the internal migrants were a disproportionately large share of total out-migration to see if a trade-off had occurred. In seven counties, (Herefordshire, Pembroke, Brecon, Montgomery, Merioneth, Devon and Cornwall) emigrants were more than 25% of all migrants. But the high level of emigration only seemed to have been at the expense of internal migration in two of the seven counties – Devon and Merioneth. In three of the counties with exceptional emigration (Herefordshire, Brecon and Montgomery) internal migration rates were higher than the mean rate for all rural counties. Internal migration was relatively low in the two remaining counties (Cornwall and Brecon) but internal and overseas movement combined was relatively high. Hence, the high level of emigration from Cornwall was not simply at the expense of internal movement. It was also because the Cornish had a high propensity to leave the county – wherever the destination.

There were more clear examples of a trade-off between emigration and internal migration among the counties where a relatively large number of the migrants did not go overseas. Internal migrants were at least 85% of all migrants from ten counties. The counties were Cambridgeshire, Norfolk, Rutland, Bedfordshire, Hertfordshire, Oxfordshire, Berkshire, Radnor, Denbigh and Derbyshire. Perhaps not surprisingly this group included many of the rural counties within easy reach of London – but not all. All of these counties had extremely low emigration rates, with the exception of Radnor and Rutland, and even these had emigration rates that were lower than the mean of all rural counties. Norfolk, Denbigh and Derbyshire however, also had relatively *low* internal migration rates. Emigration may have been low from these three counties because the population was relatively immobile not because of the superior attraction of the urban areas.

We tested the relationship between emigration rates from rural counties and total movement out of the counties to all destinations. The rank order correlations (which are significant at the 5% level) were +0.504 for males and +0.286 for females, although there was no significant relationship between internal migration and emigration rates. We took this to mean that in some counties the level of emigration depended on whether the natives were relatively mobile or immobile – irrespective of destination.

Table 8.7 is a simple contingency table which distinguishes those

Table 8.5. *Migration by natives of English and Welsh rural counties (net of returns), 1861–1900, as a % of those aged 15–24*

	Males			Females	
	To overseas %	To other counties %		To overseas %	To other counties %
Cornwall	44.8	29.7	Brecon	26.4	58.7
Brecon	28.1	60.1	Cornwall	26.2	35.5
Herefordshire	25.0	55.2	Montgomery	16.3	52.4
Pembroke	23.3	48.3	Huntingdonshire	14.6	69.4
Montgomery	22.4	50.1	Herefordshire	14.3	62.0
Westmorland	21.6	57.4	Pembroke	13.6	45.5
Devon	20.1	38.4	Merioneth	12.5	45.5
Somerset	19.5	46.0	Westmorland	12.0	58.1
Merioneth	18.5	41.5	Worcestershire	11.0	52.5
Dorset	18.3	51.5	Somerset	10.6	51.9
Cumberland	17.4	47.2	Cumberland	10.3	46.9
Huntingdonshire	16.3	59.8	Devon	9.9	41.9
Caernarvon	15.7	32.2	Radnor	9.3	63.6
Shropshire	15.7	51.7	Rutland	9.1	78.2
Worcestershire	15.7	48.1	Cardigan	9.0	44.0
Anglesey	15.2	38.0	Dorset	8.9	60.2

County		
Wiltshire	14.8	47.8
Buckinghamshire	14.7	53.5
Rutland	14.6	63.4
Cardigan	14.1	53.8
Northamptonshire	13.7	43.3
Suffolk	13.5	45.7
Oxfordshire	12.7	58.3
Carmarthen	12.6	40.7
Flint	12.6	52.2
Lincolnshire	12.3	46.9
Berkshire	12.0	55.0
Radnor	11.9	60.8
Norfolk	10.0	45.6
Cambridgeshire	9.5	56.8
Denbigh	8.6	44.0
Derbyshire	7.5	45.3
Bedfordshire	6.5	55.9
Hertfordshire	5.0	55.7
All rural counties	16.0	47.1

County		
Carmarthen	8.8	36.4
Shropshire	8.6	60.1
Anglesey	7.9	39.5
Northamptonshire	7.8	49.2
Buckinghamshire	7.7	66.5
Suffolk	7.3	52.1
Wiltshire	6.9	58.9
Flint	6.8	58.8
Lincolnshire	5.6	50.8
Oxfordshire	5.3	65.5
Derbyshire	5.1	50.3
Bedfordshire	4.3	59.7
Norfolk	3.9	49.8
Caernarvon	2.9	35.3
Denbigh	2.0	53.3
Cambridgeshire	1.0	65.1
Hertfordshire	0.4	66.9
Berkshire	0.1	68.3
All rural counties	8.5	52.6

Notes: For the definition of 'rural' see chapter 6. The population at risk is the native population of the county living within England and Wales. For the method of estimating the proportion of that population aged 15–24 see chapter 4. Migration to Scotland is included in 'emigration' except in the case of Cumberland.
Source: Appendix 1.

Table 8.6. *Migration by natives of English and Welsh rural counties (net of returns), 1861–1900, as a % of the total native population born in each county (weighted mean rate in each of four decades). Rank order of emigration rates*

	Males			Females	
	To overseas %	To other counties %		To overseas %	To other counties %
Cornwall	10.5	7.0	Brecon	5.4	12.2
Brecon	5.9	12.6	Cornwall	5.3	7.1
Herefordshire	5.2	11.4	Montgomery	3.3	10.6
Pembroke	5.1	10.7	Huntingdonshire	2.9	13.8
Cumberland	3.5	9.6	Herefordshire	2.8	12.0
Montgomery	4.8	10.7	Pembroke	2.8	9.3
Westmorland	4.3	11.6	Merioneth	2.4	9.0
Devon	4.2	8.1	Westmorland	2.4	11.5
Somerset	4.2	9.9	Somerset	2.1	10.1
Merioneth	3.8	8.5	Worcestershire	2.1	10.2
Dorset	3.8	10.8	Cumberland	2.0	9.2
Huntingdonshire	3.5	12.8	Devon	1.9	7.9
Cardigan	3.4	11.5	Radnor	1.9	13.1
Caernarvon	3.3	6.7	Cardigan	1.8	8.8
Anglesey	3.2	8.1	Carmarthen	1.8	7.5

County		
Rutland	3.2	13.9
Shropshire	3.2	10.7
Worcestershire	3.2	9.9
Buckinghamshire	3.1	11.3
Wiltshire	3.1	10.1
Carmarthen	2.8	8.9
Northamptonshire	2.8	8.7
Suffolk	2.8	9.5
Flint	2.7	11.0
Oxfordshire	2.6	12.2
Lincolnshire	2.5	9.6
Radnor	2.5	12.6
Berkshire	2.4	11.3
Norfolk	2.1	9.4
Cambridgeshire	2.0	11.9
Hertfordshire	1.9	11.8
Denbigh	1.8	9.3
Derbyshire	1.5	9.1
Bedfordshire	1.3	11.8
All rural counties	3.4	9.8

County		
Rutland	1.8	15.4
Dorset	1.7	11.5
Shropshire	1.7	11.8
Buckinghamshire	1.5	12.7
Northamptonshire	1.5	9.5
Flint	1.4	11.7
Suffolk	1.4	10.1
Wiltshire	1.3	11.4
Lincolnshire	1.1	10.1
Anglesey	1.0	7.8
Derbyshire	1.0	9.5
Oxfordshire	1.0	12.7
Bedfordshire	0.9	11.8
Hertfordshire	0.7	12.8
Norfolk	0.7	9.4
Caernarvon	0.6	6.8
Denbigh	0.4	10.6
Cambridgeshire	0.2	12.6
Berkshire	0	12.9
All rural counties	1.7	10.2

Note: Migration to Scotland is included in 'emigration' except in the case of Cumberland.
Source: Appendix 1.

Table 8.7. *Internal migration and emigration, 1861–1900*

Counties where emigration and internal migration may have been substitutes
(a) Relatively high emigration, low internal migration
　　　Pembroke, Merioneth, Devon, Cornwall; Somerset
(b) Relatively low emigration, high internal migration
　　　Rutland, Radnor, Flint, Wiltshire, Shropshire, Cambridgeshire,
　　　Bedfordshire, Buckinghamshire, Hertfordshire, Oxfordshire, Berkshire

*Counties where emigration and internal migration do not appear to have been
substitutes*
(c) Relatively high emigration, high internal migration
　　　Huntingdonshire, Herefordshire, Brecon, Montgomery,
　　　Worcestershire, Cumberland, Westmorland, Dorset
(d) Relatively low emigration, low internal migration
　　　Suffolk, Norfolk, Lincolnshire, Northamptonshire, Cardigan,
　　　Denbigh, Caernarvon, Anglesey, Carmarthen, Derbyshire

Note: 'Relatively high emigration' and 'relatively high internal migration'
means above the mean rate for rural counties (12.3% and 49.8% of the 15–24
age group, respectively).

counties where emigration and internal migration appear to have been
substitutes to some degree and those where emigration and internal
migration were positively correlated. Table 8.7 shows some important
geographical features. Relatively small numbers of migrants from the
West of England counties of Devon, Cornwall and Somerset went
to other counties but emigration was exceptional. About six out of
every ten persons left these counties of which two went overseas
and only four went to the other counties. On the other hand, all
the rural counties to the north and west of London (Bedfordshire,
Buckinghamshire, Hertfordshire, Oxfordshire, Cambridgeshire and
Berkshire) had extremely low emigration and high internal movement
– mainly to London. Nearly one in seven out of every ten natives
left their county of birth of which less than one emigrated. It seems
possible that many of the emigrants from the West of England had
considered moving to another county but had rejected it. But it is
not clear if the internal migrants from the so-called 'South-Midlands'
counties had considered emigration and rejected it. The timing of
emigration from this area suggests that relatively little information
about emigration was available to them (This issue is discussed in
chapter 7.) Hence, internal migration from the South Midlands, strictly
speaking, may not have been a substitute for emigration.
　　The population of the large eastern counties of Norfolk, Suffolk

Table 8.8. *Net migration of natives to other counties, 1861–1900 as a %*
of those aged 15–24

	Males	Females
From all urban counties	34.7	37.4
From all rural counties	47.1	52.6
From all counties	38.9	42.4

Source: Appendix 1.

and Lincolnshire were less mobile. Only about five out of every ten left for other counties and emigration was very low. This means that internal migration from the eastern counties may have decreased emigration but not because the internal migration rate was high. On the other hand, some counties, notably Dorset and Worcestershire lost relatively large numbers of internal and overseas migrants. Hence, the degree of substitution was limited. Finally, it is worth noting that the rural Welsh counties show no consistent migration pattern. (There are Welsh counties in all four categories.) It is obvious, therefore, that the relation between internal migration and emigration was very complex. There are some important instances where internal and overseas movement were substitutes but there are also many where they almost certainly were not.

There were some interesting contrasts between male and female migration. Many contemporaries thought that women were more internally mobile than men and this is confirmed by our estimates.[43] Our measure shows that relatively more females left their county of birth for another county *and did not return*. But it is not known if females made more moves than males or, to put it another way, if females were more likely to return to their county of birth. Between 1861 and 1900, the equivalent of 37.4% of the urban female young adult population (by our measure) moved internally compared with only 34.7% of males (Table 8.8). The difference between male and female migration was even greater in the rural counties. Of rural women 52.6% moved internally, but only 47.1% of rural men. In the same period, females were much less likely to emigrate from the rural counties than males (about 8.5% of females compared with 16% of males). But even if we include emigration, it is clear that rural-born

---

[43] That females were more internally mobile than males was one of Ravenstein's 'laws of migration'. In 1881, 12% more women than men were living outside their county of birth but there were only 6% more women than men in the population. Ravenstein, 'Laws of migration', p. 199.

women were not much less mobile than rural-born men. And in eleven counties, female losses were relatively greater than male, even when emigration and internal migration are combined.

We might expect female internal migration rates to be positively correlated with male emigration rates. For example, in counties where emigration was fairly common, a woman might be prepared to move to another part of the country even if she was not prepared to follow her male friends and neighbours overseas. But there was no tendency for female internal migration to be high from the rural counties that were losing large numbers of male emigrants.[44] Only three of the nine counties with the highest male emigration had female emigration rates that were above average. This is because these counties, which include Cornwall, Devon and Somerset, also had high levels of female emigration. In fact, in two of the counties that had exceptional male emigration, females were *less* likely to move internally than males.

Females were less likely to move internally than males in only five of the thirty-four rural counties – Cumberland, and the four Welsh counties of Brecon, Carmarthen, Pembroke and Cardigan. (Cumberland can be disregarded.)[45] The four Welsh rural counties lay to the immediate north and west of Glamorgan, which was the industrial centre of Wales. These counties lost about the same proportion of their male population to other counties as the rural counties as a whole – 46.8% compared with 47.1%. But they only lost 43.9% of their female population compared with an average loss for all counties of 52.6%. A possible explanation is that the South Wales coalfield attracted disproportionate numbers of men from these counties. There were more men living in Glamorgan in 1901 who had been born in Brecon, Carmarthen, Pembroke and Cardigan than there were women. But we must remember that females from these counties were more immobile than females from the other Welsh rural counties, many of which were more remote from the urban and industrial areas. The reason for the disproportionate rate of female internal migration must have

---

[44] The rank order correlation between male emigration rates from rural counties and female internal migration rates is +0.063 which is not significant.

[45] Females were only marginally less likely to move internally from Cumberland (46.9% of women, compared with 47.2% of men). But our Cumberland migration estimates may be biased by movement to Scotland which is included in 'emigration'. We attempted to remove the Scottish component from our estimate of Cumberland emigration (chapter 4). But it is possible that we slightly overestimated female migration from Cumberland to Scotland which would have the effect of reducing our estimate of female internal migration from Cumberland. (Cumberland is the only rural county outside South and West Wales where male internal migration exceeded female.)

partly been because women in West Wales and Brecon were less mobile than women in other counties.

The counties which had disproportionately high female internal migration were Cornwall, Wiltshire, Cambridgeshire, Rutland, Buckinghamshire, Hertfordshire, Berkshire and Denbigh. Females in these counties were at least 20% more likely to move internally than males in the same county. (In the rural counties as a whole females were about 8% more likely to move than males.) Three of these counties were part of the 'South Midlands'. (Buckinghamshire, Hertfordshire and Berkshire.) Female internal migration from these counties was absolutely high which may reflect the opportunities for women in London. We have seen that this part of the country had very low emigration but relatively high internal migration. This means that most of their population must have been quite informed about the advantages to be gained from moving to London. We do not know if they had also considered emigration and rejected it in favour of an internal move, however, because we do not know if they were well informed about the advantages of emigration.

V

We also tested the relationship between internal migration and emigration from rural counties by observing the changes in the relative level of migration. If internal migration was a substitute for emigration we would expect it to have tended to rise when emigration was falling (i.e. between 1861–70 and 1871–80 and between 1881–90 and 1891–1900) and to have tended to fall when emigration was rising (between 1871–80 and 1881–90). There were thirty-four rural counties which give thirty-four possible observations for each pair of decades and three pairs of decades – 102 observations in all. Unfortunately, because of estimation errors we can only be sure that the rate of emigration definitely rose and fell in sixty-three of the 102 possible male cases and fifty-six female. We do know, however, that in twenty-seven cases when male emigration definitely rose, male internal migration also *rose* in eight counties, and fell in twelve. In thirty-six cases where male emigration fell, internal migration also *fell* in twelve counties and rose in thirteen. Female migration was (slightly) more likely to conform to the expected pattern. In twenty-four cases when female emigration definitely rose, internal migration fell in seven counties and only rose in five. And in thirty-two cases where female emigration definitely fell internal migration rose in fourteen counties and definitely fell in only eight. This confirms our analysis in Section III. There

Migration in a mature economy

Table 8.9. *Internal migration and emigration (net of returns) from the 34 rural counties, decades 1861–1900, as % of total native population*

	1861–70	1871–80	1881–90	1891–1900
Males				
To overseas	3.4 ± 0.2	3.4 ± 0.3	4.4 ± 0.2	2.6 ± 0.2
To other counties	10.3 ± 0.1	10.9 ± 0.1	9.3 ± 0.2	8.9 ± 0.2
Females				
To overseas	1.6 ± 0.2	1.8 ± 0.2	2.3 ± 0.2	1.1 ± 0.2
To other counties	10.3 ± 0.2	11.6 ± 0.2	9.8 ± 0.2	9.0 ± 0.2

Source: Appendix 1.

was some trade-off between internal migration and emigration but there were many cases where internal migration and emigration cannot have been substitutes.

Migration patterns seem to have differed in each decade. It is difficult to draw any conclusions about migration in the 1870s. Male emigration from all rural counties was about 3.4% of the native population in the 1860s and 1870s, and female was about 1.6% and 1.8% (Table 8.9). Because of the degree of error in our estimates we cannot be sure whether emigration from the rural counties marginally rose or marginally fell. We can be sure that internal migration rose, however. Movement of males to other counties rose in sixteen of the thirty-four rural counties and fell in six and female internal migration rose in no less than twenty-two and fell in only three. On average the rural born were between 7% and 13% more likely to go to another county in the 1870s than they had been in the 1860s. Unless emigration was underestimated in the 1860s and overestimated in the 1870s the increase in internal migration must have been greater than the fall in emigration.

There is no doubt of the course of migration in the 1880s. Natives of the rural counties were between 10% and 50% more likely to emigrate in 1881–90 than in 1871–80. They were between 10% and 18% less likely to move to another county. (This meant that the number of internal migrants fell by more in this decade than the number of emigrants rose.) In other words, there was a trade-off between internal migration and emigration in the 1880s, as Brinley Thomas had thought.[46] There were few counties from which emigration failed to

---

[46] See the discussion of Brinley Thomas's work on pp. 220–3. Thomas's view was that the towns acted as a reservoir for the essentially rural out-migrants. Depending on the relative degree of attractiveness of the towns the rural out-migrants went

rise and internal migration failed to fall. Male emigration definitely rose in seventeen rural counties and only fell in four. Female emigration rose in fourteen and only fell in three. Net migration to other counties rose in twenty-four and twenty-seven counties for males and females respectively. In other words, the emigrants from rural counties in the 1880s probably included people who would have moved internally had opportunities abroad been less favourable. But, by our measure, there was less total migration in the 1880s than in the 1870s. Conditions were exceptionally favourable for emigration in the 1880s but the number of additional people who decided to emigrate was less than those who were deterred from internal migration. This was particularly true of females, who were between 4% and 15% less likely to leave their county of birth (for all destinations). Males were between 10% more likely and 1% *less* likely to leave their county of birth. In the 1880s, emigration was a substitute for internal migration but as we would expect – it was not a perfect substitute. The decision to emigrate presumably had to be weighted more carefully than the decision to move to another county. And compared with the 1870s, some people in the 1880s preferred not to move at all rather than to go overseas. Women were relatively more likely to stay at home in the 1880s, which is what we would expect.

The pattern of migration from the rural counties in the 1890s was quite different. Both male and female emigration fell by at least a third, but males were no more likely to move internally than they had in the previous decade and females were definitely less likely to move internally. Male emigration fell in twenty-one counties and female in twenty-three. Internal migration only rose in nine counties and five counties for males and females respectively. Male internal migration actually fell in fourteen rural counties and female in sixteen. The sharp fall in emigration from rural counties in the 1890s cannot therefore have been caused by any increase in the movement of rural born within England and Wales.

The evidence does not suggest that high emigration from rural counties was primarily at the expense of movement to other counties (i.e. to the cities). This was true of the 1880s, but in the 1890s falling emigration was associated with a *fall* in the rate of internal migration. It is difficult to analyse the 1870s decade because we do not know if emigration fell but there may have been an increase in internal migra-

either to the towns or abroad. This view is generally incorrect, since the majority of emigrants came from the urban counties, but his view that the towns affected *rural* emigration is partially correct. See Thomas, *Migration and economic growth*, pp. 124–5.

tion that was unrelated to emigration. In most counties the sum of internal migration and emigration was highest in the 1870s. We might guess that there was a secular decline in migration from rural areas which began in the 1880s and was considerable in the 1890s. In the 1890s only eighty-three people left the rural counties for every 100 who had done so in the 1870s (relative to the population). Unfortunately we cannot test whether there was a long run decline in internal migration because there is no way of analysing the decade 1901–10 when there was exceptional emigration. But if internal migration – insofar as we can measure it – was in secular decline it would be more difficult to justify the view that internal migration and emigration from rural counties were substitutes.

The fluctuations of internal migration from the rural counties in the 1870s and 1880s suggest that in these decades the attraction of the urban areas was the dominant influence on the decision to move internally – but not necessarily on the decision to emigrate. The towns attracted rural migrants at a much greater rate in the 1870s than they did in the 1880s. There were only three English counties which lost relatively more internal migrants in the 1880s than in the 1870s.[47] The pattern is less marked in rural Wales, however, especially for males.[48]

The fall in the rate of internal migration in the 1880s even included those counties that had a perverse pattern of emigration. For example, emigration from Hertfordshire, Buckinghamshire and Oxfordshire was definitely *lower* in the 1880s than it had been in the 1870s and it may not have risen in the neighbouring counties of Berkshire, Northamptonshire and Bedfordshire. Yet internal migration fell in the 1880s from all of the 'South Midland' counties except Hertfordshire. With the exception of Northamptonshire, migration from these counties was dominated by London. We can assume that the attraction of London fell in the South Midlands in the 1870s and also in the other rural counties of the South-East. But the natives of Norfolk and Suffolk,

[47] Herefordshire, Lincolnshire and Hertfordshire.
[48] Female internal migration definitely fell in the 1880s in seven of the eleven rural Welsh counties but male internal migration definitely fell in only three. Taking rural Wales as a whole, internal migrants were 1–15% higher in the 1880s but the number of female migrants was 10–20% lower. The lack of correspondence in the rate of male and female emigration was unique to Wales. It does not seem to have been connected with the relative demands for male and female labour in the heavy industry of Glamorgan and Monmouth because the counties with the perverse pattern of male internal migration were all in North and Central Wales from which the bulk of the internal migrants went to Lancashire and the West Midlands respectively. The relationship (if any) between Welsh and English migration patterns is discussed in chapter 10.

for example, were more likely to emigrate in the 1880s than they had been in the 1870s so that for them a destination overseas became relatively more attractive as London became relatively less attractive. Natives of the South Midlands, on the other hand, were not only less likely to move to the urban areas in the 1880s, they were also less likely to emigrate.

Potential migrants from the West of England counties – Devon, Cornwall, Somerset and Dorset – behaved in a similar way to those in some of the South Midlands counties. We have seen that emigration from the West of England counties was not only exceptionally high but tended to fluctuate less than from most other counties. Emigration probably rose in the 1880s, but it is unlikely that it rose from Devon and Dorset and it definitely fell from Cornwall. Yet internal migration *fell* from every county in the West of England. Similarly, internal migration from the West of England rose strongly in the 1870s although emigration was also tending to rise.

It is difficult to see how the timing of rural–urban internal migration, which we have described, could have been so regular unless it was largely determined by the relative attractiveness of the urban areas. If it had been determined by changes in the rural counties it is difficult to see how the timing of the main internal migration flows could have been similar. We might also argue that if migration from rural areas had been determined by the relative degrees of 'push' we would expect emigration to be more likely to rise in the same decades as internal migration. In fact, it was more likely to fall. But this argument would rest on an assumption that internal migrants and emigrants were drawn from the same population, which is unproven. The fluctuation in the rate of internal migration must have been caused by changes in the relative attractiveness of the towns. For example, internal migration may have been partly determined by fluctuations in the demand for building labour – i.e. of the urban building cycle. We must remember, however, that fluctuations in the rate of rural–urban migration seem to have been as marked for women as for men, which means that women were probably equally affected by changes in the relative attraction of the towns as men.

We would expect that there was a degree of inertia in the population. For example, if internal migration from a county fell by 5,000 persons we would not reasonably expect emigration to increase by equal numbers. In the 1880s, for example, the rate of male emigration from rural counties rose by between 1.5% and 0.5% compared with a fall of between 1.9% and 1.3% in the rate of internal migration. Female emigration rose by between 0.1% and 0.9%, compared with a fall of between 1.8% and 2.4% in internal migration. If we assume that emigrants and internal migrants were drawn from the same population, some of those who would have gone to the towns under more favourable conditions must have stayed at home rather than emigrate. The degree of inertia was probably rather small for males. (The rise in emigration may not have been very much less than the fall in internal migration.) But the degree of inertia for females was much greater. The number of female migrants who left the rural counties in the 1880s must have fallen by between 11% and 25%.

This degree of inertia which we have noticed in the 1880s cannot have been a permanent feature, because when emigration from the rural counties fell sharply in the 1890s (i.e. when the rate of return probably rose) the rate of movement into other counties did not recover. About 14% of natives of rural counties left their county of birth (net of returns) in the 1870s when emigration was low, and about 13% moved in the 1880s when emigration was high. But in the 1890s when emigration was very low, migration out of the rural counties was unlikely to have exceeded 11% of the native population. The relationship between internal migration and emigration was complicated by a downward trend in the rate of internal migration. Hence, the substitution between internal migration and emigration must have been limited.

The decision to emigrate in some of the rural counties seems to have been unrelated to the decision to move to another part of the country. About 17% of all emigrants between 1861 and 1900 came from the West of England and the South Midlands. This was about a half of all emigrants from rural areas. In the main, the pattern of internal migration from these areas was similar to that from the other rural counties. It was presumably equally affected by the relative attraction of the urban areas. But the emigration pattern from most of the South Midlands and most of the West of England was different to emigration from the other rural counties. There are two possible explanations for the coincidence of a perverse pattern of emigration and of 'normal' patterns of internal migration. The timing of emigration from the West and from the South Midlands may have been determined by factors which were largely specific to the region. On the other hand, the decision to emigrate in these areas may not have been related to the decision to move internally. Emigration was very low in the South Midlands and it is possible that people were largely ignorant about it. The opposite was true in the West of England, where emigration was common. The Cornish, for example, were more likely to leave the country than to go to another county. It is possible

Table 8.10. *Internal migration and emigration (net of returns) from the 18 urban counties, 1861–1900, as % of total native population*

	1861–70	1871–80	1881–90	1891–1900
To overseas	2.8 ± 0.2	2.2 ± 0.2	3.3 ± 0.2	1.3 ± 0.2
To other counties	7.0	7.3	6.6	6.8

Source: Appendix 1.

that some of the Cornish considered emigration before they considered internal migration.

VI

The data on internal migration from the urban counties are much more difficult to interpret. In the first place, the urban counties were much more varied than the rural counties. One county, London, was an urban area in its own right (even including Middlesex), whereas Leicestershire, for example, included an urban area surrounded by a rural hinterland. Native migration from an urban county was the sum of a set of different flows, just as it was from a rural county. But migration from the urban counties included flows like the movement to the suburbs – which was rare across the borders of the rural counties. There is, therefore, no significance in the variance in the rate of internal migration from the urban counties. On the other hand, changes in the rate of internal migration from urban counties are more likely to be significant.

Fluctuations in the rate of internal migration from the urban counties seem to have been roughly similar to fluctuations from the rural counties.[49] Emigration from the urban counties as a whole was 2.8 ± 0.2% in 1861–70 and 2.2 ± 0.2% in 1871–80 (Table 8.10). Emigration was almost certainly lower in the 1870s than in the 1860s. In the same decades the rate of internal migration was 7.0% and 7.3% respectively. If we assume that our estimate of internal migration is an equally good sample of all internal movement in the two decades there was

[49] On fourteen occasions when male emigration rose from urban counties, male internal migration fell in eleven and rose in only one. But on twenty-two occasions when emigration fell, internal migration rose on only seven occasions and fell in nine. On eleven occasions when female emigration rose internal migration fell in five and rose in one. On twenty-six occasions when emigration fell, internal migration rose in eleven and fell in ten. There were eighteen urban counties and hence there were fifty-four observations for each sex.

almost certainly some trade-off between emigration and internal migration. Emigration definitely fell in nine of the eighteen urban counties in the 1870s and in seven of those counties movement to other counties rose. The changes in migration rates, however, were relatively slight and there were important exceptions to the general pattern. Londoners, for example, seem to have been no more likely to go abroad or to move internally in the 1870s than in the previous decades. Our estimates of urban migration in the 1860s and 1870s neither support nor deny that internal migration and emigration were substitutes.

In the 1880s on the other hand, the sharp rise in the rate of emigration from urban counties was accompanied by a fall in the rate of internal migration. Emigration from urban counties rose to 3.3% ± 0.2%, 30% to 75% higher than in the previous decade. Movement to other counties net of returns fell from 7.3% to 6.6%. Emigration definitely rose from fourteen of the urban counties in the 1880s and internal migration definitely fell in twelve of those. The extent of the substitution between internal migration and emigration is difficult to establish, but there were at least 200,000 additional emigrants from urban counties in the 1880s. Internal migration fell by about 60,000. This would suggest that some of the emigrants from the northern industrial counties like Lancashire, Yorkshire, Cheshire and Durham (from which emigration peaked in the 1880s) were normally relatively immobile and only decided to leave their county of birth when emigration was particularly attractive. This conclusion must be very tentative. The estimates of internal migration from urban counties only capture a small proportion of total movement. Hence, some of the apparent fall of 10% in the rate of internal migration between 1871–80 and 1881–90 may merely reflect change in the direction and nature of the migration flows. There seems little doubt, however, that movement to other counties fell in the 1880s although possibly by less than the estimates suggest. This would mean that it is unlikely that much of the increase in emigration from urban counties in the 1880s was at the expense of movement to other parts of England and Wales.

Migration from the urban counties to another part of England and Wales cannot have been caused by the simple attraction of other urban counties. In our discussion of the pattern of internal migration from the rural counties it was assumed (correctly) that it was dominated by the relative degree of attraction of the towns. If this were equally true of the urban counties we would expect that internal migration from urban counties fell when rural out-migration rose. In fact, urban and rural out-migration rose and fell in parallel. This may have been a coincidence, but it is possible that urban workers were more likely to move when the towns were attracting relatively large numbers of rural-urban migrants. Alternatively, a buoyant urban labour market may have made it easier for both the rural and the urban-born migrant.

The pattern of urban migration in the 1890s was also similar to the pattern in the rural areas. Emigration fell by at least a half. Internal migration appears to have risen overall but its fall was nowhere near sufficient to make up for the shortfall in emigration. Emigration fell in fifteen of the eighteen urban counties in the 1890s but internal migration only rose in six and definitely fell in seven. Hence, the decision to emigrate in the 1890s, may not have been related to the attraction of other English and Welsh counties.

The migration pattern of industrial South Wales and London was quite different from that in the other urban counties. Emigration from South Wales seems to have fallen continuously throughout the period, from about 8% of the native population in 1861–70 to about 1% in 1891–1900. Despite falling emigration, movement to other counties from South Wales fell sharply in the 1880s. But the most striking feature was that natives became increasingly less likely to leave the area at all. This was presumably connected with the continuous expansion of coal-mining. (Coal output in Glamorgan rose by 46% in the 1870s, 36% in the 1880s and 27% in the 1890s.) This does not necessarily mean that the migration decision in South Wales was dominated by what was happening within South Wales itself. Emigration from South Wales was exceptionally heavy in the 1860s; therefore we can assume that the flow of information was high for some years. We can surmise that many potential migrants from South Wales considered emigration and made a decision *not to emigrate*. Finally, London had both a perverse emigration pattern and a perverse pattern of movement to other counties. Emigration rates tended to be stable until the 1890s and then fell. But movement of Londoners out of the county tended to rise throughout the period. This was almost certainly a consequence of the spread of the built up area into other counties and the growth of suburbs. This type of move cannot be disaggregated from the net moves of Londoners across the county boundary. If it were disaggregated we might find that London migration was not dissimilar to the other English urban counties. We cannot tell whether the perverse pattern of London emigration was associated with a 'normal' pattern of internal migration as was the case in the West of England, for example.

The pattern of internal migration and emigration from the urban counties – despite the difficulties of interpretation – tends to confirm our view of migration from the rural counties. There were occasions when emigration occurred at the expense of movement within England and Wales, for example, as from most of the rural counties in the 1880s. But when emigration was low from a county internal migration was often low as well.

VII

This chapter has examined the relationship between internal migration and emigration in late nineteenth-century England and Wales and, in particular, the effect of urban growth on the rate of emigration. Urban growth could have affected emigration in two ways. The growth of towns could have provided an alternative destination for rural migrants which would have reduced the rate of emigration. On the other hand, urban growth could have increased the rate of emigration through the spread of information, transport and trading links.

We have paid considerable attention to Professor Brinley Thomas's thesis that fluctuations in the rate of emigration in this period were determined by changes in the relative attraction of the towns and overseas. In the domestic phase of a building/investment cycle, migrants were drawn to the towns and in the overseas phase they were drawn abroad. The thesis assumes, however, that the great majority of emigrants came from the rural areas which is incorrect.

The relative attraction of the urban areas and overseas cannot have determined the rate of emigration. But, in theory, emigration and internal migration could still have been substitutes, particularly for rural migrants. If they were substitutes, we would expect that those rural counties with high long run emigration rates would have relatively low internal migration rates, and that the fluctuations in internal and overseas counties were negatively correlated.

We found that in many rural counties, relatively large numbers of emigrants were associated, in the long run, with relatively small numbers of internal migrants, but in general there was no significiant relationship between long run rates of emigration and internal migration. Emigration from the counties where it was very high was more than enough to compensate for a relatively low rate of movement to other counties. (Long run out-migration – to all destinations – was significantly correlated with emigration.) This presumably means that some emigrants had only chosen between leaving the country and staying at home and had not considered migration to an urban area.

Secondly, it is possible that in some of the counties where internal migration seems to have been a substitute for emigration, it may have been because few people knew about emigration.[50] If this is true, some of the internal migrants cannot have considered emigration. Finally, there were many important rural counties where both internal and overseas migration rates were low.

Natives of Devon, Cornwall and Somerset were exceptionally likely to emigrate and this appears *partly* to have been at the expense of internal migration. Natives of some of the counties to the immediate north and west of London (Buckinghamshire, Hertfordshire, Berkshire, Bedfordshire, Oxfordshire and Cambridgeshire) were very unlikely to emigrate but were exceptionally likely to move internally – i.e. to London. Natives of Suffolk, Norfolk and Lincolnshire seem to have been relatively immobile. They were relatively unlikely to move internally *or* to emigrate.

We tested whether the fluctuations in internal migration and emigration were negatively correlated – i.e. whether they were substitutes. In our model, we used the rate of emigration in each decade as the independent variable and the dependent variables were designed to capture the economic structure of each county and the information available to prospective emigrants.[51] We included the rate of internal migration in each decade as an additional explanatory variable. We found that there was no relationship between male internal and overseas emigration rates – the internal migration coefficient was not significant. We found that there was a correlation between female internal and overseas emigration rates and that it had the expected sign. But unfortunately, female internal migration was correlated with the emigration rate in the previous decade and the coefficient was not significant. Our understanding of these results, which are set out in detail in Appendix 7, is that these relationships do not in general support the thesis that internal migration and emigration were substitutes.

On the other hand our analysis of the fluctuations in internal and overseas migration from rural counties shows that the attractiveness of the towns was probably the most important factor in changes in the rate of internal migration. (This is confirmed by our model which

---

[50] This conclusion is not based on the low emigration rate *per se*, but on our observation of the fluctuation in the rate of emigration from the South Midlands counties. In particular, emigration was high in the 1870s when it was least attractive and low in the 1880s when it was most attractive.

[51] The independent variables were the proportion of the male labour force working in agriculture; the proportion of young adults in the population; the level of unskilled wages; the proportion of the total population living in urban areas and the proportion of persons who could sign the marriage register. We also included time and county dummies and the migration rate in the previous period. See Appendix 7.

shows that internal migration rates were correlated with the economic circumstances of the counties.) In the 1870s, internal migration from most rural counties rose, but unfortunately we cannot tell if emigration fell simultaneously. Emigration rose substantially from the majority of the rural counties in the 1880s. At the same time, there was a substantial fall in the rate of internal migration from virtually every county. The increase in the propensity to emigrate was somewhat less than the fall in the propensity to move to another county, but this could simply have been because some of the people who were deterred from moving to the towns were unwilling to take a bigger step and emigrate. The propensity to move internally fell by about 18% in the 1880s and it seems clear that the pull of the towns had substantially diminished compared with the 1870s.

But it is not clear that all the increase in emigration in the 1880s was explained by the fall in migration to the towns. Internal migration fell from every rural county but three, but it also fell from those counties where emigration failed to rise and from those where emigration *fell*. This may mean that in some counties the potential emigrants and internal migrants were not necessarily drawn from the same group of people. Finally, emigration fell from virtually every rural county in the 1890s. But internal migration from about half of the rural counties also fell.

The urban migration pattern is more difficult to interpret, but with the major exceptions of London and South Wales the fluctuations were virtually the same as from the rural counties. Emigration fell in the 1870s, rose substantially in the 1880s and fell substantially in the 1890s. Movement to other counties rose in the 1870s, fell in the 1880s and failed to rise significantly in the 1890s. Hence the fluctuations in urban–urban migration were the same as in rural–urban migration. However, in the 1880s urban emigration increased by much more than internal migration fell. This could mean that the towns became less attractive and there was nowhere for urban people to go but abroad. In general, the urban migration pattern does not contradict our interpretation of the rural migration pattern.

The relation between internal migration and emigration is complicated by the fact that the rate of internal migration appears to have been falling from the 1870s. Hence the pattern of the last three decades might be a continuous fall in movement from the rural counties to the urban areas on which was superimposed a decade of exceptional emigration.

Migration from the rural areas was probably high in the 1870s because the pull of the urban areas was high, and lower in the 1880s because the urban pull was less powerful. Some of those who might have gone to the urban areas in the 1880s emigrated, but the fall in the attractiveness of the towns does not explain all the emigration in that decade. And the extremely low emigration from the rural areas in the 1890s was *not* because rural–urban migration was more attractive. Changes in the relative attraction of the urban areas are not a sufficient explanation of changes in emigration rates. The decision to move to another part of the country or to go abroad must, in part, have been independent.

9

Rural–urban stage emigration, 1861–1900

I

There has been considerable interest in stage migration in the literature on European emigration, particularly in Scandinavia. Some of the emigrants from Norway, Sweden, Denmark and Finland may have made frequent moves within the country before they went abroad although this is extremely difficult to test.[1] Most research has concentrated on a special case of stage migration – how many of the urban emigrants had come originally from the rural areas. Rural–urban stage emigration appears to have been quite common in Scandinavia. For example, less than half of the emigrants from Bergen in the last quarter of the century had been born there.[2] Emigration rates from many of the (larger) Scandinavian towns were higher than from the rural areas and a commonly expressed view is that the towns drew most of the migrants from the surrounding rural areas, some of whom emigrated.[3] This raises the important question of where the decision to emigrate was taken. If the emigrants had decided to leave the country before they left the rural areas they can be considered to be *rural* emigrants who happened to emigrate via an urban area. But if they had lived in the towns for some years before emigrating they can reasonably be regarded as urban emigrants.[4]

---

[1] It would be necessary to have some form of a continuous population register to measure the total number of internal moves that an emigrant had made. It is possible in Sweden, for example, to trace emigrants from their place of birth to the towns but even these are only a few possible observations.

[2] Semmingsen, 'Norwegian emigration', pp. 156–7.

[3] 'Urban influence fields' are thought to have surrounded the cities of Helsinki, Copenhagen, Bergen, Oslo, Stockholm and Goteburg, among others. Semmingsen, 'Norwegian emigration', p. 154. Rundblom and Norman, *From Sweden to America*, pp. 134–6. Kero, *Migration from Finland*, p. 54.

[4] Nilsson showed that about three-quarters of the emigrants from Stockholm in the

Very little is known about the extent of stage migration in England and Wales. The only published paper – by Ross Duncan – that traces nineteenth-century emigrants through a series of moves, shows that a group of assisted migrants to Australia from Gloucestershire and Cornwall had made many moves before emigration.[5] But it is not known if the emigrants had been more mobile internally than non-emigrants. Surprisingly, there has been no attempt to estimate the probable extent of rural–urban stage emigration in England and Wales. For example, the influential work of Brinley Thomas implicitly assumed that none of the urban emigrants had been born in the rural areas.[6]

Our estimates of emigration from England and Wales in the later nineteenth century are based on the county of birth of the migrants and it is essential to know the probable extent of stage emigration. We have been able to show, for example, that the majority of emigrants had been born in the urban counties. Therefore, if rural–urban stage migration was extensive, the rural counties could not have been a significant source of emigrants. In turn, this would mean that our explanation of the increase in emigration from the rural counties in the 1880s, for example, would have to be related to conditions in the urban counties rather than in the rural counties.

It can be shown, however, that the majority of the rural-born emigrants from England and Wales could not have moved to the urban areas before they left the country. Their last (permanent) place of residence could not have been an urban area. This is because the number of rural-born lifetime migrants who were enumerated in the urban counties was insufficient to have provided the majority of rural-born emigrants. This would be true, even if internal migrants were substantially more likely to emigrate than were the natives of the rural counties who did not move to the towns.

II

An upper limit to the number of rural–urban stage emigrants can be estimated as follows. Assume, for the sake of argument, that rural–urban migration doubled the propensity to emigrate. For example, we assume that the 48,000 male natives of Norfolk who were living

1880s had been born outside the city. But nearly one half had lived in Stockholm for more than five years before emigrating. F. Nilsson, *Emigrationen från Stockholm*, p. 310. The conclusion of Tederbrand's study is similar. Half of the emigrants from the industrial towns of Vasternoerland who had been born in rural areas had lived in the towns for more than five years. Tederbrand, *Vasternoerland och Nordamerika*, p. 308.

[5] Duncan, *Case studies in emigration*, pp. 288–9.

[6] Thomas *Migration and economic growth*, pp. 124–5.

in the urban counties were twice as likely to emigrate, as the 220,000 male natives of Norfolk who were living in Norfolk and the other rural counties.[7] (The number of lifetime migrants are the median values for the years 1861–1900.)

We cannot assume, however, that if rural–urban migration doubled the propensity to emigrate, that the number of Norfolk-born emigrants who left from an urban area was proportionally twice as great as it was among Norfolk born in rural counties. The Norfolk-born population who were still in Norfolk, for example, must have been less at risk of emigration than those in London because their age distribution was different. In chapter 4 we demonstrated that the ages of current internal migrants at the time of arrival, net of returns to their county of birth, must have approximated the following distribution: 4% aged 0–4, 34% aged 5–14, 51% aged 15–24 and 11% aged 25–34. (We assumed that there were no internal migrants (net of returns) aged over 35.) The youngest migrants (aged 0–4) would have lived in their new county for about 33 years before reaching age 35, those aged 5–14 for about 25 years and so on. Hence, every 100 migrants would live about 1,800 person years before the age of 35. Each migrant was, therefore, at risk of emigrating for about 18 years.[8]

We know the number of Norfolk-born natives who were still living in the rural counties. We can estimate the mean years they were at risk of emigrating from the age distribution of the population. We assume that the number of Norfolk-born lifetime migrants in the other rural counties was approximately equal to the number of rural lifetime migrants who were living in Norfolk and also that their age distribution was similar.[9] These are both reasonable assumptions. The age

---

[7] Most Norfolk-born internal migrants were living in London and Yorkshire.

[8]

No. of migrants	Age at arrival	Person years lived to age 35
4	0–4	132
34	5–14	850
51	15–24	765
11	25–34	55
Total person years to age 35		1,802

Deaths of lifetime migrants are ignored. Since we are attempting to estimate the maximum feasible extent of stage emigration we ignore those factors which would reduce our estimates.

[9] It does not matter how many Norfolk-born migrants returned to Norfolk or to one of the other rural counties, of course, since by definition they must have been replaced by others.

distribution of the Norfolk-born population in all rural counties would then approximate the age distribution of the population of the county of Norfolk. We also assume that all emigrants from Norfolk were aged 15–34. We know the population in each decade, and the proportion aged 15–34. It is easy, therefore, to estimate the mean male population aged 15–34 in Norfolk in each year. This was about 67,500. The male Norfolk-born population living in rural areas who were at risk of emigrating between 1861 and 1900 was, therefore, 67,500 × 40 person years i.e. 2,700,000. There were 220,000 male natives of Norfolk of all ages living outside the urban areas. Hence on average, each was at risk of emigrating for 12.3 years. We know that lifetime migrants in urban areas were at risk for about 18 years, i.e. for about 1.5 times as long.

We have assumed that rural–urban migrants were twice as likely to emigrate than if they had remained in Norfolk. Therefore the ratio of person years at risk must have been about 1 to 3.[10] Total emigration of Norfolk-born males in 1861–1900 was 21,900. The median population of male Norfolk natives in urban and rural counties was 48,000 and 220,000 respectively. On these assumptions $\frac{21,900 \times 3 \times 48,000}{220,000 + (3 \times 48,000)} = 8,644$ of the male Norfolk-born emigrants must have left from the urban areas and 13,236 from the rural areas.

These calculations are rather rough and ready but they are designed only to estimate the upper limit of rural–urban stage emigration. Our method can only estimate stage emigration from counties with a small urban population because there is no way of estimating rural–urban movement within a county. This does not matter too much for the rural counties, because the uncounted migration tends to net out. Norfolk stage emigration is undercounted by the number of rural born who emigrated from Norwich. It is overcounted by the number of Norfolk born who left from the rural part of an urban county, i.e. from a town of less than 20,000 population in Essex.

III

Our estimates of the maximum extent of stage emigration from the rural counties can be seen in Table 9.1. It is unlikely that more than 311,000 (38%) of the 814,500[11] emigrants who had been born in the

[10] It could have been less. It was assumed that only persons aged 15–34 in Norfolk were at risk of emigration but that all lifetime migrants in the urban counties, aged 0–34, were at risk. This gives an upward bias to the rate of stage emigration.

[11] This is the best proxy for total emigration for the period 1861–1900 as a whole. The method of estimation is explained in chapter 4.

Table 9.1. *Maximum rural–urban stage emigration, 1861–1900 (net of returns) (000s) (assuming that rural–urban migration doubled the propensity to emigrate)*

Born in		London and Middlesex	West Midlands	Lanca-shire	York-shire	Industrial Wales	Other urban	Total rural – urban stage emigration	All emigration from rural counties	% Stage emigration
South Midlands	M	18.0	2.4	0.7	1.3	—	6.0 (1)	28.5	65.7	43.4
	F	7.4	0.7	0.2	0.4	—	0.8	9.5	24.0	39.6
East of England	M	15.1	—	3.0	10.1	—	7.5 (2)	35.7	88.2	40.5
	F	8.7	—	1.2	3.4	—	3.0	16.3	39.9	40.9
West of England	M	30.8	—	3.5	—	10.5	19.0 (3)	63.8	210.7	30.3
	F	19.8	—	2.0	—	2.4	10.5	34.7	112.4	30.3
Rural Wales and Borders	M	4.3	6.8	7.4	0.9	19.6	3.7 (4)	42.8	99.4	43.0
	F	2.5	4.0	6.1	1.0	6.6	2.8	23.0	56.8	40.5
Others	M	2.3	9.2	7.5	5.7	—	8.7 (5)	33.4	69.5	48.1
	F	1.6	6.4	5.6	3.8	—	6.0	23.4	47.5	49.3
All rural	M	70.5	18.4	22.1	18.0	30.1	44.9	204.2	533.9	38.2
	F	40.0	11.1	15.1	8.6	9.0	23.1	106.9	280.6	38.1

Key: (1) mainly the South East suburban counties
(2) Essex and Nottinghamshire
(3) Gloucestershire and Hampshire
(4) mainly Cheshire
(5) Northumberland and Durham, Nottinghamshire and Cheshire

Note: For the definition of rural counties and those included in each region see Table 6.1. 'Other urban' counties are Durham, Northumberland, Cheshire, Nottinghamshire, Gloucestershire, Leicestershire, Essex, Kent, Surrey, Hampshire and Sussex.

rural areas were stage emigrants. The proportion of males and females who are likely to have been stage emigrants was the same. This result obviously depends on our view of the effect of internal migration on the propensity to emigrate. Our assumption that a person who had moved to a city was twice as likely to emigrate can be tested by looking at the rate of emigration that it implies. For example, if male lifetime migrants from the West of England had been twice as likely to emigrate as non-migrants, the male lifetime migrants would have been going overseas at an average rate of 10.5% in each decade. In other words, the West of England would have lost overseas the equivalent of 37% of its male young adult population (net of returns). Similarly more than 27% of male lifetime migrants born in Wales and more than 19% born in the eastern counties would have emigrated and not returned. These emigration rates are extremely high and we can be fairly sure that our estimates place an upper limit on the extent of stage emigration from the rural counties.

The English counties where stage emigration may have been relatively high, were (in order) Westmorland, Hertfordshire, Shropshire and Worcestershire. It is possible (if unlikely) that a half of all emigrants from these counties had been resident in an urban area. Counties where stage emigration was probably less important were (in order) Cornwall, Bedfordshire, Huntingdon, Devon, Dorset, Somerset, Wiltshire, Suffolk and Northamptonshire. Stage emigration from these counties must have been less than 40% of all emigration, and in all probability it was much less.

Rural Wales may have produced quite a large number of stage emigrants. There were three important internal migration streams from the rural parts of Wales, to Lancashire, the West Midlands and South Wales. The equivalent of 16.3% of the rural Welsh males and 9.3% of females emigrated, of which something under 40% could have done so from one of the urban areas (Table 9.1). There were proportionately as many people from the South Midlands and the East of England living in the large towns as there were rural Welsh. But the East of England and the South Midlands produced relatively few emigrants and proportionately far fewer than rural Wales.[12] Hence, an

[12] *Emigration rates of natives of rural regions (% of total native population aged 15–24)*

	Rural Wales	South Midlands	East of England
Males	16.3	11.1	11.8
Females	9.3	4.4	5.4

English rural migrant in London – where most migrants from these regions were living – was almost certainly less likely to emigrate than a Welsh migrant living in South Wales or the West Midlands.

The second important feature is that most of the emigration from the West of England which was exceptionally heavy appears to have been direct. Only Wiltshire (for men) and Somerset and Dorset (for women) had stage emigration rates that may have been as high as the mean for England and Wales. The West of England counties did not send a large proportion of their native population to the urban counties. Stage emigration from the west must have been less than 30% of all emigration from these counties. We have already seen that this rate implies that more than 37% of *all* male West of England born lifetime migrants in the urban counties emigrated, which is virtually impossible. We are left with the fact that the West of England, which was the rural region with the highest level of emigration was the least integrated into the internal migration flow. But it is not generally true that counties with high emigration rates tended to send their emigrants directly overseas. Natives of Westmorland, Shropshire and Herefordshire may have been exceptionally likely to go to Birmingham and the Black Country or Lancashire and then to emigrate.

There is some interesting circumstantial evidence about stage emigration from London. Emigration by Norfolk and Suffolk natives increased substantially in the 1880s (emigration was at its peak from most counties in this decade). But Londoners may have been no more likely to emigrate than they had been in the previous decade.[13] This raises an interesting question. If significant numbers of the Norfolk and Suffolk-born emigrants in the 1880s had been living in London, why were they particularly likely to emigrate in the 1880s, when the Londoners were not?[14] On the other hand, the natives of all the so-called South Midland counties (Buckinghamshire, Northamptonshire, Oxfordshire, Hertfordshire, Berkshire and Bedfordshire) were no more likely to emigrate in the 1880s than in other decades. With the exception of natives of Northamptonshire, the majority of lifetime

[13] Male emigration of London born was $4.0 \pm 0.5\%$ in the 1870s and $4.7 \pm 0.4\%$ in the 1880s. Female emigration was $3.2 \pm 0.5\%$ in the 1870s and $2.9 \pm 0.4\%$ in the 1880s.

[14] Obviously, considerable stage emigration by Norfolk or Suffolk natives in the 1880s is not incompatible with relatively low emigration of London natives. The migrants who had been born in Norfolk and Suffolk could have been living in a particular part of London. For example, London is normally considered to have included three separate labour markets in the late nineteenth century. See E. Hobsbawm, 'The nineteenth-century London labour market', pp. 3–28, in R. Glass (ed.), *London, aspects of change* (Macgibbon and Kee, 1964).

migrants from these counties lived in London. Natives of London and the South Midland counties seem to have behaved rather similarly in the 1880s, which suggests that there may have been stage emigration from these counties. But the total number of stage emigrants cannot have been high, since the South Midlands counties produced few emigrants.

On the other hand, the circumstantial evidence does suggest that some of the rural Welsh may have been stage emigrants. Only four Welsh counties (Carmarthen, Pembroke, Cardigan and Brecon) sent substantial numbers of internal migrants to the two counties of industrial Wales. Natives of three of these counties were no more likely to emigrate in the 1880s, when conditions for emigration were very favourable, than in other decades.[15] This corresponds with the experience of natives of Glamorgan and Monmouth where emigration fell continuously from the 1860s to the 1890s. But natives of five of the other seven rural Welsh counties were *more* likely to emigrate in the 1880s than in other decades.[16] But most of the lifetime migrants from these counties were living in Lancashire and the West Midlands, where the natives were also more likely to emigrate in the 1880s. Hence, the circumstantial evidence supports our view that stage emigration may have been more common from rural Wales.

IV

We can also use the analysis of stage emigration to place an upper limit on the number of emigrants from the main urban counties who had been born in a rural area. This will provide an estimate of emigration *from the counties themselves*, in contrast to the emigration of the *natives* of a particular county. The calculations are rather rough and ready but the assumptions tend to overstate stage emigration and we can be fairly sure that it was not in excess of our estimates.

We assumed that the number of rural emigrants from say, Lancashire who had been born in Lancashire was roughly proportional to the rural share of the population, and that the number of Lancashire emigrants who had been born in the rural parts of the other urban counties was proportional to the share of the rural population in those counties. Hence, total (male) emigration from Lancashire was 149,000 natives less about 15,000 who went from other counties. Of these

---

[15] The exception was Brecon, where native emigration peaked in the 1880s.
[16] Emigration of natives of Montgomery, Merioneth, Flint, Caernarvon and Anglesey peaked in the 1880s. The exceptions were Denbigh and Flint.

33,000 were assumed to have been born in the rural parts of Lancashire. We have already shown that no more than 40% of emigrants from rural counties can have been rural–urban stage emigrants, so that no more than about 13,000 Lancashire-born emigrants from the urban areas can probably have been born in the countryside. About 20,000 of the emigrants from Lancashire had been born in the other urban counties. About half of these emigrants were assumed to have been born in the rural parts of these counties. We also assumed all the rural-born migrants to Lancashire went to Lancashire towns. We already know that a maximum of about 22,000 male emigrants from Lancashire had been born in the rural counties. Hence, total male emigration from the county of Lancashire in 1861–1900 was 176,000, of which not more than 45,000 (26%) can have been rural–urban stage emigrants. These calculations are rather crude, of course, but our assumptions all tend to increase the extent of stage emigration. For example, it was assumed that emigration of Lancashire born from the other counties was as likely as from (urban) Lancashire; that all the rural-born internal migrants had gone to the urban parts of Lancashire and (as before) that rural–urban and urban–urban migration doubled the propensity to emigrate. We can be fairly sure, therefore, that our estimates of stage emigration are an upper limit.

Table 9.2 shows the maximum extent of rural–urban stage emigration from the main urban counties. Rural-born stage emigrants must have been outnumbered by direct emigrants and by urban–urban stage emigrants by between two and three to one in every county except Glamorgan. In fact, rural–urban stage emigration must have been even less important. About half of the lifetime migrant population of London, for example, had been born in the neighbouring counties of Surrey, Kent and Essex. Some parts of those counties were as rural as, say, Herefordshire but others were included in the London conurbation. Most of East London was in Essex, Bromley was in Kent and Richmond in Surrey. A stage emigrant who was born in Essex may merely have moved from Stratford to Shoreditch. The London born were much more likely to emigrate than natives of Essex, Kent and Surrey and it is possible that the London emigrants from these three counties all came from the built up area. We assumed that rural-born migrants were equally likely to emigrate as urban-born migrants. This means that our estimate of the extent of stage emigration is more likely to be too high than too low.

Table 9.2 shows that total emigration from London (of natives and stage migrants) was probably more than 500,000 persons. The equivalent of 20.0% of the male population aged 15–24 must have gone abroad and not returned and 12.1% of the female population (Table 9.3). Evidence of emigration rates from the larger European cities is scarce, but Stockholm, for example, lost emigrants at an average annual rate of only 2.8% of its population between 1851 and 1930 (6.5% between 1881 and 1890). Copenhagen lost about 3.4% between 1868 and 1900.[17] These rates are difficult to compare with those from London – not least because there must be considerable double counting in the denominator. But the equivalent London emigration rate for 1861–1900 for example, would be about 3.3% of the total population in each decade *net of returns*. Copenhagen and Stockholm emigration is expressed in gross rates which means that London emigration may have been relatively higher than from these Scandinavian cities.

There is an important difference between emigration from London and the Scandinavian cities. No more than one quarter of London emigrants can have previously moved there from the rural areas. But only 25% of emigrants from Stockholm (1880–93), 55% of emigrants from Copenhagen (1910–14) and less than half the emigrants from Bergen (1875–94) had been born there.[18] The picture is similar for the other urban areas. Rural–urban stage emigrants must have been less than one-third of all emigrants from each of the main urban areas except from industrial Wales. In Lancashire, they cannot have been much more than a quarter and they may have been even less.

On the other hand, South Wales could have been an important source of rural–urban stage emigrants. We estimated that a maximum of 39,000 persons who had been born in the rural counties could have emigrated from Glamorgan and Monmouth of which about two-thirds would have been Welsh and most of the rest would have come from the West of England. About 14,000 could have been born in the rural parts of Glamorgan and Monmouth but have subsequently moved into the urban areas. Stage emigrants could have been as much as a half of all male emigrants from industrial Wales and a third of all female. It is perhaps worth noting at this point that this aspect of Welsh emigration has not been anticipated by the majority of the literature. Most writers on Welsh emigration have been at pains to point out that there was heavy migration in the late nineteenth century from rural Wales to the mining districts. They have assumed that Welsh rural

---

[17] Hvidt, *Flight to America*, pp. 58–9. S. Carlsson, 'Chronology and composition of Swedish emigration to America', in Rundblom and Norman, *From Sweden to America*, p. 122.

[18] Nilsson, *Emigrationen från Stockholm*, p. 365. Semmingsen, 'Norwegian emigration', p. 156.

Table 9.2. *Upper limit of stage emigration from the main urban counties (net of returns), 1861–1900 (000s)*

| | Emigration from | | | | | | | | | | |
| Characteristics of emigrants | London and Middlesex | | Stafford-shire and Warwick-shire | | Lanca-shire | | York-shire | | Industrial Wales | | All the main urban counties | |
	M	F	M	F	M	F	M	F	M	F	M	F
Natives												
(i) Direct from urban areas	210	154	61	39	101	61	54	35	24	15	450	304
(ii) Direct from rural areas	5	4	20	13	20	12	27	17	14	9	86	55
(iii) Rural stage emigration	4	2	13	8	13	8	18	11	9	5	57	34
Stage Migrants												
(iv) Born in rural counties	70	40	18	11	22	15	18	9	30	9	158	84
(v) Born in rural parts of other urban counties	11	5	4	2	10	7	7	4	—	—	32	18
(vi) Born in urban parts of other urban counties	11	5	4	2	10	7	7	4	—	—	32	18

(vii) All emigration	311	210	120	75	176	110	131	80	77	38	815	513
(viii) Total rural–urban stage emigration (iii) + (iv) + (v)	85	47	35	21	45	30	43	24	39	14	247	136
Rural–urban stage emigration as a % of all emigration, i.e. [(viii)/(vii)] × 100	27	22	29	28	26	27	33	30	51	37	30	27

Notes: Rural counties are defined as those having less than 35% of their population at any time in urban areas containing more than 20,000 persons. The table should be read as follows, 311,000 male emigrants left London and Middlesex. Of these (i) 210,000 were natives of the urban part and left from it; (ii) 5,000 were natives of the rural part and left from it and (iii) 4,000 were natives of the rural part who left from the urban part. In addition, there was a maximum of 92,000 emigrants from London and Middlesex who had been born in another county. [(iv) + (v) + (vi)] of those, 70,000 had been born in a rural county (iv); 11,000 had been born in the rural part of an urban county (v); and 11,000 had been born in the urban part of an urban county (vi). The maximum number of emigrants from London and Middlesex who had been born in a rural area is therefore (iii) + (iv) + (v), i.e. 85,000 persons.

Note that the emigration of natives of London and Middlesex [(i) + (ii) + (iii)], i.e. 219,000 is not the same as the emigration of London natives given in Appendix 1 – i.e. 243,000; since it *excludes* our maximum estimate of the emigration of London natives from other counties. That is, it excludes London-born stage emigrants.

Table 9.3. *Estimate of total emigration (net of returns) from the main urban counties (including rural-born stage emigrants), 1861–1900 (000s)*

	Males	Females
London and Middlesex	311	210
Staffordshire and Warwickshire	120	75
Lancashire	176	110
Yorkshire	131	80
Industrial Wales	77	38
All emigration from the main urban counties	815	513
England and Wales	1,485	864

Note: Includes an estimate of the maximum extent of stage emigration – see text. The estimates also include those persons who are assumed to have emigrated *directly* from the rural parts of the urban counties. We estimate these to have numbered about 141,000 persons or about 11% of all emigrants from these counties.
Source: Calculated from Table 9.2. and Appendix 1.

Table 9.4. *Estimate of total emigration (net of returns) from the main urban counties (including rural-born stage emigrants), 1861–1900, as a % of those aged 15–24)*

	Male %	Female %
London and Middlesex	20.0	12.1
Staffordshire and Warwickshire	16.7	10.4
Lancashire	13.7	7.7
Yorkshire	11.9	6.8
Industrial Wales	23.0	12.2
England and Wales	15.4	8.9

Note: Includes an estimate of the maximum extent of stage emigration – see text.
Source: Calculated from Table 9.2 and Appendix 1.

emigration was low and Welsh urban emigration was negligible.[19] In fact, industrial Wales was one of the most important emigration regions in Britain. It could have lost the equivalent of about 23.0%

[19] For example, Brinley Thomas (ed.) *The Welsh economy. Studies in expansion* (University of Wales Press, Cardiff, 1962), chapter 1, pp. 9–29. The major exception is Alan Conway who conjectured that the rural Welsh may have emigrated via South Wales. Alan Conway, 'Welsh emigration to the United States', *Perspectives in American History*, 7, 1973, p. 226.

of its male young adult population (net of returns) and 12.2% of females. This issue is discussed in detail in chapter 10.

Our estimates of the maximum extent of stage emigration make it possible to compare the probable extent of emigration from the industrial counties as a whole. The data are summarised in Tables 9.3 and 9.4.[20] About 815,000 males and 513,000 females must have emigrated from London, the West Midlands, Lancashire, Yorkshire and South Wales. This was more than 54% of all male emigrants from England and Wales and more than 58% of all female emigrants. Hence, emigration rates from some of these counties exceeded those from rural counties. Of these, something under 600,000 males and 400,000 females were natives of one of these urban counties and emigrated from it. No more than 200,000 males and 100,000 females or about 25% of all emigrants from the main urban areas can have been born in one of the other urban counties or in one of the rural counties. Even so, emigration from both Lancashire and Yorkshire must have been below the mean rate from England and Wales (Table 9.4). But the rate of emigration from London and South Wales was probably well above the mean rate for England and Wales and they were emigration regions of major importance, as to a somewhat lesser extent, was the West Midlands.

The relatively low emigration from Lancashire and Yorkshire cannot have been because those counties did not attract internal migrants, of course. The share of stage emigrants was probably about the same in all industrial areas except in South Wales where it was probably high. The reason why emigration from Lancashire and Yorkshire was relatively low was because people who had been *born* in those counties seem to have been less prone to consider emigration than natives of London, Staffordshire and South Wales. More instructive, is our observation that emigration from Lancashire and Yorkshire was more concentrated in one decade than emigration from London, South Wales and in some other urban counties.[21] This was in the 1880s, when the benefits to be expected from emigration were exceptional. We might conjecture that the emigration threshold in London and South Wales was low whereas in Lancashire and Yorkshire (and

---

[20] The estimates imply that London was losing male and female emigrants at an average rate of 4.8% and 2.2%; Lancashire at 2.7% and 1.6%; Yorkshire 2.4% and 1.4% and industrial South Wales at 4.8% and 2.6%.

[21] About 30% of all emigration from London and about 20% of emigration from South Wales in the four decades 1861–1900 occurred in 1881–90 compared with about 37% for Yorkshire and Lancashire. These estimates are corrected for the population at risk.

several other industrial areas) people were more resistant to emigration and it tended to be high only under exceptional circumstances.

V

It is now possible to put an upper limit on the extent of rural–urban
stage emigration for England and Wales as a whole. Our assumptions
are maintained that the number of rural emigrants was proportional
to the share of the rural population in the county in which they were
born, and that rural–urban migration doubled the propensity to emigrate. This would imply that about 290,000 emigrants came from the
rural parts of the urban counties of which about 96,000 went directly
overseas and about 194,000 had previously moved to the cities. We
estimated that, at most, about 311,000 emigrants from the rural counties were stage emigrants. Therefore, no more than 500,000, or less
than a quarter of all emigrants can have moved from a rural area
to a city and then emigrated in the period 1861–1900. The bulk of
the emigrants from England and Wales did not come from the rural
areas, and the rate of emigration cannot have been dominated by
the relative attraction of the English cities for rural migrants. The more
interesting finding is that relatively few of the emigrants from English
cities seem to have been born in the countryside.[22]

The main features of English and Welsh emigration are summarised
in Table 9.5. Since the purpose of our calculation was to estimate
the maximum extent of stage emigration, assumptions were used that
were generous to stage migration which is, therefore, probably overestimated.

We can see from Table 9.5 that the 2⅓ million emigrants from England
and Wales between 1861 and 1900 were predominantly *urban*. Up
to two-thirds of all emigrants must have come from the towns and
cities and not much more than a third from the rural areas. In addition,
the majority of the urban emigrants could not have previously moved
there from the rural areas. There were more than 1½ million urban
emigrants of which no more than 500,000 can have been born in a
rural area. This means that at least 45% of *all* English and Welsh
emigrants in the period must have been both *born and brought up* in
an urban enivronment.

[22] The only writer who seems to have anticipated this result is Habakkuk. Habakkuk,
'Fluctuations in housebuilding', pp. 124–5. (This was a conjecture of course.) Professor Erickson was the first to point out that the majority of the emigrants in the
1880s came from the urban areas. She suspected, but could not prove that the urban
emigrants had been born there. Erickson, 'Who were?' (1972).

Table 9.5. *Estimate of emigration (net of returns) by place of last residence (including an estimate of stage emigration), 1861–1900 (000s and % of total emigration)*

	Emigrating from			
Born in	Towns and cities	Rural areas of urban counties	Rural counties	All emigrants
Towns and cities	1065 (45%)	—	—	1065 (45%)
Rural areas of urban counties	194 (8%)	290 (12%)	—	484 (21%)
Rural counties	311 (13%)	—	489 (21%)	800 (34%)
Total emigration	1570 (67%)	290 (12%)	489 (21%)	2349 (100%)
Upper limit of rural–urban stage emigration	505 (c.21%) of all emigration and c.20% of all emigration from urban areas)			

Notes: 'Towns and cities' are defined as continuous urban areas containing at least 20,000 persons. Rural counties are those where the urban population was less than 35% of the total population. The main assumptions are: that rural–urban migration doubled the propensity to emigrate; that there was no urban–rural migration (net of returns); that the share of emigration from the rural parts of an urban county was the same as the rural share of total population, and that emigration from the urban parts of rural counties (e.g. from Norwich) was equal to the emigration of rural born from the rural parts of other counties.

The estimate of stage emigration is an upper limit.

10

Wales and the Atlantic economy, 1861–1900

I

A common view in recent years is that Welsh migration in the late nineteenth and early twentieth century was qualitatively different from English. The main contributions have been made by Professor Brinley Thomas in 1959 and 1961[1] and (in an important restatement of his view) in 1972.[2] They have been taken up by several Welsh historians.[3]

The hypothesis of a distinctive Welsh migration pattern rests on the existence of a distinct Welsh economy and on the position of South Wales within it. Brinley Thomas argued that Welsh industry was geared almost entirely to the export trade in coal and that the 'rate or growth of output of coal in Wales synchronised with fluctuations in the British export sector'.[4] According to Brinley Thomas this had two consequences. In the first place, Wales had an inverse migration cycle and second the rate of emigration from Wales was low. Expansion in the South Wales coalfield was fastest in the decades 1881–90 and 1901–10, that is, in the decades when the long swing in English domestic investment turned down, and the North American long swing turned up. Hence, emigration from Wales was low when emigration from England was high. Similarly, rural–urban migration was relatively low in England in the 1880s and 1900s but relatively high in Wales. The main evidence used by Professor Thomas is the net gains and losses by migration in English and Welsh urban and

---

[1] Thomas, *The Welsh economy*, chapter 1, pp. 9–29. 'Wales and the Atlantic economy', pp. 169–92.
[2] Thomas, *Migration and urban development*, chapter 6, pp. 170–81.
[3] For example, Jones, 'Background to emigration from Great Britain', pp. 81–2. Conway, 'Welsh emigration to the United States', pp. 264–5.
[4] Thomas, *Migration and urban development*, p. 175.

Table 10.1. *Decennial net gains and losses by migration from English and Welsh rural and urban areas, 1871–1911 (000s)*

	1871–80	1881–90	1891–1900	1901–10
England				
Rural	−769	−731	−596	−251
Urban	+673	+132	+551	−346
	−96	−599	−45	−597
Wales				
Rural	−65	−106	−57	−38
Urban	+13	+88	+48	+132
	−52	−18	−9	−94

Source: Thomas, *Migration and urban development*, p. 176. Calculated from Cairncross, 'Internal migration in Victorian England', Welton, *England's recent progress*. Coalfield migration was recalculated by Professor Thomas.

rural areas. These are the familiar Welton/Cairncross estimates,[5] slightly amended. Professor Thomas's interpretation of the estimates (which are reproduced in Table 10.1) is as follows: in the 1870s, 'practically the whole of the rural exodus in England was absorbed in the urban sector of that country, whereas only one-fifth of the rural exodus in Wales was absorbed internally'.[6] In the 1880s, 82% of the 731,000 English migrants emigrated, while 83% of the 106,000 Welsh rural migrants were 'absorbed in the Welsh urban sector'. In the 1890s, emigration was low and only 8% of English rural migrants and 16% of Welsh were not absorbed by their respective urban centres. But, according to Professor Thomas, in the 1901–10 decade, about 40% of the 597,000 net English emigrants were from the rural sector and 60% from the urban. On the other hand, net migration from the rural parts of Wales was only 38,000 in the 1900s when the urban areas absorbed 132,000 migrants. Net immigration to Wales in that decade must have been 94,000 or 4.5% of the mean population.

Professor Thomas's view is that emigration from Wales as a whole was low after the 1870s because most of the rural Welsh migrants went to South Wales. The South Wales coalfield expanded fastest when the Atlantic cycle was in its 'North American' phase which provided the rural Welsh with an alternative destination which was

[5] The essentials are contained in Cairncross, 'Internal migration in Victorian England'. They were partly based on estimates in Welton, *England's recent progress*.
[6] Thomas, *Migration and urban development*, p. 175–6.

less available to the English. He pointed out the contrast between Welsh and Scottish migration. Professor Thomas believed that over the whole period 1871–1911, Wales had retained all its natural increase of 986,000 people and gained a further 20,000 migrants. In the same period Scotland had lost 31% of its natural increase of 2,019,000.

The American immigration data also seem to show that emigration from Wales was low. In the decade 1881–90, only 12,600 Welsh were recorded as having entered the United States or only 0.8% of the Welsh population in that decade. In the next two decades Welsh migration was only 0.6% and 0.8% of the Welsh population. This compared with English immigration into the U.S.A. in the three decades of 2.5%, 0.8% and 1.2% of the home population and Scottish immigration of 3.9%, 1.4% and 2.9% of the home population.[7]

The thesis that most of the surplus population of rural Wales in the late nineteenth and early twentieth centuries was absorbed into the industrial parts of the country was a most important result, not least because of its cultural implications. An important theme of Welsh political and cultural history had been the effect of continuous out-migration on the Welsh-speaking rural communities. Since most Welsh historians had also seen 'industrialisation as an anglicising force', it followed that Wales must have suffered from a cultural disaster in the late nineteenth and early twentieth centuries.[8] If, on the other hand, the surplus rural population had been able to move to the South Wales coalfield, their essential Welshness may have been preserved. Brinley Thomas argued that it was preserved. He pointed to the dominance of the non-conformist chapels and the survival of spoken Welsh in the valleys. He agreed with the existing view that the Welsh heritage could not have survived the problems of rural Wales. Hence, the industrialisation of Wales was not the enemy of Welsh culture and traditions but its saviour.

II

The Brinley Thomas thesis that the pattern of Welsh migration was qualitatively different from English, depends on several propositions.

---

[7] See, Thomas, 'Wales and the Atlantic economy', p. 11 reprinted in *Migration and urban development*, p. 177. This view has recently been re-affirmed by Berthoff. See R. Berthoff, 'Welsh' in S. Thernstrom (ed.), *The Harvard encyclopaedia of American ethnic groups* (Harvard University Press, 1980), p. 1013.

[8] See, for example, the view of David Williams in his *History of modern Wales* (John Murray, 1950) which was restated in his chapter in A. J. Roderick (ed.), *Wales through the ages*, vol. II (Christopher Davies, Llandybie, Carmarthen, 1960). Quoted in Thomas, *Migration and urban development*, p. 179.

Table 10.2. *Emigration from Wales, 1861–1900 (000s)*

	1861–70	1871–80	1881–90	1891–1900
Rural Wales	33.3 ± 2.8	12.0 ± 2.8	40.6 ± 3.0	16.9 ± 3.0
Monmouth	14.4 ± 1.1	9.0 ± 1.1	7.5 ± 1.1	2.4 ± 1.2
Glamorgan	17.6 ± 1.3	15.7 ± 1.6	14.0 ± 1.9	3.5 ± 2.3
All Wales and Monmouth	65.3 ± 5.2	36.7 ± 5.5	62.1 ± 6.0	22.8 ± 6.5

Note: Rural Wales: all Welsh counties except Monmouth and Glamorgan.
Source: Appendix 1.

Table 10.3. *Emigration from Wales, 1861–1900 (% of total native population)*

	1861–70	1871–80	1881–90	1891–1900
Rural Wales	3.6 ± 0.3	1.2 ± 0.3	4.2 ± 0.3	1.7 ± 0.3
Monmouth	9.4 ± 0.7	5.0 ± 0.6	3.6 ± 0.5	1.0 ± 0.5
Glamorgan	6.7 ± 0.5	4.7 ± 0.5	3.2 ± 0.4	0.6 ± 0.4
All Wales and Monmouth	4.9 ± 0.4	2.5 ± 0.4	3.8 ± 0.4	1.3 ± 0.4
England	2.5	2.3	3.5	1.5

Note: Rural Wales: all Welsh counties except Monmouth and Glamorgan.
Source: Appendix 1.

First, that Welsh emigration was low after the 1870s, and in particular that there were relatively few Welsh emigrants in the large movements of the 1880s and early twentieth century. Second, the dominant migration stream into South Wales was from Welsh-speaking rural Wales. Third, the dominant migration stream from rural Wales was towards the South Wales coalfield. The thesis also depends on an implicit assumption that all migration was either rural–urban or rural–overseas. In this case Professor Thomas assumes that there was no emigration from industrial Wales.[9] Any reader who has managed to reach this far will know that our estimates of Welsh migration, which are set out in Appendix 1, do not substantiate any of these propositions.

Our new estimates of Welsh migration in 1861–1900 are summarised in Tables 10.2 and 10.3 . (Unfortunately, there is no way of analysing migration by county of birth in the decade 1901–10.) Tables 10.2 and

[9] Thomas, *Migration and urban development*, p. 178.

10.3 show that emigration from Wales was much higher in the 1860s and 1870s than it was in the 1880s and 1890s. In the first two decades, between 91,000 and 113,000 Welsh born emigrated, net of returns. (That is, they went outside England and Wales.) This was, on average, 3.7% (±0.4%) of Welsh born in England and Wales in each decade. In the 1880s and 1890s, however, Welsh emigration was much less. Between 72,000 and 98,000 left the country, or only the equivalent of 2.5% (±0.3%) of the Welsh-born population in each decade. But even in the 1880s, the Welsh were more likely to emigrate than the English. Therefore, emigration from Wales did not cease after the 1870s, despite the rapid growth of the South Wales coalfield in that decade. The apparent collapse of Welsh immigration into the U.S.A. in the 1880s which appears in the American immigration records was almost certainly because most of the Welsh immigrants were returned as English.[10]

The reason for the high level of emigration from Wales in the 1880s was that emigration from rural Wales was exceptionally high. In the forty years 1861–1900, more than 100,000 natives of the rural Welsh counties went overseas (net of returns) or the equivalent of more than 12% of the young adult population. Between 38,000 and 43,000 of these emigrants left in the 1880s. This was 4.2% of the total population (±0.3%) and was relatively (20% to 40%) *higher* than emigration from England. Hence, emigration from rural Wales was at its peak in the decade when the South Wales coalfield was at its maximum rate of expansion in the century. On the other hand, emigration from rural Wales in the 1870s was exceptionally low, and possibly only half as great as emigration from England. The 1870s was a decade when expansion in South Wales was relatively slow. The pattern of emigration from rural Wales was no different from the pattern from most of the English urban and rural counties. Consequently, the industrialisation of Wales cannot have seriously affected either the rate or the timing of emigration from the Welsh rural counties.

It is difficult to define industrial Wales using only the county boundaries. Glamorgan was already highly urbanised in 1861 but Monmouth was less so. But a large part of the coalfield was in Monmouth (and is included in the Welsh coalfield areas in the Welton/Cairncross estimates). Industrial South Wales will be considered to be Monmouth

---

[10] Assuming the Welsh went to the U.S.A., which was very likely. Welsh emigrants had nearly all gone to the U.S.A. in the past and they were particularly unlikely to have changed destinations in the 1880s. Both Scots and English emigrants were more likely to go to the U.S.A. in that decade.

and Glamorgan and the two counties will be considered separately. There is, however, little difference in the migration history of the two counties in the period.

Emigration from Monmouth and Glamorgan was considerably higher than from any industrial area in England in the 1860s. Between 13,000 and 15,000 natives of Monmouth left the country which was no less than 9–10% of the Monmouth-born population. In the same decade, between 15,000 and 18,000, or 6.7% of the population, emigrated from Glamorgan. This may have been connected with the decline of the iron industry. It is possible that many iron workers preferred emigration to moving into the coal mines in the next valley.[11] Emigration from South Wales was lower in the 1870s but it was still considerably higher than from most English counties. There is also some qualitative evidence that there was emigration from the coal-mining areas in the 1870s.[12] Emigration from Glamorgan and Monmouth fell again in the 1880s. But even in the 1880s the counties were losing between 2.9% and 3.9% of their native population, i.e., at about the same rate as from the average English county in the decade. South Wales only began to lose emigrants at substantially below the English rate in the 1890s. Emigration from rural Wales (technically, of rural Welsh born) was higher than from England in the 1860s, the 1880s and (marginally) in the 1890s (Table 10.3). Hence, the effect of the industrialisation of South Wales seems not to have reduced emigration from rural Wales but to have reduced emigration of natives of the Welsh industrial areas themselves.

It is probable that some of the rural Welsh emigrants were stage emigrants who had been living in the industrial part of South Wales.[13] The Welsh rural counties with a substantial proportion of lifetime migrants in Monmouth and Glamorgan were Carmarthen, Pembroke, Cardigan and Brecon. Natives of these counties, with the exception of Brecon, were more likely to emigrate in the 1860s than in the 1880s, that is their migration pattern corresponded to that of Monmouth and Glamorgan more closely than to the great majority of the English

[11] Conway, 'Welsh emigration to the United States', pp. 249–54, 258.
[12] Professor Conway gave several examples of emigration from Methyr, Aberdare, Pontypridd and the Rhondda in the 1860s and 1870s but assumed that they had been born in the rural areas and that emigration by natives of industrial South Wales was small. Conway, 'Welsh emigration to the United States', pp. 264–5.
[13] This point was taken up by Conway. He suggested that the growth of industrial South Wales may not have inhibited emigration from rural Wales because it allowed the rural-born emigrants to make only a 'knight's move' in their emigration to the United States. Conway, 'Welsh emigration to the United States', p. 226.

urban counties.[14] On the other hand, natives of most of the counties
of North and Central Wales were much more likely to emigrate in
the 1880s than they had been in the 1860s.[15] The greater proportion
of lifetime migrants from these counties were living in the West Midlands and Lancashire – areas from which emigration was at its peak
in the 1880s. This evidence is not very firm, of course, but it suggests
that some of the rural Welsh emigrated *via* the industrial areas of
South Wales, the West Midlands and Lancashire. But since there were
more rural Welsh migrants living in England than there were in Monmouth and Glamorgan, it is likely that stage emigration from rural
Wales *via* English urban areas was more important than it was *via*
South Wales.[16]

The probability that some of the rural Welsh went to South Wales
and then overseas does not support the Brinley Thomas thesis. The
thesis assumes that *all* Welsh emigration was low. And if South Wales
was merely a staging post for rural Welsh emigrants they were unlikely
to have been the agent that transferred Welsh culture to the area.

It is clear that Brinley Thomas seriously misinterpreted the Welton/
Cairncross estimates of the net migration gains and losses of the Welsh
urban and rural areas. In effect, he assumed that migrants from the
rural areas could only move to the industrial parts of Wales or overseas. And migrants from the urban areas could only emigrate. He
ignored the possibility that the Welsh rural migrants might have gone
to England or that substantial migration from England into South
Wales would mask the emigration of Welsh natives from that area.

[14]
*Emigration of natives of Welsh counties (net of returns), 1861–1900. (% of total native popula-
tion)*

	1861–70	1871–80	1881–90	1891–1900
Monmouth and Glamorgan	7.7 ± 0.6	4.8 ± 0.5	3.4 ± 0.5	0.7 ± 0.4
Carmarthen, Pembroke, Cardigan and Brecon	5.3 ± 0.4	1.2 ± 0.4	3.8 ± 0.5	2.9 ± 0.4
Other Welsh rural counties	2.2 ± 0.5	1.4 ± 0.5	4.4 ± 0.5	0.8 ± 0.5

[15] The exceptions were Radnor and Flint. Anglesey, Caernarvon, Denbigh, Merioneth
and Montgomery all had peak emigration in the 1880s.
[16] All the Welsh rural counties had more lifetime emigrants outside Wales than in
Glamorgan and Monmouth.

In other words, Brinley Thomas assumed that Wales was a discrete economy with its own migration pattern which was largely unrelated to the pattern of English migration. This was a rather unrealistic assumption, which we can now show to be false.

III

The estimates of migration from Glamorgan in 1861–70 and 1871–80 are subject to a boundary adjustment. Our analysis of the relative growth of the lifetime migrant population (POPij) in the fifty-two counties in England and Wales suggested that there had been a serious misenumeration in the census of Glamorgan in 1871. This was because the number of lifetime migrants in Glamorgan was no larger in 1871 than it had been in 1861, but in 1881 it was 50% and 35% higher for males and females respectively (Table 10.4). If the 1871 census was correct, the male native population of Glamorgan (POPii) would have been 73% of the total population (POPqi), whereas in every other census between 1861 and 1901 it was between 66% and 68%. The female native population (POPii) was 68% of the total population in 1871, and 59–62% in all other censuses. The main groups affected were the natives of Wiltshire, Devon, Gloucestershire, Somerset, Monmouth and Cardigan. These data imply that migration into Glamorgan from the other counties of England and Wales was about 13,000 males and 8,000 females in the 1860s and about 48,000 males and 40,000 females in the 1870s.

There are three reasons why we suspected that there had been a serious enumeration error. Firstly, if we assumed that the enumeration was correct, then the emigration of Glamorgan natives in 1861–70 must have been about +4,000 males and +2,000 females. That is 6,000 more natives of Glamorgan had returned to England and Wales than had left it. But in 1871–80, emigration of Glamorgan natives must have been about 19,000 males and 14,000 females (net of returns). The uncorrected enumeration also implies that in-migration into Glamorgan was exceptionally high in the 1870s. But it is difficult to envisage circumstances that would have encouraged 98,000 natives of other English and Welsh counties to have entered Glamorgan in the 1870s, and 33,000 natives of Glamorgan, or 10% of the native population to emigrate. It is much more likely that some natives of English and Welsh counties were incorrectly enumerated as natives of Glamorgan in 1871 (see Table 10.4). The error would have the effect of decreasing the apparent number of in-migrants in the 1860s and increasing it in the 1870s, and also of decreasing the out-migration

Table 10.4. *Lifetime migrants and natives enumerated in Glamorgan,*
1861–1881

	1861	1871	1881
Males			
Born in Glamorgan	98,592	139,547 (131,947)	162,900
Born in other counties	64,907	66,113 (73,713)	99,769
Females			
Born in Glamorgan	102,349	140,408 (133,508)	167,739
Born in other counties	51,814	51,791 (58,691)	81,115

Source: The enumeration of the 'Birthplaces of the people' in the 1861, 1871
and 1881 Census of England and Wales. The figures in brackets assume that
7600 males and 6900 females who were natives of other counties were mis-
enumerated as Glamorgan natives in 1871.

(and hence the emigration) of Glamorgan born in the 1870s. Our
second reason for suspecting that the enumeration was incorrect is
that it implies that more migrants entered Glamorgan in the 1870s
than in the boom decade of the 1880s. And third, it implies that more
than 12% of the male natives of Monmouth emigrated and 11% of
the females emigrated in 1861–70 which is also unlikely. We estimated
that about 7,600 males and 6,900 females who were migrants to
Glamorgan had been incorrectly enumerated as Glamorgan natives
in 1871. This meant that the sum of the enumerated lifetime population
of natives of Wiltshire, Devon, Gloucestershire, Somerset, Monmouth
and Cardigan were about 14,500 over-estimated. We assumed that
the lifetime migrant population of these counties grew equally fast
in 1861–70 as in 1871–80.

Table 10.5 shows the effect of the correction. Emigration from
Glamorgan becomes 8,500 higher in the 1870s than in the 1860s compared with the uncorrected estimates. Emigration from Monmouth
becomes 3,400 lower. Of course, total emigration from the two
counties in the two decades is similar. The effect on emigration from
rural Wales is to increase emigration in the 1860s by something under
1,000, and to reduce it in the 1870s by a similar amount.[17] Our estimate,

---

[17] The error also affects emigration from the West of England. It increases emigration
in the 1860s at the expense of the 1870s. In other words, our conclusion that emigration
from the rural West was much less liable to fluctuation does not depend on the
adjustment. In fact, the adjustment biases the results against the hypothesis.

Table 10.5. *Effect of error correction in the lifetime migrant population in Glamorgan, 1871 (000s) – mid-point estimates*

(i) Assuming enumeration was correct

	1861–70		1871–80	
	Migration to other counties	Emigration	Migration to other counties	Emigration
Glamorgan	12.2	+5.7	19.5	32.4
Monmouth	12.4	17.8	23.9	6.3

(ii) Assuming 14,500 lifetime migrants were incorrectly enumerated as Glamorgan born

	1861–70		1871–80	
	Migration to other counties	Emigration	Migration to other counties	Emigration
Glamorgan	10.6	17.6	19.0	15.8
Monmouth	15.8	14.4	21.1	9.0

Source: Appendix 1.

that emigration from rural Wales was exceptionally low in the 1870s does not, therefore, depend on this correction. Needless to say, our conclusion that emigration from all parts of Wales was high until the 1880s is unaffected, as is our conclusion that emigration from rural Wales peaked at the time when the South Wales coalfield was apparently at its most attractive.

Our result resolves an important paradox between a well-known early paper by Brinley Thomas and his later work on Welsh migration patterns. In his early paper he estimated that migration into Glamorgan by natives of other counties was 21,000 in 1861–70, 74,700 in 1871–80 and 108,500 in 1881–90, i.e., that in-migration was relatively high in the 1870s.[18] A relatively high rate of in-migration in the 1870s was obviously incompatible with Brinley Thomas's later view that Glamorgan attracted more migrants in the decades when emigration from England was high – particularly since there was a serious mining contraction in South Wales in 1875–9. Brinley Thomas's explanation of high 'in-migration' in the 1870s was that migration from the more distant counties fell in that decade, and that the contraction of 1875–9

[18] Thomas, 'Migration into the Glamorganshire coalfield', p. 284.

Table 10.6. *Lifetime migrants in Glamorgan, 1861 and 1901 (000s)*

Born in	1861	1901
Rural Wales	49.9 (15.7%)	100.6 (11.7%)
Monmouth	11.4 (3.6%)	34.4 (4.0%)
England	35.9 (11.3%)	135.9 (15.8%)
Other	19.4 (6.1%)	26.7 (3.1%)
Glamorgan	201.5 (63.4%)	562.4 (65.4%)
Total population	317.8 (100.0%)	859.9 (100.0%)

Notes: 'Other' includes Scotland and Ireland. 'Rural Wales' includes all Welsh counties except Glamorgan and Monmouth.

'drove many of the newcomers back to their homes'.[19] The latter cannot be the explanation, of course, since all his migration estimates are net of returns. We now know that Brinley Thomas's estimates of the in-migration into Glamorgan were almost certainly affected by a serious error in the 1871 census which he did not detect. His original estimate of in-migration in the 1860s was too low and his estimate of in-migration in the 1870s was too high.

IV

The second element in Brinley Thomas's hypothesis that Welsh migration was qualitatively different from English, rests on the movement of natives of rural Wales into the South Wales coalfield – a migration which in his view transferred Welsh culture and traditions to the industrial areas. Table 10.6 shows the distribution of lifetime migrants in Glamorgan in 1861 and 1901. Less than half of the 116,000 migrants living in Glamorgan in 1861 had been born in rural Wales, and the rural Welsh born were only 15.7% of the total population. In 1901, only one-third of the migrants in Glamorgan had been born in rural Wales and they were only 11.7% of the total population.[20] If we assume that the fertility and mortality of the rural Welsh and the English in Glamorgan were roughly the same, there must have been as many people of English extraction in Glamorgan by 1901 as there were

[19] Ibid., p. 285.
[20] It is assumed that natives of Monmouth were not rural, or if they were, they were not Welsh speaking. Note that there were almost certainly more people of non-Welsh descent in Glamorgan in 1901 than there were of Monmouth and rural-Welsh descent put together.

Table 10.7. *Rural Welsh in England and Wales, 1861 and 1901 (000s)*

Enumerated in	1861	1901
Glamorgan	49.7 (26.2%)	98.9 (33.5%)
Monmouth	16.4 (8.7%)	16.4 (5.6%)
England	123.7 (65.2%)	180.2 (61.0%)

(Welsh-speaking) natives of rural Wales. In addition, there were many people of Irish and Scots and foreign descent.[21]

Welsh culture cannot therefore have been transferred to the valleys by the weight of numbers of rural Welsh migrants. It could be equally argued that the South Wales coalfield was converted to English institutions by the weight of English migrants. Of course, this does not disprove the fact that, by the late nineteenth century, South Wales was the centre of Welsh culture (which is Professor Thomas's position). The rural Welsh might have been relatively more successful in imposing Welshness on the English than vice-versa. Or possibly, the Welsh traditions were retained by the original Welsh population of Glamorgan. But the migration of rural Welsh to Glamorgan and Monmouth cannot of *itself* disprove the view that industrial Wales was anglicised in the late nineteenth and early twentieth centuries.[22]

The reason why relatively few of the rural Welsh went to South Wales was because the majority of them preferred to go to England. In 1861, two-thirds of the 190,000 persons who had left rural Wales (and not emigrated) were living in England and only about a quarter

[21] Of course, the bulk of Welsh in-migrants may have gone to the coalfield and the bulk of the non Welsh to the 'anglicised' towns of Cardiff and Swansea. But P. N. Jones showed that this could not have been the case. The large towns did attract a larger proportion of non-Welsh migrants. More than 70% of lifetime migrants in Cardiff and Swansea in 1891 and 1911 were not Welsh born. But 43% of the lifetime migrants on the coalfield were not Welsh born in 1891 and 53% in 1911. Hence, Wales had admitted a 'Trojan horse'. P. N. Jones, 'Aspects of internal migration to the Glamorganshire coalfield 1881–1911', *Transactions of the Honourable Society of Cymmrodorion*, 2, 1969, pp. 92–4.

[22] Professor Thomas's evidence that the valleys were the centre of Welsh culture is unconvincing. It does not follow from the fact that the Rhondda had 151 nonconformist chapels containing 85,105 seats which 'alone could accommodate three-quarters of the entire population of the Rhondda Urban District', that the seats were filled, or that they were filled by Welshmen. (Many of the English migrants came from the West of England.) According to the Census, 34% of the inhabitants of the Rhondda in 1891 could not speak Welsh at all, and 43% in 1911. Moreover, the non-Welsh speakers were relatively younger than the Welsh speakers. See E. D. Lewis, *The Rhondda Valleys* (Phoenix House, 1959), pp. 241–2, and Thomas, *Migration and urban development*, p. 180.

were in Glamorgan (Table 10.7). In 1901, the proportion had hardly changed. 180,000 rural Welsh or 61% of the migrants were living in England and only 99,000 (33.5%) were in Glamorgan. Industrial South Wales (Glamorgan and Monmouth) drew migrants in any numbers only from the nearby counties of Carmarthen, Pembroke, Cardigan and Brecon. Even these counties had more migrants living outside Wales than in Glamorgan and Monmouth in 1901. The main destination of migrants from Central Wales was the West Midlands and from North Wales was Merseyside. It is possible that many of these migrants subsequently emigrated. The English industrial areas were far more accessible from North and Central Wales than were Glamorgan and Monmouth. The view that industrial Wales was the dominant destination of rural Welsh migrants seems to neglect the relative remoteness of South Wales from Central and North Wales.

V

It is clear that Professor Thomas's view of the pattern of Welsh migration rests on a misinterpretation of the estimates of the net balance of migration in the urban and rural areas. In effect, he assumed that Wales was a closed migration system with only two important destinations, industrial Wales and overseas.[23] But the high rate of net movement into South Wales subsumed important additional flows. There were as many migrants to industrial Wales from outside Wales as from the rural counties of Wales (which Professor Thomas himself had pointed out in an earlier paper).[24] And the net migration into Glamorgan and Monmouth concealed heavy emigration of people who had been born there. Similarly, the net losses of the rural areas concealed the fact that the rural Welsh were twice as likely to go to England as to industrial Wales. Hence, migration to South Wales was not a substitute for emigration from rural Wales which remained high, and highest in the 1880s when the South Wales coalfield developed very fast. Welsh migration was not distinctive, but integrated into the main pattern of English migration. This means that the rate and pattern of Welsh migration provide no evidence for the existence of the so-called 'Welsh economy'.

[23] In fact he frequently uses 'emigration' as if it were synonymous with movement out of Wales.
[24] Thomas, 'Migration into the Glamorganshire coalfield'.

A summary of conclusions

Our main views about the nature of emigration from England and Wales in the late nineteenth century are set out below. Our conclusions do not depend on our migration estimates achieving exceptional accuracy and would all hold at the limits of the errors inherent in the estimates.

Between 1861 and 1900 about 4¼ million natives of England and Wales sailed from English and Welsh ports for a destination outside Europe. A very large number of these passengers were not emigrants or were temporary emigrants. Since nearly 50% of outward passengers returned, permanent emigrants from England and Wales must have numbered about 2¼ million persons in the period. The rate of return rose sharply in the 1870s, which was the first decade when virtually all emigrants on the North Atlantic were carried by steamships. From the 1870s until 1914 it is likely that about 40% of *emigrants* returned. This was probably the highest rate in Europe for those forty-five years.

About 35% of all the permanent emigrants from England and Wales in the period had been born in London, the West Midlands or Lancashire, and just under 25% had been born in other counties that were highly urbanised. It is likely that the majority of emigrants had been born and brought up in an urban environment. The heavy emigration from England and Wales in the last forty years of the nineteenth century cannot, therefore, have been mainly caused by the decline of rural industry or by the supposed problems of agriculture in the 1870s and 1880s. In fact, people who had been born in the rural counties were, on average, only marginally more likely to emigrate than natives of the urban counties.

There were wide variations in emigration rates between individual urban counties and between rural counties, but differential emigration rates do not seem to be correlated with the degree of urbanisation, real income levels or the proportion of the population working in agriculture. But it is clear that the variation in emigration rates from the counties was not random but followed a pattern. In particular, emigration rates were related to the level of previous emigration. We take this to mean that chain migration and the flow of information back to England were probably very important and that there may have been local factors which are not captured by the data.

On the other hand, we were able to relate internal migration to a set of variables that captures economic and social conditions in the counties. Our ability to explain internal migration rates but not emigration rates could imply that the decision to move to another part of the country was unrelated to the decision to emigrate. Or that the emigrants and internal migrants were drawn from different groups of people.

Emigration from England and Wales (net of returns) varied in the four decades. In particular, it rose markedly in the 1880s for most counties and fell in the 1890s. The low rate of net emigration in the 1890s was partly because of a further rise in the rate of return. These fluctuations affected most parts of the country simultaneously and must, largely, have been caused by changes in the degree of attraction of the countries to which the emigrants normally went.

The buoyant economies of the U.S.A., Canada and Australia in the 1880s attracted large numbers of additional emigrants from most parts of the country. This means that we can assume that people living in most counties were aware of the advantages of emigration. But emigration from London, industrial South Wales and from Devon and Cornwall did not increase substantially in the 1880s. This was probably because there were important countervailing factors which affected the regional economy of these areas. But London, South Wales and the West of England nearly always had heavy emigration and can be thought of as emigration regions of the highest importance. Most of the *additional* emigrants in the 1880s came from counties where there had been no recent tradition of heavy emigration. In other words, potential emigrants from these counties would only go when it was exceptionally favourable. The group included the rural East of England, the counties to the south and east of London, and most of the remaining urban counties including Lancashire and Yorkshire. The effect was that an even greater share of the emigrants in the 1880s (when emigration was at its peak) had been born in the urban counties.

The attraction of the urban areas seems to have determined the pattern and timing of rural–urban migration (as far as it could be measured). But the rate of emigration from England and Wales was, in the main, not determined by the relative attraction of the English towns and the countries of immigration. Hence, the internal migration phase of the 'Atlantic economy' collapses. There were occasions when potential migrants from the rural counties seem to have chosen between a move to the cities and a move overseas – but it must be remembered that rural-born emigrants were probably a minority of all emigrants – even if we include those who left from an urban area.

The strongest evidence for the view that emigrants were partly composed of people who had rejected internal migration occurred in the 1880s, when internal migration fell from virtually every county. But it also fell from those counties where emigration failed to rise. In the 1890s, however, internal migration fell from nearly all the rural counties so that the low emigration of that decade could not have been because more people were moving to the towns. (Nor was it because of a shortfall in the number of young adults in the rural population.) Hence, there was no general trade-off between rural–urban migration and emigration, and they could not normally be considered to be substitutes.

Rural–urban stage emigration must have been relatively rare in England and Wales – unlike from many European countries. Less than a third of all the emigrants who had been born in a rural area are likely to have lived in an urban area. Our estimates suggest that about a third of all emigrants left from rural areas (including the rural parts of urban counties) and up to two-thirds of all emigrants left from the towns and cities. Hence, if we include stage emigrants, emigration rates from the urban areas may have been higher than from the rural areas. Of the urban emigrants, at least two-thirds had been born there, so that rural–urban stage emigrants cannot have been more than one-third of urban emigrants and about 20% of all emigrants. At least 45% of all emigrants had known *no* other environment than a substantial town.

There is no evidence that the development of the South Wales coalfield reduced emigration from Wales and no evidence of a distinctive Welsh migration pattern. On the contrary, Wales had both heavy emigration and heavy movement to England both of which were integrated into English migration.

It is obvious that emigration from England and Wales in the late nineteenth century cannot be easily explained. The majority of emigrants must have come from places that were in the mainstream of economic change, not, for example, from the remote rural areas that had benefited less from the industrialisation of the country. We can also assume that there was a general awareness of emigration in many parts of the country. It is difficult to see how the inhabitants of Lancashire and Yorkshire, for example, could have been relatively unaware of the advantages of emigration before the 1880s when emigration from these counties rose to a high level. And even the remote rural areas had large numbers of migrants living in cities like London which were losing many of their own natives overseas. There is, however, a difference between being aware of emigration and doing it.

A possible explanation of the variation in emigration rates is that some parts of England and Wales contained a large number of people (i.e. families) who may have been actively involved in emigration before 1861 and had good contacts overseas. People in these parts of the country could be considered to have a relatively low emigration threshold and they might have been prepared to emigrate for relatively small advantage. The rate of return migration to England and Wales in the late nineteenth century was probably consistently higher than to anywhere else in Europe and it is probable that many English and Welsh emigrants left the country with the specific intention of returning. This meant, among other things, that English and Welsh migrants into the U.S.A. were, in this regard, not very different from the later immigrants who entered the U.S.A. from eastern and southern Europe. In other parts of England and Wales the population may have had a higher emigration threshold and tended to go overseas only when conditions were exceptionally favourable, as for example, they were in the 1880s. Put crudely, a marginal increase in the expected gains from emigration would draw more additional emigrants from London than from Lancashire.

Our work suggests that it is likely that virtually all the emigrants from England and Wales in the last forty years of the nineteenth century had made a rational choice which was based on a considerable amount of information. In the main, the emigrants were not fleeing from problems at home nor were they going blindly overseas. Most of the English and Welsh emigrants of the later nineteenth century must have been going to parts of the world which they knew something about.

Net migration of natives into other counties (IMIGij) and overseas (EMIGio), 1861–1900 (000s and % of mean decade population)

Appendix 1 shows the net migration of the natives of each county in each decade between 1861 and 1900, to two destinations: other counties within England and Wales (IMIGij), and overseas which includes Scotland and Ireland (EMIGio). The table also shows migration from each county as a percentage of the mean native population living within England and Wales in each decade. There are two important sources of error in these estimates, the death rate of lifetime migrants ($\overline{Dji}$ or $\overline{Dij}$) and enumeration errors. The estimates of net native migration in Appendix 1 are shown between limits determined by 5% errors in lifetime migrant deaths (i.e. the sum of a 5% error in Dij and Dji). An error larger than 5% is unlikely, because it would imply an unrealistic assumption of the age distribution of current migrants which is the critical assumption (see chapter 4 pp. 99–108).

Appendix 1 also shows which of the estimates of migration are affected by enumeration errors. Several errors were identified in the census – usually lifetime migrants who were returned as natives of the counties in which they were living (see chapter 4 pp. 96–7). The probable errors were corrected by extrapolation and the estimates of migration |ows in this table are based on the adjusted data. The effect of an adjustment can be seen from the following example. Assume it was discovered that 500 inhabitants of county m in 1871 (census 2), who had been born in county i (POPim²), were incorrectly enumerated as natives of county m (POPmm²). POPim² would then be increased by 500 and POPmm² reduced by 500 to compensate for the enumeration error. Four migration flows would be affected. After the error had been adjusted, the migration of natives of county i into all other counties in 1861–70 (IMIGij¹) would be something over 500 higher, and emigration (EMIGio¹) something under 500 lower. In 1871–80 IMIGij² would be something under 500 less and EMIGio² something over 500 more. Emigration from county m would be something under 500 more in 1861–70 and something over 500 less in 1871–80. Migration into other counties would be unaffected. The exact value of the adjusted EMIGio and IMIGio is determined by the appropriate level of migrant deaths (Dji and Dij) in the two decades, since the adjustments affect the lifetime migrant population at risk. (If the appropriate emigrant death rates were 20 per 1,000, for example, then IMIGij[1] would be increased by 550 and EMIGio[1] reduced by 450.) Thirteen of the fifty-two counties were affected in some way by enumeration adjustments, but usually in only two decades. The most important affect Gloucestershire, Monmouth and Glamorgan. The migration flows affected by boundary changes are denoted by asterisks (*).

The counties are arranged in the same order as in the enumeration of the 'Birthplace of the People' in the census. In that table London was always first, followed by the regions next to London and finishing with the northern counties and Wales.

County of Birth	IMIGij		EMIGio	
	000s	%	000s	%
1. London and Middlesex				
1861–1870 M	81.0 ± 1.3	(7.1 ± 0.1)	44.5 ± 7.7	(3.9 ± 0.7)
F	90.0 ± 1.4	(7.0 ± 0.1)	46.9 ± 6.2	(3.6 ± 0.5)
1871–1880 M	90.2 ± 1.8	(6.4 ± 0.1)	56.4 ± 7.4	(4.0 ± 0.5)
F	100.8 ± 1.7	(6.4 ± 0.1)	50.0 ± 7.3	(3.2 ± 0.5)
1881–1890 M	121.5 ± 2.1	(7.1 ± 0.1)	80.6 ± 7.0	(4.7 ± 0.4)
F	144.3 ± 2.2	(7.6 ± 0.1)	54.8 ± 7.4	(2.9 ± 0.4)
1891–1900 M	165.7 ± 2.8	(8.2 ± 0.1)	61.7 ± 7.6	(3.1 ± 0.4)
F	187.8 ± 2.9	(8.4 ± 0.1)	24.8 ± 8.0	(1.1 ± 0.4)
2. Surrey (extra-metropolitan)[a]				
1861–1870 M	17.7 ± 0.4	(14.7 ± 0.3)*	+1.4 ± 0.8	(+1.2 ± 0.7)*
F	19.7 ± 0.4	(15.5 ± 0.3)*	+2.2 ± 0.9	(+1.7 ± 0.7)*
1871–1880 M	20.4 ± 0.4	(13.8 ± 0.3)	3.7 ± 1.1	(2.5 ± 0.7)
F	22.9 ± 0.5	(14.5 ± 0.3)	2.1 ± 1.0	(1.3 ± 0.6)
1881–1890 M	21.4 ± 0.5	(12.0 ± 0.3)	6.8 ± 1.2	(3.8 ± 0.7)
F	22.5 ± 0.5	(11.9 ± 0.3)	5.5 ± 1.5	(2.9 ± 0.8)
1891–1900 M	26.6 ± 0.5	(12.5 ± 0.2)	1.2 ± 1.3	(0.6 ± 0.6)
F	30.0 ± 0.6	(13.2 ± 0.3)	4.4 ± 1.7	(1.9 ± 0.7)
3. Kent (extra-metropolitan)				
1861–1870 M	24.0 ± 0.7	(8.4 ± 0.2)	7.1 ± 1.5	(2.5 ± 0.5)
F	29.6 ± 0.7	(9.7 ± 0.2)	3.0 ± 1.2	(1.0 ± 0.4)
1871–1880 M	30.7 ± 0.8	(9.6 ± 0.2)	8.3 ± 1.5	(2.6 ± 0.5)
F	33.2 ± 0.8	(9.7 ± 0.2)	6.4 ± 1.4	(1.9 ± 0.4)
1881–1890 M	30.4 ± 0.8	(8.5 ± 0.2)	17.1 ± 1.6	(4.8 ± 0.4)
F	35.8 ± 0.9	(9.3 ± 0.2)	4.5 ± 1.7	(1.2 ± 0.5)
1891–1900 M	31.3 ± 0.9	(7.8 ± 0.2)	5.9 ± 1.9	(1.5 ± 0.5)
F	38.3 ± 1.0	(8.9 ± 0.2)	+3.0 ± 1.9	(+0.7 ± 0.4)
4. Sussex[b]				
1861–1870 M	14.5 ± 0.5	(7.5 ± 0.2)	3.1 ± 1.0	(1.6 ± 0.5)
F	17.5 ± 0.5	(8.7 ± 0.2)	1.2 ± 0.9	(0.6 ± 0.4)
1871–1880 M	19.3 ± 0.5	(9.0 ± 0.2)*	2.9 ± 0.9	(1.3 ± 0.4)*
F	21.0 ± 0.5	(9.3 ± 0.2)*	2.7 ± 1.0	(1.2 ± 0.4)*
1881–1890 M	20.6 ± 0.5	(8.7 ± 0.2)*	11.0 ± 1.0	(4.6 ± 0.4)*
F	22.2 ± 0.5	(8.9 ± 0.2)*	10.1 ± 1.0	(4.0 ± 0.4)*
1891–1900 M	23.6 ± 0.6	(9.1 ± 0.2)	4.0 ± 1.1	(1.5 ± 0.4)
F	26.0 ± 0.6	(9.4 ± 0.2)	0.7 ± 1.4	(0.3 ± 0.5)

County of Birth	IMIGij		EMIGio	
	000s	%	000s	%
5. Hampshire[b]				
1861–1870 M	21.7 ± 0.5	(9.6 ± 0.2)	8.3 ± 1.4	(3.7 ± 0.6)
F	18.8 ± 0.6	(7.6 ± 0.2)	9.6 ± 1.0	(3.9 ± 0.4)
1871–1880 M	28.2 ± 0.6	(11.0 ± 0.2)*	10.7 ± 1.4	(4.2 ± 0.5)*
F	32.2 ± 0.6	(11.7 ± 0.2)*	3.5 ± 1.2	(1.3 ± 0.4)*
1881–1890 M	25.7 ± 0.7	(8.9 ± 0.2)*	11.1 ± 1.4	(3.9 ± 0.5)*
F	29.3 ± 0.7	(9.4 ± 0.2)*	5.1 ± 1.4	(1.6 ± 0.4)*
1891–1900 M	27.0 ± 0.7	(8.4 ± 0.2)	6.9 ± 1.6	(2.1 ± 0.5)
F	30.7 ± 0.8	(8.7 ± 0.2)	+2.0 ± 1.7	(+0.6 ± 0.4)
6. Berkshire[c]				
1861–1870 M	12.2 ± 0.3	(12.0 ± 0.3)*	+1.3 ± 0.5	(+1.3 ± 0.5)*
F	13.8 ± 0.4	(13.2 ± 0.4)*	+4.0 ± 0.6	(+3.8 ± 0.6)*
1871–1880 M	12.8 ± 0.4	(11.5 ± 0.4)*	3.6 ± 0.7	(3.2 ± 0.6)*
F	15.9 ± 0.4	(13.7 ± 0.3)*	1.3 ± 0.7	(1.1 ± 0.6)*
1881–1890 M	12.6 ± 0.4	(10.6 ± 0.3)	4.4 ± 0.7	(3.7 ± 0.6)
F	15.8 ± 0.5	(12.4 ± 0.4)	1.8 ± 0.8	(1.4 ± 0.6)
1891–1900 M	14.3 ± 0.4	(11.3 ± 0.3)	4.6 ± 0.7	(3.6 ± 0.6)
F	16.9 ± 0.5	(12.3 ± 0.4)	1.0 ± 0.8	(0.7 ± 0.6)
7. Hertfordshire				
1861–1870 M	10.7 ± 0.3	(10.9 ± 0.3)	1.7 ± 0.5	(1.7 ± 0.5)
F	12.8 ± 0.4	(12.3 ± 0.4)	+0.5 ± 0.6	(+0.5 ± 0.6)
1871–1880 M	12.6 ± 0.4	(11.9 ± 0.4)	4.9 ± 0.6	(4.6 ± 0.5)
F	15.3 ± 0.4	(13.5 ± 0.4)	2.5 ± 0.6	(2.2 ± 0.5)
1881–1890 M	13.8 ± 0.4	(12.2 ± 0.4)	1.2 ± 0.6	(1.1 ± 0.5)
F	15.7 ± 0.4	(12.9 ± 0.3)	0.4 ± 0.7	(0.3 ± 0.6)
1891–1900 M	14.4 ± 0.4	(11.9 ± 0.3)	0.6 ± 0.7	(0.5 ± 0.5)
F	16.3 ± 0.5	(12.3 ± 0.4)	+2.0 ± 0.8	(+1.5 ± 0.6)
8. Buckinghamshire				
1861–1870 M	11.5 ± 0.3	(11.6 ± 0.3)	3.1 ± 0.5	(3.1 ± 0.5)
F	12.6 ± 0.4	(12.4 ± 0.4)	1.3 ± 0.6	(1.3 ± 0.6)
1871–1880 M	12.5 ± 0.4	(11.9 ± 0.4)	5.4 ± 0.5	(5.1 ± 0.5)
F	16.0 ± 0.4	(14.7 ± 0.4)	2.3 ± 0.6	(2.1 ± 0.6)
1881–1890 M	12.1 ± 0.4	(11.0 ± 0.4)	1.9 ± 0.5	(1.7 ± 0.5)
F	13.4 ± 0.4	(11.6 ± 0.3)	2.2 ± 0.6	(1.9 ± 0.5)
1891–1900 M	12.5 ± 0.4	(10.9 ± 0.3)	3.0 ± 0.6	(2.6 ± 0.5)
F	14.9 ± 0.4	(12.3 ± 0.3)	0.8 ± 0.7	(0.7 ± 0.6)

County of Birth	IMIGij		EMIGio	
	000s	%	000s	%
9. Oxfordshire[c]				
1861–1870 M	11.4 ± 0.3	(11.2 ± 0.3)*	2.6 ± 0.5	(2.6 ± 0.5)*
F	13.9 ± 0.4	(13.3 ± 0.4)*	0.2 ± 0.6	(0.2 ± 0.5)*
1871–1880 M	13.8 ± 0.4	(12.8 ± 0.4)*	3.7 ± 0.6	(3.4 ± 0.6)*
F	15.0 ± 0.4	(13.5 ± 0.4)*	2.3 ± 0.6	(2.1 ± 0.5)*
1881–1890 M	12.7 ± 0.4	(11.4 ± 0.4)	1.8 ± 0.5	(1.6 ± 0.4)
F	14.0 ± 0.4	(11.9 ± 0.3)	0.6 ± 0.6	(0.5 ± 0.5)
1891–1900 M	15.3 ± 0.4	(13.3 ± 0.3)	3.5 ± 0.6	(3.0 ± 0.5)
F	15.4 ± 0.5	(12.5 ± 0.4)	1.6 ± 0.7	(1.3 ± 0.6)
10. Northamptonshire				
1861–1870 M	13.1 ± 0.3	(10.2 ± 0.2)	4.4 ± 0.5	(3.4 ± 0.4)
F	14.4 ± 0.4	(11.1 ± 0.3)	1.9 ± 0.6	(1.5 ± 0.5)
1871–1880 M	14.0 ± 0.4	(10.0 ± 0.3)	3.5 ± 0.6	(2.5 ± 0.4)
F	16.2 ± 0.4	(11.2 ± 0.3)	1.9 ± 0.6	(1.3 ± 0.4)
1881–1890 M	12.8 ± 0.4	(8.3 ± 0.3)	3.8 ± 0.7	(2.5 ± 0.5)
F	14.8 ± 0.4	(9.3 ± 0.3)	3.3 ± 0.7	(2.1 ± 0.4)
1891–1900 M	11.7 ± 0.4	(7.0 ± 0.2)	4.6 ± 0.7	(2.7 ± 0.4)
F	12.6 ± 0.5	(7.2 ± 0.3)	2.1 ± 0.8	(1.2 ± 0.5)
11. Huntingdon				
1861–1870 M	4.5 ± 0.1	(12.2 ± 0.3)	1.7 ± 0.2	(4.6 ± 0.5)
F	5.3 ± 0.1	(13.8 ± 0.3)	1.5 ± 0.2	(3.9 ± 0.5)
1871–1880 M	6.1 ± 0.1	(16.0 ± 0.3)	1.5 ± 0.2	(3.9 ± 0.5)
F	6.7 ± 0.2	(16.7 ± 0.5)	1.3 ± 0.2	(3.2 ± 0.5)
1881–1890 M	4.3 ± 0.1	(11.1 ± 0.3)	1.5 ± 0.2	(3.9 ± 0.5)
F	5.3 ± 0.2	(12.9 ± 0.5)	1.4 ± 0.2	(3.4 ± 0.5)
1881–1900 M	4.6 ± 0.1	(11.6 ± 0.3)	0.6 ± 0.2	(1.5 ± 0.5)
F	5.0 ± 0.2	(12.0 ± 0.5)	0.5 ± 0.3	(1.2 ± 0.7)
12. Bedfordshire				
1861–1870 M	9.1 ± 0.2	(12.2 ± 0.3)	1.6 ± 0.3	(2.1 ± 0.4)
F	8.2 ± 0.2	(10.9 ± 0.3)	1.1 ± 0.3	(1.5 ± 0.4)
1871–1880 M	12.1 ± 0.2	(14.7 ± 0.2)	1.3 ± 0.3	(1.6 ± 0.4)
F	12.4 ± 0.2	(14.7 ± 0.2)	1.0 ± 0.4	(1.2 ± 0.5)
1881–1890 M	9.9 ± 0.3	(11.1 ± 0.3)	1.2 ± 0.4	(1.3 ± 0.4)
F	10.9 ± 0.3	(11.8 ± 0.3)	1.2 ± 0.4	(1.3 ± 0.4)
1890–1900 M	9.2 ± 0.3	(9.7 ± 0.3)	0.6 ± 0.4	(0.6 ± 0.4)
F	9.9 ± 0.3	(9.9 ± 0.3)	+0.3 ± 0.5	(+0.3 ± 0.5)

County of Birth	IMIGij		EMIGio	
	000s	%	000s	%
13. Cambridgeshire				
1861–1870 M	10.7 ± 0.3	(10.8 ± 0.3)	1.5 ± 0.2	(1.5 ± 0.2)
F	12.8 ± 0.3	(12.3 ± 0.3)	— ± 0.5	(— ± 0.5)
1871–1880 M	15.7 ± 0.3	(14.6 ± 0.3)	2.4 ± 0.5	(2.2 ± 0.5)
F	17.2 ± 0.3	(15.2 ± 0.3)	0.7 ± 0.5	(0.6 ± 0.4)
1881–1890 M	12.2 ± 0.4	(10.7 ± 0.4)	3.1 ± 0.5	(2.7 ± 0.4)
F	14.4 ± 0.3	(11.9 ± 0.2)	0.5 ± 0.5	(0.4 ± 0.4)
1891–1900 M	13.6 ± 0.4	(11.4 ± 0.3)	1.7 ± 0.6	(1.4 ± 0.5)
F	14.3 ± 0.4	(11.2 ± 0.3)	+0.3 ± 0.6	(+0.2 ± 0.5)
14. Essex				
1861–1870 M	22.7 ± 0.3	(10.1 ± 0.1)	3.6 ± 0.7	(1.6 ± 0.1)
F	28.5 ± 0.7	(12.0 ± 0.3)	+1.6 ± 1.0	(+0.7 ± 0.4)
1871–1880 M	28.6 ± 0.6	(11.4 ± 0.2)	4.2 ± 1.1	(1.7 ± 0.4)
F	31.5 ± 0.7	(11.8 ± 0.3)	0.7 ± 1.1	(0.3 ± 0.4)
1881–1890 M	23.8 ± 0.7	(8.1 ± 0.2)	8.4 ± 1.4	(2.9 ± 0.5)
F	31.0 ± 0.8	(10.0 ± 0.3)	0.8 ± 1.5	(0.3 ± 0.5)
1891–1900 M	27.6 ± 0.8	(7.9 ± 0.2)	10.7 ± 1.9	(3.1 ± 0.5)
F	33.2 ± 0.9	(8.9 ± 0.2)	2.6 ± 1.9	(0.7 ± 0.5)
15. Suffolk				
1861–1870 M	20.4 ± 0.5	(10.1 ± 0.2)	4.0 ± 0.7	(2.0 ± 0.3)
F	22.4 ± 0.6	(10.6 ± 0.3)	3.4 ± 0.8	(1.6 ± 0.4)
1871–1880 M	26.1 ± 0.6	(12.3 ± 0.3)	2.5 ± 0.8	(1.2 ± 0.4)
F	24.5 ± 0.6	(11.0 ± 0.3)	3.1 ± 0.8	(1.4 ± 0.4)
1881–1890 M	16.3 ± 0.7	(7.4 ± 0.3)	9.9 ± 0.9	(4.5 ± 0.4)
F	23.2 ± 0.7	(9.8 ± 0.3)	1.8 ± 1.0	(0.8 ± 0.4)
1891–1900 M	19.7 ± 0.5	(8.6 ± 0.2)	8.0 ± 0.7	(3.5 ± 0.3)
F	22.3 ± 0.6	(9.1 ± 0.2)	4.6 ± 0.9	(1.9 ± 0.4)
16. Norfolk				
1861–1870 M	25.5 ± 0.6	(10.2 ± 0.2)	4.8 ± 0.8	(1.9 ± 0.3)
F	29.3 ± 0.6	(10.9 ± 0.2)	+0.7 ± 0.8	(+0.3 ± 0.3)
1871–1880 M	26.0 ± 0.7	(9.9 ± 0.3)	3.7 ± 0.9	(1.4 ± 0.3)
F	26.4 ± 0.7	(9.4 ± 0.2)	3.7 ± 0.9	(1.3 ± 0.3)
1881–1890 M	22.7 ± 0.7	(8.3 ± 0.3)	8.9 ± 0.9	(3.3 ± 0.3)
F	26.3 ± 0.8	(8.9 ± 0.3)	4.8 ± 1.0	(1.6 ± 0.3)
1891–1900 M	25.7 ± 0.4	(9.1 ± 0.1)	4.5 ± 0.6	(1.6 ± 0.2)
F	26.7 ± 0.8	(8.7 ± 0.3)	0.7 ± 1.1	(0.2 ± 0.4)

County of Birth	IMIGij		EMIGio	
	000s	%	000s	%
17. Wiltshire[d]				
1861–1870 M	15.5 ± 0.5	(10.2 ± 0.3)*	3.6 ± 0.7	(2.4 ± 0.5)*
F	18.8 ± 0.5	(11.7 ± 0.3)*	1.3 ± 0.7	(0.8 ± 0.4)*
1871–1880 M	17.9 ± 0.6	(11.3 ± 0.4)*	5.3 ± 0.8	(3.4 ± 0.5)*
F	21.4 ± 0.6	(12.8 ± 0.4)*	3.2 ± 0.8	(1.9 ± 0.5)*
1881–1890 M	15.2 ± 0.5	(9.4 ± 0.3)	5.9 ± 0.7	(3.6 ± 0.4)
F	18.4 ± 0.6	(10.6 ± 0.3)	2.4 ± 0.8	(1.4 ± 0.5)
1891–1900 M	15.9 ± 0.4	(9.6 ± 0.2)	5.2 ± 0.6	(3.1 ± 0.4)
F	18.8 ± 0.6	(10.5 ± 0.3)	2.2 ± 0.9	(1.2 ± 0.5)
18. Dorset				
1861–1870 M	10.6 ± 0.3	(10.1 ± 0.3)	3.7 ± 0.4	(3.5 ± 0.4)
F	13.2 ± 0.3	(11.7 ± 0.3)	1.3 ± 0.4	(1.2 ± 0.4)
1871–1880 M	15.0 ± 0.3	(13.6 ± 0.3)	4.3 ± 0.5	(3.9 ± 0.5)
F	16.5 ± 0.3	(13.8 ± 0.3)	2.5 ± 0.4	(2.1 ± 0.3)
1881–1890 M	11.6 ± 0.3	(10.1 ± 0.3)	4.0 ± 0.5	(3.5 ± 0.4)
F	13.8 ± 0.4	(11.1 ± 0.3)	2.0 ± 0.5	(1.6 ± 0.4)
1891–1900 M	11.2 ± 0.4	(9.5 ± 0.3)	5.2 ± 0.5	(4.4 ± 0.4)
F	12.7 ± 0.4	(9.9 ± 0.3)	2.5 ± 0.6	(1.9 ± 0.5)
19. Devon[e]				
1861–1870 M	28.1 ± 0.7	(9.2 ± 0.2)*	14.2 ± 1.2	(4.6 ± 0.4)*
F	32.1 ± 0.8	(9.4 ± 0.2)*	5.7 ± 1.2	(1.7 ± 0.4)*
1871–1880 M	30.8 ± 0.8	(9.6 ± 0.3)*	15.7 ± 1.3	(4.9 ± 0.4)*
F	33.3 ± 0.8	(9.3 ± 0.2)*	8.7 ± 1.2	(2.4 ± 0.4)*
1881–1890 M	21.7 ± 0.8	(6.6 ± 0.2)	16.2 ± 1.3	(4.9 ± 0.4)
F	24.2 ± 0.9	(6.5 ± 0.2)	8.9 ± 1.4	(2.4 ± 0.4)
1891–1900 M	24.9 ± 0.8	(7.3 ± 0.2)	9.2 ± 1.4	(2.7 ± 0.4)
F	25.3 ± 0.9	(6.6 ± 0.2)	4.0 ± 1.4	(1.0 ± 0.4)
20. Cornwall				
1861–1870 M	11.8 ± 0.3	(6.4 ± 0.2)	24.5 ± 0.4	(13.3 ± 0.2)
F	14.4 ± 0.3	(6.9 ± 0.2)	13.6 ± 0.4	(6.5 ± 0.2)
1871–1880 M	18.0 ± 0.4	(10.0 ± 0.2)	21.6 ± 0.6	(12.0 ± 0.3)
F	22.8 ± 0.4	(10.8 ± 0.2)	14.0 ± 0.5	(6.6 ± 0.2)
1881–1890 M	7.9 ± 0.4	(4.5 ± 0.2)	19.6 ± 0.6	(11.3 ± 0.3)
F	10.2 ± 0.4	(4.9 ± 0.2)	10.4 ± 0.6	(5.0 ± 0.3)
1891–1900 M	11.8 ± 0.3	(6.8 ± 0.2)	8.8 ± 0.5	(5.1 ± 0.3)
F	12.2 ± 0.4	(5.9 ± 0.2)	6.0 ± 0.6	(2.9 ± 0.3)

County of Birth		IMIGij		EMIGio	
		000s	%	000s	%
21. Somerset[f,g]					
1861–1870	M	25.0 ± 0.7	(10.2 ± 0.3)*	6.1 ± 1.0	(2.5 ± 0.4)*
	F	29.4 ± 0.8	(10.9 ± 0.3)*	1.6 ± 1.3	(0.6 ± 0.5)*
1871–1880	M	29.0 ± 0.8	(11.3 ± 0.3)*	11.0 ± 1.2	(4.3 ± 0.5)*
	F	32.2 ± 0.8	(11.4 ± 0.3)*	8.0 ± 1.2	(2.8 ± 0.4)*
1881–1890	M	25.3 ± 0.9	(9.5 ± 0.3)	14.3 ± 1.3	(5.4 ± 0.5)
	F	27.7 ± 0.9	(9.4 ± 0.3)	8.1 ± 1.4	(2.8 ± 0.5)
1891–1900	M	23.6 ± 0.8	(8.6 ± 0.3)*	12.3 ± 1.2	(4.5 ± 0.4)
	F	26.7 ± 0.9	(8.7 ± 0.3)*	6.0 ± 1.5	(2.0 ± 0.5)
22. Gloucestershire[f,h,i]					
1861–1870	M	23.2 ± 0.7	(9.3 ± 0.3)*	4.8 ± 1.3	(1.9 ± 0.5)*
	F	25.9 ± 0.7	(9.7 ± 0.3)*	2.9 ± 1.4	(1.1 ± 0.5)*
1871–1880	M	32.8 ± 0.8	(11.8 ± 0.3)*	3.1 ± 1.4	(1.1 ± 0.5)*
	F	34.5 ± 0.8	(11.6 ± 0.3)*	1.8 ± 1.5	(0.6 ± 0.5)*
1881–1890	M	30.3 ± 0.8	(10.0 ± 0.3)	8.3 ± 1.4	(2.7 ± 0.5)
	F	32.3 ± 0.9	(9.8 ± 0.3)	5.8 ± 1.6	(1.8 ± 0.5)
1891–1900	M	30.1 ± 0.8	(9.3 ± 0.2)*	1.7 ± 1.4	(0.5 ± 0.4)*
	F	30.5 ± 1.0	(8.6 ± 0.3)*	+0.7 ± 1.7	(+0.2 ± 0.5)*
23. Herefordshire					
1861–1870	M	7.4 ± 0.2	(10.6 ± 0.3)	3.2 ± 0.4	(4.6 ± 0.6)
	F	8.4 ± 0.3	(11.7 ± 0.4)	1.3 ± 0.4	(1.8 ± 0.6)
1871–1880	M	9.2 ± 0.2	(12.9 ± 0.3)	4.3 ± 0.4	(6.0 ± 0.6)
	F	10.4 ± 0.3	(14.0 ± 0.4)	2.5 ± 0.4	(3.4 ± 0.5)
1881–1890	M	9.2 ± 0.2	(12.8 ± 0.3)	3.9 ± 0.4	(5.4 ± 0.6)
	F	9.4 ± 0.3	(12.4 ± 0.4)	2.1 ± 0.4	(2.8 ± 0.5)
1891–1900	M	6.6 ± 0.3	(9.2 ± 0.4)	3.3 ± 0.5	(4.6 ± 0.7)
	F	7.8 ± 0.3	(10.2 ± 0.4)	2.4 ± 0.5	(3.1 ± 0.7)
24. Shropshire					
1861–1870	M	14.4 ± 0.5	(10.0 ± 0.3)	4.5 ± 0.8	(3.1 ± 0.6)
	F	16.8 ± 0.5	(11.3 ± 0.3)	2.4 ± 0.7	(1.6 ± 0.5)
1871–1880	M	17.7 ± 0.5	(11.8 ± 0.3)	4.2 ± 0.7	(2.8 ± 0.5)
	F	21.8 ± 0.5	(13.9 ± 0.3)	2.2 ± 0.7	(1.4 ± 0.4)
1881–1890	M	17.9 ± 0.5	(11.7 ± 0.3)	7.5 ± 0.7	(4.9 ± 0.5)
	F	19.2 ± 0.6	(11.9 ± 0.4)	5.0 ± 0.8	(3.1 ± 0.5)
1891–1900	M	14.1 ± 0.6	(9.1 ± 0.4)	3.3 ± 0.9	(2.1 ± 0.6)
	F	16.6 ± 0.6	(10.1 ± 0.4)	1.0 ± 0.8	(0.6 ± 0.5)

County of Birth	IMIGij		EMIGio	
	000s	%	000s	%
25. Staffordshire				
1861–1870 M	32.2 ± 0.6	(8.7 ± 0.2)	16.6 ± 1.7	(4.5 ± 0.5)
F	36.8 ± 0.7	(9.7 ± 0.2)	12.5 ± 1.6	(3.3 ± 0.4)
1871–1880 M	41.7 ± 0.9	(9.4 ± 0.2)	16.4 ± 2.1	(3.7 ± 0.5)
F	47.1 ± 0.8	(10.3 ± 0.2)	11.1 ± 1.8	(2.4 ± 0.4)
1881–1890 M	38.8 ± 1.0	(7.6 ± 0.2)	22.4 ± 2.1	(4.4 ± 0.4)
F	46.4 ± 1.0	(8.7 ± 0.2)	17.5 ± 2.0	(3.3 ± 0.4)
1891–1900 M	38.8 ± 1.0	(6.6 ± 0.2)	11.6 ± 2.1	(2.0 ± 0.4)
F	47.3 ± 1.1	(7.7 ± 0.2)	+0.2 ± 2.1	(— ± 0.3)
26. Worcestershire				
1861–1870 M	18.0 ± 0.5	(11.0 ± 0.3)	5.3 ± 0.9	(3.2 ± 0.5)
F	16.4 ± 0.5	(9.6 ± 0.3)	6.8 ± 0.9	(4.0 ± 0.5)
1871–1880 M	20.2 ± 0.5	(11.1 ± 0.3)	5.2 ± 0.9	(2.9 ± 0.5)
F	24.0 ± 0.6	(12.6 ± 0.3)	2.7 ± 1.0	(1.4 ± 0.5)
1881–1890 M	19.3 ± 0.6	(9.7 ± 0.3)	11.3 ± 1.0	(5.7 ± 0.5)
F	21.8 ± 0.6	(10.3 ± 0.3)	8.3 ± 1.1	(3.9 ± 0.5)
1891–1900 M	17.8 ± 0.6	(8.2 ± 0.2)	2.7 ± 1.1	(1.2 ± 0.5)
F	20.2 ± 0.6	(8.6 ± 0.3)	+0.6 ± 1.1	(+0.3 ± 0.5)
27. Warwickshire				
1861–1870 M	26.4 ± 0.5	(10.0 ± 0.2)	8.3 ± 1.4	(3.1 ± 0.5)
F	28.5 ± 0.6	(10.2 ± 0.2)	7.5 ± 1.5	(2.7 ± 0.5)
1871–1880 M	31.2 ± 0.7	(10.0 ± 0.2)	5.2 ± 1.6	(1.7 ± 0.5)
F	33.5 ± 0.7	(10.2 ± 0.2)	3.9 ± 1.7	(1.2 ± 0.5)
1881–1890 M	34.9 ± 0.7	(9.6 ± 0.2)	12.1 ± 1.6	(3.3 ± 0.4)
F	38.8 ± 0.8	(10.1 ± 0.2)	5.5 ± 1.8	(1.4 ± 0.5)
1891–1900 M	33.2 ± 0.8	(8.2 ± 0.2)	12.3 ± 1.8	(3.0 ± 0.4)
F	36.4 ± 0.9	(8.4 ± 0.2)	8.3 ± 2.0	(1.9 ± 0.5)
28. Leicestershire				
1861–1870 M	12.3 ± 0.4	(8.9 ± 0.3)	0.9 ± 0.6	(0.7 ± 0.4)
F	11.9 ± 0.4	(8.4 ± 0.3)	0.7 ± 0.6	(0.5 ± 0.4)
1871–1880 M	12.5 ± 0.4	(8.1 ± 0.3)	0.2 ± 0.6	(0.1 ± 0.4)
F	12.1 ± 0.4	(7.6 ± 0.3)	0.4 ± 0.6	(0.3 ± 0.4)
1881–1890 M	12.2 ± 0.4	(7.2 ± 0.2)	5.5 ± 0.7	(3.2 ± 0.4)
F	12.4 ± 0.4	(6.9 ± 0.2)	3.1 ± 0.7	(1.7 ± 0.4)
1891–1900 M	12.3 ± 0.3	(6.3 ± 0.2)	3.0 ± 0.6	(1.5 ± 0.3)
F	12.0 ± 0.4	(5.9 ± 0.2)	0.9 ± 0.8	(0.4 ± 0.4)

County of Birth	IMIGij		EMIGio	
	000s	%	000s	%
29. Rutland				
1861–1870 M	1.8 ± 0.1	(13.1 ± 0.1)	0.4 ± 0.1	(2.9 ± 0.7)
F	2.4 ± 0.1	(17.8 ± 0.1)	+0.1 ± 0.1	(+0.7 ± 0.7)
1871–1880 M	2.2 ± 0.1	(15.6 ± 0.1)	0.4 ± 0.1	(2.8 ± 0.7)
F	2.3 ± 0.1	(16.2 ± 0.1)	0.4 ± 0.1	(2.8 ± 0.7)
1881–1890 M	2.0 ± 0.1	(14.1 ± 0.1)	0.5 ± 0.1	(3.5 ± 0.7)
F	1.9 ± 0.1	(13.2 ± 0.1)	0.5 ± 0.1	(3.5 ± 0.7)
1891–1900 M	1.8 ± 0.1	(12.6 ± 0.1)	0.5 ± 0.1	(3.5 ± 0.7)
F	2.0 ± 0.1	(13.7 ± 0.1)	0.2 ± 0.1	(1.4 ± 0.7)
30. Lincolnshire				
1861–1870 M	24.1 ± 0.5	(10.4 ± 0.2)	5.1 ± 0.8	(2.2 ± 0.3)
F	25.3 ± 0.6	(10.6 ± 0.3)	2.9 ± 0.8	(1.2 ± 0.3)
1871–1880 M	25.0 ± 0.6	(9.9 ± 0.2)	5.5 ± 1.0	(2.2 ± 0.3)
F	28.1 ± 0.6	(10.7 ± 0.2)	3.2 ± 0.9	(1.2 ± 0.3)
1881–1890 M	27.0 ± 0.7	(10.0 ± 0.3)	11.2 ± 1.0	(4.1 ± 0.4)
F	29.8 ± 0.7	(10.6 ± 0.2)	5.2 ± 1.0	(1.8 ± 0.4)
1891–1900 M	23.6 ± 0.7	(8.3 ± 0.2)	4.3 ± 1.1	(1.5 ± 0.4)
F	25.0 ± 0.7	(8.6 ± 0.2)	0.6 ± 1.0	(0.2 ± 0.3)
31. Nottinghamshire				
1861–1870 M	17.0 ± 0.4	(10.8 ± 0.3)	2.9 ± 0.7	(1.8 ± 0.4)
F	15.2 ± 0.4	(9.4 ± 0.2)	4.0 ± 0.7	(2.5 ± 0.4)
1871–1880 M	12.9 ± 0.5	(7.3 ± 0.3)	2.7 ± 0.8	(1.5 ± 0.5)
F	13.7 ± 0.4	(7.6 ± 0.2)	2.3 ± 0.7	(1.3 ± 0.4)
1881–1890 M	19.4 ± 0.5	(9.6 ± 0.2)	8.7 ± 0.9	(4.3 ± 0.4)
F	18.3 ± 0.4	(8.8 ± 0.2)	5.4 ± 0.8	(2.6 ± 0.4)
1891–1900 M	16.1 ± 0.5	(7.1 ± 0.2)	7.4 ± 1.0	(3.3 ± 0.4)
F	17.2 ± 0.5	(7.3 ± 0.2)	4.2 ± 1.0	(1.8 ± 0.4)
32. Derbyshire				
1861–1870 M	22.5 ± 0.5	(12.4 ± 0.3)	2.3 ± 0.9	(1.3 ± 0.5)
F	19.4 ± 0.4	(10.5 ± 0.2)	2.7 ± 0.8	(1.5 ± 0.4)
1871–1880 M	18.6 ± 0.6	(8.8 ± 0.3)	1.6 ± 1.1	(0.8 ± 0.5)
F	21.6 ± 0.5	(10.1 ± 0.2)	0.5 ± 0.9	(0.2 ± 0.4)
1881–1890 M	20.5 ± 0.6	(8.5 ± 0.2)	7.2 ± 1.1	(3.0 ± 0.4)
F	23.2 ± 0.5	(9.4 ± 0.2)	4.1 ± 1.0	(3.0 ± 0.4)
1891–1900 M	21.5 ± 0.6	(7.8 ± 0.2)	2.7 ± 1.2	(1.0 ± 0.4)
F	24.6 ± 0.6	(8.6 ± 0.2)	1.7 ± 1.1	(0.6 ± 0.4)

County of Birth		IMIGij		EMIGio	
		000s	%	000s	%
33. Cheshire					
1861–1870	M	25.6 ± 0.7	(10.4 ± 0.3)	11.1 ± 1.5	(4.5 ± 0.6)
	F	26.9 ± 0.6	(10.7 ± 0.2)	9.5 ± 1.4	(3.8 ± 0.6)
1871–1880	M	28.4 ± 0.8	(10.2 ± 0.3)	6.2 ± 1.7	(2.2 ± 0.6)
	F	29.4 ± 0.7	(10.2 ± 0.2)	3.5 ± 1.6	(1.2 ± 0.6)
1881–1890	M	24.1 ± 0.7	(7.7 ± 0.2)	15.3 ± 1.6	(4.9 ± 0.5)
	F	26.3 ± 0.7	(8.0 ± 0.2)	10.4 ± 1.6	(3.2 ± 0.5)
1891–1900	M	31.4 ± 0.8	(9.0 ± 0.2)	8.3 ± 1.8	(2.4 ± 0.5)
	F	32.7 ± 0.8	(8.9 ± 0.2)	4.1 ± 1.8	(1.1 ± 0.5)
34. Lancashire					
1861–1870	M	41.1 ± 1.0	(3.9 ± 0.1)	31.1 ± 4.3	(3.0 ± 0.4)
	F	42.1 ± 0.9	(3.8 ± 0.1)	25.8 ± 4.4	(2.3 ± 0.4)
1871–1880	M	44.8 ± 1.2	(3.6 ± 0.1)	23.4 ± 4.0	(1.9 ± 0.3)
	F	44.8 ± 1.0	(3.4 ± 0.1)	16.4 ± 4.8	(1.2 ± 0.4)
1881–1890	M	45.8 ± 1.2	(3.1 ± 0.1)	62.8 ± 4.9	(4.2 ± 0.3)
	F	50.4 ± 1.1	(3.2 ± 0.1)	40.1 ± 5.2	(2.5 ± 0.3)
1891–1900	M	66.9 ± 1.4	(3.9 ± 0.1)	31.7 ± 5.1	(1.8 ± 0.3)
	F	68.7 ± 1.3	(3.7 ± 0.1)	7.6 ± 5.4	(0.4 ± 0.3)
35. Yorkshire					
1861–1870	M	36.1 ± 1.3	(3.4 ± 0.1)	19.0 ± 2.8	(1.8 ± 0.3)
	F	38.6 ± 1.1	(3.5 ± 0.1)	12.2 ± 2.6	(1.1 ± 0.2)
1871–1880	M	59.6 ± 1.4	(4.9 ± 0.1)	19.1 ± 3.4	(1.6 ± 0.3)
	F	56.1 ± 1.2	(4.4 ± 0.1)	16.4 ± 3.0	(1.3 ± 0.2)
1881–1890	M	58.4 ± 1.5	(4.2 ± 0.1)	46.5 ± 3.6	(3.3 ± 0.3)
	F	62.4 ± 1.4	(4.3 ± 0.1)	34.0 ± 3.6	(2.3 ± 0.2)
1891–1900	M	68.7 ± 1.7	(4.4 ± 0.1)	24.1 ± 4.9	(1.5 ± 0.3)
	F	72.2 ± 1.6	(4.4 ± 0.1)	7.0 ± 3.8	(0.4 ± 0.2)
36. Durham					
1861–1870	M	10.8 ± 0.3	(4.7 ± 0.1)	17.1 ± 1.4	(7.5 ± 0.6)
	F	13.8 ± 0.3	(5.8 ± 0.1)	11.0 ± 1.1	(4.6 ± 0.5)
1871–1880	M	22.2 ± 0.4	(7.4 ± 0.1)	12.0 ± 1.8	(4.0 ± 0.6)
	F	22.8 ± 0.3	(7.4 ± 0.1)	6.7 ± 1.2	(2.2 ± 0.4)
1881–1890	M	22.2 ± 0.4	(5.8 ± 0.1)	20.7 ± 1.7	(5.4 ± 0.4)
	F	24.8 ± 0.4	(6.3 ± 0.1)	14.4 ± 1.4	(3.7 ± 0.4)
1891–1900	M	26.9 ± 0.5	(5.7 ± 0.1)	9.4 ± 1.8	(2.0 ± 0.4)
	F	29.8 ± 0.5	(6.1 ± 0.1)	0.8 ± 1.5	(0.2 ± 0.3)

County of Birth	IMIGij		EMIGio	
	000s	%	000s	%
37. Northumberland				
1861–1870 M	18.4 ± 0.4	(10.7 ± 0.2)	2.7 ± 0.8	(1.6 ± 0.5)
F	18.1 ± 0.4	(10.1 ± 0.2)	2.8 ± 0.8	(1.6 ± 0.4)
1871–1880 M	20.7 ± 0.5	(10.5 ± 0.3)	2.7 ± 1.0	(1.4 ± 0.4)
F	21.0 ± 0.4	(10.3 ± 0.2)	2.1 ± 0.8	(1.0 ± 0.4)
1881–1890 M	14.8 ± 0.4	(6.6 ± 0.2)	7.7 ± 0.9	(3.5 ± 0.4)
F	15.8 ± 0.5	(6.8 ± 0.2)	5.0 ± 1.0	(2.2 ± 0.4)
1891–1900 M	15.2 ± 0.5	(6.0 ± 0.2)	4.6 ± 1.1	(1.8 ± 0.4)
F	17.4 ± 0.5	(6.6 ± 0.2)	0.8 ± 1.1	(0.4 ± 0.4)
38. Cumberland[j]				
1861–1870 M	12.1 ± 0.3	(11.3 ± 0.3)*	2.9 ± 0.5	(2.7 ± 0.5)*
F	12.6 ± 0.3	(10.8 ± 0.3)*	1.4 ± 0.5	(1.2 ± 0.4)*
1871–1880 M	10.2 ± 0.3	(8.7 ± 0.3)*	2.7 ± 0.6	(2.3 ± 0.5)*
F	10.4 ± 0.3	(8.3 ± 0.2)*	1.5 ± 0.5	(1.2 ± 0.4)*
1881–1890 M	10.3 ± 0.3	(7.9 ± 0.2)	7.2 ± 0.6	(5.5 ± 0.5)
F	10.2 ± 0.3	(7.5 ± 0.2)	5.0 ± 0.5	(3.7 ± 0.4)
1891–1900 M	15.0 ± 0.3	(10.8 ± 0.2)	4.8 ± 0.5	(3.4 ± 0.4)
F	15.0 ± 0.3	(10.2 ± 0.2)	2.7 ± 0.5	(1.8 ± 0.3)
39. Westmorland[j]				
1861–1870 M	4.2 ± 0.1	(11.9 ± 0.3)*	1.6 ± 0.2	(4.5 ± 0.6)*
F	4.3 ± 0.2	(11.8 ± 0.6)*	0.9 ± 0.2	(2.5 ± 0.6)*
1871–1880 M	4.5 ± 0.1	(12.1 ± 0.3)*	1.5 ± 0.2	(4.0 ± 0.5)*
F	4.5 ± 0.2	(11.7 ± 0.5)*	0.8 ± 0.2	(2.1 ± 0.5)*
1881–1890 M	4.4 ± 0.1	(11.3 ± 0.3)	2.0 ± 0.2	(5.1 ± 0.5)
F	4.5 ± 0.2	(11.2 ± 0.5)	1.1 ± 0.2	(2.7 ± 0.5)
1891–1900 M	4.4 ± 0.2	(11.1 ± 0.5)	1.5 ± 0.1	(3.8 ± 0.3)
F	4.6 ± 0.2	(11.1 ± 0.5)	0.9 ± 0.3	(2.2 ± 0.7)
40. Monmouth[k]				
1861–1870 M	7.4 ± 0.2	(9.9 ± 0.3)*	7.6 ± 0.6	(10.1 ± 0.8)*
F	8.4 ± 0.2	(10.8 ± 0.3)*	6.8 ± 0.5	(8.8 ± 0.6)*
1871–1880 M	10.3 ± 0.2	(11.7 ± 0.2)*	4.0 ± 0.6	(4.6 ± 0.7)*
F	10.9 ± 0.2	(12.0 ± 0.2)*	5.0 ± 0.5	(5.5 ± 0.6)*
1881–1890 M	8.1 ± 0.2	(7.9 ± 0.2)	4.7 ± 0.6	(4.6 ± 0.6)
F	9.5 ± 0.2	(8.9 ± 0.2)	2.8 ± 0.5	(2.6 ± 0.5)
1891–1900 M	11.3 ± 0.2	(9.3 ± 0.2)	2.6 ± 0.6	(2.1 ± 0.5)
F	13.0 ± 0.3	(10.2 ± 0.2)	+0.2 ± 0.6	(+0.2 ± 0.5)

County of Birth	IMIGij		EMIGio	
	000s	%	000s	%
41. Glamorgan[1]				
1861–1870 M	4.0 ± 0.1	(3.1 ± 0.1)*	10.3 ± 0.7	(8.0 ± 0.5)*
F	6.5 ± 0.2	(4.9 ± 0.1)*	7.3 ± 0.6	(5.5 ± 0.5)*
1871–1880 M	9.6 ± 0.2	(5.8 ± 0.1)*	9.0 ± 0.9	(5.5 ± 0.5)*
F	9.5 ± 0.2	(5.5 ± 0.1)*	6.7 ± 0.7	(3.9 ± 0.4)*
1881–1890 M	8.5 ± 0.2	(4.0 ± 0.1)	8.5 ± 1.1	(4.0 ± 0.5)
F	10.5 ± 0.2	(4.8 ± 0.1)	5.5 ± 0.8	(2.5 ± 0.4)
1891–1900 M	16.8 ± 0.2	(6.1 ± 0.1)	5.3 ± 1.3	(1.9 ± 0.5)
F	17.0 ± 0.3	(6.0 ± 0.1)	+1.8 ± 1.0	(+0.6 ± 0.4)
42. Carmarthen				
1861–1870 M	6.7 ± 0.3	(9.8 ± 0.4)	2.1 ± 0.3	(3.1 ± 0.4)
F	5.2 ± 0.2	(7.2 ± 0.3)	2.3 ± 0.2	(3.2 ± 0.3)
1871–1880 M	6.6 ± 0.3	(9.3 ± 0.4)	1.0 ± 0.4	(1.4 ± 0.6)
F	7.8 ± 0.2	(10.4 ± 0.3)	+1.3 ± 0.3	(+1.7 ± 0.4)
1881–1890 M	6.4 ± 0.3	(8.6 ± 0.4)	2.5 ± 0.4	(3.4 ± 0.5)
F	5.1 ± 0.2	(6.5 ± 0.3)	2.0 ± 0.3	(2.5 ± 0.4)
1891–1900 M	6.1 ± 0.3	(7.9 ± 0.4)	2.4 ± 0.3	(3.1 ± 0.4)
F	5.1 ± 0.2	(6.2 ± 0.2)	2.6 ± 0.2	(3.2 ± 0.2)
43. Pembroke				
1861–1870 M	5.1 ± 0.1	(9.9 ± 0.2)	5.0 ± 0.2	(9.7 ± 0.4)
F	5.2 ± 0.2	(8.9 ± 0.3)	3.0 ± 0.2	(5.1 ± 0.3)
1871–1880 M	6.6 ± 0.2	(12.6 ± 0.4)	1.0 ± 0.3	(1.9 ± 0.6)
F	6.9 ± 0.2	(11.7 ± 0.3)	0.3 ± 0.2	(0.5 ± 0.3)
1881–1890 M	6.4 ± 0.2	(11.9 ± 0.4)	2.6 ± 0.2	(4.8 ± 0.4)
F	5.8 ± 0.2	(9.7 ± 0.3)	1.5 ± 0.2	(2.5 ± 0.3)
1891–1900 M	4.5 ± 0.2	(8.2 ± 0.4)	2.3 ± 0.3	(4.2 ± 0.5)
F	4.2 ± 0.1	(6.9 ± 0.2)	1.8 ± 0.1	(3.0 ± 0.2)
44. Cardigan[m]				
1861–1870 M	3.9 ± 0.1	(9.6 ± 0.2)*	1.6 ± 0.2	(3.9 ± 0.5)*
F	2.8 ± 0.1	(6.2 ± 0.2)*	1.1 ± 0.1	(2.4 ± 0.2)*
1871–1880 M	5.5 ± 0.1	(12.0 ± 0.2)*	1.2 ± 0.1	(2.9 ± 0.2)*
F	4.6 ± 0.1	(9.9 ± 0.2)*	0.3 ± 0.1	(0.6 ± 0.2)*
1881–1890 M	6.2 ± 0.1	(15.0 ± 0.2)	1.8 ± 0.2	(4.4 ± 0.5)
F	5.6 ± 0.1	(12.0 ± 0.2)	1.0 ± 0.2	(2.2 ± 0.4)
1891–1900 M	3.7 ± 0.1	(9.3 ± 0.3)	0.9 ± 0.2	(2.3 ± 0.5)
F	3.2 ± 0.1	(7.1 ± 0.2)	0.9 ± 0.2	(2.0 ± 0.4)

County of Birth		IMIGij		EMIGio	
		000s	%	000s	%
45. Brecon					
1861–1870	M	4.3 ± 0.1	(13.2 ± 0.3)	3.2 ± 0.2	(9.8 ± 0.6)
	F	3.4 ± 0.1	(10.4 ± 0.3)	3.3 ± 0.2	(10.1 ± 0.6)
1871–1880	M	4.6 ± 0.1	(14.0 ± 0.3)	1.6 ± 0.2	(4.9 ± 0.6)
	F	5.5 ± 0.1	(16.6 ± 0.3)	0.9 ± 0.2	(2.7 ± 0.6)
1881–1890	M	3.8 ± 0.1	(11.6 ± 0.3)	2.3 ± 0.2	(7.0 ± 0.6)
	F	3.3 ± 0.1	(9.9 ± 0.3)	2.4 ± 0.2	(7.2 ± 0.6)
1891–1900	M	4.0 ± 0.1	(11.8 ± 0.3)	0.7 ± 0.2	(2.1 ± 0.6)
	F	4.0 ± 0.1	(11.6 ± 0.3)	0.7 ± 0.2	(2.0 ± 0.6)
46. Radnor					
1861–1870	M	2.7 ± 0.1	(15.2 ± 0.6)	+0.1 ± 0.1	(+0.6 ± 0.6)
	F	2.1 ± 0.1	(12.1 ± 0.6)	0.5 ± 0.1	(2.9 ± 0.6)
1871–1880	M	2.2 ± 0.1	(12.5 ± 0.6)	0.8 ± 0.1	(4.6 ± 0.6)
	F	2.9 ± 0.1	(16.9 ± 0.6)	— ± 0.1	(— ± 0.6)
1881–1890	M	2.2 ± 0.1	(13.3 ± 0.6)	0.6 ± 0.1	(3.6 ± 0.6)
	F	2.1 ± 0.1	(12.7 ± 0.6)	0.4 ± 0.1	(2.4 ± 0.6)
1891–1900	M	1.6 ± 0.1	(9.8 ± 0.6)	0.4 ± 0.1	(2.5 ± 0.6)
	F	1.8 ± 0.1	(10.9 ± 0.6)	0.4 ± 0.1	(2.4 ± 0.6)
47. Montgomery					
1861–1870	M	4.4 ± 0.1	(10.9 ± 0.2)	1.1 ± 0.2	(2.7 ± 0.5)
	F	3.6 ± 0.1	(8.7 ± 0.2)	1.4 ± 0.2	(3.4 ± 0.5)
1871–1880	M	4.0 ± 0.1	(9.8 ± 0.2)	2.4 ± 0.2	(5.9 ± 0.5)
	F	5.3 ± 0.2	(12.7 ± 0.5)	0.8 ± 0.2	(1.9 ± 0.5)
1881–1890	M	5.2 ± 0.1	(13.1 ± 0.3)	2.9 ± 0.2	(7.3 ± 0.5)
	F	4.6 ± 0.2	(11.2 ± 0.5)	2.2 ± 0.2	(5.4 ± 0.5)
1891–1900	M	3.6 ± 0.2	(9.4 ± 0.5)	1.3 ± 0.2	(3.4 ± 0.5)
	F	3.9 ± 0.2	(9.7 ± 0.5)	1.0 ± 0.2	(2.5 ± 0.5)
48. Flint					
1861–1870	M	4.6 ± 0.2	(11.1 ± 0.5)	— ± 0.3	(— ± 0.7)
	F	4.2 ± 0.2	(9.9 ± 0.5)	0.7 ± 0.3	(1.7 ± 0.7)
1871–1880	M	4.2 ± 0.2	(9.6 ± 0.5)	1.9 ± 0.3	(4.4 ± 0.7)
	F	5.6 ± 0.2	(12.7 ± 0.5)	0.2 ± 0.3	(0.5 ± 0.7)
1881–1890	M	5.6 ± 0.1	(12.6 ± 0.2)	2.1 ± 0.2	(4.7 ± 0.5)
	F	5.8 ± 0.2	(12.8 ± 0.4)	1.3 ± 0.3	(2.7 ± 0.7)
1891–1900	M	5.0 ± 0.2	(10.9 ± 0.4)	0.7 ± 0.3	(1.5 ± 0.7)
	F	5.2 ± 0.2	(11.1 ± 0.4)	0.2 ± 0.3	(0.4 ± 0.6)

County of Birth	IMIGij		EMIGio	
	000s	%	000s	%
49. Denbigh				
1861–1870 M	5.9 ± 0.2	(10.5 ± 0.4)	1.7 ± 0.3	(3.0 ± 0.5)
F	6.7 ± 0.2	(11.7 ± 0.3)	0.4 ± 0.3	(0.7 ± 0.5)
1871–1880 M	5.8 ± 0.2	(9.8 ± 0.3)	1.1 ± 0.3	(1.9 ± 0.5)
F	6.9 ± 0.2	(11.5 ± 0.3)	0.4 ± 0.3	(0.7 ± 0.5)
1881–1890 M	4.9 ± 0.2	(8.0 ± 0.3)	1.6 ± 0.3	(2.6 ± 0.5)
F	6.2 ± 0.2	(9.9 ± 0.3)	0.6 ± 0.3	(1.0 ± 0.5)
1891–1900 M	5.9 ± 0.2	(8.9 ± 0.3)	— ± 0.3	(— ± 0.5)
F	6.4 ± 0.2	(9.4 ± 0.3)	+0.4 ± 0.3	(+0.6 ± 0.4)
50. Merioneth				
1861–1870 M	1.7 ± 0.1	(7.5 ± 0.4)	0.2 ± 0.1	(0.9 ± 0.4)
F	1.4 ± 0.1	(6.0 ± 0.4)	0.7 ± 0.1	(3.0 ± 0.4)
1871–1880 M	1.2 ± 0.1	(4.9 ± 0.4)	0.7 ± 0.1	(2.9 ± 0.4)
F	2.4 ± 0.1	(9.6 ± 0.4)	0.3 ± 0.1	(1.2 ± 0.4)
1881–1890 M	2.6 ± 0.1	(10.3 ± 0.4)	2.6 ± 0.1	(10.3 ± 0.4)
F	2.5 ± 0.1	(9.5 + 0.4)	1.3 ± 0.1	(4.9 ± 0.4)
1891–1900 M	2.8 ± 0.1	(10.9 ± 0.4)	0.2 ± 0.1	(0.8 ± 0.4)
F	2.8 ± 0.1	(10.2 ± 0.4)	0.2 ± 0.1	(0.7 ± 0.4)
51. Caernarvon				
1861–1870 M	2.2 ± 0.1	(4.6 ± 0.2)	3.0 ± 0.2	(6.2 ± 0.4)
F	2.2 ± 0.1	(4.2 ± 0.2)	1.1 ± 0.2	(2.1 ± 0.4)
1871–1880 M	2.8 ± 0.1	(5.4 ± 0.2)	0.5 ± 0.2	(1.0 ± 0.4)
F	4.2 ± 0.1	(7.5 ± 0.2)	+1.1 ± 0.1	(+1.8 ± 0.2)
1881–1890 M	4.9 ± 0.1	(8.9 ± 0.2)	4.0 ± 0.2	(7.2 ± 0.4)
F	4.6 ± 0.1	(7.7 ± 0.2)	1.8 ± 0.2	(3.0 ± 0.3)
1891–1900 M	4.5 ± 0.1	(7.7 ± 0.2)	+0.5 ± 0.2	(+0.9 ± 0.3)
F	4.7 ± 0.1	(7.4 ± 0.2)	+0.5 ± 0.2	(+0.8 ± 0.3)
52. Anglesey				
1861–1870 M	3.1 ± 0.1	(10.5 ± 0.3)	1.2 ± 0.1	(4.1 ± 0.3)
F	2.8 ± 0.1	(8.9 ± 0.3)	+0.2 ± 0.1	(+0.6 ± 0.3)
1871–1880 M	3.2 ± 0.1	(10.8 ± 0.3)	+0.2 ± 0.1	(+0.7 ± 0.3)
F	3.6 ± 0.1	(11.3 ± 0.3)	+0.5 ± 0.1	(+1.6 ± 0.3)
1881–1890 M	1.6 ± 0.1	(5.4 ± 0.3)	2.0 ± 0.1	(6.8 ± 0.3)
F	1.7 ± 0.1	(5.4 ± 0.3)	1.1 ± 0.1	(3.5 ± 0.3)
1891–1900 M	1.6 ± 0.1	(5.5 ± 0.3)	0.8 ± 0.1	(2.8 ± 0.3)
F	1.9 ± 0.1	(6.0 ± 0.3)	0.8 ± 0.1	(2.5 ± 0.3)

Notes

a   Some Surrey born in London may have been incorrectly enumerated as London born in 1861.

b   Assumes that 800 males and 500 females who were born in Sussex and living in Hampshire in 1881 were incorrectly enumerated as Hampshire natives.

c   Assumes that 2,300 males and 2,100 females who were born in Oxfordshire and living in Berkshire in 1871 were incorrectly enumerated as Berkshire natives.

d   Assumes that 500 males and 457 females who were born in Wiltshire and living in Glamorgan in 1871 were incorrectly enumerated as Glamorgan natives.

e   Assumes that 1,277 males and 1,185 females who were born in Devon and living in Glamorgan in 1871 were incorrectly enumerated as Glamorgan natives.

f   Assumes that 3,000 males and 3,500 females who were born in Gloucestershire and living in Somerset in 1871 were incorrectly enumerated as Somerset natives and that 7,500 males and 7,500 females who were born in Gloucestershire and living in Somerset in 1901 were incorrectly enumerated as Somerset natives. This was presumably because the conurbation of Bristol lay on both sides of the River Avon which was the county boundary.

g   Assumes that 2,650 males and 2,169 females who were born in Somerset and living in Glamorgan in 1871 were incorrectly enumerated as Glamorgan natives.

h   Assumes that 1,200 males and 1,000 females who were born in Gloucestershire and living in Glamorgan in 1871 were incorrectly enumerated as Glamorgan natives.

i   Assumes that 200 males and 500 females who were born in Gloucestershire and living there in 1881 were incorrectly enumerated as Monmouth born.

j   Assumes that 600 males and 500 females who were born in Westmorland and living in Cumberland in 1871 were incorrectly returned as Cumberland natives.

k   Assumes that 1,449 males and 1,662 females who were born in Monmouth and living in Glamorgan in 1871 were incorrectly enumerated as Glamorgan natives.

l   See notes d, e, g, h, k and m.

m   Assumes that 535 males and 427 females who were born in Cardigan and living in Glamorgan in 1871 were incorrectly enumerated as Glamorgan natives.

APPENDIX 2

Minimum estimates of English and Welsh emigration (gross outward passenger movement), 1825–1853

	English, Welsh and Irish 000s	% assumed to be English and Welsh	English and Welsh 000s	Per 1000 of the estimated mid-year population
1825–29	23.5	80	18.9	0.4
1830–34	69.8	80	55.8	1.0
1834–39	56.2	60	33.7	0.7
1840–44	106.6	40	42.6	1.3
1845–49	172.2	25	43.0	2.0
1850–53	312.6	25	78.2	4.3

Source: Calculated from Carrier and Jeffery, *External migration*, p. 93, and Mitchell, *Abstract of British historical statistics*, Table 3, pp. 8–9. The table assumes that no English and Welsh sailed from a Scottish or Irish port and that all the Irish sailing via an English port sailed via Liverpool. The table understates English and Welsh emigration probably by more than 50%. See chapter 3, p. 49.

APPENDIX 3

Emigration (outward passenger movement) from Scottish ports, 1825–1853

	Annual sailings (000s)	Per 1000 of estimated mid-year population
1825	2.0	0.9
1826	1.7	0.8
1827	2.8	1.1
1828	5.2	2.3
1829	3.2	1.4
1830	4.4	1.9
1825–30	19.3	1.4
1831	7.6	3.2
1832	9.1	3.8
1833	7.8	3.2
1834	5.2	2.1
1835	2.7	1.1
1836	3.7	1.5
1837	3.7	1.5
1838	4.0	1.6
1839	3.7	1.4
1840	4.1	1.6
1831–40	51.6	2.1
1841	12.1	4.6
1842	8.9	3.4
1843	6.9	2.6
1844	2.9	1.1
1845	3.4	1.2
1846	2.7	1.0
1847	5.2	1.9
1848	5.1	1.8
1849	7.9	2.8
1850	4.5	1.6
1841–50	59.6	2.2
1851	8.9	3.1
1852	19.5	6.7
1853	15.4	5.2
1851–53	43.8	5.0

Note: As in Appendix 2. Irish emigration from Scottish ports before 1853 is assumed to be negligible.

APPENDIX 4

Emigration (outward passenger movement) by natives of England and Wales, 1853–1930

	Total emigration			Net outward		
	Annual passengers (000s)	Per 1,000 of estimated mid-year population	Per 1,000 of the natural increase	Annual passengers (000s)	Per 1,000 of estimated mid-year population	Per 1,000 of the natural increase
1853	62.9	3.4	271			
1854	91.0	4.9	401			
1855	57.1	3.0	241			
1856	64.5	3.4	219			
1857	78.6	4.1	291			
1858	40.0	2.1	173			
1859	33.9	1.7	124			
1860	26.4	1.3	93			
1853–60	454.4	2.4	222			
1861	22.2	1.1	79			
1862	35.3	1.7	120			
1863	61.2	3.0	225			
1864	56.6	2.7	216			
1865	61.3	2.9	225			
1866	58.9	2.8	219			
1867	55.5	2.6	178			
1868	58.3	2.7	183			
1869	90.4	4.1	313			
1870	105.3	4.7	367			
1861–70	605.2	2.8	385			
1871	102.5	4.5	353			
1872	118.2	5.2	347			
1873	123.3	5.3	358			
1874	116.5	4.9	348			
1875	84.5	3.5	273			
1876	73.4	3.0	192			
1877	63.7	2.6	163			
1878	72.3	2.9	203			
1879	104.3	4.1	293			
1880	111.8	4.4	315			
1871–80	970.6	4.0	281			

(cont. next page)

APPENDIX 4 (*cont.*)

	Total emigration			Net outward		
	Annual passengers (000s)	Per 1,000 of estimated mid-year population	Per 1,000 of the natural increase	Annual passengers (000s)	Per 1,000 of estimated mid-year population	Per 1,000 of the natural increase
1881	140.0	5.4	358			
1882	163.0	6.2	438			
1883	183.2	6.9	498			
1884	147.7	5.5	393			
1885	126.3	4.7	340			
1886	146.3	5.3	399			
1887	168.2	6.1	474			
1888	170.8	6.1	463			
1889	163.5	5.8	444			
1890	140.0	4.9	455			
1881–90	1549.0	5.6	425			
1891	137.9	4.8	422			
1892	133.8	4.6	396			
1893	134.0	4.5	388			
1894	99.6	3.3	255			
1895	112.5	3.7	319	43.3	1.4	123
1896	102.8	3.3	265	34.6	1.1	89
1897	94.7	3.0	249	28.7	0.9	75
1898	90.7	2.9	244	28.4	0.9	77
1899	87.4	2.7	251	17.7	0.6	51
1900	102.4	3.2	302	36.0	1.1	106
1891–1900	1095.9	3.6	306	188.7 (1895–1900)	0.6	87
1901	111.6	3.4	295	42.8	1.3	113
1902	137.1	4.2	338	64.7	2.0	159
1903	177.6	5.3	409	98.8	3.0	228
1904	175.7	5.2	445	78.4	2.3	198
1905	170.4	5.0	417	85.9	2.5	210
1906	219.8	6.4	544	129.1	3.8	320
1907	265.2	7.7	673	153.1	4.4	389
1908	177.0	5.1	443	68.2	1.9	163
1909	185.5	5.3	468	92.7	2.6	234
1910	255.6	7.2	617	152.7	4.3	369
1901–10	1875.5	5.5	463	966.4	2.8	239

APPENDIX 4 (*cont.*)

	Total emigration			Net outward		
	Annual passengers (000s)	Per 1,000 of estimated mid-year population	Per 1,000 of the natural increase	Annual passengers (000s)	Per 1,000 of estimated mid-year population	Per 1,000 of the natural increase
1911	302.7	8.4	858	185.1	5.1	524
1912	314.5	8.7	815	225.4	6.2	584
1913	276.8	7.6	734	211.0	5.8	560
1914	149.6	4.1	412	69.4	1.9	191
1915	51.5	1.5	204	21.4	0.6	85
1916	34.7	1.0	125	11.3	0.3	41
1917	8.1	0.2	48	2.1	0.1	12
1918	9.2	0.3	18	1.9	0.1	4
1919	125.9	3.6	670	53.2	1.5	283
1920	206.1	5.5	419	136.4	3.7	277
1911–20	1479.1	4.0	508	917.2	2.5	315
1921	132.0	3.5	358	75.7	2.0	194
1922	113.1	3.0	386	59.6	1.6	203
1923	145.4	3.8	465	98.6	2.6	315
1924	108.1	2.8	422	58.1	1.5	227
1925	94.0	2.4	395	48.8	1.3	205
1926	105.1	2.7	436	63.3	1.6	263
1927	98.1	2.5	580	53.4	1.4	316
1928	88.3	2.2	444	40.9	1.0	206
1929	88.2	2.2	795	42.7	1.1	385
1930	97.0	1.4	294	5.2	0.1	27
1921–30	1029.2		428	546.3	1.4	227

Source: Calculated from Carrier and Jeffery, *External migration*, Table C (1), pp. 92–3, and Mitchell, *Abstract of British historical statistics*, Table 3, pp. 8–10, Table 10, pp. 29–30 and Table 11, pp. 34–5.

It was assumed that births were 5% under-registered in 1853, 3% in 1861, 1% in 1871. Registration was assumed to have been complete in 1881. The total population for the years 1915–20 is the civilian population only.

APPENDIX 5

Emigration (outward passenger movement) by Scottish natives 1853–1930

	Total emigration			Net outward		
	Annual passengers (000s)	Per 1,000 of estimated mid-year population	Per 1,000 of the natural increase	Annual passengers (000s)	Per 1,000 of estimated mid-year population	Per 1,000 of the natural increase
1853	22.0	7.5				
1854	25.9	8.8				
1855	14.0	4.7	388			
1856	12.0	4.0	249			
1857	16.3	5.4	355			
1858	11.8	3.9	265			
1859	10.2	3.4	209			
1860	8.7	2.8	213			
1853–60	120.9	4.0	276 (1855–60)			
1861	6.7	2.2	139			
1862	12.6	4.1	291			
1863	15.2	4.9	374			
1864	15.0	4.8	369			
1865	12.9	4.1	287			
1866	12.3	3.8	276			
1867	12.9	4.0	274			
1868	15.0	4.6	330			
1869	22.6	6.8	578			
1870	23.0	6.9	540			
1861–70	148.2	4.6	340			
1871	19.2	5.7	450			
1872	19.5	5.7	436			
1873	21.3	6.2	486			
1874	20.3	5.8	462			
1875	14.7	4.2	345			
1876	10.1	2.8	191			
1877	8.7	2.4	163			
1878	11.1	3.1	220			
1879	18.7	5.1	355			
1880	22.1	6.0	446			
1871–80	165.7	4.7	345			

APPENDIX 5 (*cont.*)

	Total emigration			Net outward		
	Annual passengers (000s)	Per 1,000 of estimated mid-year population	Per 1,000 of the natural increase	Annual passengers (000s)	Per 1,000 of estimated mid-year population	Per 1,000 of the natural increase
1881	26.8	7.2	497			
1882	32.2	7.2	497			
1883	31.1	8.2	653			
1884	22.0	5.7	407			
1885	21.4	5.5	416			
1886	25.3	6.5	466			
1887	34.4	8.8	689			
1888	35.9	9.1	689			
1889	25.4	6.4	512			
1890	20.7	5.2	487			
1881–90	275.2	7.1	541			
1891	22.2	5.5	524			
1892	23.3	5.7	472			
1893	22.6	5.5	477			
1894	14.4	3.5	271			
1895	18.3	4.3	410	4.2	0.9	94
1896	16.9	4.0	289	4.1	1.0	70
1897	16.1	3.7	323	4.9	1.1	98
1898	15.6	3.6	297	4.9	1.1	93
1899	16.1	3.7	315	4.6	1.0	90
1900	20.5	4.6	418	8.9	2.0	181
1891–1900	186.0	4.4	373	31.6 (1895–1900)	0.7	188
1901	20.9	4.7	401	9.0	2.0	173
1902	26.3	5.8	484	14.7	3.3	271
1903	36.8	8.1	640	22.8	5.0	397
1904	37.4	8.2	685	19.5	4.3	357
1905	41.5	9.0	729	25.4	5.5	446
1906	53.2	11.5	943	34.4	7.4	610
1907	66.4	14.3	1289	44.2	9.5	858
1908	42.3	9.0	791	19.1	4.1	357
1909	52.9	11.2	978	33.4	7.1	617
1910	79.8	16.8	1538	58.4	12.3	1125
1901–10	457.5	9.9	843	280.9	6.1	518

APPENDIX 5 (*cont.*)

	Total emigration			Net outward		
	Annual passengers (000s)	Per 1,000 of estimated mid-year population	Per 1,000 of the natural increase	Annual passengers (000s)	Per 1,000 of estimated mid-year population	Per 1,000 of the natural increase
1911	88.9	18.7	1771	61.3	12.9	1221
1912	72.6	15.3	1440	55.0	11.6	1091
1913	68.2	14.4	1439	54.2	11.5	1143
1914	34.3	7.2	682	17.8	3.7	354
1915	10.1	2.1	310	−4.3	−0.9	−132
1916	8.3	1.7	212	0.3	0	8
1917	1.1	0.2	39	−0.2	0	−7
1918	1.1	0.2	54	0	0	0
1919	16.8	3.5	538	4.4	0.9	141
1920	48.5	10.0	709	38.2	7.9	558
1911–20	349.9	7.3	837	226.7	4.7	542
1921	41.4	8.5	726	30.8	6.3	540
1922	39.9	8.1	945	30.8	6.3	730
1923	88.6	18.1	1823	80.1	16.4	1648
1924	39.2	8.1	1074	26.9	5.5	737
1925	37.9	7.8	982	28.3	5.8	733
1926	48.6	10.0	1259	40.6	8.3	1052
1927	43.5	9.0	1408	34.1	7.0	1104
1928	38.3	7.9	1216	28.4	5.9	902
1929	42.9	8.9	1950	33.9	7.0	1541
1930	26.0	5.4	858	14.0	2.9	462
1921–30	446.3	9.2	1186	347.9	7.2	925

Source: As for Appendix 4. Under-registration of births in Scotland is assumed to be the same as in England.

APPENDIX 6

Male and female lifetime emigrants and lifetime internal migrants from Northumberland, Durham, Cumberland and Westmorland, 1861–1900

Born in	To other English and Welsh counties		Overseas	
	Males	Females	Males	Females
Durham	82.1 (47%)	91.2 (53%)	59.2 (64%)	32.9 (36%)
Northumberland	62.1 (49%)	65.3 (51%)	24.7 (58%)	17.7 (42%)
Westmorland	17.5 (49%)	17.9 (51%)	6.6 (64%)	3.7 (36%)
Cumberland	40.6 (50%)	41.2 (50%)	24.6 (58%)	17.6 (42%)
England and Wales			1498.9 (63%)	877.8 (37%)
Glamorgan	38.9 (47%)	43.5 (53%)	33.1 (65%)	17.7 (35%)
Yorkshire	222.8 (49%)	229.5 (51%)	108.7 (61%)	69.6 (39%)
West of England	370.8 (47%)	424.1 (53%)	210.7 (65%)	112.4 (35%)

Note: see chapter 4, pp. 121–2.

APPENDIX 7

A model of internal and overseas migration by natives of English and Welsh counties, 1861–1900
(by Dr Mary Morgan)

This appendix presents an econometric analysis of the overseas and internal migration series reported in Appendix 1. It proposes a model, based on the traditional theories of economists and economic historians, that is appropriate for the explanation of domestic and overseas migration on a cross section basis. Data which incorporate both cross section and time series dimensions present particular, but well recognised, econometric problems both in modelling and in estimation. These problems are discussed in order to justify the use of covariance analysis in this instance. The results of this analysis of the data are presented and their implications discussed.

The model

Although economists' and economic historians' theories of migration tend to differ, the econometric models derived from both theories are basically similar. The *economist* postulates a micro-economic theory of migration which depends on the individual's reaction to opportunities at home versus opportunities in an alternative environment (either another country or another area of the same country). In this model, the individual maximises his or her welfare by migrating when the expected gains from moving (allowing for the cost of the move) outweigh the expected gains from not moving. A comparison is therefore made at each point in time between job opportunities, expected earnings, etc., which in turn depend on the supply and demand factors at work, in the two (or more) alternative labour markets.

The economic historian is concerned with explaining mass migration movements of the past and the traditional migration theory is couched in terms of push and pull factors which operate to cause these aggregate movements. The push factors refer to unpleasant employment (or other, non-economic) conditions in the home country and pull factors to the attractive conditions in another country. As Gould[1] has pointed out, this basically 'supply push – demand pull' model is misconceived since the 'push' conditions will depend on both the supply and demand factors in the home labour market and similarly the 'pull' conditions are dependent on both supply and demand factors in the alternative labour market. Gould has represented the individual's migration decision as a balance between these conditions (including the cost of moving) – when the balance shifts, the decision to migrate which may have been made much earlier, is then carried out. So it is the change in this balance which determines the timing of migration movements. The migration historian also has a strong preference for explaining present migration by the behaviour of past migration. This theory, known as chain migration, depends on information flows from previous migrants and the presence of already established migrant communities and thus involves both the stock of previous migrants and the most recent flow of migrants. (See chapter 2.)

The difference between the economist's model of the individual maximising his welfare and the economic historian's model of push and pull factors determining mass movement largely disappears in applied econometric work on migration. This is firstly because most migration series relate to aggregate movements rather than to individuals. So the economist is forced to treat the aggregated figures as a sum of individuals who behave as the average individual in responding to average labour market conditions represented by average wages, unemployment levels, etc. Secondly, the historian, when using standard multiple regression techniques, no longer treats push and pull factors as separate but incorporates them both in the same model, thus taking both influences into account at the same time. To this extent, the micro-theory of the economist produces a very similar model in the aggregate to the macro push-pull model of the economic historian. However, the presence of the additional chain migration theory in the economic historian's model differentiates the two econometric models. Effectively, therefore, the economist's model is a special case of the more general economic historian's model – namely one where the chain migration theory does not hold. The most general tentative working model derived from all the theories discussed here is therefore the economic historian's model:

Migration = F[labour market conditions at home and at destination, costs of moving, chain effect of previous migration]

[1] J. D. Gould, *European inter-continental emigration.*

The economist's theories result in a restricted version of the same model:

Migration = F[labour market conditions at home and at destination, costs of moving]

However, the derived econometric model should not only be coherent with the economist's and/or the economic historian's theories (i.e. incorporate the basic features of these theories and not have features which contradict them), but also be an accurate representation of the data generation process for the migration data in use. So the tentative working model of the previous paragraph must now be adapted to be conformable with the migration data series in use. Firstly, these series only relate to half the migration story since we have the overseas and domestic migration figures only for the sending county. We have no matching information on emigrant destinations so we cannot model labour market conditions at the destination area, as both economists and economic historians would ideally like to do. We must assume instead that the opportunities and conditions in the labour market in the alternative environment (i.e. the historian's 'pull' factors) are constant for all migrants. We can incorporate directly in the model only the labour market conditions at home – i.e. in each country of origin. If the destination of migrants is unknown it also makes it difficult to incorporate either a cost of migration variable into the model or certain possible measures of the chain migration effect, namely the stock or recent flow of previous migrants at a destination area. The second important feature of the migration data set is that it provides net migration flows for arbitrarily defined time periods and geographical units. The data in this instance are flows per decade for four decades between 1861 and 1901 (using census dates) rather than per year so we are not in a position to model the effect on migration of short-term changes in labour market conditions over the business cycle. (Gould has recently surveyed the econometric work on this subject.) The limitation of only four data points over time means that the model must instead concentrate on the cross section differences in emigration flows. The cross section unit of measurement is by county, which may not be the ideal economic unit but does provide a good sized data set.

Given the constraints enforced by the migration data series that we want to explain, we first considered factors which would reflect the labour market environment in each county. The factors we wanted to incorporate were – a demographic variable to reflect the absolute labour supply available, a measure of local underemployment or the stock of labour in a local reserve labour pool and a variable to indicate local labour skills and reflect the type of jobs being sought by potential migrants. We also required some measure of local wages and some indicator of the variety and density of employment opportunities available. Any migration model incorporating these variables will suffer from the problem that the local labour market conditions will be affected by migration as well as influencing it. We must therefore choose the actual variables to be used carefully to reduce this problem as far as possible.

Secondly, we wanted to incorporate the chain migration theory in some form. Although we cannot make use of a previous migration stock variable because of lack of information on migrant destination, we can proxy the information flow and chain migration effect of previous migrants by using the previous outflow of migration from a county. So our tentative econometric model now becomes:

Migration = F[conditions in the home labour market variables, chain migration variable]

The data and the econometric model

The *Dependent Variables* consisted of the four migration series:

MEMIGio – male emigration from county i to overseas destinations
FEMIGio – female emigration from county i to overseas destinations
MIMIGij – male migration from county i to all other counties (denoted j)
FIMIGij – female migration from county i to all other counties

The data are net flows of migrants per decade for four decades, 1861–70 to 1891–1900, and for the fifty-two counties of England and Wales. (These are the estimated flows reported in Appendix 1.)

The explanatory variables

Home labour market conditions
'*Age*' – For the demographic variable to denote available labour supply, we used the proportion of the population in the age group 10–20 years at the beginning of the decade (from census data – males and females separately). This age group was chosen since it includes all those individuals who pass through the age of twenty years in the decade and is the group most likely to react to conditions of population pressure on job opportunities by migrating. The coefficient is expected to have a positive sign – the higher the proportion in the age group the higher the migration.

'*ΔAgric*' – For a measure of underemployment or the local reserve labour pool we took the change from the beginning of each decade to the next in the percentage of the male labour force defined as being employed in agricultural occupations (taken from Lee and the census).[2] We used the first difference (or change) in the agricultural labour force because the decision to migrate and its timing is based on changes in local labour market conditions. Since the equivalent figures for women are rather poor, we used the male figures and assumed that the female variable was a constant proportion of the male figure. We expect the sign to be negative – i.e. a fall in the agricultural labour force would be associated with a rise in migration.

'*ΔLiteracy*' – For a measure of the skill of the labour force we used the proportion of men and women (taken separately) signing the marriage register with a mark as opposed to a signature. The data are the annual average per decade from the *Registrar General's Annual Reports*. Although this variable is an admittedly crude indicator of the labour force skill, literacy is normally positively associated with mobility. In the context of a migration model, therefore, literacy may also be a measure of the information effect in chain migration, i.e. the more literate the population, the better communication with the home county and the more migrants go to join friends and relatives elsewhere. It was a period of sharply falling illiteracy (by this measure) and for the reasons argued above we used the change in average literacy rather than its level. We expect a rise in literacy to be associated with a rise in migration from both the skill effect and the information effect.

'*ΔWages*' – For the local wage rate we used the agricultural labourer's wage rate for men for both male and female dependent variable regressions. This we take to be a proxy for the local minimum wage rate. Very few wage details are available by county and the source for this series is taken from Hunt.[3] This provided us with two data points for each county – 1868 and 1897/8 which we used for the first and last decades. We interpolated data for the two intervening decades using a log linear trend (i.e. a constant rate of increase) between the two points. This variable was also used in change (i.e. first differences) form and we expect an increase in reserve or minimum wages, indicating an increased demand for labour in that county, to lead to a decrease in migration – i.e. a negative sign.

'*Urban*' – For a measure of the variety and density of job opportunities we used the percentage of people in the county living in contiguous

[2] Lee, *British regional employment statistics*.   [3] Hunt, *Regional wage variations*, pp. 62–4.

urban areas of over 20,000 inhabitants. (Obviously we used the same variable for both male and female dependent variable regressions.) The source was the census, and figures were means for the decade. Because changes in this variable were likely to be highly collinear with 'Agric', we left this variable as a level and expect a high level of urbanisation to have a negative impact on internal migration but its impact on external migration is unclear.

Chain migration
'Mlag' – The dependent variable lagged one period. We expect that previous overseas migration will be positively related to present overseas migration because of the chain migration theory, but that previous internal migration, by releasing pressure of labour supply on local job opportunities will be negatively related to present internal migration.

A straightforward linear function of the explanatory variables was used because there seemed to be no reason to believe that the relationship was multiplicative. [Indeed, a log linear form would have provided some problems since some of the migration observations were negative (i.e. positive inflows) and some observations for the explanatory variables were zero.] The *econometric model* used was therefore:

$$\text{Net migration} = F[B_1\text{Age} + B_2\Delta\text{Agric} + B_3\Delta\text{Literacy} + B_4\Delta\text{Wages} + B_5\text{Urban} + B_6\text{MLag}]$$

Covariance analysis
We have specified an econometric equation to explain the migration data from fifty-two counties over four decades. It may be that our model will not completely explain the migration data due to the omission of non-economic variables from the equation. Two different approaches have been developed in econometrics to deal with this problem of errors due to omitted variables when the data is both cross section and time series.

We can consider the error in the relationship for each county at each time period, u_{it}, to be made up of three uncorrelated components. That is:

$$u_{it} = v_i + w_t + e_{it} \text{ (where } i \text{ subscript refers to the county, } t \text{ subscript to the time period and } e_{it} \text{ is a random error).}$$

We then have the choice of treating v_i and w_t as fixed or random effects. If we assume the cross-section effect, v_i, to be a fixed effect we are assuming that each county unit has its own particular omitted variable that is constant for all time periods and that is different from all other counties. In other words that there is something specific to Cornwall, for instance, which we have not included in our model, and that is different from other counties, that causes Cornish people to migrate consistently over the four decades – i.e. a fixed 'Cornish' parameter. Alternatively, we can assume that the v_i are random variables – i.e. that the 'Cornish' parameter is not fixed but a random variable. Specific time period effects, w_t can be treated in a similar manner – the fixed effects model specifying a different constant term for each time period and the error component model a random component for each time period.

In the circumstances of this model it is reasonable to assume that the v_i and the w_t are correlated with the explanatory variables in the model, in which case the fixed effects approach is regarded as preferable to the error components model. The fixed effect parameters $_i$ and w_t are incorporated into the econometric model by using dummy variables; so each equation specification includes county dummies, γ_i, or time dummies, δ_t, or both. This gives us the following set of equation specifications, starting with the most general – number 6 (which is the econometric model plus both county and time dummies) and ending with the most restricted – number 1. Specification 2 is the econometric model with no dummies in at all.

6. $M_{it} = \alpha + \gamma_i + \delta_t + X\beta + e_{it}$
5. $M_{it} = \alpha + \delta_t + X\beta + e_{i\tau}$
4. $M_{it} = \alpha + \gamma_i + X\beta + e_{it}$
3. $M_{it} = \alpha + \gamma_i + \delta_t + e_{it}$
2. $M_{it} = \alpha + X\beta + e_{it}$
1. $M_{it} = \alpha + e_{it}$

(Where M_{it} is the pooled dependent variable (i.e. the complete migration data series for all counties at all points of time), α is a simple constant term, γ_i is a dummy variable which incorporates a different intercept term for each country, δ_t is a similar dummy variable for time periods, $X\beta$ is the matrix of explanatory variables of our econometric model and their coefficients, and e_{it} is assumed to be a well behaved error term.)

Covariance analysis consists of estimating and comparing the different fixed effects specifications (the equations above) for each of our migration models. The method of comparison of the different model specifications is illustrated by the diagrams and the explanations below. Each numbered box in the diagram is a different model specification (as listed above the diagram) – specification 6 is the most

Nest 1

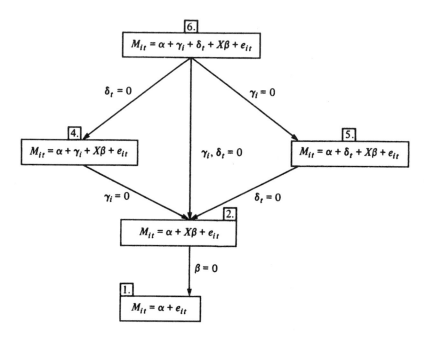

general (because it includes all the explanatory and dummy variables) and specification 1 is the most restricted (because it includes only a constant term). The specifications are compared by testing a relatively restricted version of a model against a more general version (i.e. less restricted) of the same model using standard 'F' tests. Only nested specifications (i.e. specifications where one version is a more restricted version of another) – represented on the diagram by joining arrows, are tested by covariance analysis. The restrictions which are being tested are written beside each arrow on the diagram. So, for example, specification 1 can be tested against specification 2 and the restriction being tested is that $\beta = 0$, but specification 2 cannot be tested against specification 3 since they are not nested versions of the same model – i.e. one is not a restricted version of the other. Similarly, we can test specification 4 versus 6 (testing whether $\delta_t = 0$) or 5 versus 6 (testing whether $\gamma_i = 0$) but we cannot test specification 4 versus 5 since they are not nested.

Covariance analysis is concerned with comparison of these different model specifications. What inference can we draw from the test results? Obviously, in the top section of nest 1:

the more zero restrictions (i.e. that γ_i and $\delta_t = 0$) we cannot reject the better since this implies our initial specification (the explanatory variables – number 2), with no fixed effects, is well specified. The alternative, namely a rejection of such zero restrictions on the dummy variables implies a failure of that initial specification in so far as it suggests that our explanatory variables require the help of the dummies to explain the variance in the dependent variable.

However, another possibility is that our initial specification (our explanatory variables) are less successful in explaining the dependent variables than the dummies. Covariance analysis also allows us to test this possibility as can be seen from nest 2.

Nest 2

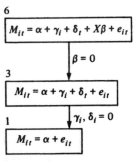

If we cannot reject the restriction that $\beta = 0$ in specification 3 versus 6 in nest 2, then this implies a total failure of our model since it implies that the dummy variables explain migration better than our theories. On the other hand, if we cannot reject the restrictions in testing 1 against 3 then we know that the migration behaviour does have a certain regular pattern which can therefore, at least in principle, be explained, as opposed to being completely random around a given constant term as implied by specification 1.

In the context of this migration model, the dummy variable intercept terms can be interpreted as our missing information on conditions in the destination countries or counties. We assumed that this was constant for all counties at all times, however if for example, we accept specification 5 on the basis of the covariance analysis we might infer that this missing information was constant to all counties at each point in time, but that the information changed for each time period.

The results

The main results are shown in Tables 1–4 of this appendix with explanatory notes at the foot of each table. All the equations have been estimated by ordinary least squares. The dummy variable intercept terms have not been reported.

We first estimated the econometric model for all four dependent variables – i.e. overseas male and female migration (MEMIGio and FEMIGio), and internal male and female migration (MIMIGij and FIMIGij, labelled A to D respectively in Tables 1 and 2). We have reported the results for the 'best' specification (as indicated by the covariance analysis) of each model in Table 1. This proved to be specification 6 for all except the female overseas migration model (model B) in which it was specification 5. The 'F' tests for these specifications compared to specification 2 are reported in Table 4.

The results for the overseas migration series (models A and B) show reasonably high levels of explanation ($\bar{R}^2$) for cross section data. But, of those variables whose coefficients are significant, only 'ΔLiteracy' in model A and the lagged dependent variable in model B have the expected sign. The models of internal migration are more successful with higher levels of explanation ($\bar{R}^2$) and more significant coefficients of the expected sign. In fact, only 'ΔAgric' has an unexpected sign.

Specification 2 has also been reported for all four dependent variables for comparison in Table 2. It was in all cases preferable to specification 1 and the appropriate 'F' test results for the comparison are given in Table 4. A comparison of the results in Tables 1 and 2 reveals that the dummy variables are correlated to some extent with the explanatory variables. In the overseas migration models, this correlation leads to a reduction in significance of the explanatory variables when the dummies are added, whereas in the internal migration models the level of significance of the explanatory variables improves.

Covariance analysis on these models has suggested that our theoretical model was successful (in that specification 2 was preferable to specification 1) – but also that it could be improved upon. The fact that the 'best' specifications included dummy variables indicated that the variables omitted from our original econometric model have some regular pattern (otherwise the dummy variables would not have improved the fit of the equations). The behaviour of the explanatory variables (see Tables 1 and 2) for the female overseas migration series suggests that this model is particularly poorly specified although these same variables appear to be successful for the internal female migration model. This may be because female internal and overseas migration respond to different stimuli. The male overseas migration model is more successful than its female counterpart, but even so the model proves more satisfactory for internal than for overseas male migration.

The fact that the lagged dependent variable – our chain migration effect variable – is significant and the correct (i.e. expected) sign in the simple econometric version of models A and B (see Table 2) gives some support for the historian's theories over the rival economic theories which omit the chain effect. However, this support is reduced in the 'best' specifications by the change in sign to the unexpected negative in model A (Table 1). All the models support the importance of previous migration but it may not be a single chain effect at work.

We then tested several subsidiary hypotheses and these results are reported in Table 3 with the 'F' tests in Table 4. Firstly, in order to see whether overseas and internal migration were substitutes or complements, we specified that the overseas migration models should also include internal migration as an explanatory variable. Model E incorporates internal male migration into the model for male overseas migration (model A). Here we find that there is no significant connection between male overseas and internal migration since the coefficient is not significant and the model is rejected when compared with model A by an 'F' test. Model F incorporates internal female migration as an explanatory variable in the female overseas migration model. Here the 'best' specification is number 6. This can be compared with model 8, specification 5 (the 'best' for that model) because the two equations are nested both in explanatory and in dummy variables. The 'F' test comparison shows that model F is significantly better than model B and we find that female internal and overseas migration are substitutes. However, it is clear that the internal migration variable is correlated with the lagged dependent variable which is now no longer significant.

Secondly, we also tested the importance of family ties in migration patterns by specifying the female migration variables to be dependent additionally on male migration. (These results are also reported in Table 3.) Models G and H include the male migration variable as an explanatory variable for female migration and are compared with models B and D. We find that male migration is positively associated with female migration to a significant degree. The coefficients are strongly significant and the 'F' tests firmly reject models B and D. However, it is also clear that the positive influence of male migration (or perhaps family ties) is not independent of the other explanatory variables. In the overseas migration model (G), this can be seen in the lack of significance of any other variable, even the lagged dependent variable, which might imply that male migration provides a better chain migration variable than the lagged dependent variable. Thus male migration may be a better predictor of female overseas migration than the explanatory model but may tell us little about the causes of such migration.

Although the addition of male migration to the internal female migration model also reduces the significance of the other explanatory variables to a considerable degree, the coefficient on the lagged dependent variable remains stable in sign and size. Since, in this case, the male migration variable does not provide a substitute for the chain migration variable (the lagged dependent variable) we can justifiably consider that it may capture family migration effects. This would not be incompatible with the fact that its presence substitutes for the other explanatory variables since male and female labour market variables are likely to be highly correlated.

Conclusions

Econometric analysis of migration in the late nineteenth century has tended to concentrate on the push–pull mechanism within a business cycle framework. This emphasis on the short term dynamic behaviour of overseas migration flows makes it difficult to compare our results on cross section behaviour with other work in the field. However, it is clear from the discussion of our results that our basic theoretical model (which is similar to those used for time series work mentioned above) is unable to explain fully the behaviour of overseas migration data. The chances of improving our understanding of overseas migration for England and Wales in this period through the econometric analysis of cross section data seem likely to depend on finding and analysing systematic information on individual migrants and their characteristics. Our model was more successful for the internal migration data and our results compare well with cross section studies of internal migration in less-developed countries in a more recent period which was surveyed by L. Y. L. Yap.[4]

The results of our subsidiary models on internal and overseas migration are interesting and suggest the importance, at least for cross section studies, of further econometric analysis of the relationship between internal and overseas migration and more particularly between male and female migration.

[4] L. Y. L. Yap, 'Internal migration in less developed countries: a survey of the literature' *International Bank for Reconstruction and Development*, Bank Staff Working Paper No. 215, September 1975.

Results

Table 1

Model label	Dependent variable	Specification number[a]	Explanatory variables[b]						R̄²
			'Age'	'ΔAgric'	'ΔLiteracy'	'ΔWages'	'Urban'	Lagged dependent	
A	MEMIGio	6	-1.03** (.32)	.69** (.20)	.07 (.04)	-1.47 (2.42)	.06* (.04)	-.23** (.08)	.5755
B	FEMIGio	5	-.06 (.17)	.27** (.09)	.01 (.03)	-.20 (.23)	-.01 (.00)	.21** (.06)	.3193
C	MIMIGij	6	.60* (.33)	.56** (.19)	.02 (.04)	-2.73 (2.42)	-.08** (.04)	-.32** (.09)	.7587
D	FIMIGij	5	.47** (.22)	.26* (.16)	.07** (.03)	-4.02** (1.99)	-.03 (.03)	-.24** (.08)	.8554

a In this table, the 'best' specification for each model (based on 'F' tests) is reported. Specification 6 includes explanatory variables and additionally both time and county dummies, specification 5 includes additional time dummies only.

b The regression coefficients are given with standard errors in brackets: ** denotes a coefficient significantly different from zero at 5% and * at 10%.

Table 2

Model label	Dependent variable	Specification number[a]	Explanatory variables[b]						$\bar{R}^2$
			'Age'	ΔAgric'	ΔLiteracy'	ΔWages'	'Urban'	Lagged dependent	
A	MEMIGio	2	−.42** (.18)	.34** (.11)	.11** (.04)	−.15 (.33)	−.02** (0.1)	.16** (.07)	.1644
B	FEMIGio	2	−.33** (.17)	.28** (.08)	.08** (.03)	−.43* (.25)	−.01 (.00)	.19** (.07)	.1681
C	MIMIGij	2	.01 (.18)	−.21** (.10)	.01 (.04)	−.49 (.33)	−.03** (.01)	.53** (.06)	.5422
D	FIMIGij	2	−.03 (.21)	−.41** (.10)	−.01 (.03)	−.39 (.32)	−.03** (.01)	.54** (.06)	.6260

a Specification 2 includes explanatory variables only.
b The regression coefficients are given with standard errors in brackets; ** denotes a coefficient significantly different from zero at 5% and * at 10%.

321

Table 3

Model label	Dependent variable	Specification number[a]	Explanatory variables[b]							R̄²
			'Age'	'ΔAgric'	'ΔLiteracy'	'ΔWages'	'Urban'	Lagged dependent	Other	
E	MEMIGio	6	-1.03** (.32)	.68** (.20)	.06 (.04)	-1.38 (2.45)	.07* (.04)	-.23** (.09)	MIMIGij: .03 (.09)	.5715
F	FEMIGio	6	-.21 (.24)	.57** (.16)	.04 (.04)	.11 (2.14)	-.03 (.04)	-.14 (.09)	FIMIGij: -.24** (.10)	.4419
G	MIMIGij	5	.11 (.12)	.09 (.06)	-.02 (.02)	-.13 (.16)	.00 (.00)	.07 (.04)	MEMIGio: .55** (.04)	.6663
H	FIMIGij	6	.23 (.15)	-.12 (.10)	-.02 (.02)	-2.43* (1.28)	.03* (.02)	-.23** (.05)	MIMIGij: .65** (.06)	.9403

a In this table, the 'best' specification for each model (based on 'F' tests) is reported. Specification 6 includes explanatory variables and additionally both time and county dummies, specification 5 includes additional time dummies only.

b The regression coefficients are given with standard errors in brackets: ** denotes a coefficient significantly different from zero at 5% and * at 10%.

Table 4. 'F' tests

Restricted equation		Unrestricted equation		
Model label	Specification number	Model label	Specification number	'F' statistic[a]
A	2	A	6	$F(53,96) = 3.72^{**}$
B	2	B	5	$F(2,147) = 17.55^{**}$
C	2	C	6	$F(53,96) = 3.52^{**}$
D	2	D	6	$F(53,96) = 5.26^{**}$
A	1	A	2	$F(6,149) = 6.08^{**}$
B	1	B	2	$F(6,149) = 6.22^{**}$
C	1	C	2	$F(6,149) = 31.59^{**}$
D	1	D	2	$F(6,149) = 44.24^{**}$
A	6	E	6	$F(1,95) = .11$
B	5	F	6	$F(52,95) = 1.62^{*}$
B	5	G	5	$F(1,146) = 153.89^{**}$
D	6	H	6	$F(1,95) = 137.52^{**}$

Notes: These reported 'F' tests are used to test different specifications of the same basic model or to test different models (provided they are nested in both the explanatory variables and included dummy variables).

a   The 'F' statistics are calculated as follows:

$$(F(g, n - k)) = \frac{(RSS_R - RSS_U)/(g)}{RSS_U/(n - k)}$$

where RSS_R = residual sum of squares of the restricted equation

RSS_U = residual sum of squares of the unrestricted equation

g = no. of restrictions

$n - k$ = no. of observations − no. of parameters (of the unrestricted equation)

** indicates that the 'F' value lies within the upper 1% zone of the 'F' distribution.

* indicates that the 'F' value lies within the upper 5% zone of the 'F' distribution. For both symbols, the inference is that zero restrictions involved should be rejected and that the specifications are significantly different.

Table 5. *'Male age'. Male population aged 10–20 at beginning of decade
(counties) 1861–1891 (%)*

	1861	1871	1881	1891
1. London and Middlesex	19.30	19.62	19.74	20.43
2. Surrey	19.86	20.26	21.31	22.16
3. Kent	20.60	20.48	21.58	22.12
4. Sussex	21.57	21.12	21.53	22.35
5. Hampshire	20.83	20.30	20.97	21.61
6. Berkshire	21.34	20.99	22.18	21.92
7. Hertfordshire	21.84	21.61	22.80	23.19
8. Buckinghamshire	21.73	21.13	22.83	22.49
9. Oxfordshire	21.29	21.69	22.31	22.30
10. Northamptonshire	20.54	21.08	21.35	22.04
11. Huntingdon	22.47	21.83	22.65	22.50
12. Bedfordshire	22.32	21.90	22.87	23.24
13. Cambridgeshire	22.27	21.00	22.15	22.81
14. Essex	21.45	21.34	21.82	22.01
15. Suffolk	21.34	21.60	21.95	22.28
16. Norfolk	21.06	20.95	21.50	21.66
17. Wiltshire	22.11	21.68	22.29	21.97
18. Dorset	21.27	21.78	22.01	22.12
19. Devon	21.10	21.57	22.73	22.16
20. Cornwall	23.36	23.51	24.66	23.12
21. Somerset	21.95	22.01	22.64	22.73
22. Gloucestershire	21.02	21.15	22.39	22.63
23. Herefordshire	20.42	20.54	21.93	21.47
24. Shropshire	20.31	20.83	21.99	22.31
25. Staffordshire	20.34	21.35	21.64	23.00
26. Worcestershire	20.60	21.40	21.83	22.67
27. Warwickshire	20.27	21.25	21.19	22.45
28. Leicestershire	20.79	21.12	20.94	22.06
29. Rutland	21.05	23.54	22.94	24.72
30. Lincolnshire	21.27	20.60	21.46	22.30
31. Nottinghamshire	20.22	20.93	20.37	21.79
32. Derbyshire	20.65	20.85	21.37	22.07
33. Cheshire	20.04	20.99	20.69	22.06
34. Lancashire	20.46	20.90	20.58	22.01
35. Yorkshire	20.46	20.78	20.89	22.02
36. Durham	20.40	20.51	21.02	22.15
37. Northumberland	20.65	20.89	20.91	21.92
38. Cumberland	21.08	20.91	20.98	22.21
39. Westmorland	20.37	20.51	21.57	21.30
40. Monmouth	20.37	20.48	21.44	21.74
41. Glamorgan	20.15	21.02	21.08	21.47
42. Carmarthen	22.66	22.26	22.69	23.63
43. Pembroke	23.01	22.33	22.89	22.21
44. Cardigan	22.07	22.11	23.48	23.18

	1861	1871	1881	1891
45. Brecon	20.62	20.52	21.26	22.23
46. Radnor	20.83	21.46	21.63	21.12
47. Montgomery	20.89	21.24	22.51	22.19
48. Flint	22.36	20.69	21.70	22.12
49. Denbigh	21.45	21.08	21.92	22.14
50. Merioneth	21.20	19.85	20.14	22.08
51. Caernarvon	21.73	20.66	21.42	21.97
52. Anglesey	21.85	21.65	20.65	21.28

Source: Census of England and Wales

Table 6. *'Female age'. Female population aged 10–20 at beginning of decade (counties) 1861–1891 (%)*

	1861	1871	1881	1891
1. London and Middlesex	18.28	18.56	21.95	19.50
2. Surrey	19.08	18.97	19.80	20.00
3. Kent	19.76	19.42	20.25	20.39
4. Sussex	20.03	19.62	20.04	20.10
5. Hampshire	19.40	19.08	19.75	19.63
6. Berkshire	19.85	19.01	19.67	19.86
7. Hertfordshire	20.70	19.32	19.76	19.90
8. Buckinghamshire	19.90	19.66	20.02	20.22
9. Oxfordshire	19.95	20.53	20.22	20.59
10. Northamptonshire	20.06	20.18	20.26	21.23
11. Huntingdon	21.02	19.96	20.51	20.32
12. Bedfordshire	21.79	20.56	20.47	20.54
13. Cambridgeshire	20.70	19.70	20.13	20.46
14. Essex	20.15	19.73	20.15	20.71
15. Suffolk	20.15	19.62	20.12	20.18
16. Norfolk	19.58	19.08	19.63	19.87
17. Wiltshire	19.93	19.73	19.85	19.99
18. Dorset	20.07	19.50	20.15	19.80
19. Devon	19.18	19.17	19.78	19.29
20. Cornwall	20.53	20.36	20.67	19.17
21. Somerset	19.81	19.82	20.14	20.28
22. Gloucestershire	19.91	19.84	20.38	20.75
23. Herefordshire	19.24	19.54	20.42	20.16
24. Shropshire	19.99	19.78	20.51	20.52
25. Staffordshire	19.96	20.81	20.91	22.16
26. Worcestershire	20.05	20.41	20.65	21.31
27. Warwickshire	19.43	20.24	20.23	21.49
28. Leicestershire	19.78	20.03	20.03	21.61
29. Rutland	19.07	19.87	19.64	20.27
30. Lincolnshire	20.43	19.92	20.45	21.09
31. Nottinghamshire	19.69	20.57	20.23	21.16
32. Derbyshire	19.90	19.85	20.45	21.09
33. Cheshire	19.67	19.94	20.17	21.46
34. Lancashire	19.79	20.00	20.01	21.28
35. Yorkshire	19.85	20.18	20.34	21.35
36. Durham	19.82	20.54	21.23	22.43
37. Northumberland	19.88	20.09	20.59	21.72
38. Cumberland	19.88	20.04	20.26	21.51
39. Westmorland	20.32	21.00	18.56	21.38
40. Monmouth	20.21	20.54	20.64	21.45
41. Glamorgan	19.82	20.46	21.16	21.63
42. Carmarthen	21.60	20.91	20.98	21.68
43. Pembroke	20.50	20.52	20.57	20.30
44. Cardigan	20.25	19.30	19.86	19.73

	1861	1871	1881	1891
45. Brecon	20.10	20.62	21.08	21.32
46. Radnor	20.08	21.01	21.90	21.09
47. Montgomery	20.30	20.32	21.00	21.64
48. Flint	19.72	18.95	20.49	20.85
49. Denbigh	19.97	19.63	20.51	20.92
50. Merioneth	20.10	19.01	19.95	20.82
51. Caernarvon	20.19	19.28	19.64	19.87
52. Anglesey	20.54	19.87	18.98	19.90

Source: Census of England and Wales

Table 7. *'Male literacy'. Mean % of males who signed the marriage register with a mark (counties) 1861–1900*

	1861–70	1871–80	1881–90	1891–1900
1. London and Middlesex	10.1	8.3	5.6	2.9
2. Surrey	18.4	10.8	6.1	2.4
3. Kent	20.2	14.4	8.5	3.3
4. Sussex	19.2	14.0	7.9	3.5
5. Hampshire	17.5	12.1	7.4	2.9
6. Berkshire	25.4	16.8	10.4	3.9
7. Hertfordshire	33.9	25.4	16.3	5.7
8. Buckinghamshire	28.8	22.3	14.0	5.4
9. Oxfordshire	23.8	17.5	10.8	4.6
10. Northamptonshire	23.1	16.9	10.2	3.7
11. Huntingdon	31.0	21.9	15.1	5.7
12. Bedfordshire	34.7	25.6	15.3	5.1
13. Cambridgeshire	29.4	23.4	16.1	6.8
14. Essex	29.6	18.7	11.2	4.1
15. Suffolk	34.1	25.8	17.9	6.7
16. Norfolk	32.3	24.6	16.3	6.0
17. Wiltshire	26.4	18.8	11.3	4.6
18. Dorset	24.6	18.5	11.5	4.7
19. Devon	18.4	12.5	7.6	2.9
20. Cornwall	28.8	21.3	15.5	6.9
21. Somerset	25.7	19.2	12.5	5.3
22. Gloucestershire	20.2	15.5	10.6	4.3
23. Herefordshire	30.8	22.1	15.4	5.8
24. Shropshire	30.5	22.4	13.8	6.2
25. Staffordshire	36.6	29.9	17.4	5.9
26. Worcestershire	26.4	20.6	13.3	4.9
27. Warwickshire	23.1	19.8	11.4	4.2
28. Leicestershire	21.8	16.8	9.1	3.0
29. Rutland	19.3	16.0	7.8	3.8
30. Lincolnshire	21.2	15.2	10.0	3.8
31. Nottinghamshire	24.1	18.6	11.1	4.2
32. Derbyshire	21.7	16.1	10.1	3.5
33. Cheshire	22.6	16.0	10.1	3.7
34. Lancashire	23.5	17.5	10.1	4.0
35. Yorkshire	20.7	16.2	10.2	4.4
36. Durham	23.9	20.1	13.4	5.1
37. Northumberland	15.7	12.3	7.7	3.2
38. Cumberland	17.7	13.8	9.1	3.4
39. Westmorland	11.8	7.8	4.0	1.9
40. Monmouth	38.6	30.5	2.1	7.4
41. Glamorgan	38.0	27.4	11.9	6.3
42. Carmarthen	30.1	20.5	7.4	5.0
43. Pembroke	21.6	15.6	7.4	4.8
44. Cardigan	21.2	15.2	5.2	3.9

	1861–70	1871–80	1881–90	1891–1900
45. Brecon	36.8	21.0	13.6	7.7
46. Radnor	31.6	23.9	9.3	5.0
47. Montgomery	30.4	23.9	9.8	9.1
48. Flint	42.3	31.1	17.0	8.0
49. Denbigh	38.5	28.4	14.5	7.5
50. Merioneth	27.5	19.6	8.0	4.2
51. Caernarvon	28.3	23.4	9.9	6.4
52. Anglesey	36.6	28.9	14.3	10.7

Source: Registrar General's Annual Reports

Table 8. *'Female literacy'. Mean % of females who signed the marriage register with a mark (counties) 1861–1900*

	1861–70	1871–80	1881–90	1891–1900
1. London and Middlesex	16.0	12.2	7.2	3.7
2. Surrey	14.6	8.4	3.9	1.6
3. Kent	19.3	12.3	6.2	2.3
4. Sussex	14.8	8.9	4.0	1.6
5. Hampshire	16.8	10.9	5.1	2.0
6. Berkshire	20.6	12.1	6.0	2.1
7. Hertfordshire	28.7	20.9	11.2	3.7
8. Buckinghamshire	31.1	21.4	10.6	2.7
9. Oxfordshire	21.2	13.0	7.0	2.4
10. Northamptonshire	25.7	18.0	9.3	3.4
11. Huntingdon	27.4	16.0	9.0	2.8
12. Bedfordshire	40.9	31.0	16.9	4.9
13. Cambridgeshire	29.0	18.3	10.4	3.9
14. Essex	23.5	14.1	7.5	3.2
15. Suffolk	26.9	18.2	10.4	3.8
16. Norfolk	27.5	18.9	10.4	3.6
17. Wiltshire	23.7	14.0	7.2	2.3
18. Dorset	22.3	14.1	6.7	2.3
19. Devon	22.4	15.2	8.1	2.9
20. Cornwall	36.6	24.6	15.6	6.2
21. Somerset	25.5	17.5	10.2	3.8
22. Gloucestershire	22.5	16.0	9.9	4.1
23. Herefordshire	25.6	16.7	8.5	3.7
24. Shropshire	32.7	23.3	12.2	4.9
25. Staffordshire	46.3	36.6	20.9	7.0
26. Worcestershire	31.2	23.2	14.7	5.5
27. Warwickshire	30.4	25.3	14.9	5.5
28. Leicestershire	29.6	21.8	11.7	3.4
29. Rutland	16.3	9.9	3.5	1.5
30. Lincolnshire	22.1	14.3	8.2	3.0
31. Nottinghamshire	33.8	26.1	13.4	4.7
32. Derbyshire	29.5	21.3	11.1	3.7
33. Cheshire	36.4	25.5	13.3	4.4
34. Lancashire	45.1	32.8	18.0	6.5
35. Yorkshire	36.6	27.5	15.0	6.0
36. Durham	37.2	30.8	18.7	6.5
37. Northumberland	26.7	20.7	12.0	5.0
38. Cumberland	28.9	22.3	13.0	4.4
39. Westmorland	16.5	10.4	4.9	1.8
40. Monmouth	46.5	34.3	21.6	8.4
41. Glamorgan	54.9	40.2	15.8	8.3
42. Carmarthen	54.0	41.3	16.0	8.9
43. Pembroke	37.1	29.3	11.2	7.3
44. Cardigan	51.1	36.6	14.7	9.2

	1861–70	1871–80	1881–90	1891–1900
45. Brecon	48.2	27.0	14.9	8.7
46. Radnor	30.9	25.8	8.1	3.9
47. Montgomery	40.2	29.0	10.5	6.1
48. Flint	47.1	33.7	14.6	8.5
49. Denbigh	48.1	33.5	15.1	9.0
50. Merioneth	44.8	30.9	11.4	5.4
51. Caernarvon	45.5	35.1	12.1	7.5
52. Anglesey	53.3	37.4	15.6	9.9

Source: Registrar General's Annual Reports

Table 9. *'Wages'. Mean wage rates for agricultural labourers (counties)*
1861–1900 – shillings per week

	1861–70	1871–80	1881–90	1891–1900
1. London and Middlesex	17.25	17.94	18.67	19.42
2. Surrey	17.50	17.98	18.49	19.00
3. Kent	17.00	17.90	18.84	19.83
4. Sussex	16.50	16.93	17.38	17.83
5. Hampshire	14.00	14.81	15.67	16.58
6. Berkshire	13.50	14.01	14.53	15.08
7. Hertfordshire	13.50	14.31	15.17	16.08
8. Buckinghamshire	14.25	14.55	14.86	15.17
9. Oxfordshire	13.50	13.88	14.27	14.67
10. Northamptonshire	15.25	15.71	16.18	16.67
11. Huntingdon	14.25	14.60	14.96	15.33
12. Bedfordshire	14.25	14.86	15.50	16.17
13. Cambridgeshire	14.25	14.94	15.66	16.42
14. Essex	14.25	14.65	15.07	15.50
15. Suffolk	14.42	14.42	14.42	14.42
16. Norfolk	14.75	14.75	14.75	14.75
17. Wiltshire	13.00	13.64	14.30	15.00
18. Dorset	11.50	12.49	13.58	14.75
19. Devon	12.50	13.66	14.94	16.33
20. Cornwall	12.50	13.73	15.09	16.58
21. Somerset	12.25	13.34	14.53	15.83
22. Gloucestershire	12.75	13.48	14.26	15.08
23. Herefordshire	12.75	13.70	14.73	15.83
24. Shropshire	12.25	13.78	15.49	17.42
25. Staffordshire	14.00	15.20	16.50	17.92
26. Worcestershire	13.50	14.60	15.79	17.08
27. Warwickshire	15.00	15.38	15.77	16.17
28. Leicestershire	13.50	14.63	15.85	17.17
29. Rutland	13.50	14.63	15.85	17.17
30. Lincolnshire	16.25	16.74	17.24	17.75
31. Nottinghamshire	15.00	16.28	17.66	19.17
32. Derbyshire	15.50	16.85	18.32	19.92
33. Cheshire	16.00	16.64	17.31	18.00
34. Lancashire	17.75	18.25	18.79	19.33
35. Yorkshire	17.50	17.85	18.21	18.58
36. Durham	20.00	20.25	20.50	20.75
37. Northumberland	17.50	18.35	19.24	20.17
38. Cumberland	18.50	18.58	18.67	18.75
39. Westmorland	18.50	18.58	18.67	18.75
40. Monmouth	13.50	14.48	15.54	16.67
41. Glamorgan	14.00	15.52	17.21	19.08
42. Carmarthen	11.50	12.99	14.68	16.58
43. Pembroke	11.50	12.79	14.23	15.83
44. Cardigan	11.50	12.49	13.58	14.75

	1861–70	1871–80	1881–90	1891–1900
45. Brecon	13.50	14.48	15.54	16.67
46. Radnor	13.50	14.14	14.80	15.50
47. Montgomery	13.50	14.11	14.75	15.42
48. Flint	13.50	14.65	15.90	17.25
49. Denbigh	13.50	14.51	15.59	16.75
50. Merioneth	13.50	14.41	15.38	16.42
51. Caernarvon	13.50	14.63	15.85	17.17
52. Anglesey	11.50	12.70	14.03	15.50

Notes: Dr Hunt's figures are based on Bowley's estimates for 1867 and 1897–8. His data for 1867 and 1897–8 are used for the two decades 1861–70 and 1891–1900 respectively. The data for the two intervening decades were interpolated, on the assumption that wages increased at a constant rate between 1861–70 and 1891–1900.
Source: Hunt, *Regional wage variations,* pp. 62–4.

Table 10. *'Urban'. Mean urban population, counties 1861–1900*
(population living in contiguous urban areas containing at least 20,000
persons) %

	1861–70	1871–80	1881–90	1891–1900
1. London and Middlesex	95.1	95.8	95.2	96.5
2. Surrey	17.7	25.4	35.5	45.2
3. Kent	21.5	27.5	35.5	41.2
4. Sussex	30.2	34.8	41.6	45.7
5. Hampshire	33.6	38.2	44.1	50.2
6. Berkshire	15.3	19.4	23.7	26.4
7. Hertfordshire	0	0	0	5.6
8. Buckinghamshire	0	0	0	0
9. Oxfordshire	17.2	18.5	21.9	26.1
10. Northamptonshire	15.4	23.4	31.6	38.6
11. Huntingdon	0	0	0	0
12. Bedfordshire	0	8.1	26.1	39.0
13. Cambridgeshire	15.4	17.4	19.2	19.8
14. Essex	28.5	35.6	44.8	55.0
15. Suffolk	11.8	16.1	20.8	23.3
16. Norfolk	26.6	29.1	31.7	36.4
17. Wiltshire	0	4.4	10.7	14.5
18. Dorset	0	0	5.4	17.0
19. Devon	27.2	29.9	33.1	37.4
20. Cornwall	0	0	0	0
21. Somerset	16.7	19.0	21.0	23.2
22. Gloucestershire	35.9	38.5	47.0	55.5
23. Herefordshire	0	8.3	16.9	19.2
24. Shropshire	13.5	9.9	11.0	11.6
25. Staffordshire	51.7	60.8	67.8	73.2
26. Worcestershire	31.5	33.4	36.4	34.6
27. Warwickshire	65.9	71.0	79.2	88.9
28. Leicestershire	32.0	39.0	44.8	50.4
29. Rutland	0	0	0	0
30. Lincolnshire	8.0	13.6	18.5	22.8
31. Nottinghamshire	36.1	47.1	50.4	53.7
32. Derbyshire	14.4	19.0	24.8	30.4
33. Cheshire	45.8	48.7	53.7	55.2
34. Lancashire	68.3	74.2	79.6	82.0
35. Yorkshire	47.0	53.4	59.0	62.6
36. Durham	39.6	45.9	52.2	55.8
37. Northumberland	45.3	45.3	52.4	57.6
38. Cumberland	14.1	14.4	19.4	25.3
39. Westmorland	0	0	0	0
40. Monmouth	18.6	20.4	23.4	37.7
41. Glamorgan	44.1	53.6	60.3	67.1
42. Carmarthen	0	8.0	17.2	18.8
43. Pembroke	0	0	0	0

	1861–70	1871–80	1881–90	1891–1900
44. Cardigan	0	0	0	0
45. Brecon	0	0	0	0
46. Radnor	0	0	0	0
47. Montgomery	0	0	0	0
48. Flint	0	0	0	0
49. Denbigh	0	0	0	0
50. Merioneth	0	0	0	0
51. Caernarvon	0	0	0	0
52. Anglesey	0	0	0	0

Note: The boundaries of the urban areas were established by cartographic evidence. They include, *inter alia,* registration districts, urban sanitary districts, municipal boroughs and parishes.
Source: Census of England and Wales

Table 11. *'Agric'. Mean % of the male labour force in agricultural*
occupations, 1861–1900

	1861–70	1871–80	1881–90	1891–1900
1. London and Middlesex	1.84	1.38	1.19	1.08
2. Surrey	16.80	11.83	9.79	8.09
3. Kent	20.00	16.59	14.39	11.86
4. Sussex	23.83	19.72	16.52	14.12
5. Hampshire	16.92	14.50	11.86	9.32
6. Berkshire	27.72	22.49	18.91	14.90
7. Hertfordshire	28.74	23.13	20.95	17.19
8. Buckinghamshire	29.99	25.17	21.80	19.16
9. Oxfordshire	30.36	26.07	22.95	19.99
10. Northamptonshire	25.97	20.36	16.15	12.96
11. Huntingdon	37.46	34.93	33.67	31.79
12. Bedfordshire	31.23	26.52	23.34	19.57
13. Cambridgeshire	34.11	30.51	29.12	28.24
14. Essex	28.01	21.12	14.71	10.06
15. Suffolk	32.04	28.79	27.13	24.36
16. Norfolk	29.95	26.52	25.40	23.36
17. Wiltshire	30.16	25.43	22.40	19.43
18. Dorset	26.53	23.55	21.41	18.73
19. Devon	20.92	18.29	16.71	14.84
20. Cornwall	19.15	20.15	20.42	19.00
21. Somerset	22.51	18.89	16.77	15.81
22. Gloucestershire	15.60	12.47	10.70	8.78
23. Herefordshire	31.73	28.71	27.64	27.10
24. Shropshire	25.07	21.60	20.73	19.62
25. Staffordshire	7.74	5.89	4.85	4.15
26. Worcestershire	14.92	12.14	10.77	9.87
27. Warwickshire	10.11	7.91	6.44	4.99
28. Leicestershire	18.55	13.53	10.51	8.29
29. Rutland	34.17	30.41	28.44	25.42
30. Lincolnshire	33.34	29.32	26.94	25.26
31. Nottinghamshire	15.34	11.22	8.75	7.47
32. Derbyshire	12.18	9.37	7.75	6.45
33. Cheshire	13.91	10.74	9.28	8.21
34. Lancashire	5.17	3.78	3.03	2.61
35. Yorkshire	11.18	8.59	7.10	6.04
36. Durham	5.10	3.47	2.87	2.36
37. Northumberland	11.33	8.84	7.19	5.77
38. Cumberland	18.15	14.94	13.27	12.46
39. Westmorland	24.61	22.15	21.49	20.56
40. Monmouth	11.20	8.70	7.40	5.80
41. Glamorgan	6.60	4.70	3.30	2.40
42. Carmarthen	24.10	19.40	16.70	16.30
43. Pembroke	21.70	20.30	19.30	19.10
44. Cardigan	30.70	28.20	28.40	28.10

	1861–70	1871–80	1881–90	1891–1900
45. Brecon	26.90	24.10	22.80	20.40
46. Radnor	39.20	37.60	37.00	35.40
47. Montgomery	32.70	29.30	30.10	31.40
48. Flint	13.40	10.90	10.30	11.30
49. Denbigh	23.20	18.80	16.80	15.60
50. Merioneth	28.20	22.60	20.90	20.40
51. Caernarvon	20.40	17.50	15.50	14.20
52. Anglesey	27.60	26.60	27.00	26.50

Note: 'Agricultural occupations' include all those in industrial order 1 'Agriculture, forestry and fishing'.
Source: Lee, *British regional employment statistics*.

Select bibliography of works cited in footnotes

(Place of publication is London, unless stated otherwise.)

Abramovitz, M. 'The nature and significance of Kuznets' cycles', *Economic Development and Cultural Change*, 9, 1961.

Adamic, L. *From many lands* (Harper and Row, New York, 1940).

Adams, M. 'The causes of the Highland emigrations of 1783–1803', *Scottish Historical Review*, 17, 1920.

Anderson, M. *Family Structure in nineteenth-century Lancashire* (Cambridge University Press, 1971).

'Urban migration into nineteenth-century Lancashire: Some insights into two competing hypotheses' in M. Drake (ed.), *Historical Demography. Problems and Projects* (Open University, 1974).

Armstrong, W. A. *Stability and change in an English county town. A social study of York 1801–1851* (Cambridge University Press, 1974.)

Baines, D. E. 'The use of published census data in migration studies' in E. A. Wrigley (ed.), *Nineteenth-century society, essays in the use of quantitative data* (Cambridge University Press, 1972).

'Emigration and internal migration in England and Wales 1861–1901' (unpublished paper, MSSB/SSRC Conference, Harvard University, 10–12 September, 1973).

'Birthplace statistics and the analysis of internal migration' in R. Lawton (ed.), *British censuses of the nineteenth century* (Cass, 1978).

'The labour market, 1860–1914', in Floud, R. and McCloskey, E. (eds.), *The economic history of Britain since 1700* (Cambridge University Press, 1981).

Banks, C. E. 'English sources of emigration to the New England colonies in the 17th century', *Proceedings of the Massachusetts Historical Society*, 60, 1927.

Berthoff, B. T. *British immigrants in industrial America* (Harvard University Press, Cambridge, Mass., 1953).

Blegen, T. C. (ed.) *Land of their choice. The immigrants write home* (University of Minnesota Press, Minneapolis, 1955).

Bobinska, C. and Pilch, A. (eds.) *Employment-seeking emigrations of the Poles world wide. XIXth and XXth centuries* (Polonia Educational Research Centre, 1976).

Bowley, A. L. 'Rural population in England and Wales. A study of the changes in density, occupations and ages, *Journal of the Royal Statistical Society*, LXXVII, 1914.

Brattne, B. *Bröderne Larsson. En studie i Svensk emigrant agent verksamket inder 1880 talet (The Larsson Brothers. A study of the activity of Swedish emigrant agencies during the 1880s)* (Almqvist and Wiksell, Uppsala, 1973).

Brattne, B. and Akerman, S. 'The importance of the transport sector for mass emigration', in H. Rundblom and H. Norman (eds.), *From Sweden to America. A history of the migration* (University of Uppsala Press, 1976).

Bridenbaugh, C. *Vex'd and troubled Englishmen, 1590–1642* (Oxford University Press, 1968).

Brown, A. J. *The framework of regional economics in the United Kingdom* (NIESR, Cambridge University Press, 1972).

Brown, J. S., Swartzweller, H. K. and Magalam, J. F. J. 'Kentucky mountain migration and the stem family', *Rural Sociology*, 28, 1963.

Butlin, N. G. 'Growth in a changing world. The Australian economy, heavily disguised', *Business Archives and History*, 4, 1964.

Bythell, D. *The handloom weavers* (Cambridge University Press, 1969).

Cairncross, A. K. 'Internal migration in Victorian England', *Manchester School*, 17 (1), 1949.

Home and foreign investment, 1870–1913 (Cambridge University Press, 1953).

Campbell, M. 'English emigration on the eve of the American Revolution', *American Historical Review*, 61, 1955.

'Social origins of some early Americans', in J. M. Smith (ed.), *Seventeenth-century America* (University of North Carolina Press, Chapel Hill, 1959).

Carlsson, S. 'Chronology and composition of Swedish emigration to America', in Rundblom, H. and Norman, H. (eds.), *From Sweden to America. A history of the migration* (University of Uppsala Press, 1976).

Caroli, B. B. *Italian repatriation from the United States* (Centre for Migration Studies, New York, 1973).

Carrothers, W. A. *Emigration from the British Isles* (D. S. King, 1929).

Chmelar, J. 'The Austrian emigration, 1900–1914', *Perspectives in American History*, 7, 1973.

Citroën, H. A. *European emigration overseas, past and future* (Research group in European migration problems. The Hague, 1951).

Clements, R. V. 'Trade unions and emigration 1840–1880', *Population Studies*, 9, 1955–6.

Coleman, T. *Passage to America* (Hutchinson, 1972).

Connell, K. H. 'Peasant marriage in Ireland: its structure and development since the Famine', *Economic History Review*, 14, 1962.

Conway, A. *The Welsh in America* (University of Wales Press, Cardiff, 1961).

'Welsh emigration to the United States', *Perspectives in American History*, 7, 1973.

Cooney, E. W. 'Long waves in building in the British economy in the nineteenth century', *Economic History Review*, 13 (2), 1960.

Cousens, S. M. 'The regional pattern of emigration during the great Irish Famine', *Transactions of the Institute of British Geographers*, 28, 1960.

Cowan, H. I. *British emigration to British North America, the first hundred years* (revised edition, Toronto University Press, 1961).

Craven, W. F. *White, red and black: the seventeenth-century Virginia* (University Press of Virginia, Charlottesville, Virginia, 1971).

Cromar, P. 'Labour migration and suburban expansion in the north of England: Sheffield in the 1860s and 1870s', in White, P. and Woods, R. (eds), *The geographical impact of migration* (Longman, 1980).

Cullen, L. M. *An economic history of Ireland* (Batsford, 1962).

Curti, M. and Birr, K. 'The immigrant and the American image in Europe, 1860–1914', *Mississippi Valley Historical Review*, 37, 1950.

Darby, H. C. 'The movement of population to and from Cambridgeshire 1851–61', *Geographical Journal*, 107 (3), 1943.

Daniel, G. H. 'Labour migration and age composition', *Sociological Review*, 30, 1939.

Davie, M. R. *World Migration* (MacMillan, New York, 1949).

Devine, T. M. 'Temporary migration and the Scottish Highlands in the nineteenth century', *Economic History Review*, 32 (3), 1979.

Diaz Alezandro, C. *Essays on the economic history of the Argentine Republic* (Yale University Press, New Haven, 1970).

Dodd, A. H. *The character of early Welsh emigration to the USA* (University of Wales Press, Cardiff, 1957).

Duncan, R. 'Case studies in emigration. Cornwall, Gloucestershire and New South Wales, 1877–1886', *Economic History Review*, 16, 1963.

'Late nineteenth-century migration into New South Wales from the United Kingdom', *Australian Economic History Review*, 1974.

Dunkley, P. 'Emigration and the state, 1803–1842: the nineteenth-century revolution in government reconsidered', *Historical Journal*, 23 (2), 1980.

Easterlin, R. A. 'Influences in overseas emigration before World War I', *Economic Development and Cultural Change*, 9 (3), 1961.

Easterlin, R. *Population, labour force and long swings in economic growth: the American experience*, (NBER, Columbia University Press, New York, 1968).

Eddie, S. M. 'The changing pattern of landownership in Hungary', *Economic History Review*, 20, 1967.

Erickson, C. 'The encouragement of emigration by British trade unions, 1850–1900', ·*Population Studies*, 3, 1949–50.

American industry and the European immigrant 1860–1885 (Harvard University Press, Cambridge, Mass., 1957).

'Agrarian myths of English immigrants', in Ander, O. F. *In the track of the immigrants* (Augustana College, Rock Island, Illinois, 1964).

'Who were the English and Scots emigrants in the 1880s?', in Glass, D. V. and Revelle, R. (eds.), *Population and Social Change* (Arnold, 1972).

Invisible immigrants: the adaptation of English and Scottish immigrants in nineteenth-century America (L.S.E., Weidenfeld and Nicholson, 1972).

(ed.), *Emigration from Europe, 1815–1914. Select documents* (Adam and Charles Black, 1976).

'Who were the English emigrants of the 1820s and 1830s? A preliminary analysis' (unpublished research paper, California Institute of Technology, 1977).

'The English', in Thernstrom, S. (ed.), *The Harvard encyclopedia of American ethnic groups* (Harvard University Press, Cambridge, Mass., 1980).

'Emigration from the British Isles to the USA in 1831', *Population Studies*, 35, 1981.

Ferenczi, I. and Willcox, W. F. *International migrations* (National Bureau of Economic and Social Research, New York, 1929–31).

Fletcher, T. W. 'The Great Depression in English agriculture 1873–1896', *Economic History Review*, 13, 1961.

Flinn, M. W. 'Malthus, emigration and potatoes in the Scottish North West 1770–1870', in Cullen, C. M. and Smout, T. C. (eds.), *Comparative aspects of Scottish and Irish economic and social history 1600–1900* (John Macdonald, Edinburgh, 1977).

Flinn, M. W. (ed.), *Scottish population history from the seventeenth century to the 1930s* (Cambridge University Press, 1977).

Foerster, R. F. *The Italian emigration of our times* (Harvard University Press, Cambridge, Mass., 1919).

Forsyth, W. D. *The myth of the open spaces* (Melbourne University Press, 1942).

Friedlander, D. and Roshier, R. J. 'A study of internal migration in England and Wales, Part 1', *Population Studies*, 19, 1966.

'A study of internal migration in England and Wales, Part II. Recent internal movements', *Population Studies*, 19, 1966.

Galenson, D. W. '"Middling people" or "common sort"? The social origins of some early Americans re-examined', *William and Mary Quarterly*, 3rd Series, 35, 1978.

White servitude in colonial America. An economic analysis (Cambridge University Press, 1981).

Gallaway, L. E. and Vedder, R. K. 'Emigration from the United Kingdom to the United States, 1860–1913', *Journal of Economic History*, 31, 1971.

Gallaway, L. E., Vedder, R. K. and Shulka, V., 'The distribution of the immigrant population in the United States: an economic analysis', *Explorations in Economic History*, 11, 1974.

Gandar, J. M. 'New Zealand net migration in the latter part of the nineteenth century', *Australian Economic History Review*, 19 (2) 1979, pp. 151–68.

Gartner, L. D. *The Jewish immigrant in England, 1870–1914* (Wayne State University Press, Detroit, 1960).

Gemery, H. A., 'Emigration from the British Isles to the New World, 1630–1700: inferences from colonial populations', in Uselding, P. (ed.), *Research in Economic History*, vol. V (JAI Press, Greenwich, Conn., 1980).

Glass, D. V. *Population policies and movements in W. Europe* (Oxford University Press, 1940, reprinted Cass, 1967).

'Changes in fertility in England and Wales', in Hogben, L. (ed.), *Political Arithmetic* (Allen and Unwin, 1938).

'A note on the under-registration of births in the nineteenth century', *Population Studies*, 5, 1951–2.

'Population', in Glass, D. V. and Taylor, P. A. M. (eds.), *Population and emigration in 19th century Britain* (Irish University Press, Dublin, 1976).

Glass, D. V. and Grebenik, E. 'World population 1800–1950' in Habakkuk, H. J. and Postan, M. (eds.), *The Cambridge economic history of Europe*, vol. VI (Cambridge University Press, 1966).

Gould, J. D. 'European inter-continental emigration, 1815–1914: patterns and causes', *Journal of European Economic History*, 8 (3), 1979.

'European inter-continental emigration. The road home: return emigration from the USA', *Journal of European Economic History*, 9 (1), 1980.

Graham, I. C. C. *Colonists from Scotland* (Cornell University Press, Ithaca, NY, 1956).

Graham, P. A. *The rural exodus* (Methuen, 1892).

Gray, M. *The Highland economy 1750–1850* (Oliver and Boyd, Edinburgh, 1957).

'The social impact of agrarian change in the rural lowlands 1775–1875', *Perspectives in American History*, 7, 1973.

Grigg, D. B. 'E. G. Ravenstein and the laws of migration', *Journal of Historical Geography*, 3, 1977.

'Migration and overpopulation', in White, P. and Woods, R., *The geographical impact of migration* (Longmans, 1980).

Groniowski, K. *Polska emigracja Zarobkova in Brazylii, 1871–1914* (Polska Akademia Nauk, Instytut Historii, Warsawa, 1972).

Guillet, E. *The great migration* (Toronto University Press, 1937).

Habakkuk, H. J. 'Fluctuations in housebuilding in Britain and the United States in the twentieth century', *Journal of Economic History*, 22, 1962.

Haggard, H. Rider *Rural England* (Longmans, 1902).

Hall, P. G. *The industries of London since 1861* (Hutchinson, 1962).

Hammerton, A. *Emigrant gentlewomen* (Croom Helm, 1979).

Hammond, P. E. 'The migrating sect: an illustration from early Norwegian immigration', *Social Forces*, 41 (3), 1963.

Hance, W. A. *Population, migration and urbanisation in Africa* (New York, 1970).

Handley, J. E. *The Irish in modern Scotland* (Cork University Press, 1947).

Hansen, M. L. *The Atlantic migration, 1607–1860* (Harvard University Press, Cambridge, Mass., 1940).

Hasbach, W. *History of the English agricultural labourer* (reprinted Cass, 1966).

Heaton, H. 'The industrial immigrant in the United States, 1783–1812', *Proceedings of the American Philosophical Society*, 95, 1951.

Hutchens, F. M. *The Colonial Land and Emigration Commission* (University of Pennsylvania Press, Philadelphia, 1931).

Hobsbawm, E. J. 'The nineteenth-century London labour market', in Glass, R. (ed.), *London, aspects of change* (Macgibbon and Kee, 1964).

Hollingsworth, T. H. *Migration. A study based on Scottish experience between 1939 and 1964* (Oliver and Boyd, Edinburgh, 1970).

'Historical studies of migration', *Annales de Démographie Historique 1970* (Paris, 1971).

Horn, P. 'Gloucester and the Brazilian emigration movement, 1872–1873', *Transactions of the Bristol and Gloucester Antiquarian Society*, 89, 1970.

'Agricultural trade unionism and emigration 1872–1881', *Historical Journal*, 15 (1), 1972.

Hunt, E. H. *Regional wage variations in Britain 1850–1914* (Clarendon Press, Oxford, 1973).

British Labour History, 1815–1914 (Weidenfeld and Nicholson, 1980).

Hutchinson, E. P. *Immigrants and their children, 1850–1950* (SSRC Chapman and Hall, New York, 1956).

'Notes on immigration statistics of the United States', *Journal of the American Statistical Association*, 53, 1957.

Hvidt, K. 'Danish emigration prior to 1914. Trends and problems', *Scandinavian Economic History Review*, 14, 1966.

Flight to America. The social background of 300,000 Danish emigrants (Academic Press, New York, 1975).

Hyde, F. E. *Cunard and the North Atlantic 1840–1973. A history of shipping and financial management* (Macmillan, 1975).

Innes, J. W. *Class fertility trends in England and Wales* (Princeton University Press, 1938).

Jackson, J. A. *The Irish in modern Britain* (Routledge, 1963).

Jansen, C. 'Some sociological aspects of migration' in Jackson, J. A. (ed.), *Migration* (Cambridge University Press, 1969).

Jefferies, J. R. *Hodge and his masters* (reprinted Faber, 1948).

Jeremy, D. *Transatlantic industrial revolution: the diffusion of textile technologies between Britain and America, 1790–1830s* (Blackwell, Oxford, 1981).

Jerome, H. *Migration and business cycles* (National Bureau of Economic Research, New York, 1926).

Johnson, J. H. 'Harvest migration from nineteenth-century Ireland', *Transactions of the Institute of British Geographers*, 41, 1967.

Johnson, J. H., Salt, J. and Wood, P. A. *Housing and the migration of labour in England and Wales* (Saxon House, Farnborough, 1974).

Johnson, S. C. *A history of emigration from the United Kingdom to North America, 1763–1912* (Routledge, 1913, reprinted Cass, 1966).

Johnston, H. J. M. *British emigration policy, 1815–1830. Shovelling out paupers* (Oxford University Press, 1972).

Jones, M. A. 'The role of the United Kingdom in the trans-Atlantic emigrant trade', D.Phil. thesis, Oxford University Press, 1955.

American immigration (University of Chicago Press, Chicago, 1965).

'The background to emigration from Great Britain in the nineteenth century', *Perspectives in American History*, 7, 1973).

Jones, P. N. 'Aspects of internal migration to the Glamorganshire Coalfield 1881–1911', *Transactions of the Honourable Society of Cymmrodorion*, 1969.

Kelley, A. G. 'International migration and economic growth. Australia, 1865–1935', *Journal of Economic History*, 25, 1965.

Kennedy, R. E. *Ireland: fertility, emigration and marriage since the Famine* (University of California Press, Los Angeles, 1974).

Kenwood, A. G. and Lougheed, A. L. *The growth of the international economy, 1820–1960* (Allen and Unwin, Sydney, 1971).

Kero, R. *Migration from Finland to North America in the years between the United States Civil War and the First World War* (Yliopisto Turun, Turku, 1974).

Kerr, B. M. 'Irish seasonal migration to Great Britain 1800–1838', *Irish Historical Studies*, 3, 1942.

Knodel, J. E. *The decline of fertility in Germany, 1871–1939* (Princeton University Press, 1974).

Köllmann, W. 'The process of urbanisation in Germany at the height of the industrialisation period', *Journal of Contemporary History*, 4, 1969.

Kosa, J. 'A century of Hungarian emigration 1850–1950', *American Slavic and East European Review*, 16, 1957.

Kuznets, S. *Secular movements in production and prices* (Houghton Mifflin, Boston, Mass., 1930).

'Long swings in the growth of population and related variables', *Proceedings of the American Philosophical Society*, CII, 1958.

Law, C. M. 'The growth of urban population in England and Wales 1801–1911', *Transactions of the Institute of British Geographers*, 41, 1967.

Lawton, R. 'Rural depopulation in nineteenth-century Britain', in Steel, R. W. and Lawton, R. (eds.), *Liverpool essays in geography* (Longmans, 1967).

'Population changes in England and Wales in the late nineteenth century: an analysis of trends by registration districts', *Transactions of the Institute of British Geographers*, 44, 1968.

'Population and society, 1730–1900', pp. 313–66 in Dodgshon, R. A.and Butler, R. A., *An historical geography of England and Wales* (Academic Press, 1978).

Lawton, R. and Pooley, C. G. *Individual appraisals of nineteenth-century Liverpool*, Social Geography of Liverpool: Working Paper No. 3 (1975).

Lee, C. H. (ed.), *British regional employment statistics, 1841–1971* (Cambridge University Press, 1979).

Lee, W. R. (ed.), *European demography and economic growth* (Croom Helm, 1979).

Lewis, E. D. *The Rhondda Valleys* (Phoenix House, 1959).

Lewis, W. A. *Growth and fluctuations 1870–1913* (Allen and Unwin, 1978).

Lipman, V. D. 'The development of areas and boundary changes 1888–1939', in Wilson, C. H. (ed.), *Essays in local government* (Blackwell, Oxford, 1948). *Local government areas 1834–1945* (Blackwell, Oxford, 1949).

Livi Bacci, M. *L'Immigrazione e l'Assimilazione degli Italiani negli Stati Uniti secondo la statistiche demografiche Americana* (Guiffre, Milan, 1961).

Ljingmark, L. *For sale, Minnesota. Organised promotion of Scandinavian immigration, 1866–1873* (Scandinavian University Books, 1971).

Lucas, H. S. *Netherlanders in America* (University of Michigan Press, 1955).

Ludlow, J. M. 'The growth of American influence in England', *Atlantic Monthly*, 42, 1894.

MacDonagh, O. *A pattern of government growth: The Passenger Acts and their enforcement 1800–1860* (McGibbon and Kay, 1961).

MacDonald, D. F. *Scotland's shifting population, 1770–1850* (Jackson, Glasgow, 1937).

MacDonald, J. S. 'Some socio-economic emigration differentials in rural Italy 1902–1913', *Economic Development and Cultural Change*, 7, 1958.
'Agricultural organisation, migration and labour militancy in rural Italy', *Economic History Review*, 16 (1), 1963.

MacDonald, N. *Canada: immigration and colonisation 1841–1903* (Aberdeen University Press, 1966).

Malchow, H. L. 'Trade unions and emigration in late Victorian England: a national lobby for state aid', *Journal of British Studies*, 15 (2), 1976.

Mellor, G. R. 'Emigration from the British Isles to the New World, 1765–1775', *History*, 40, 1955.

Mendras, H. 'The rural exodus and industrialisation', *Diogenes*, 30, 1960.

Mitchell, B. R. *Abstract of British historical statistics* (Cambridge University Press, 1962).
European historical statistics, 1750–1975 (Macmillan, 1981).

Moe, T. 'Some economic aspects of Norwegian population movements: an econometric study', *Journal of Economic History*, 30 (1), 1970.

Musgrove, F. *The migratory elite* (Heinemann, 1963).

Neal, L. 'Cross spectral analysis of long swings in Atlantic migration', in Uselding, P. (ed.), *Research in Economic History*, vol. 1 (Greenwich, Connecticut, 1976).

Nelli, H. S. 'Italians in America', *International Migration Review*, New Series, 1, 1967.

Nilsson, F. *Emigrationen från Stockholm till Nordamerika 1880–1893* (Studia Historica Upsaliensis, 1973).

Norman, H. 'Causes of emigration. An attempt at a multivariate analysis' in Rundblom, H. and Norman, H., *From Sweden to America, A history of the migration* (University of Uppsala Press, 1976).

Oden, B. 'Scandinavian emigration prior to 1914', *Scandinavian Economic History Review*, 20, 1972.

Ogle, M. 'The alleged depopulation of the rural districts of England, 1851–1881', *Journal of the Royal Statistical Society*, 52, 1889.

Olssen, N. W. *Swedish passenger arrivals in New York City, 1820–1850* (Norstedt and Soners, Stockholm, 1967).

Page, T. W. 'The transportation of immigrants and reception arrangements in the nineteenth century', *Journal of Political Economy*, 19, 1911.

Palairet, M. 'The "New" migration and the newest; Slavic migration from the Balkans to America and industrial Europe since the late nineteenth century', pp. 43–65 in Smout, T. C. (ed.), *The search for wealth and stability. Essays in economic and social history presented to M. W. Flinn* (Macmillan, 1979).

Parenti, G. 'Italian emigration' in Thomas, B. (ed.), *The economics of international migration* (MacMillan, 1958).

Parr, J. *Labouring children: British immigrant apprentices to Canada, 1869–1924* (Croom Helm, 1980).

Parry, P. J. *British farming in the Great Depression, 1870–1914* (David and Charles, Newton Abbot, 1974).

Parry Lewis, J. 'Growth and inverse cycles: a two country model', *Economic Journal*, 74, 1964.

Building cycles and Britain's growth (Macmillan, 1965).

Patten, J. *Rural–urban migration in pre-industrial England* (Oxford University, School of Geography, Research Papers No. 6, 1973).

Plant, G. F. *Oversea settlement* (Oxford University Press, 1951).

Pooley, C. G. 'The residential segregation of migrant communities in mid-Victorian Liverpool', *Transactions of the Institute of British Geographers*, New Series, 1977.

Pope, D. 'Empire migration to Canada, Australia and New Zealand, 1910–1929', *Australian Economic Papers*, 11, 1968.

'The push–pull model of Australian migration', *Australian Economic History Review*, 16 (2), 1976.

Potter, J. 'The growth of population in America', in Glass, D. V. and Eversley, D. E. C.(eds.), *Population in history* (Arnold, 1965).

Poulson, B. W. and Holyfield, J. 'A note on European migration to the United States. Cross spectral analysis', *Explorations in Economic History*, 11 (3), 1974.

Quigley, J. M. 'An econometric model of Swedish emigration', *Quarterly Journal of Economics*, 86 (1), 1972.

Ravenstein, E. G. 'The laws of migration', *Journal of the Royal Statistical Society*, 48, 1885 and 52, 1889.

Redford, A. *Labour migration in England* (Manchester University Press, 1926, revised 1964).

Richards, J. H. and Parry Lewis, J. 'Housebuilding in the South Wales coalfield, 1851–1913', *Manchester School*, 24, 1956.

Richardson, H. W. 'British emigration and overseas investment 1870–1914', *Economic History Review*, 25, 1972.

Rohdahl, B. *Emigration folk emflyttning och säsongarbete i att saguvorksdistrikt i sodra Haslinghand, 1865–1910* (Sondia Historia Upsalusia 41, Almqvist and Wiksell, Stockholm, 1972).

Rowe, J. *Cornwall in the age of the Industrial Revolution* (Liverpool University Press, 1953).

The Hard Rock Men: Cornish migrants and the North American mining frontier (Liverpool University Press, 1974).

Rowse, A. L. *A Cornish childhood* (Jonathan Cape, 1942).

Rundblom, H. and Norman, H. (eds.), *From Sweden to America. A history of the migration* (University of Minnesota Press, Minneapolis, and Acta Universitatis Upsaliensis, 1976).

Saloutos, T. *They remember America. The story of the repatriated Greek–Americans* (University of California, Berkeley, 1956).

Saul, S. B. 'Housebuilding in England, 1890–1914', *Economic History Review*, 15, 1962.

Sauvy, P. *The general theory of population* (Weidenfeld, 1969).

Saville, J. *Rural depopulation in England and Wales 1851–1951* (Routledge, 1957).

Schofield, R. S. 'Dimensions of illiteracy 1750–1850', *Explorations in Economic History*, 10 (4), 1973.

Schrier, A. *Ireland and the American emigration, 1850–1900* (University of Minnesota Press, Minneapolis, 1959).

Scott, F. D. 'The study of the effects of emigration', *Scandinavian Economic History Review*, 8, 1960.

Semmingsen, I. 'Norwegian emigration in the nineteenth century', *Scandinavian Economic History Review*, 7, 1960.

'Emigration and the image of America in Europe', in Commanger, H. S. (ed.), *Immigration and American history. Essays in honour of Theodore C. Blegen* (University of Minnesota Press, Minneapolis, 1961).

'Emigration from Scandinavia', *Scandinavian Economic History Review*, 20 (1), 1972.

Shannon, H. A. 'Migration and the growth of London 1841–1891', *Economic History Review*, 5, 1935.

Shepperson, W. S. 'Industrial emigration in early Victorian Britain', *Journal of Economic History*, 13, 1953.

British emigration to North America (Blackwell, Oxford, 1957).

Emigration and disenchantment (University of Oklahoma Press, 1966).

Snow, C. E. 'British emigration', in Ferenczi, I. and Willcox, W. (eds.), *International Migration* (NBER, New York, 1929–31).

Souden, D. 'Rogues, whores and vagabonds? Indentured servant emigrants to North America and the case of mid-seventeenth-century Bristol', *Social History*, 3, 1978.

Stankiewicz, Z. 'The economic emigration from the Kingdom of Poland. Portrayed on the European background', pp. 27–52 in Bobinska, C. and Pilch, A., *Employment-seeking emigrations of Poles world wide. XIXth and XXth centuries* (Polonia educational research centre, 1976).

Stouffer, S. A. 'Intervening opportunities. A theory relating mobility and distance', *American Sociological Review*, 5, 1940.

Sundbärg, G. *Emigrationsutredningen. Bilaga IV, Utvandringsstatistick* (Stockholm, 1910).

Sundin, J. 'The demographic data-base at the University of Umea' in Sundin J. and Soderlund E. (eds.), *Time, Space and Man* (Almqvist and Wiksell, Stockholm, 1979).

Swierenga, R. P. and Stout, H. S. 'Social and economic patterns of migration from the Netherlands in the nineteenth century', in Uselding, Paul, *Research in Economic History*, vol. I (Greenwich, Connecticut, 1976).

Taylor, P. A. M. *Expectations westward, The Mormons and the emigration of the British converts in the nineteenth century* (Oliver and Boyd, Edinburgh, 1965).

The distant magnet (Eyre and Spottiswoode, 1971).

'Emigration', in Glass, D. V. and Taylor, P. A. M. (eds.), *Population and emigration in 19th-century Britain* (Irish Universities Press, Dublin, 1976).

Taylor, R. C. 'Migration and motivation. A study of determinants and types', in Jackson, J. A. (ed.), *Migration* (Cambridge University Press, 1969).

Tederbrand, L.-G. *Vasternoerland och Nordamerika, 1875–1913* (Studia Historica Upsalensia, 42, Almqvist and Wiksell, Uppsala, 1972).

'Sources for the history of Swedish emigration' in Rundblom, H. and Norman, H. (eds.), *From Sweden to America, A history of the migration* (University of Uppsala Press, 1976).

Teitelbaum, M. S. 'Birth under-registration in the constituent counties of England and Wales 1841–1910', *Population Studies*, 28, 1974.

Thistlethwaite, F. 'Migration from Europe overseas in the nineteenth and twentieth centuries', in *XIe Congrès International des Sciences Historiques, Stockholm, 1960, V: Histoire Contemporaine* (Almqvist and Wiksell, Stockholm, 1960).

Thernstrom, S. (ed.), *The Harvard encyclopaedia of American ethnic groups* (Harvard University Press, Cambridge, Mass., 1980).

Thomas, B. 'Migration into the Glamorganshire coalfield, 1861–1911', *Economica*, 30, 1930.

'Migration and international investment', in Thomas, B. (ed.), *The economics of international migration* (Macmillan, 1958).

'Wales and the Atlantic Economy', *Scottish Journal of Political Economy*, 1959.

'Long swings in international migration and capital formation', *Bulletin of the International Statistical Institute, Proceedings of the 34th Session*, 40, book 1 (Toronto, 1964).

Migration and economic growth. A study of Great Britain and the Atlantic Economy (NIESR, Cambridge University Press, 1954, 2nd edition, 1973).

Migration and urban development. A reappraisal of British and American long cycles (Methuen, 1972).

(ed.), *The Welsh economy. Studies in expansion* (University of Wales Press, Cardiff, 1962).

Thomas, D. S. *Research memorandum on migration differentials* (New York, Social Science Research Council, No. 43, 1938).

Social and economic aspects of Swedish population movements 1750–1933 (Macmillan, New York, 1941).

Thomas, W. I. and Znaniecki, F. *The Polish peasant in Europe and America* (Knopf, New York, 1918).

Tilley, C. 'Migration in modern European history', in Sundin, J. and Söderlund, E. (eds.), *Time, space and man* (Almqvist and Wiksell, Stockholm, 1979).

Tillot, P. M. 'Sources of error in the 1851 and 1861 census' in Wrigley, E. A. (ed.), *Nineteenth-century society. Essays in the use of quantitative data* (Cambridge University Press, 1972).

Tipton, F. B. *Regional variations in economic development in Germany during the nineteenth century* (Weslyan University Press, Middletown, Connecticut, 1976).

Toivonen, A.-Z. *Etëla-Pohjanmaan Valtamoven-Takaineen Sürtolaisuus 1857–1930* (Emigration overseas from South Ostrobothnia) (Suomen Historiallisia Tutkimuksia, Helsinki, 1963).

Tomaske, J. A. 'International migration and economic growth: the Swedish experience', *Journal of Economic History*, 25, 1965.

'The determinants of inter-country differences in European emigration 1881–1900', *Journal of Economic History*, 31, 1971.

United Nations. *The determinants and consequences of population trends* (UN New York, 1953).

U.S.A. *Historical Statistics of the USA* (American Government Printing Office, 1957).

Vedder, R. K. and Gallaway, L. E. 'The settlement preferences of Scandinavian emigrants to the United States, 1850–1960', *Scandinavian Economic History Review*, 18 (2), 1970.

Vogel, E. F. 'Kinship structure, migration to the city and modernisation' in Dore, R. P. (ed.), *Aspects of social change in modern Japan* (Princeton University Press, 1967).

Walker, M. *Germany and the emigration, 1816–85* (Harvard University Press, Cambridge, Mass., 1964).

Wander, H. 'Migration and the German economy', in Thomas, B. (ed.), *The economics of international migration* (MacMillan, 1958).

Warriner, D. (ed.) *Contrasts in emerging societies* (Athlone Press, 1965).

Weber, B. 'A new index of residential construction, 1838–1950', *Scottish Journal of Political Economy*, 2, 1955.

Welton, T. A. *England's recent progress: an investigation of the statistics of migration, mortality etc. in the twenty years from 1881 to 1901, as indicating tendencies towards the growth and decay of particular communities* (Chapman and Hall, 1911).

Werthenbaker, T. J. *The first Americans. 1607–1690. A history of American life*, vol. II (Macmillan, New York, 1927).

White, P. and Woods, R. (eds.). *The geographical impact of migration* (Longmans, 1980).

Wilkening, E. A., Jao Bosco and Jose Pastor, 'Role of the extended family in migration and adaptation in Brazil, *Journal of Marriage and the Family*, 30, 1968.

Wilkinson, M. 'Evidence of long swings in the growth of Swedish population and related economic variables', *Journal of Economic History*, 27 (1) 1967.

'European migration to the United States, an econometric analysis of aggregate labour supply and demand', *Review of Economics and Statistics*, 52, 1970.

Williams, D. *History of modern Wales* (John Murray, 1950).

Williams, G. *The desert and the dream. A study of Welsh colonization in Chubut. 1865–1915* (University of Wales Press, Cardiff, 1975).

Williamson, J. G. 'The Long Swing: comparison and interaction between the British and American balance of payments', *Journal of Economic History*, 22 (1) 1962.

American growth and the balance of payments, 1820–1913 (University of North Carolina Press, Chapel Hill, 1964).

'Migration to the New World. Long term influences and impact', *Explorations in Economic History*, 2 (4), 1974.

Late nineteenth-century American development. A general equilibrium history (Cambridge University Press, 1974).

Wood, J. D. 'Scottish migration overseas', *Scottish Geographical Magazine*, December 1964.

Wrigley, E. A. (ed.), *Nineteenth-century society, essays in the use of quantitative data* (Cambridge University Press, 1972).

Wrigley, E. A. and Schofield, R. S. *The population history of England, 1541–1871. A reconstruction* (Arnold, 1981).

Youngson, A. J. *After the Forty-Five. The economic impact on the Scottish Highlands* (Edinburgh University Press, 1973).

Youngson Brown, A. J. 'Trade union policy in the Scots coalfields, 1855–1885', *Economic History Review*, 2nd series, 1953–4.

Zimmerman, C. C. 'American roots in an Italian village', *Genus*, 11, 1955.

Zubrzycki, J. 'Emigration from Poland in the nineteenth and twentieth centuries', *Population Studies*, 6, 1953.

BRITISH GOVERNMENT PUBLICATIONS

Census of England and Wales, Scotland and Ireland, 1841–1961.

Annual Reports of the Registrar General (and Decennial Supplements) for England, Scotland and Ireland.

Annual Reports of the Colonial Land and Emigration Commissioners.

Royal Commission on Labour, The agricultural labourer, 1893–4, XXXV and XXXVI.

Royal Commission on the Agricultural Depression, 1894, XVII and XVIII.

Report on decline in the agricultural population of Great Britain 1881–1906, 1906, XCVI.

Hill, A. B. *Internal migration and its effects on the death rates with special reference to the County of Essex* (Medical Research Council, 1925).

Interdepartmental Committee on Social and Economic Research (Feery, L. M.), *Guide to official sources, No. 2. Census reports of Great Britain 1801–1931* (HMSO 1951).

Newton, M. P. and Jeffery, J. R. *Internal Migration* (General Register Office, Studies on medical and population subjects, No. 5, HMSO, 1951).

Carrier, N. H. and Jeffery, J. R. *External migraion, A study of the available statistics, 1815–1950* (General Register Office, Studies on medical and population subjects, No. 6, HMSO, 1953).

Harris, A. and Clausen, R. *Labour mobility in Great Britain, 1953–63* (Ministry of Labour and National Service, 1967).

Index

Printed in the United Kingdom
by Lightning Source UK Ltd.
119772UK00001BA/49

9 780521 891547